Literature and Music

ESSAYS ON FORM

Literature and Music

Brigham Young University Press

EDITED BY

NANCY ANNE CLUCK

Library of Congress Cataloging in Publication Data
Main entry under title:

Literature and music.

Bibliography: p. 253
Includes index.
1. Music and literature—Addresses, essays, lectures. 2. Musical form—Addresses,
essays, lectures. 3. Literature, Modern—History and criticism—Addresses, essays,
lectures. I. Cluck, Nancy Anne, 1936–
PN56.M87L5   1981   809'.93357   81-1070
ISBN 0-8425-1943-2   AACR2

International Standard Book Number: 0-8425-1943-2
Brigham Young University Press, Provo, Utah 84602
© 1981 by Brigham Young University Press. All rights reserved
Printed in the United States of America
7/81   49711

Table of Contents

Preface

This book is intended for those who enjoy the discovery of relationships between unlike phenomena. The dissimilarities between music and literature are obvious; much more enticing to the curious and creative mind are the similarities. To find these resemblances, however, one must clearly identify the vital common areas between the two arts. One area that may serve as a focal point is the use of music *in* literature, as in the works of Thomas Mann; another is the use of literature *in* music, as in the opera or in program music. More fundamental than these approaches, however, are those which proceed from the central question of *form*. This book offers a long-overdue inquiry into the analogous structures of music and literature.

Stated simply, the forms of music and literature invite comparison because both arts happen in time. They require the medium and material of time for their meaning just as the arts of painting and sculpture require space. Unlike the arts of space, which may be perceived as completed and even tangible entities, the arts of time are in a continual state of becoming. Striving toward the state of being through the accretion of designs that may be perceived only in time, literature and music behave comparably. The means by which they acquire their structures are remarkably similar.

Explicit structures of time are most apparent in the musical forms of the eighteenth century. The fugue, the theme and variations, and, especially, the sonata-allegro form provided public models or genres for the composers much as the sonnet, the elegy, and the epic had for the poets of the Renaissance. These particular musical structures or genres, then, were assimilated into the literary scene during the nineteenth and twentieth centuries and underscored the basic similarities between musical and literary forms.

This study progresses from discussions of the fundamental techniques of structure through examinations of the theme and variation form to studies of the sonata form in poetry, short fiction, and the novel. It concludes with a consideration of the aesthetic trend beyond classical form. Because this collection brings many viewpoints to bear upon the idea of structure, the subject in all of its complexity is opened and illuminated. My purpose in selecting these essays has not been to pursue a single stance; on the contrary, it has been to argue for a rich variety of approaches.

Through the selection and organization of these essays into considerations of particular musical and literary genres, I have attempted to provide the reader with an ongoing conversation among critics who represent the many angles from which the question of musico-literary forms may be approached. Participation in this dialogue should better enable him to discern the affinities between the sister arts.

I wish to express my gratitude to those whose aid in the preparation of this volume attests to their own enthusiasm for the interrelationships between humanistic disciplines. I am indebted to The University of Texas at Dallas for a research grant which provided me with support for this project. I am especially grateful for the advice, criticism, and encouragement offered by my colleague Professor Rainer Schulte; for the suggestions of the outstanding pioneer in this field, Dr. Calvin S. Brown; for the bibliographical services of my research assistant, Mrs. Ann Farrell; for the many tasks, in addition to typing the manuscript, performed by my patient secretary, Mrs. Audrey Kirst; and for the excellent editorial advice of Miss Elizabeth Wilkinson of Brigham Young University Press.

Nancy Anne Cluck
The University of Texas at Dallas

Introduction

The affinities between literature and music have attracted inquisitive minds for centuries. Although evidence of this fascination appears early in artistic history, it was not until the twentieth century that extensive, analytical investigations brought this field of study into focus.[1] Such interdisciplinary studies seem to arise naturally from the proximity of the arts. The practice of joining literature and music in song and opera, as well as borrowing from one of the arts to furnish a model for the other in works of fiction and in program music, encourages comparative thought. Moreover, their temporal structures invite inquiries into the means by which they achieve form.

Critical examinations of musico-literary relationships confront certain hazards, however. The fundamental difficulty arises from the self-evident fact that literary training does not necessarily equip one to deal with music, nor musical preparation to deal with literature. However, the language of one discipline can often be used advantageously to illuminate another, especially when the two disciplines have as much common ground as these two.

Given proper disciplinary preparation, the inquirer must develop a vocabulary which will effectively treat the relationships between the arts. Although no conclusive interdisciplinary lexicon has yet been developed, Professor Ulrich Weisstein has voiced his intention to offer at some later date a "Dictionary of Critical Terms Relevant to the Interdisciplinary Study of the Arts," written from a comparatist's point of view.[2] Steven Paul Scher attributes the scepticism which often accompanies the comparative study of music and literature to the lack of a precise vocabulary: "But it must be conceded that a sceptical attitude toward interart parallels is to some extent justifiable. I see the major reason for such scepticism in the lack of a clearly defined critical terminology and in the predilection of some critics for a set of terms based on little more than metaphorical impressionism."[3]

Despite these inherent difficulties, many highly original and thought-provoking inquiries have advanced this field of study. The most comprehensive is Calvin S. Brown's book, *Music and Literature: A Comparison of the Arts*. In his preface, Brown issues an invitation to other scholars: "This book was written with the hope that it might open up a field of thought which has not yet been systematically explored. Though various articles and books have dealt separately with many of the problems here brought together, there has been no survey of the entire field. This book attempts to supply such a survey."[4] As an overview it deals with the major systems for the comparison of music and literature, moving from the basic elements of melody, harmony, and rhythm through the union of these fundamentals with words to the influence of music on literature and, finally, the influence of literature on music.

Few contemporary scholars have attempted such a vast enterprise, preferring instead to concentrate on one category. For example, many critics concern themselves with the relationship between words and music in vocal settings. Others work with the musical contributions of a literary figure, such as E. T. A. Hoffmann, or the literary importance of a musical figure, such as Robert Schumann. Still others inquire into the influence of literature upon music, exploring, for example, programmatic music which relies on particular Shakespearean plays; or, conversely, they trace the influence of music upon literature in the works of Gide, Proust, Rousseau, Mann, or Huxley, to name only a few.

Stemming from such considerations but proceeding beyond documented evidence of influence is the study of interrelationships through structure. Those critics who concern themselves primarily with formal relationships follow the direction indicated by T. S. Eliot, Northrop Frye, René Wellek, and Steven Scher. Their central hypothesis is that the real juncture of music and literature is in structure and that this common area offers the most fruitful potential for interdisciplinary inquiry. René Wellek asserts that, "obviously, the most central approach to a comparison of the arts is based on an analysis of the actual objects of art, and thus of their structural relationships. There will never be a proper history of an art, not to speak of a comparative history of the arts, unless we concentrate on an analysis of the works themselves and relegate to the background studies in the psychology of the reader and the spectator or the author and the artist as well as studies in the cultural and social background, however illuminating they may be from their own point of view."[5] Steven Scher assumes a similar stance in his discussion, written nearly thirty years later, of the term "musical" as applied to literature:

> Ignoring those instances when the term is employed in such a muddled way that in the end it signifies nothing, we may distinguish three possibilities of implicated meaning: the acoustic, the evocative, and the structural. . . . Only in the case of the third type of response—alluding to structural phenomena, to artistic arrangement in musiclike sequence—are we dealing with literary techniques which can be proven more or less analogous to certain techniques in actual music. Thus, when we try to demonstrate the semblance of a specifically musical structure or device present in a literary work, the use of the term "musical" seems to me legitimate.[6]

It makes little difference in the consideration of formal similarities whether or not the writer *intended* to borrow a musical form; the crucial point is that music and literature often reveal analogous forms.

The temporal nature of musical and literary structures adds further value to comparative analyses. Because these two arts order themselves through time, they tend to trace similar designs. These patterns, constantly in a state of becoming, are thus fundamentally different from structures of the fine arts—painting, sculpture, and architecture—which stand as completed entities, wholly observable in space. The entire, fulfilled, form of the temporal arts, because they are in a perennial state of becoming, may be perceived only in the memory, after the time of the work itself is over.

It is this experience of becoming without attaining closed form that the temporal arts share with human experience. The aesthetic experience heightens and reflects time as it functions in human lives; passage, duration, and mutability are made comprehensible. In art the extraneous elements or experiences are deleted and the integral characteristics are heightened and refined as they assume their position in relation to the whole. For example, in a literary work, only the past events and impressions which bear an essential distinctive relation to the present and the future are presented; extrinsic or irrelevant material is eliminated. In music the clarification process is even more dramatic because the original musical ideas furnish the sole material for present and future development within a composition. The development section of the first movement of Beethoven's Fifth Symphony, for example, would be meaningless without the preceding exposition. Musical and literary forms, then, establish and concentrate abstract experiences in time. Aesthetic time transforms the nebulous and meaningless constituents of human time into purposeful designs that outline the progressive movement toward being.

Paradoxically, the human perceiver seems to escape time through the aesthetic experience which makes it more meaningful. Obviously, the temporal arts require chronological time in order to unfold; yet, in their very development through time they go beyond it and transmit the essence of internal, subjective time. The movement toward form—this process of becoming—in the temporal arts, then, momentarily impels the perceiver beyond chronological time and provides him with the illusion of wholeness, of completed design which has achieved being. The interest of a work of art relies largely on this interplay between aesthetic time and chronological time. J. T. Fraser further illustrates this point with his comment on rhythm in music: "The subjective, human experience we are most likely to associate with the various manifestations of musical rhythm and often with rhythmic motion in general, is a change in the apparent rate of the flow of time. The curious situation thus obtains that the most striking effect of the temporal arts on man is a feeling of transcending time."[7] Eudora Welty echoes Fraser with her similar remark on time in literature: "Fiction penetrates chronological time to reach our deeper version of time that's given to us by the way we think and feel."[8] Although accomplished in chronological time, aesthetic time transcends the clock and reflects the internal, subjective time of human experience. It purifies and refines the chronological experience and, in so doing, provides the model that reflects the structures of becoming in internal, human time. The temporal arts furnish the paradigm for mutability that constantly strives for immutability.

The forms of music and literature do not exist as static molds into which musical and literary ideas may be poured; rather they are the *strategies* of western art for dealing with the dialectics of human experience—with the dichotomies of same and other, god and man, the individual and the universal. These antitheses find expression in such principles as repetition and change in the theme and variation model, the pattern of separation and return in the three-part song form, and the dialectical tensions resolved into unity in the sonata form, to name only a few. Temporal forms afford ways for dealing with the conflicts inherent in time. They supply the boundaries within which conflict can occur; or, in Fraser's words, "Through the many means at his command, the artist conveys the experience of structured conflict rather than mere orderliness of the world. Thus he imitates the cosmic emergence of creative conflicts from the primordial chaos."[9]

Ultimately, the value of structural analyses of musico-literary inter-relationships comes from the recognition that both aesthetic and human experience strive for form in remarkably similar ways. In shaping the conflicts of human experience and furnishing the parameters of aesthetic time, the dynamic structures of art afford a wholeness not available in the chronological time of human existence. They create a new order and a new means for understanding; for, as Jacob Bronowski explains, "a man becomes creative, whether he is an artist or a scientist, when he finds a new unity in the variety of nature. He does so by finding a likeness between things which were not thought alike before, and this gives him a sense at the same time of richness and understanding. The creative mind is one that looks for unexpected likeness."[10]

The purpose of this collection of essays is to offer to all of those who "find pleasure in unexpected likeness" the best and most thought-provoking inquiries into musico-literary form. Because they have been assembled under one cover, these essays may be more easily seen as a conversation among the most astute thinkers on this particular subject. The collection provides scholars with more accessible tools for their own research, and it allows students to enter the discussion. It offers interested laymen a focused introduction and a variety of structural methodologies for examining the affinities between music and literature.

The essays chosen for the collection primarily address the larger questions of form rather than the smaller components from which it is achieved. The first four essays, however, give more than passing attention to elemental matters such as rhythm, counterpoint, and the problem of simultaneity in literature. The second section includes the essays on theme and variation form in music and poetry, while the third attends to sonata form in poetry. In the fourth section the conversational qualities become most apparent with the subject gravitating around one poet: T. S. Eliot. From this central argument the reader may garner the fundamental agreements and disagreements upon which critics build cogent and ever more penetrating insights; because it focuses upon one central figure, this section should most successfully fulfill the secondary purpose of exploring and illuminating interdisciplinary methodology. The fourth section carries the discussion of sonata form into the realm of short fiction, while the fifth deals with the sonata in longer prose fiction. The last section may be considered an appendix to the collection: one of its two essays concerns sonata form in drama and is appended because it is one of the surprisingly few studies of musical form in drama; and the final essay concerns the movement of both literature and music beyond classical form.

These six sections achieve coherence and unity through their progressive consideration of musico-literary form. Although the essays may be read independently from one another, they should ultimately be considered as one study arguing that formal comparisons between music and literature offer a useful means for the study of these two arts.

In the first section, which deals with some of the techniques for achieving and perceiving patterns that lead to larger forms, Marden J. Clark explores one of the fundamental problems of temporal form: the idea that structure in music and literature can be fully perceived only in retrospect, after the aesthetic time of the work has ceased. He finds that the key to the reflective experience is provided by the resonating of the rhythmic patterns presented in the immediate experience. These immediate rhythmic patterns, then, combine in memory to create the overall structural patterns.

This point echoes and carries forward that of an earlier critic, T. S. Eliot, who states in his famous essay "The Music of Poetry" that "a poem, or a passage of a poem, may tend to realize itself first as a particular rhythm before it reaches expression in words, and . . . this rhythm may bring to birth the idea and the image; and I do not believe that this is an experience peculiar to myself."[11] The primary difference between Eliot and Clark is that Eliot writes of the inception of the poem in its creator's mind, while Clark considers the form of the work in the perceiver's mind. Clark convincingly supports his thesis through an analysis of the recurring rhythms in sentence structure, paragraphs, and chapters that lead to the perception of patterns in the retrospective mode of memory.

A study of a related peculiarity of temporal form follows Clark's treatment of rhythmic resonances. The sounding of tones or passages simultaneously is possible in music but not in literature. Yet, according to William Freedman in the second essay "*Tristram Shandy:* The Art of Literary Counterpoint," various ideas and emotions pervade the consciousness at the same time, and literature must in some way record these simultaneous impressions. Sterne achieves the semblance of musical simultaneity and counterpoint through the frequent intrusions and digressions of his narrator that bring another part of the plot current while, theoretically, the original part continues and is overtaken and retrieved at later points.

The difficulties of literary counterpoint are further explored in Stephen J. Adams's "Are the *Cantos* a Fugue?" Unlike Freedman, Adams asserts that counterpoint cannot really exist in literature and that Pound's statements regarding the similarity between the fugal form and his *Cantos* do not ratify such a comparative analysis. Pound does not attempt a formal fugue; rather, he refers to its special temporal behavior as a way of explaining that his themes are not bound to historical or chronological time. Little is to be gained, then, from the consideration of the fugal structure of *Cantos;* such an analogy can offer only a limited explanation for Pound's poetry.

Patricia Haas Stanley approaches the idea of counterpoint in literature from another standpoint in her "Verbal Music in Theory and Practice." Primarily concerned with the polyphonic basis of the toccata in Wolfgang Hildersheimer's *Tynset,* she describes literary conterpoint as a "rapid shifting from one image to another." Her close reading of the text results in the discovery that verbal polyphony arises from principles of subordination and coordination, repetition of words and images, and a limited use of onomatopoeia. Thus, to the previous studies of counterpoint through plot incidents and time sequences, Stanley adds her derivation of polyphony from patterns of words and phrases themselves.

Discussions of the problems of and techniques for achieving pattern in the temporal arts lead to studies of larger and more formal musico-literary structures. In the first essay of the second section, Northrop Frye sets the theme and variation form in its theoretical or philosophical context. He argues in "Wallace Stevens and the Variation Form" that the polarity between reality and the imagination provides the dialectic of this structure. Changing ideas, emotions, and images furnish a sequence of imaginative settings through which immutable reality may be perceived. For Stevens the imagination transforms reality and confers variety upon it.

Calvin S. Brown precedes his discussion of theme and variation form in poetry with a short historical and analytical account of that form in music. In his article, "Theme and Variations as a Literary Form," he outlines the problems inherent in the borrowing of musical form for use in literature and then analyzes the structure of Josef Weinheber's "Variationen auf eine hölderlinische Ode" and Robert Browning's *The Ring and the Book*. Brown notes that the two writers start from different premises. Weinheber's purpose is to transfer as nearly as possible the technique of the musical theme and variation form to literature; Browning's goal, on the other hand, is to transform into poetry a basic truth in human life, and he chose the theme and variation form to do so. Brown concludes that the poet should borrow only what is useful rather than making a fetish of following a particular form point for point.

Proceeding to the more complex sonata-allegro form in poetry, the next series of essays clusters about one figure: T. S. Eliot. Although additional poets and critics could have been selected to illustrate this area, this purposeful concentration on a single writer allows comparison of a variety of formal methodologies and stimulates a spirited critical conversation.

In "The Music of *The Waste Land*," Paul Chancellor analyzes the work as a symphonic poem in sonata form with an interwoven narration. He moves from the poem's aural qualities, such as "rhythm, sonority, verbal orchestration, and tempo," to the interplay of the basic symbols and leitmotifs that supply the pattern of the entire poem.

Helen Gardner traces the symphonic form of *Four Quartets* in her essay "The Music of *Four Quartets*." As the "poetic equivalent" of a symphony, quartet, or sonata, each poem contains five movements: the first in sonata form, the second containing a single subject handled in opposite ways, the third an exploration with "a twist of the ideas of the first two movements," the fourth a lyrical treatment affording a transition to the final movement, and the fifth movement recapitulating the themes of the poem and resolving the conflicts.

D. Bosley Brotman agrees essentially with Gardner. In his "T. S. Eliot: 'The Music of Ideas'," he names the conflicting theme groups as "the spiritual conditions of man, the aspects and paradoxes of time within eternity, and man's concern with them." While the individual poems develop the whole, each one is also complete in itself, as Brotman demonstrates in his analysis of "East Coker." In her essay, Gardner describes the behavior of each movement but refers to a particular musical structure in relation only to the first; Brotman goes further and argues that, at least in "East Coker," the second movement is a rondo, the third theme and variation, and the fourth a transition, much like Beethoven's

Quartet No. 15 in A Minor. Surprisingly, he does not give a name to the last movement, but he does agree that it serves to recapitulate and resolve the themes.

Brotman's reference to the late Beethoven quartets, especially the one in A minor, receives expanded treatment in the next essay, "Eliot, Beethoven, and J. W. N. Sullivan" by Herbert Howarth. Concerned specifically with the connections, available from biographical evidence, between the Beethoven A Minor Quartet and the *Four Quartets,* Howarth refers to Eliot's own words and to his position as editor of the *Criterion.* Because he was a conscientious editor, he probably read J. B. Trend's piece on appropriate and inappropriate literary approaches to music, which singled out J. W. N. Sullivan's *Beethoven: His Spiritual Development* as a desirable method. Howarth ties some of the phrases of the *Four Quartets* to some of Sullivan's phrases and furthers his argument with the fact that Eliot, like Beethoven, had passed through a period of physical and spiritual sickness which prompted his desire to write a poem of gratitude to God as Beethoven did in the A Minor.

Harvey Gross adds to the discussion with his "Music and the Analogue of Feeling: Notes on Eliot and Beethoven." Rather than the A Minor Quartet of Beethoven, Gross chooses the C# Minor, op. 131, because of its cyclical nature. No attempt is made to show a direct influence or an intentional imitation of this particular string quartet, but the manner for achieving form appears to be very similar. Both Eliot's *Quartets* and Beethoven's C# Minor evolve from a single controlling idea: for Beethoven this idea is the opening fugue; for Eliot it is the central theme dealing with the nature of time, the meaning of history, and the paradox of the seasons. Both Beethoven and Eliot capture a root experience: the perception and understanding of the universe as the expression of disorder in an overriding order.

In the final essay of the section, Thomas R. Rees warns in "The Orchestration of Meaning in T. S. Eliot's *Four Quartets*" against an excessively rigid insistence on musical form. He does agree that the quartet, symphony, and sonata forms afford one sort of pattern to Eliot's work; but rather than seeing each separate quartet as a complete musical quartet, he argues that all four must be taken together before the analogy with the string quartet is valid. In other words, Rees prefers to consider Eliot's entire *Four Quartets* as one quartet. He bases his thoughts on the recurrence of basic themes, images, and strategies throughout the work.

From poetry, the contributors of the fourth section turn to the sonata form in short fiction. In "Thomas Mann's Use of Musical Structure and Techniques in *Tonio Kröger,*" H. A. Basilius notes Mann's frequent allusions to his interest in music and his use of the leitmotif in both *Tonio Kröger* and *The Magic Mountain.* Basilius is not satisfied merely with Mann's testament to musical influence, however, but systematically points out that the short novel achieves the three-part exposition/development/recapitulation progression of the sonata-allegro form. This form is evident not only in plot or fable but also in patterns of images and language.

That sonata form can be usefully applied to an author who had little if anything to say about musical form in his own writing is demonstrated by Robert K. Wallace in the next essay, "'The Murders in the Rue Morgue' and Sonata

Form." Certainly the poetry of Edgar Allan Poe frequently imitates musical devices and sounds, but there is no evidence that any of his fiction was deliberately cast in a musical structure. Intention is not fundamental to analogies between music and literature, however; as Wallace explains, his objective is to demonstrate that prose fiction and classical music can "work in the same way" even though neither author nor composer models his work on that of the other. These remarks recall those of Gross in indicating that, although Eliot's "Four Quartets" is not intentionally patterned after Beethoven's C# Minor Quartet, the two works are inherently similar. Wallace chooses the first movement of Beethoven's "Pathétique Sonata," op. 13, to illustrate his thesis. Making no claim for conscious borrowing, he maintains that structural similarities arise as a result of the temporal nature of these arts that depend so heavily on the memory of the perceiver.

The fifth section of the collection expands discussion of the sonata form in literature from short fiction to the novel. In "*Great Circle:* Conrad Aiken's Musico-Literary Technique," Robert Emerson Carlile traces the pattern of musical allusions within the novel and concludes that the novelist's ordering of them resembles the ordering of theme groups characteristic of sonata form. Although he does not argue rigorously that the novel is "in" sonata form, Carlile suggests that it tends toward that form. Especially interesting is his implication that music in the novel provides a way back to the past; this aspect of his argument recalls Proust's and Eliot's use of music as a means for recovering the past.

Theodore Ziolkowski carries Carlile's thesis further in his "Herman Hesse's *Steppenwolf:* A Sonata in Prose" by meticulously showing how the novel, rather than merely tending toward sonata-allegro or first-movement form, may be compared with the overall sonata form. That is, the conflict between the Bürger and Haller provides the dialectic of the first movement, while the double perception, or counterpoint, furnishes the material for a second movement. Finally, the pattern derived from the "tractate," which details the multifaceted elements in Haller's personality, supplies material for the theme and variation structure of the third movement. Ziolkowski considers the primary similarity between *Steppenwolf* and the modern symphony to be that both employ the themes of the first movement in subsequent sections.

The final essay of this group again refers to specific musical form in a literary work. Don Noel Smith analyzes the sonata form of *Ulysses* in his "Musical Form and Principles in the Scheme of *Ulysses.*" Many critics have discussed the musical techniques of Joyce's work, but few have assimilated these views into the pattern of the sonata form. Smith postulates that the exposition consists of chapters one through six; the development, of chapters seven through fifteen; and the recapitulation, of chapters sixteen to seventeen; with chapter eighteen appending a coda. As interesting as his formal analysis is Smith's suggestion that the musical analogy goes beyond the formal—that the interpretation of reality as a whole in *Ulysses* is one in which "events bear essentially the same relation to time, space, and motion that sounds bear to them in music." He sees the octave as the basic ordering principle, with Stephen and Bloom at the extremes pulled toward the middle by love.

Finally, two essays furnish a kind of appendix to the collection. Surprisingly, few studies have been made of musical form in the drama. Perhaps it seems closer to music because it is a performer's art and is necessarily perceived in a self-contained expanse of time during its production. For whatever reason, drama has not elicited many formal analyses of its musico-literary structure. Raymond Jarvi's "Strindberg's *The Ghost Sonata* and Sonata Form" supplies a unique example. Jarvi briefly summarizes Strindberg's interest in and knowledge of music as Basilius did for Mann. Surely, Strindberg intended *The Ghost Sonata* to be in sonata form, and he seems to have been particularly aware of Beethoven's D Minor Piano Sonata during the time he was writing it. Jarvi explains that the requisite conflict of themes stems from opposing characters—Arkenholz and Hummel. He argues that the former is "the savior of human lives in a world where accident and chance are the fundamental laws" while the latter, Hummel, is "the well-to-do businessman who claims to look mildly on the shortcomings of, and flaws in, his fellow human beings, but whose grasp literally sucks the life force from Arkenholz."

The final essay, "Parallel Attitudes to Form in Late Beethoven and Late Goethe: Throwing Aside the Appearance of Art," by R. T. Llewellyn, brings the collection full circle. From the discussions of techniques for patterning in the first four essays, through the formal analyses of the middle section, it now moves out to a comparison of the conscious formlessness of Beethoven's late quartets and Goethe's *Wilhelm Meister*. For these artists, in their full maturity, classical form was no longer adequate to their vision of reality; both moved to fragmentation, shorthand, allegory, and even the conventional cliché to achieve their orders of reality.

The subjects of this conversation, then, range from the elemental techniques underlying musico-literary structures through examples of the theme and variation and sonata form in literature to speculations concerning the movement beyond classical form. Rather than affording only one point of view in a kind of monologue, the entire collection affirms a variety of stances that unfold the complex problem of structural relationships. This study does not concern the question of influence or intention so much as it does the innate similarities that result from the *ways* by which these temporal arts attain form. The peculiar nature of chronological and aesthetic time is inherent in all of the discussions. Literature and music require the interplay between chronological and aesthetic time, or, in other words, between objective and subjective time. This tension is the material through which the temporal arts *become*. Form in literature and music provides the core of this dialogue, which offers the basis for a new apprehension of the similarities between the dissimilar arts of music and literature.

Notes

1.   For a concise historical summary of critical work in musico-literary relationships see Calvin S. Brown, "The Relations between Music and Literature as a Field of Study," *Comparative Literature* 22 (1970):97–107.

2.   Weisstein alludes to this study in his article "Collage, Montage, and Related Terms: Their Literal and Figurative Use in and Application to Techniques in Various Arts," *Comparative Literature Studies* 15 (1978):124.

3.   Steven Paul Scher, "How Meaningful is 'Musical' in Literary Criticism?" *Yearbook of Comparative and General Literature* 21 (1972):52.

4.   Calvin S. Brown, *Music and Literature: A Comparison of the Arts* (Athens: University of Georgia Press, 1948), p. xi.

5.   René Wellek and Austin Warren, *Theory of Literature,* 3d ed. (New York: Harcourt, Brace and World, 1970), p. 130.

6.   Scher, p. 56.

7.   J. T. Fraser, "A Note on Rhythm and Time," in *The Voices of Time,* edited by J. T. Fraser (New York: George Braziller, 1966), p. 201.

8.   Eudora Welty, "Some Notes on Time in Fiction," 1973; reprinted in Eudora Welty, *The Eye of the Story* (New York: Random House, 1978), p. 168.

9.   J. T. Fraser, *Of Time, Passion, and Knowledge: Reflections on the Strategy of Existence* (New York: George Braziller, 1975), p. 404.

10.   Jacob Bronowski, "The Creative Process," 1958; reprinted in *A Sense of the Future: Essays in Natural Philosophy,* edited by Peiro E. Ariotti in collaboration with Rita Bronowski (Cambridge, Mass.: The MIT Press, 1977), p. 12.

11.   T. S. Eliot, "The Music of Poetry," 1942; reprinted in T. S. Eliot, *On Poetry and Poets* (New York: The Noonday Press, 1943), p. 32.

One

Techniques of Structure

Blending Cadences:
Rhythm and Structure in *Moby-Dick*

Marden J. Clark

> . . . lulled into such an opium-like listlessness of vacant, unconscious reverie is this absent-minded youth by the blending cadence of waves with thoughts.
>
> Herman Melville, *Moby-Dick*

Once we have completed *Moby-Dick* and set it aside to let it work on us, perhaps the most insistent single impression is the sense of increasing, building, pervasive resonances. They may strike us even stronger in the retrospective experience of the novel than in the actual reading of it. Part of the magic of *Moby-Dick* must lie in these resonances: resonances in sounds, in patterns, in images and metaphors and symbols, in ideas and meanings. And resonance in rhythms. For rhythms can resonate in something of the way sounds do, and our sense of that resonance is crucial to many of the cumulative effects of *Moby-Dick*. In this essay I explore some of the rhythmic resonances as they build toward structural patterns. I use as a springboard a concept of rhythm developed almost concurrently with the Melville revival—and rather "nervously"—by E. M. Forster.[1]

Forster thinks of rhythm as something beyond what we usually think of as prose rhythms. Even in its "easy sense," he defines rhythm as "repetition plus variation" and exemplifies it by the "little phrase" from the Vinteuil sonata that keeps recurring in Marcel Proust's *Remembrance of Things Past*. But Forster teases us with a larger concept of rhythm, wondering if there is not "any effect in novels comparable to the effect of the Fifth Symphony as a whole, where, when the orchestra stops, we hear something that has never actually been played," something "achieved mainly (though not entirely) by the relation between the three big blocks of sound which the orchestra has been playing." Forster cannot find such an analogy, though he wonders whether there might not be something of it in *War and Peace:* "Yet, as we read it, do not great chords begin to sound behind us, and when we have finished does not every item—even the catalogue of strategies—lead a larger existence than was possible at the time?" Surely such "great chords" *do* begin to sound in *War and Peace*, in *The Brothers Karamazov*,

Reprinted from *Studies in the Novel* 8 (1976):158–71.

in nearly every great novel. In few novels do we sense such chords more profoundly than in *Moby-Dick*.

I cannot help feeling, however, that in his concern for the big effects Forster passed too easily over the smaller ones. The great chords of the reflective experience have to develop from the immediate chords of the immediate experience. "Prose rhythms" develop into the resonating rhythms. And rhythmic patterns develop into structural patterns.

We all know some of the immediate rhythms in *Moby-Dick:* the Shakespeare-like blank verse—or something close to it—that characterizes many of the dramatic scenes and soliloquies, the looser cadenced prose-verse that owes much to biblical rhythms, the wavelike periodic sentences that break against each other or against the rocks or against a gentle sloping shore to roll up the sands. The blank verse is perhaps the least effective of these, certainly the most derivative. Most readers have probably shared the reservations of F. O. Matthiessen that "as it breaks down again into the ejaculatory prose, it seems never to have belonged to the speaker."[2] But once one grants the Shakespearean origins and then lets the lines work in a way analogous to the allusive techniques in T. S. Eliot or Ezra Pound, they become the vehicle for highly dramatic and often very effective scenes, even when they are shrill as here from "The Candles":

> The lightning flashes through my skull;
> Mine eye-balls ache and ache; my whole beaten brain
> Seems as beheaded, and rolling on some
> Stunning ground.
> Oh, oh! Yet blindfolded, yet will I talk to thee.
> Light though thou be, thou leapest out of darkness;
> But I am darkness leaping out of light,
> Leaping out of thee! The javelins cease;
> Open eyes; see, or not? There burn the flames! [119:472][3]

Matthiessen's example from "Sunset"—beginning "I leave a white and turbid wake" (37:157)—can be extended in more or less regular blank verse almost through the brief chapter, including along the way such regular—and poignant—lines as, "This lovely light it lights not me." Even with the irregularity of some of it, one can hardly miss the controlling rhythmic feel. The iambic beat, with its echo of Ahab's pacing on that whalebone leg, suffuses nearly all of the dramatic scenes in the novel, even those which arrange much more satisfactorily into a loose, cadenced verse, like the following from "The Symphony":

> Oh, Starbuck!
> It is a mild, mild wind, and a mild looking sky.
> On such a day—very much such a sweetness as this—
> I struck my first whale—a boy harpooner of eighteen!
> Forty—forty—forty years ago!—ago!
> Forty years of continual whaling!
> Forty years of privation, and peril, and storm-time!
> ....
> Here, brush this old hair aside; it blinds me, that I seem to weep.
> Locks so grey did never grow but from out some ashes!
> But do I look very old, so very, very old, Starbuck?
> I feel deadly faint, bowed, and humped,

> As though I were Adam, staggering beneath the piled centuries
> Since paradise. [132:501–2]

We hardly need labor the examples. We can find them almost any place in the novel where men are speaking in any degree of passion. Such rhythms serve the immediate dramatic effect much more than they do any broad structural purposes. Yet the recurring rhythms do help us sense the broader unity of the dramatic scenes, do underscore the relationships among these scenes, do help us experience the novel as a basically dramatic experience.

Even so, these are not the most characteristic sentences and rhythms of *Moby-Dick*. For those we turn to the sentences and sequences of sentences that build and roll and break. Most often, they are Ishmael's sentences. They tend to come when he is most involved with his materials and their meanings. But they can come anywhere in the novel—the first paragraph, for instance:

> Whenever I find myself growing grim about the mouth; whenever it is a
> damp, drizzly November in my soul; whenever I find myself involuntarily
> pausing before coffin warehouses, and bringing up the rear of every funeral I
> meet; and especially whenever my hypos get such an upper hand of me, that it
> requires a strong moral principle to prevent me from deliberately stepping into
> the street, and methodically knocking people's hats off—then, I account it high
> time to get to sea as soon as I can. [1:3]

They are showpiece sentences, of course. But individually, and especially as a repeated pattern, they are the sentences that catch the famous Melville feel of the sea. The rhythm hardly needs emphasizing. But we can visualize it by laying it out like this:

> Whenever I find myself growing grim about the mouth;
> Whenever it is a damp, drizzly November in my soul;
> Whenever I find myself involuntarily
>   pausing before coffin warehouses, and
>   bringing up the rear of every funeral that I meet;
>   and especially
> Whenever my hypos get such an upper hand of me, that it requires
>   a strong moral principle to prevent me from
>   deliberately stepping into the street, and
>   methodically knocking people's hats off—
> then, I account it high time to get to sea as soon as I can.

I visualize such a sentence as a series of waves cresting with each clause, then finally breaking with the enclosing sentence either sharply against the rocks or less abruptly against the slope of the shore and then gently rolling up the sandy beach. Ishmael's playful tone in this one keeps it from developing the energy implicit in the structure. There is a mocking quality—almost an implied self-parody in advance. But one does not have to wait very long to find such sentences carrying real vigor, for example, in Ishmael's meditation on the dead, beginning, "In what census of living creatures. . . ." Not even the shifting structure of the clauses (some direct questions, some indirect) vitiates the building energy, though the anticlimax of the enfolding sentence does somewhat: "All these things are not without their meanings" (7:35–36).

Father Mapple can swing such a sentence with real effect, too, as witness the third paragraph from the end of his sermon. The series is set up as individual sentences, each beginning, in biblical fashion. "Woe to him ..." (9:46). But the rhetorical effect of the paragraph is almost precisely the same as I have described above.

Perhaps the best-known of these series, and certainly one which develops the full energy implicit in the form, comes at the end of "Brit":

> Consider the subtleness of the sea; how its most dreaded creatures glide un-
> der water, unapparent for the most part, and treacherously hidden beneath the
> loveliest tints of azure. Consider also the devilish brilliance and beauty of many
> of its most remorseless tribes, as the dainty embellished shape of many species
> of sharks. Consider once more, the universal cannibalism of the sea; all whose
> creatures prey upon each other, carrying on eternal war since the world began.
> Consider all this; and then turn to this green, gentle, and most docile
> earth; consider them both, the sea and the land; and do you not find a strange
> analogy to something in yourself? For as this appalling ocean surrounds the
> verdant land, so in the soul of man there lies one insular Tahiti, full of peace
> and joy, but encompassed by all the horrors of the half known life. God keep
> thee! Push not off from that isle, thou canst never return! [58:261]

Laying this out schematically gives immediate emphasis to the structure of the first paragraph. But I found it of little help with the final one. We can sense the crest, certainly, but it is a kind of hovering crest through the repeated *Consider* which breaks and rolls with the question and answer, but rolls to some kind of sharp obstruction with the imperative at the end. "God keep thee!" and the im-perative would both be merely shrill rhetoric without the building force of the series behind them. With it and with the developing image of the sea, we sense it as one of the most moving warnings in the novel—perhaps especially moving since it strikes us finally as almost totally ironic: all Melville mariners *must* push off from that isle, in spite of the dangers.

The sentences recur just often enough to become a kind of trademark of Melville's oceangoing style at its best—the guarantee that this is the genuine ar-ticle. Once conscious of them, we watch for them. And their recurrence has something of the same effect, for me at least, as the recurring phrase from Vintueil's sonata has for Forster. So that we are hardly surprised to see Ishmael introduce that prodigy of symbolic analysis, "The Whiteness of the Whale," with a virtuoso sentence-paragraph nearly five hundred words long made up of a series of twelve clauses, each introduced by "though" or "and though" and some containing within themselves long rhythmically patterned parallel phrases. In the parallel rolling building clauses Ishmael summarizes all those positive values and connotations of whiteness against which, this enfolding clause tells us, his own reservations and fears are going to play: "yet for all these accumulated associ-ations, with whatever is sweet, and honorable, and sublime, there yet lurks an elusive something in the innermost idea of this hue, which strikes more of panic to the soul than that redness which affrights in blood" (42:177). This "thought of whiteness," the "innermost idea" of it, is what Ishmael must explain, "else all these chapters might be nought" (p. 176). He spends the rest of the chapter de-veloping this innermost idea in a series of examples, usually a paragraph each, that build with an analogous rhythm to break in the final paragraph of the chapter.

All this should suggest something of what I am after in my title, "Rhythm *and* Structure." If I am right that these wavelike sentences form the most characteristic rhythms of the novel, then we might expect these rhythms to carry over into larger effects, into larger resonating rhythms.[4] "The Whiteness of the Whale" may be the best single chapter to analyze in detail for such larger effects (42:176 ff.).

The chapter begins with a kind of anticipatory chord: "What the white whale was to Ahab, has been hinted; what, at times, he was to me, as yet remains unsaid." The next paragraph leads into the long rhythmic one—analyzed above—by expressing the difficulty of trying to explain the "Mystical and well-nigh ineffable" horror in the "whiteness of the whale that above all things appalled" Ishmael.

Taken together, these three paragraphs develop an urgent context for the examples that follow. The examples themselves of the horror of whiteness build in groups to some kind of transitional enfolding paragraph, then start over again:

> Witness the white bear of the poles, and the white shark of
>   the tropics . . .
> Bethink thee of the albatross . . .
> . . . the White Steed of the Prairies . . .

Then the enfolding transitional sentence-paragraph:

> But there are other instances where this whiteness loses
>   all that accessory and strange glory which invests it in the
> White Steed and Albatross. [p. 179]

And the next series begins:

> What is it that in the Albino man . . .
> . . . the gauntleted ghost of the Southern Seas has been
>   denominated the White Squall. . . . The desperate White
>   Hoods of Ghent . . .
> . . . the one visible quality of the aspect of the dead . . .

Again the enfolding paragraph:

> Therefore, in his other moods, symbolizes whatever grand
>   or gracious thing he will by whiteness, no man can deny
>   that in its profoundest idealized significance it calls up
>   a peculiar apparition to the soul. [p. 180]

And after two paragraphs of meditation on the difficulty and subtlety of his problem (paragraphs which resonate rhythmically with the chapter's introductory paragraph), Ishmael sets up a new series that builds in parallel crests through the white-hooded "slow-pacing pilgrims," the "White Tower of London," and sad "tearless Lima." The series breaks in another transitional paragraph in which Ishmael admits again the difficulty of showing to "the common apprehension" and "the unimaginative mind" how whiteness exaggerates "the terror of objects otherwise terrible." Ishmael then tries with another series of two examples to "elucidate" the quality of whiteness to the *un*common apprehension: the mariner who awakens to find his ship "sailing through a midnight sea of milky whiteness," and the sailor in the Antarctic who "views what seems a boundless church-yard grinning upon him with its lean ice monuments and splintered crosses." The enfolding paragraph this time ties together in a somewhat lighter tone the immediately preceding examples, but also the chapter thus far:

> But thou sayest, methinks this white-lead chapter about whiteness is but a
> white flag hung out from a craven soul; thou surrenderest to a hypo, Ishmael.
> [p. 183]

The paragraph also leads into a series of four brief paragraphs that themselves build rhythmically to the remarkable crescendoing final paragraph of the chapter. These four brief paragraphs develop rather as wavelets before the real crest. Whiteness is to Ishmael what the mere shaking of a fresh buffalo robe is to a young colt: "the instinct of the knowledge of the demonism in the world," the evidence that "though in many of its aspects this visible world seems formed in love, the invisible spheres were formed in fright." But not even yet, the last of the four sentence-paragraphs tells us, "have we solved the incantation of this whiteness," have we learned why it can be at once "the very veil of the Christian's Deity" and "the intensifying agent in things the most appalling to mankind." Such a solution the final paragraph attempts—the enfolding paragraph for this brief series and for the chapter as a whole. It needs quoting almost in full:

> Is it that by its indefiniteness it shadows forth the heartless voids and im
> mensities of the universe, and thus stabs us from behind with the thought of
> annihilation, when beholding the white depths of the milky way? Or is it, that
> as in essence whiteness is not so much a color as the visible absence of color,
> and at the same time the concrete of all colors: is it for these reasons that there
> is such a dumb blankness, full of meaning, in a wide landscape of snows—a col
> orless, all-color of atheism from which we shrink? And when we consider that
> other theory of the natural philosophers, that all other earthly hues—every
> stately or lovely emblazoning ... all these are but subtile deceits, not actually
> inherent in substances, but only laid on from without; so that all deified Na
> ture absolutely paints like the harlot, whose allurements cover nothing but the
> charnel-house within; and when we proceed further, and consider that the mys
> tical cosmetic which produces every one of her hues, the great principle of
> light, forever remains white or colorless in itself, and if operating without me
> dium upon matter, would touch all objects, even tulips and roses, with its own
> blank tinge—pondering all this, the palsied universe lies before us a leper; and
> like wilful travellers in Lapland, who refuse to wear colored and coloring
> glasses upon their eyes, so the wretched infidel gazes himself blind at the mon
> umental white shroud that wraps all the prospect around him. And of all these
> things the Albino whale was the symbol. Wonder ye then at the fiery hunt?
> [pp. 183–84]

The paragraph itself builds internally with two basic series of patterned sentences: (1) "Is it that ...? Or is it, that ... ; is it for these reasons ...?" and (2) "And when we consider ... ; and when we proceed further, and consider ...—pondering all this, the palsied universe. ..." These two patterns build to break in the final two sentences of the paragraph. The paragraph functions as the enfolding paragraph of the brief series preceding it, which in turn wraps up all the series leading up to it and the chapter as a whole. The display of rhythmic virtuosity is almost as impressive as the display of symbolic exploration: rhythms within rhythms, rhythms breaking against and growing into other rhythms, rhythms building and building in resonance to finally break and wrap themselves up in those two short final sentences. Wonder ye then at the fiery hunt?

Considered rhythmically as well as other ways, the chapter may be the most impressive in *Moby-Dick*. But it is by no means the only one that builds like this. I have examined above the ending paragraphs of "Brit." The chapter is much briefer than "The Whiteness," but these paragraphs wrap up a chapter that begins in straight narrative, moves to factual description of the brit, builds through a particularly fine patterned sentence-paragraph ("But though ... ; though ... ; though ... ; yet....."), and finally breaks in those two final paragraphs that catch so much of Melville's feel for the contrast between sea and land, and so much of the symbolic suggestiveness of the novel. This may be the best of the "factual" chapters. But most of the others build the same way: through the factual material to some kind of enclosing statement of the chapter's import, often factual and nearly always symbolic–through, for example, the fine technical analysis of "The Line" (ch. 40) or of "Fast Fish and Loose Fish" (ch. 89), to broader applications, to metaphysical suggestion.

Sometimes the pattern is not so easily recognizable. But even the primarily narrative chapters often build in analogous patterns. The rhythmically building frenzy of action in "Stubb Kills a Whale" breaks with the final "flurry," to roll quietly to Stubb's comment, "Yes; both pipes smoked out" (61:272). The individual comments on the doubloon build and subside and build again to be wrapped up by Pip's mad-wise comments on the commentators (99:407-8). Father Mapple's sermon (9:40 ff.) builds in waves to break in the climactic series of "Woe to him" and to recede through the series "Delight is to him" through the benediction and the withdrawal of the people, leaving him alone in his maintop of a pulpit.

Each of the final three chapters of the novel makes especially fine use of this broad rhythmic pattern. Each follows essentially the same wavelike development in action and tension, building through the search to a crest at the sighting of Moby Dick, subsiding somewhat as the ship chases the whale, then building again to a crest at the lowering and chase by the boats, subsiding again at the whale's sounding as the crews wait, then building to a final crest and breaking with the encounter and destruction, to roll up the shore as evening approaches and finally to ebb with the abandonment of the chase for that day. The cresting of the encounter with Moby Dick on the third day is itself rhythmically divided into three increasingly furious encounters: in the first the whale destroys the other boats but only grazes Ahab's; in the second he cants Ahab's boat, throws Ishmael out of the boat, and snaps the harpoon line; in the third he destroys the ship and pulls Ahab, caught in the line, to his death. The action recedes as the ship sinks and "the great shroud of the sea rolled on as it rolled five thousand years ago."

But we are not yet done with rhythm and structure. Starbuck comments on the essential unity of this three-day chase: "For when three days flow together in one continuous intense pursuit; be sure the first is the morning, the second the noon, and the third the evening and the end of that thing—be that end what it may" (135:524). In other words, as the analysis of parallels above must have suggested, the three chapters taken together form a larger rhythmic and structural unit than any we have looked at yet, and one that builds with remarkable effectiveness and energy to the final catastrophe. It may be the most apparent and the tightest of the larger units, but again it is far from the only one. Looking back over the novel, we can see many analogous units as the novel has developed. Chapters 41, "Moby Dick," and 42, "The Whiteness of the Whale," form such a unit: the first defining Moby Dick as Ahab sees him, the second as Ishmael sees him. The "Moby Dick" chapter builds and swells internally in only less impressive ways than does "The Whiteness of the Whale." Taken together, they define the two complementary qualities of horror in *Moby-Dick*. But they also act both together and separately as climax of still larger patterns of associations and allusions that finally tell us all we can know of Moby Dick's destructive power and of his whiteness.

"The Quarter-Deck" and "The Candles," though widely separated in the novel, form a similar unit. They develop in similar patterns internally, swelling and receding and swelling again to break in the infernal sacrament at the end of "The Quarter-Deck," in Ahab's infernal fire worship at the end of "The Candles." Each is highly dramatic, though set in narrative form. Each introduces a sequence of chapters set in dramatic form, but ebbing or receding rhythmically from the high drama.[6] Together, the two chapters define the heights of Ahab's hubris and his demonism. All the first part of the novel builds *to* the first quarterdeck scene; all the final part builds *from* the second. Between them they frame the bulk of the novel: the routine killing and processing of whales, most of the cetological and structural description, most of the gams, and so forth. Finally, each acts as the enfolding chapter for several large patterns of imagery, allusion, and symbolism, notably, in "The Quarter-Deck," the building pattern of awesome references to Captain Ahab, and, in "The Candles," the intricate pattern of fire symbolism that has already had mighty crests in "The Try-Works" and "The Forge."[7]

Many other chapter sequences work as rhythmic and structural units and as parts of larger units. All the early chapters build with finely controlled tonal and narrative rhythms to that Christmas sailing. We can recognize crests at least in Father Mapple's sermon, in Ishmael's signing with Captain Peleg, and in the sailing itself, where one senses that the wave is breaking hard against the rocks. The factual chapters, cetological and otherwise, function as a unit, though individually they generally indicate a lull, a break in the narrative movement of the novel. They spread the rhythm of the whale-catch over the bulk of the novel. They develop as almost nothing else could the illusion of passing time by filling the large gaps of time between significant actions. They follow essentially the sequence of the kill, the processing, and the stowing away and cleaning up, but they build, in appropriate rhythmical increments, our knowledge of whaling as both physical and metaphysical fact until we can follow with some assurance the fastest and most complex narrative action and the most complex allusions during it, and even the most complex soundings of Ishmael's and Melville's metaphysical explorations.

While looking at some of the contiguous sequences of chapters that form rhythmic and structural units, I have moved inevitably out to larger, discontinuous sequences. These discontinuous sequences of chapters and lesser elements function rhythmically, I have noted, in Forster's "easy sense." Each pattern works nearly always with incremental force. That is, the patterns get their energy not merely from repetition, but, as in musical repetition and variation, from incremental development. When a sea-hawk rather improbably snatches Ahab's hat just before the final chase and apparently drops it into the sea at the furthest point of sight, Ishmael contrasts it with the eagle that took and replaced Tarquin's hat, indicating that Tarquin would be king of Rome. But we sense also deeper resonances: Ahab has very early thrown his pipe overboard—pipes are "meant for sereneness"—and much later destroyed his quadrant, the most precise of his instruments of navigation, because it "casts man's eyes aloft to that heaven, whose lividness but scorches him," and because it can tell nothing of where Moby Dick is or where Ahab will be tomorrow. Possibly in retaliation the storm destroys the compass, but Ahab proves himself master of the level loadstone. Just how all this works is hard to say, but the contrast between the voluntary loss of pipe and quadrant and the involuntary loss of compass and hat sets up fascinating resonances. And at least the bird snatching the hat is related to that sky-hawk which Tashtego, again improbably, catches with his hammer and pulls down, this "bird of heaven," with the ship.

On a much larger scale, the series of meetings with other ships, resulting but seldom in the expected "gam," functions with fine rhythmical effect in the novel, but much more subtly than is at first apparent. James Dean Young has demonstrated how subtly they work as a unit and how they relate to the developing novel: they provide a series of warnings to Ahab and the *Pequod*, warnings which of course go unheeded; they provide a series of alternative attitudes toward Moby Dick, culminating in that of the *Delight*, whose captain has lost men to Moby Dick and therefore knows and believes in him but, in contrast to Ahab, takes no action; and they underscore the increasing isolation of the *Pequod* and form a major part of the increasingly intense pattern of omens.[8]

The pattern of omens itself works rhythmically throughout the novel, beginning with Ishmael's fascination in chapter one with "such a portentous and mysterious monster," developing somewhat playfully and with appropriate ebbings through the introductory chapters with their paintings of destruction from whales, their marble tablets "Sacred to the Memory of" dead whalemen, their mysterious whispered warnings, and all the rest, to be climaxed in the ominous Christmas sailing, then ebbing somewhat during the long sections largely made up of factual matter, but building with increasing intensity and rapidity up to and through the final chase. A parallel pattern, intimately related, is the pattern of explicit, if highly ambiguous, prophecies that begins with Elijah's taunting warnings, includes Gabriel's similar but more specific ones, Fedallah's echoes of the Weird Sisters as he outlines the three conditions for Ahab's death, and Pip's mad warning about the sharks. Another parallel and intimately related pattern is that of madness: Elijah and Gabriel are consciously projected as mad prophets; Ahab's demonic monomania plays against their mad foreknowledge as it does against Pip's mad wisdom and Fedallah's mad calmness (to the extent that

Fedallah comes through as character); and Pip's madness from being lost overboard contrasts with Ishmael's being saved by being lost overboard.

We can trace analogous rhythms and structural patterns in the developing ideas, themes, and symbols of the novel. One brief example will suggest the others. Ishmael's seriocomic meditations on his new bedmate, "this headpeddling harpooneer" (3:21), introduce a theme of brotherhood that crests, notably when Ishmael wakes to find himself in the "bridegroom clasp" of Queequeg, "as though naught but death should part us twain" (p. 27); crests again, when in the process of squeezing the spermacetti Ishmael feels "divinely free from all ill-will" and finds himself squeezing the hands of his colaborers and finally exclaiming, "let us squeeze ourselves universally into the very milk and sperm of kindness" (94:391); and finally in the "Epilogue" breaks gently in that fascinating revelation that Ishmael has been saved by Queequeg's unused coffin—a final gift of salvation from the Queequeg who had, on the voyage to Nantucket, saved first the boat from its loose and wildly swinging spar and then the young greenhorn who had been swept overboard. Truly, as Queequeg seems to be thinking after this event, "It's a mutual, jointstock world, in all meridians. We cannibals must help these Christians" (13:59). Such a system of rhythms plays throughout the novel in a gentle and sane counterpoint to the mad violence of Ahab, who binds the crew to him with his diabolic rites and, at the same time that he increasingly isolates himself from human brotherhood, still draws both crew and ship to destruction.

From such large patterns we turn easily to the whole novel.[9] The slighter rhythms build to the larger ones, the lesser patterns to the greater, until we sense Moby-Dick as a large pattern developing with this same wavelike rhythm from the remarkable blending and building and resonating patterns we have been tracing. In retrospective experience of the novel we can identify with comparative ease the major crests which break and roll and ebb to build again: from the signing-on with its mock ceremony; to the Christmas sailing; to the appearance of Ahab, when "Reality outran apprehension"; to the demonic ceremony on the quarterdeck; ebbing through the metaphysical speculations on the meaning of Moby Dick and his whiteness and then building to the minor excitement of the first lowering; moving rather quietly with minor crestings through all the physical and metaphysical facts about whales and whaling to Ishmael's crisis before the fire of the try-works; thence through more factual materials to the final scene on the quarterdeck where Ahab challenges and controls the fire; to a lesser crest when Ahab denies help to the Rachel; through the quiet of the Symphony to the great building and climaxing crest of the three-day chase; to the quiet ebbing in the epilogue.

And of course the rhythms, the resonances, the reverberations do not stop here. I may not even yet be talking about Forster's "great chords" that begin to sound behind us and that "lead a larger existence" in retrospect than in the immediate experience. But I must be—if it is possible at all to talk about such things. Our sense of such rhythm and resonance comes to us largely in retrospect. I even suspect that the sense itself builds and crests and ebbs, then builds and crests and ebbs in a way somewhat analogous to the rhythms of Moby-Dick that I have been analyzing.

Regardless of how the rhythms work their magic, they work it. And it is an amazing achievement. We can no longer talk condescendingly of the loose or sprawling or careless structure of *Moby-Dick*. We can call it large, or different, or even exasperatingly inclusive. But within the controlling structure of the voyage, the novel sets up too many rhythms that build and resonate and clash with one another and support one another in ever-enlarging patterns of both rhythm and structure for us to sense them any longer as loose. Rather, the developing patterns of rhythm and resonance taken together attest to a profound kind of integrity—a "little lower layer"—that makes the apparent surface problems of structure fade into insignificance—if it does not make them into positive strengths. The voyage ends in disaster. But the disaster culminates and resolves nearly every developing pattern that I have commented on and hence itself acts as the final breaking and rolling of waves that by now have achieved at once both tidal proportions and the sense of total control. And following that quiet ebbing of the "Epilogue," in which Ishmael steps forth to explain his own survival, we are left with the building sense of resonating rhythms and symbols that tease us *into* thought and awareness, "as doth eternity."

Notes

1. E. M. Forster, *Aspects of the Novel* (New York: Harcourt, Harvest Books, 1927), pp. 164–69.

2. F. O. Matthiessen, *American Renaissance* (New York: Oxford University Press, 1941), p. 426. Matthiessen talks about other qualities of Melville's style, but with primary attention to diction and metaphors, emphasizing the influence of Shakespeare. There have been many comments on Melville's rhythmic prose, such as Walter Bezanson's on the "cadenced voice" of Ishmael, in "*Moby-Dick:* Work of Art," from *Moby-Dick: Centennial Essays,* edited by Tyrus Hillway and Luther S. Mansfield (Dallas: Southern Methodist University Press, 1953), p. 3. But I have found surprisingly little detailed analysis of rhythmic effects. Both John Erskine in *The Delight of Great Books* (Indianapolis: Bobbs-Merrill, 1928), p. 230, and Lewis Mumford in *The Golden Day* (New York: Norton, 1934), p. 146, made early comments on the book as poetry. Bezanson goes on to examine four levels of rhetoric: the expository; the poetic, for which he simply reproduces part of Matthiessen's arrangement in blank verse; the idiomatic; and the composite, which reaches toward some of the rhythmic effects I analyze here. Edgar A. Dryden also suggests some of them, though only indirectly, in his analysis of Ishmael's weaving of reality from words, "Ishmael as Teller," in his book *Melville's Thematics of Form: The Great Art of Telling the Truth* (Baltimore: Johns Hopkins Press, 1968), pp. 83–113. Warner Berthoff has a good chapter, "Words, Sentences, Paragraphs, Chapters," in his *The Example of Melville* (Princeton, N.J.: Princeton University Press, 1962), pp. 159–82; but he has little concern with rhythmic effects. Nathalia Wright's chapter "Style" in *Melville's Use of the Bible* (Durham, N.C.: Duke University Press, 1949), pp. 137–72, relates many qualities of Melville's style to the Bible, especially commenting on parallelism and antiphonalism in Father Mapple's sermon and in "The Whiteness of the Whale."

3. The first number in parentheses refers throughout this essay to chapter numbers in *Moby-Dick,* the second (or a single number on occasion) to page numbers in the Willard Thorpe edition of *Moby-Dick* (New York: Oxford University Press, 1947).

4. Lincoln Colcord, "Notes on *Moby-Dick*," in *The Merrill Studies in Moby-Dick,* edited by Howard Paton Vincent (Columbus, Ohio: Merrill, 1969), pp. 32–43, suggests something of the feel I am after here with his comment on the "purposeful suspense which

flows through the tale from beginning to end in a constantly swelling current." His "Notes" are suggestive but do not go very deep.

5. Most of the discussion of the structure of *Moby-Dick* has involved the problems posed by the mass of materials not immediately part of the quest for the whale. Responses have ranged all the way from Somerset Maugham's dogmatism, in *"Moby-Dick," Atlantic Monthly* 181 (1943):104, that "it would be stupid" to call the novel "well constructed," to the eulogizing exclamation of Van Wyck Brooks: "What variety one found, moreover, in the admirable unity of *Moby-Dick,"* in *Times of Melville and Whitman* (New York: Dutton, 1947), p. 174. Early analyses tried to find "something like design," as John Freeman puts it in *Herman Melville* ("English Men of Letters") (New York: Macmillan, 1926), p. 120. More recent studies have focused on related groups of chapters. See especially Bezanson's essay and Howard C. Horsford, "The Design of the Argument in *Moby-Dick," Modern Fiction Studies* 8 (1962):233–51; this essay has a strong emphasis on structural metaphors.

6. Dan Vogel, "The Dramatic Chapters in *Moby Dick," Nineteenth-Century Fiction* 13 (1958):239–47, analyzes the dramatic chapters as forming their own complete dramatic rhythm, which he schematizes in five acts. Glauco Cambden also focuses on these and other "chapter clusters," in "Ishmael and the Problem of Formal Discontinuities in *Moby-Dick," Modern Language Notes* 76 (1961):516–23.

7. Much attention has been given to the patterns of fire symbolism. See Charles C. Walcutt, "The Fire Symbolism in *Moby-Dick," Modern Language Notes* 59 (1944):304–10, and Paul V. Miller, "Sun and Fire in Melville's *Moby-Dick," Nineteenth-Century Fiction* 13 (1958):139–44. Probably the most authoritative such study of the fire symbolism as it relates to Zoroastrianism is M. A. Isani's "Zoroastrianism and the Fire Symbolism in *Moby-Dick," American Literature* 44 (1972):385–97.

8. James Dean Young, "The Nine Gams of the *Pequod," American Literature* 25 (1954):449–63. See also Bezanson.

9. Almost from the beginning attempts to define the large structure of *Moby-Dick* have evoked forms like epic and tragedy and the word *myth,* counterpointed by a recurrent commonsense insistence that the voyage itself determines the structure. Matthiessen's (pp. 417–21) division of the novel into five units, along with his use of the language of drama, suggests that he thinks of the book as tragedy, though he ties his analysis to the voyage structure. Charles Olson, in *Call Me Ishmael* (New York: Reynal and Hitchcock, 1947), divides the book into five acts, with "a rise and fall comparable to an Elizabethan tragedy" (p. 66). Newton Arvin, in *Herman Melville* ("American Man of Letters") (New York: Sloane, 1950), pp. 155–58, responds rather vigorously to such analyses, insisting on the basic voyage structure but seeing the form as closer to epic than to drama; he speaks of "crests and troughs" of the voyage. More recently Herbert G. Eldridge, " 'Careful Disorder': The Structure of *Moby-Dick," American Literature* 39 (1967):145–62, sees the novel as spatially organized around six parts of the voyage. From my standpoint, perhaps the most interesting and immediately pertinent discussion of the recent analyses is that of Warwick Wadlington, "Ishmael's Godly Gamesomeness: Selftaste and Rhetoric in *Moby-Dick," ELH: A Journal of English Literary History* 39 (1972):309–31. He envisions the story as "a great spiral of repeating cycles leading to the final paradigmatic image of Ishmael captured and released. . . ." He also analyzes "alternating centripetal and centrifugal pressures of the book." The word *myth* carries a rhythmic and structural suggestion about it. Along with the many casual or brief references by critics to myth in *Moby-Dick,* three explicit analyses will indicate something of the range of mythical resonance in the novel. R. W. B. Lewis in his brief discussion of *Moby-Dick* in *The American Adam* (Chicago: University of Chicago Press, 1955), pp. 139–45, ties the novel to Homer, especially

to the *Odyssey*. Daniel Hoffman, *Form and Fable in American Fiction* (New York: Oxford University Press, 1961), has two chapters (pp. 221–78) on Moby-Dick, both concerned in part with various archetypal and mythical qualities. And H. Bruce Franklin, *The Wake of the Gods: Melville's Mythology* (Stanford, Calif.: Stanford University Press, 1965), has a long chapter, "Moby-Dick: An Egyptian Myth Incarnate" (pp. 53–98), in which he analyzes the novel as a version of the Isis and Osiris myth.

Tristram Shandy:
The Art of Literary Counterpoint

William Freedman

By now we have grown quite accustomed to attempts at what Aldous Huxley termed the "musicalization of fiction."[1] Thomas Mann, for example, conceived his *Tonio Kröger* as a literary sonata,[2] and he used a variety of musical principles in *The Magic Mountain* and *Buddenbrooks,* notably the Wagnerian leitmotiv. Proust used "symphonic" principles of theme development and interplay in *Remembrance of Things Past,* the first volume of which begins with an "Overture." Paul-Emile Cadilhac, a French novelist of the twenties, attempted what he called the "symphonic novel," similarly based on the development of themes, and asserted that such a novel "will create a musical atmosphere by the use of images, comparisons, and words borrowed from the musical vocabulary."[3] Huxley's *Point Counter Point* is an attempt, as the title suggests, at literary counterpoint. Joyce ventured a literary fugue in *Ulysses.* And Conrad Aiken conceives his poems as verbal music and has employed an almost endless variety of musical forms and techniques. In *The Square,* the contemporary French novelist Marguerite Duras has essayed what one critic aptly called "a kind of three-voice fugue."[4]

Generally, this kind of pursuit has been traced back to the German romantic poets of the early nineteenth century, who were the first to express their intent to musicalize their writing. Writers like Tieck, Hoffmann, Novalis, and Wackenroder frequently modeled their works after musical forms and applied musical principles to literature in order, they said, to capture the rapidly shifting moods and emotions music best conveys. Tieck's play, *Topsy Turvy World,* for example, contains a verbal prelude, or "symphony" as Tieck called it, and makes use of verbal passages instead of music between the acts. The last of these interludes consists of a thematic statement with three variations.

Although the German romantics were the first to discuss at length the application of musical techniques and patterns to literature, the desire to unite music with poetry—or literature in general—considerably antedates them. In England it ran parallel with the rise of sentimentalism and romanticism, which had begun to dominate the literary scene after 1750. It was widely believed that among the

Reprinted from *Modern Language Quarterly* 32 (1971):268–80.

three "sister arts"–poetry, painting, and music–poetry (or literature) and music
were the most intimately related, and largely as a result writers made frequent demands for their union in a single form. Eighteenth-century attempts to reunify
music and literature did not typically involve the application of musical principles to literature or the extensive use of musical language or metaphors.
Rather, the object was simply to unite the basically conceptual or rational character of poetry (which was also thought to have considerable emotive power) with
the essentially emotional character of music–usually in opera or song. Although
most eighteenth-century theorists envisioned nothing beyond this limited objective, the attempt to achieve musical effects in literary forms, through both language and structure, actually had its roots in the eighteenth century, specifically
in the writings of Laurence Sterne. Sterne, himself an accomplished gambist, has
earned an honor so far denied him: recognition as the true father of that ingenious bastard-child, the musical novel.

Music is everywhere in *Tristram Shandy*. "In my opinion," Tristram
volunteers,

> to write a book is for all the world like humming a song–be but in tune with
> yourself, madam, 'tis no matter how high or how low you take it.
> –This is the reason, may it please your reverences, that some of the lowest
> and flattest compositions pass off very well. ... (4:25)[5]

And again: "Attitudes are nothing, madam–'tis the transition from one attitude
to another–like the preparation and resolution of the discord into harmony,
which is all in all" (4:6). In both of these revealing and far from incidental analogies with music, Tristram helpfully articulates what his autobiography repeatedly bears out: that for him the business of writing is very much a musical enterprise. More specifically, they state figuratively what he states more literally
elsewhere (1:22; 9:12): that it is the balance, the equipoise, the harmony that
counts, and that his book, if it seems to conform to no a priori rules of literary
production, is at least consistent and harmonious with itself. In short, in *Tristram Shandy* as in music, the criterion of truth and value is not so much external
correspondence as internal coherence and consistency.

In Tristram's view, however, the musicality of his book is not confined to
the special relationship between its parts; it extends to the parts themselves. Volume seven–literally a frenzied flight from death and structurally a digression
from the main plot–is characterized as, and reads like, "a dance," not of death
but from it (7:1). Stories within the story, no less than the story itself, must be
in tune with themselves. Before beginning the never-to-be-finished "Story of the
king of Bohemia and his seven castles," Trim must first "hem" twice "to find in
what key his story would best go, and best suit his master's humour" (8:19; see
also 9:6). Sermons too are to be read and evaluated as musical compositions:
"I'm to preach at court next Sunday, said *Homenas*–run over my notes–so I
humm'd over doctor *Homenas*'s notes–the modulation's very well–'twill do.
Homenas, if it holds on at this rate–so I humm'd–and a tolerable tune I thought
it was ..." (4:25). Yorick's sermons are likewise as much music as rhetoric; they
are, in fact, like much of *Tristram Shandy* itself, musically rhetorical. Some contain the musical notations *lentamente, tenute, grave,* and *adagio,* while others are
marked *l'octava alta!, Con strepito, Siciliana, Alla capella, Con l'arco,* and *Senza*

l'arco. "All I know," says Tristram with misleading naïveté, "is, that they are musical terms, and have a meaning;—and as he was a musical man, I will make no doubt, but that by some quaint application of such metaphors to the compositions in hand, they impressed very distinct ideas of their several characters upon his fancy . . ." (6:11).

That his ingenuousness is indeed deceptive is revealed by Tristram's own irresistible tendency to describe arguments and conversations as if they were passages in a musical rather than a literary composition. Uncle Toby has his "Argumentum Fistulatorium," while his brother Walter alternates between "that soft and irresistible *piano* of voice, which the nature of the *argumentum ad hominem* absolutely requires," and "a sudden and spirited EPIPHONEMA, or rather EROTESIS, raised a third, and sometimes a full fifth, above the key of the discourse . . ." (1:19). Here is a typical exchange between Walter and Mrs. Shandy:

> Amen: said my mother, *piano.*
> Amen: cried my father, *fortissimè.*
> Amen: said my mother again—but with such a sighing cadence of personal pity at the end of it, as discomfited every fibre about my father. . . . [9:11]

Tristram knows very well what it means to apply musical notation to language.

All this is hardly the beginning. Music, as I have said, is everywhere in *Tristram Shandy,* and on every level. An exhaustive study of the musicality of the novel, however, is the work of a small book—a great deal more than I want to try here. My hope is that even this brief accounting of music's pervasive presence in the novel will provide a context for a less ambitious enterprise—a discussion of one facet of the novel's prismatic musicality, one of the most influential and certainly the most uncannily original and predictive: its contrapuntal texture. Counterpoint, if Sterne could somehow manage it, would serve him perfectly. It would strengthen the grip of his prose on effects music handled with such enviable ease: emotivism and simultaneity. The first—the power to render and stir the passions and affections—was the mysterious power of all music and the principal tool of Sterne in the role of sentimentalist. The latter was the special province of contrapuntal music and an invaluable tool for Sterne in his role as self-conscious author of the novel of consciousness.

In principle the problem of simultaneity in literature is insuperable. Try as an author may, unlike the composer he cannot present to his audience more than one event at a time. A number of recent authors, confronted or simply infatuated with this irrevocable fact, have tried in various ways to get around it. Most often the attempt takes the form, as in much of Aiken's poetry and in Huxley's *Point Counter Point,* of a rapid shifting back and forth between contrasting tones, themes, emotions, and events to achieve, as Aiken has put it, "a kind of underlying simultaneity in dissimilarity."[6] More ambitious, if necessarily doomed, is Sacheverell Sitwell's "On Hearing Four Bands Play at Once in a Public Square," in which Sitwell presents the reader with four parallel columns of verse to be read—somehow—simultaneously. Whereas Aiken and Huxley try merely to simulate the effect of counterpoint by rapid juxtaposition. Sitwell strives gamely if hopelessly to reproduce it. Some two centuries earlier, faced with much the same puzzle to solve, Laurence Sterne evolved in *Tristram Shandy* a technique that lies somewhere between these two.

Unlike most authors and especially autobiographers, Tristram has far more than one story to tell. There is the story of young Tristram, to be sure, but there is also the story of Uncle Toby and Trim, their campaigns on the bowling green, and Toby's amours with the Widow Wadman. And he must also tell the related tale of Uncle Toby's wound, the story of Aunt Dinah, of Trim's poor incarcerated brother, of Yorick, and many others. Furthermore, as the epigraph to the novel informs us, *Tristram Shandy* is not about the adventures of men, but their opinions. So these too must be included. And what about the adult Tristram, the man whose responsibility it is to relate all these tales and opinions? His presence is the most, if not the only, pervasive element in the book, so we must be supplied with a heavy dose of his opinions and with accounts of his own adventures, principally the writing of his book. Clearly, Tristram has his problems.

All this would be perplexing enough for an ordinary author, but for Tristram the difficulties are compounded many times over. For he diligently (if foolhardily) persists in his attempt to present everything in the form truest to his conception of subjective reality, namely, as coexisting facets of the intricate totality of human experience. In presenting his history of the mind, he takes it upon himself to make clear that past, present, and future, that events, emotions, and opinions all impinge upon one another as arbitrarily differentiated bands in the same experiential spectrum. Nor does Tristram wish to be unfair to physical reality. The occurrences of the external world, he knows, occur simultaneously no less than the events of the mind, and Tristram, who shrinks from no task except perhaps that of going easy on his readers, undertakes to present an accurate empirical account here as well. Thus, in order to be genuinely true to experience— both physical and mental—Tristram must confront the problem of simultaneity, a problem that only music has the equipment to handle—through harmony and, more important for Tristram, through counterpoint.[7]

Tristram Shandy is contrapuntal in essentially two ways. The first results from Tristram's alternate and at times simultaneous consciousness of himself both as the teller of his story and as a character in the story he is telling. It results from the intrusions of Tristram's adult self into a tale ostensibly about his early life.

Actually, Tristram need not intrude in order to make his presence felt. In an important sense the adult Tristram, the narrator of this wandering tale, is always present: first, because the whole book, by virtue of its shape, is a reflection of its unpredictable author; and second, because the erratic character of the book is a direct consequence of the errant conditions of his heredity and conception, an account of which begins the autobiography. These conditions insured that poor Tristram would "neither think nor act like any other man's child . . ." (1:3). The adult Tristram, therefore, is always implicitly there, and in that sense perhaps the book is, like much of the music of J. S. Bach, always implicitly contrapuntal: two distinct voices coexist on a single line. But this is perhaps a bit too subtle: our main interest is in the overt manifestations of a contrapuntal technique.

Like Huxley and Aiken, Sterne sometimes attempts to suggest the contrapuntal texture of his narrative by leaping back and forth between himself and his story, the two contrasted but related lines of simultaneous development. Take, for example, this account of Uncle Toby's and Trim's approach to the Widow Wadman's house to begin their amorous "siege" of the widow and her maid: "As Mrs. *Bridget*'s finger and thumb were upon the latch, the Corporal did not knock as oft as perchance your honour's taylor . . ." (9:17). That is as far as Tristram gets with his characters in this chapter, for at this point he jumps, by association, to himself: "–I might have taken my example something nearer home; for I owe mine, some five and twenty pounds at least, and wonder at the man's patience." Tristram then embarks on an explanation of his philosophy of "keeping straight with the world," his Rousseauan natural simplicity and economy. "True philosophy," he congratulates himself; but having done so, he leaves off, responding to the weight of his narrative obligations: "–but there is no treating the subject whilst my uncle is whistling Lillabullero.–Let us go into the house" (9:17).

Here as elsewhere, then, Tristram rapidly vacillates between the story he has ostensibly set out to tell and the only one he ever really tells at all, the story of his own mind and opinions. This is the Aiken-Huxley technique, but Sterne goes beyond it. For while he cannot literally present simultaneity–as Sitwell tried but failed to do–he can at least verbally suggest it. He can tell the reader what he cannot quite show him: that the story he is supposed to be telling and the story of the teller are going on together. The last lines of the passage above exemplify this procedure, for they bring in a new event, one which is taking place on the narrative line, and present it as if it has been going on all the time Tristram was talking about himself. "There is no treating the subject whilst my uncle is whistling Lillabullero," he remarks, and the implication is obvious that the two events were occurring together.

Uncle Toby's whistle furnishes an interesting sidelight to this passage further illustrative of its contrapuntal character. Uncle Toby whistles "Lillabullero" only in response to ineffably absurd comments or situations. And it is clear that in Sterne's typically punning fashion the act has a dual application. Toby himself is responding to the absurdity of his amorous "attack" on Mrs. Wadman; but, as Tristram clearly perceives, the whistling is equally applicable to his own philosophical pretensions. Hence the two simultaneous lines fulfill very nicely the requirements of counterpoint. They are contrasted in their respective reference to different chronological times (past and present) and to different characters (Uncle Toby and Tristram), in their subject matter (love and "philosophy"), and in their mode of presentation (dramatic and expository). They are related, not only by their initial association which led Tristram from his uncle to himself, but by the presence of a common element or motive, the whistling of "Lillabullero."

That simultaneity is involved here is, I think, quite clear. But Sterne is usually more explicit, as he is in the remarks following Tristram's oft-cited lament over the insuperable disparity between real duration and the time required to write about it. Here Tristram implicates his readers in their mutual misfortune by compelling them to realize that as a result of this disparity "the more your worships read, the more your worships will have to read." He then inquires:

> Will this be good for your worships eyes?
> It will do well for mine; and, was it not that my OPINIONS will be the death of me, I perceive I shall lead a fine life of it out of this self-same life of mine; or, in other words, shall lead a couple of fine lives together. (4:13)[8]

There can be no question about it: Tristram is indeed leading his lives together. The prime instance of this side of the novel's treatment of simultaneity is found in the following passage, where three such levels are fused into a single experience. Tristram, with understandable pride, all but refers to this narrative technique as counterpoint:

> —Now this is the most puzzled skein of all—for in this last chapter, as far at least as it has help'd me through *Auxerre,* I have been getting forwards in two different journies together, and with the same dash of the pen—for I have got entirely out of *Auxerre* in this journey which I am writing now, and I am got half way out of *Auxerre* in that which I shall write hereafter—There is but a certain degree of perfection in every thing; and by pushing at something beyond that, I have brought myself into such a situation, as no traveller ever stood before me; for I am this moment walking across the market-place of *Auxerre* with my father and my uncle *Toby,* in our way back to dinner—and I am this moment also entering *Lyons* with my post-chaise broke into a thousand pieces—and I am moreover this moment in a handsome pavillion built by *Pringello,* upon the banks of the *Garonne,* which Mons. *Sligniac* has lent me, and where I now sit rhapsodizing all these affairs.
> —Let me collect myself, and pursue my journey. (7:28)

If the first aspect of the novel's contrapuntal movement is an outgrowth of the narrator's digressive intrusions of self, the second stems from its digressiveness in general, the fact that Tristram has many stories to tell and many opinions to relate, his own being only the most important.[9] *Tristram Shandy* has beneath the seeming chaos two chief narrative sequences which overlap, but which are internally chronological. The first deals primarily with Walter Shandy's household and with young Tristram—his conception, birth, and nose-smashing, his naming, window-sash circumcision, and consequent breeching. The second is mainly concerned with the campaigns of Uncle Toby and his affair with the Widow Wadman. Together, these two sequences provide the framework from which spring Tristram's endless digressions (or in Walter Bagehot's image, the plot "to hang plums on"). Of course Tristram cannot literally keep both his main plot and his digressions moving simultaneously before his reader's eyes any more than he can keep both himself and his story present together. But it is important to note that once again Tristram is aware of the problem; that he constantly juggles the two lines of movement, bringing first one then the other into view; and, perhaps most important of all, that he repeatedly reminds us that the events from which he has digressed have not squealed to a halt simply because he has temporarily stopped describing them. There are a great many instances of this contrapuntal technique, but two are particularly relevant, one for its immediate concern with the vexatious problem of time, the other for its handling of time as well as for its overt employment of a music analogy.

In the first, the frantic Tristram, discovering that he has spent more time on his digressions than the inexorable laws of time allow, cries out:

> But there is no time to be lost in exclamations.—I have left my father lying across his bed, and my uncle *Toby* in his old fringed chair, sitting beside him, and promised I would go back to them in half an hour, and five and thirty minutes are laps'd already.—Of all the perplexities a mortal author was ever

seen in,—this certainly is the greatest,—for I have *Hafen Slawkenbergius*'s folio, Sir, to finish—a dialogue between my father and my uncle *Toby,* upon the solution of *Prignitz, Scroderus, Ambrose Paraeus, Ponocrates* and *Grangousier* to relate,—a tale out of *Slawkenbergius* to translate, and all this in five minutes less, than no time at all;—such a head!—would to heaven! my enemies only saw the inside of it! (3:38)

In the second example, that involving a musical analogy, Tristram finds himself somewhat less harried. His lines of movement are in rhythmic harmony, and he need only inform his readers of that fact to secure both their understanding and proper admiration:

Consider that it is but poor eight miles from *Shandy-Hall* to Dr. *Slop,* the man midwife's house;—and that whilst *Obadiah* has been going those said miles and back, I have brought my uncle *Toby* from *Namur,* quite across all *Flanders,* into *England:*—That I have had him ill upon my hands near four years;—and have since travelled him and Corporal *Trim,* in a chariot and four, a journey of near two hundred miles down into *Yorkshire;*—all which put together, must have prepared the reader's imagination for the entrance of Dr. *Slop* upon the stage,— as much, at least (I hope) as a dance, a song, or a concerto between the acts. (2:8)

The deftness with which Tristram often juggles plot and digression justifies his self-congratulatory description, a description which also clearly elucidates the analogy with counterpoint:

Tho' my digressions are all fair, as you observe,—and that I fly off from what I am about, as far and as often too as any writer in *Great-Britain;* yet I constantly take care to order affairs so, that my main business does not stand still in my absence.

I was just going, for example, to have given you the great out-lines of my uncle *Toby*'s most whimsical character;—when my aunt *Dinah* and the coachman came a-cross us, and led us a vagary some millions of miles into the very heart of the planetary system: Notwithstanding all this you perceive that the drawing of my uncle *Toby*'s character went on gently all the time;—not the great contours of it,—that was impossible,—but some familiar strokes and faint designations of it, were here and there touch'd in, as we went along, so that you are much better acquainted with my uncle *Toby* now than you was before.

By this contrivance the machinery of my work is of a species by itself; two contrary motions are introduced into it, and reconciled, which were thought to be at variance with each other. In a word, my work is digressive, and it is progressive too—and at the same time. (1:22)[10]

Since Tristram himself has so handsomely resolved the problem of simultaneity in literature, he is righteously (and comically) intolerant of writers who have had less success than he and expresses contempt for those who keep only either the main line or the digressions moving at any given time. It is to avoid just such a deplorable confinement, he explains, that

from the beginning of this, you see, I have constructed the main work and the adventitious parts of it with such intersections, and have so complicated and involved the digressive and progressive movements, one wheel within another, that the whole machine, in general, has been kept a-going. . . .(1:22)

In these two passages Tristram has all but named his method contrapuntal. As Robert Erickson defines it: "In the balance of the lines, at once independent and dependent, forming a larger whole, yet each contributing its perfect wholeness, is the essence of counterpoint."[11]

Most of the digressions, we have said, arise with varying degrees of directness out of one or the other of the two main story lines. Slawkenbergius's tale, for example, a digression one could hardly call integral to the story of our young hero, does in fact owe its telling, however indirectly, to that story. Tristram tells the tale because his father translated it, which he did because little if anything interested him more than noses. His interest, in turn, is a result of a lamentable tradition of short noses in the Shandy family, which, in its turn, was only recounted in the first place because Tristram's nose was smashed during his unhappy delivery into this world—and with that we are back to young Tristram. Though there are exceptions to this rule—occasions when the narrator feels a strong propensity "to begin nonsensically"—most of the digressions do spin away from one of the two basic story threads. And the chronological plot sequence persists contrapuntally with the digressions.

In its rather consistent adherence to this formal procedure—the digression from a persistent foundation—Tristram's narrative technique resembles one of the dominant contrapuntal procedures of the first half of the eighteenth century: the use of a ground bass (or variant thereof) as the foundation over and around which the melodies could be invented, expanded, and even improvised.[12] The passacaglia, the chaconne, the cantata, the choral prelude, and a variety of other musical forms were built upon the principle of the ground bass. In his innumerable chorales, Bach was particularly fond of deriving both the designs and the details of large movements from the chorale tunes they were based on. And the typically "Handelian" melody is one in which "a pregnant motive is placed upon a sequentially running bass" (often a ground bass) and in which, as in *Tristram Shandy,* sudden halts and rests interrupt the melodic flow.[13] The use of the ground bass was a very popular procedure indeed. In polyphonic music, the melodies—the horizontal lines—are of course paramount, but at least a minimal relationship is always maintained between the independently developing threads. In both the essentially horizontal emphasis and the retention of harmonic relationships the analogy with *Tristram Shandy* holds up. The separate stories are of the greatest immediate interest, but the fact of their simultaneity in the mind of the narrator and their relationships by association is never completely forgotten.

The stories Tristram wants to tell, then, are simultaneous in the perplexed mind of the narrator. He cannot present them together, but he can do his best to suggest their actual co-occurrence. The point is that the mind works this way. The mind does not receive ideas and impressions in neatly outlined sequences, and if Tristram is to present an accurate picture of the mind—at least his own— he must come to grips with the intractable fact of simultaneity. By doing so in musical fashion, by employing a variety of contrapuntal techniques (as Huxley and others have sought to do), Sterne achieved two compatible results: first, the desired suggestion of mental and physical simultaneity; and second, the suggestion of a musical atmosphere, of the feeling that we are somehow in the presence of something more evocative than descriptive, more emotive than cognitive, more suggestive than comprehensible—in short, that we are in the presence of something musical. This last, perhaps, accounts as much as anything else for the historic unaccountability of *Tristram Shandy*.

Notes

1.   Contemplating his projected novel, Philip Quarles enters in his notebook: "The musicalization of fiction. Not in the symbolist way, by subordinating sense to sound. . . . But on a large scale, in the construction." See Aldous Huxley, *Point Counter Point* (New York, 1928), pp. 349–50.

2.   Calvin Brown. *Music and Literature: A Comparison of the Arts* (Athens: University of Georgia Press, 1948), pp. 213–17. See also H. A. Basilius, "Thomas Mann's Use of Musical Structure and Techniques in *Tonio Kröger*," *Germanic Review* 19 (1944):284–308. In the preface to *Stories of Three Decades*, trans. H. T. Lowe-Porter (New York: Alfred A. Knopf, 1936), Mann wrote that it was probably in *Tonio Kröger* that "I first learned to employ music as a shaping influence in my art. The conception of epic prose-composition as a weaving of themes, as a musical complex of associations, I later on largely employed in *The Magic Mountain*. Only that there the verbal leitmotiv is no longer, as in *Buddenbrooks*, employed in the representation of form alone, but has taken on a less mechanical, more musical character, and endeavours to mirror the emotion and the idea" (p. vi).

3.   Preface to *La Pastorale* (1924), as quoted by Brown, p. 174.

4.   Germaine Brée, review of *The Square*, by Marguerite Duras, *New York Times Book Review* 64 (8 November 1959):62.

5.   Laurence Sterne, *The Life and Opinions of Tristram Shandy, Gentleman*, ed. James Aiken Work (New York: Odyssey Press, 1940); citations are to volume and chapter.

6.   Conrad Aiken, "Counterpoint and Implication," *Poetry* 14 (1919):155.

7.   According to at least one view, the simultaneity of past, present, and future is integral to the very nature of musical time, so that in a sense the peculiar flow of time through Tristram's consciousness, whether or not it is presented in a literary analogue of counterpoint, is always essentially musical. Joan Stambaugh, "Music as a Temporal Form," *Journal of Philosophy* 61 (1964):276, argues: "Musical time does not have an objective, abstract, 'non-musical' future and past as its orientation. It sets up, so to speak, its own future and past, and it does this *constantly in the process of its own motion.* . . . This is the very essence of musical motion: the constant creation of a future and a past in the actual present moment, in *each* present moment. Even this moment is not present in the strict sense: it is not there in front of the listener in the manner of an object. The moment of musical time is not present, it is at best present*ing*, creating the temporal tension of what has gone before and what is to come, the tension of the whole in the moment."

8.   Actually, though it is not sufficiently pervasive to warrant full treatment, there is yet another source of simultaneity and counterpoint in *Tristram Shandy*, namely, the relationship between the writing and other activities of the author, Tristram, and his reading audience: "What a tract of country have I run!—how many degrees nearer to the warm sun am I advanced, and how many fair and goodly cities have I seen, during the time you have been reading, and reflecting, Madam, upon this story!" (7:26).

9.   Tristram's self-conscious attempts to include all things expected and unexpected of an author in his book provide further illustration of his awareness of simultaneity. For example, he reports: "As for my uncle *Toby*, his smoak-jack had not made a dozen

revolutions, before he fell asleep also.—Peace be with them both.—Dr. *Slop* is engaged with the midwife, and my mother above stairs.—*Trim* is busy in turning an old pair of jack-boots into a couple of mortars to be employed in the siege of *Messina* next summer,—and is this instant boring the touch holes with the point of a hot poker.—All my heroes are off my hands;—'tis the first time I have had a moment to spare,—and I'll make use of it, and write my preface" (3:20). At a later stage in the progress of his book he finds himself similarly freed of his characters, but this time: "I wish I could write a chapter upon sleep. A fitter occasion could never have presented itself, than what this moment offers, when all the curtains of the family are drawn—the candles put out—and no creature's eyes are open but a single one, for the other has been shut these twenty years of my mother's nurse. It is a fine subject!" (4:15).

10.   In the language of music, "contrary motion" is the melodic progression of two voice parts, one rising, the other falling. Contrary motion introduces the maximum of linear independence, so that Tristram is justifiably proud of having reconciled the two lines of motion. It is possible that Sterne was actually addressing some contemporary composers as well as authors with this criticism. As early as 1737, polyphony was under attack; as Alfred Einstein observes, the works of such composers as Nardini and Pugnani were characterized by "their repetitions that protracted without enhancing, their windy effeminacy, their impotence in expression, and their substitution of noise for vigour. The change of taste can be read in their basses. These had once been part of the thematic structure, but now they move inconsequently in support of the harmonies with unwilling feet, at the most enlivened by subdivision into idle semi-quavers. With that, all melodic expression evaporated in endless *furniture.*" See *A Short History of Music,* 4th Amer. ed. (New York: Alfred A. Knopf, 1954), p. 114.

11.   Robert Erickson, *The Structure of Music: A Listener's Guide* (New York: Noonday Press, 1955), p. 201.

12.   Of all the various uses of the ground bass, that generally found in the Chorale Concertato is perhaps most nearly parallel to the procedure in *Tristram Shandy.* There the bass is usually cut up into phrases, each of which (like the main events in Tristram's life) is given a separate contrapuntal elaboration.

13.   For a fuller discussion of this point, see Manfred F. Bukofzer, *Music in the Baroque Era* (New York: W. W. Norton, 1947), p. 310.

Are the *Cantos* a Fugue?

Stephen J. Adams

One of the ways in which music can have a bearing on poetry is as an analogy for poetic structure. Pound compared the structure of the *Cantos* to fugue, and a number of critics have alluded to this supposed resemblance in defense of the poem's supposed incoherence; but no one, I think, has ever examined the analogy closely. I do not intend here an analysis of the *Cantos* using the vocabulary of "subject," "response," "countersubject" that Pound proposes. I do intend to examine the limits of the fugal analogy in order to discover what was in Pound's head when he suggested it, how it may be applied justly, and, perhaps more important, how it may not.

For musical structure in poetry is a subject much bandied but rarely, it seems to me, rewarding. Critics who suggest musical analogies too often have a naïve textbook understanding of musical form as a *donnée* with no flexibility, no inner necessity of its own. Analogies are suggested casually, with no explanation of what verbal phenomena the analogy is supposed to single out. The various manipulations of harmony, tonality, melody, and rhythm that govern most musical structures simply correspond to nothing in a verbal text. When a text is said to have a musical structure, the question must be asked whether the structure is molded to a textbook paradigm (as in a *jeu d'esprit* like Wallace Stevens's "Peter Quince at the Clavier"), or if the structure is verbal, with perhaps certain necessarily vague resemblances to some musical procedure.

Pound, who once prided himself on refusing to define one art in terms of another,[1] was cautious in his own use of the musical analogy. He never declared the analogy in print. The references are all made in private correspondence; or in one case reported from private conversation by W. B. Yeats in *A Packet for Ezra Pound* (1929). All of Pound's references are themselves tentative. On the two occasions in his published letters when he refers to Yeats's report of his fugal idea, he disavows it angrily: "God damn Yeats' bloody paragraph. Done more to prevent people reading Cantos for what is *on the page* than any other one smoke screen."[2] Pound evidently regarded the analogy as something of a red herring.

Reprinted from *University of Toronto Quarterly* (1975):67–74, by permission of *University of Toronto Quarterly*.

During the thirties, two articles appeared on the musicality of the *Cantos*, one by Louis Zukofsky, which Pound approved, and the other by Dudley Fitts, which he dismissed as uncomprehending; Fitts speaks at some length on the subject of "counterpoint," while Zukofsky, who knew of Pound's fugue idea, never mentions it.[3]

Equally significant, though, is the want of evidence that the fugal notion had ever occurred to Pound before 1927, the date of his earliest extant allusion to it in a letter to his father. At this date the first twenty-seven cantos were already written. Yeats must have received Pound's explanation early in 1928 when he was in Rapallo. For some reason Bach's fugues were on Pound's mind around this time: there is a reference in "How to Read" (published January 1929) to taking a fugue apart and putting it together again.[4] None of Pound's references to "fugue" or "counterpoint" before 1927 relates in any direct way to the *Cantos;* the significance which he attached to the word "fugue" around 1917, when the *Cantos* were begun in earnest, was even less definite, as we shall see, than the usage he discovered later. When Pound was writing the first cantos, he was notoriously vague as to their eventual structure. He wrote to James Joyce in 1917:

> I have begun an endless poem, of no known category. Phanopoeia or something or other, all about everything. "Poetry" may print the first three cantos this spring. I wonder what you will make of it. Probably too sprawling and unmusical to find favour in your ears. Will try to get some melody into it further on. Though we have not *ombra* and *ingombra* to end our lines with, or poluphloisbious thallassas to enrich the middle feet.[5]

Melody, but no fugue. The *Cantos* have been subject to many generalized approaches by analogy, but the fact remains that they did turn out to be a poem "of no known category," and whatever structure they may possess must be demonstrated from the text.

Still, Pound did propose the fugal analogy himself, and the notion held enough meaning for him to repeat it in years after the war.[6] So it seems fair to ask what light it may shed on the thought processes embodied in the poem. Pound, however, always averse to the accepted categories, attached personal meanings to common terms like "harmony" and "melody," and the terms "fugue" and "counterpoint" also had special associations for him.[7] Working from Pound's fairly extensive music criticism, one concludes that fugue appealed because it is (1) abstract, (2) melodic, or horizontal, and (3) intellectual. With an eye to the *Cantos*, we may add that fugue is (4) founded on a principle of juxtaposition, and that it is both (5) "elastic" and (6) open-ended.

To say that fugue is abstract is simply to say that it is not program music. Despite Pound's fascination with Jannequin (Canto 75), his musical aesthetic favored what he calls "pattern music" as opposed to "impressionist" or "emotional" music:

> I do not mean that Bach is not emotional, but the early music starts from the mystery of pattern; if you like, with the vortex of pattern; with something which is, first of all, music, and which is capable of being, after that, many things. What I call emotional, or impressionist music, starts with being emotion or impression and then becomes only approximately music. . . .

> Programme music is only a weaker, more flabby and descriptive kind of impressionist music, needing, perhaps, a guide and explanation.[8]

Not bound in the *Cantos* by mimesis, Pound is free, for instance, with historical time. While historical events in the poem all have a date and a place, Pound rearranges them achronologically, just as a vorticist painter rearranges vision into meaningful form. This is what Pound called "the musical conception of form," "the understanding that you can use form as a musician uses sound, that you can select motives of form from the forms before you, that you can recombine them and 'organize' them into new form."[9] Consistently, Pound prefers horizontal music to vertical music, melody to harmony. He rejected Debussy's impressionism, for example, as music which "ascends like steam from a morass," and declared, "In the creation of music: FIRST, melody."[10] Naturally, fugue is the epitome of horizontal music, calling on the intellect to perceive and synthesize in time not one but several melodies at once. Fugue, then, is intellectual music, appealing to more than the passively receptive senses.

Pound's vorticism insists strenuously on this distinction:

> You may think of a man as that toward which perception moves. You may think of him as the TOY of circumstance, as the plastic substance receiving impressions.
>
> OR you may think of him as DIRECTING a certain fluid force against circumstance, as CONCEIVING instead of merely observing and reflecting.[11]

In the Wagnerian aesthetic, "you confuse the spectator by smacking as many of his senses as possible at every possible moment," while in the Vorticist, you aim "at focusing the mind on a given definition of form, or rhythm."[12] Fugue is the least sensuous of musical genres. It depends upon a grasp of its procedures, and it does not overwhelm the listener with Wagnerian sonorities. Debate continues over what instrument Bach had in mind for *Die Kunst der Fuge,* and Beethoven's *Grosse Fuge* is notoriously ill conceived for its string quartet medium; both works were long considered *Augenmusik,* much admired on paper, but little performed before recent times. Pound's poem likewise demands an intellectual grasp of its procedures, and, despite all his talk about the sound of verse, it is most un-Poundian merely to loll in the sonority of his melopoeia.

Fugue is obviously founded on a kind of juxtaposition; but Pound was aware, as we shall see, that literature is not really capable of "counterpoint" or simultaneity but must place its themes in succession. There is nothing in verse parallel to melodies combined as in fugue, just as there is nothing in drama like the operatic ensemble. To say that fugue is "elastic" and open-ended means only the commonplace that fugue is not a predetermined form in the same sense as sonata-allegro or minuet, but a musical procedure founded on certain principles. Bach treated fugue more freely than Haydn or Beethoven treated sonata form. By calling the *Cantos* fugal, Pound implied that they were an ongoing process, an unfolding development, not the filling out of a mould, and that he could bring them to an end at any time. With all these attributes of fugue in mind, we can turn to Pound's statements on the subject with a clearer idea of how they may have been intended.

The most detailed explanation of the *Cantos* in fugal terms comes not directly from Pound but from Yeats:

Now at last he explains that it will, when the hundredth canto is finished, display a structure like that of a Bach Fugue. There will be no plot, no chronicle of events, no logic of discourse, but two themes, the Descent into Hades from Homer, a Metamorphosis from Ovid, and, mixed with these, medieval or modern historical characters. He has tried to produce that picture Porteous commended to Nicolas Poussin in *Le chef d'oeuvre inconnu* where everything rounds or thrusts itself without edges, without contours—conventions of the intellect—from a splash of tints and shades; to achieve a work of art as characteristic of our time as the paintings of Cézanne, avowedly suggested by Porteous, as *Ulysses* and its dream association of words and images, a poem in which there is nothing that can be taken out and reasoned over, nothing that is not a part of the poem itself. He has scribbled on the back of an envelope certain sets of letters that represent emotions or archetypal events—I cannot find any adequate definition—ABCD and then JKLM, and then each set of letters repeated, and then ABCD inverted and this repeated, and then a new element XYZ, and then certain letters that never recur, and then all sorts of combinations of XYZ and JKLM and ABCD and DCBA, and all set whirling together. . . .[13]

Pound called this passage a "smoke screen," and said elsewhere,

You are right that Blackmur et sim. do *not,* etc. If Yeats knew a fugue from a frog, he might have transmitted what I told him in some way that would have helped rather than obfuscated *his* readers. Mah!!![14]

Yeats betrays his partial comprehension of Pound in several phrases, but the only essential difference, I think, between his version of the fugal analogy and Pound's own is that Yeats, tone deaf and musically naïve, puts his in the form of an unqualified assertion: the poem will, when finished, "display a structure like that of a Bach fugue." So monstrous a fugue was never known. Pound is more guarded:

Afraid the whole damn poem is rather obscure, especially in fragments. Have I ever given you the outline of main scheme ::: or whatever it is?
    1.   Rather like, or unlike subject and response and counter subject in fugue.
A.A.   Live man goes down into world of Dead
C.B.   The "repeat in history"
B.C.   The "magic moment" or moment of metamorphosis, bust thru from quotidien into "divine or permanent world." Gods, etc.[15]

Pound is equally tentative in his only other prewar allusion to the subject, in a letter of 1937, exactly ten years after the first:

Take a fugue: theme, response, contrasujet. *Not* that I mean to make an exact analogy of structure.
    Vide, incidentally, Zukofsky's experiment, possibly suggested by my having stated the Cantos are in a way fugal. There *is* at start, descent to the shades,

metamorphosis, parallel (Vidal-Actaeon). All of which is mere matter for little
. . . Harvard instructors, *unless* I pull it off as reading matter, singing matter,
shouting matter, the tale of the tribe.[16]

Pound's version corresponds to Yeats's in certain obvious ways. We see the
same "theme" and "response" of the first two cantos–the descent, the metamorphosis–singled out. We see the same algebraic use of letters to represent the
themes. Pound apparently even reversed the letters to represent fugal inversion
(or retrograde?), attempting to show how his themes reappear in various guises.
Nothing is gained, however, from pressing a comparison of Pound's treatment
of his themes to fugal devices of inversion or retrograde; these musical procedures correspond to nothing that can happen in language. Pound is merely
declaring that his themes are not static, not bound to historical or sequential
time. Perhaps in telling Yeats that the themes in the end would all be "set whirling together," Pound suggested something like a fugal stretto, which is in a
vague sense what happens. Yeats also stresses the notion, clearly in Pound's
mind, that the poem would have no necessary linear progression; his themes
were free to appear and disappear at will, rather like themes in a fugue, which
have not the relatively fixed positions for first or second or codetta themes as in
sonata-allegro. Pound was aware of fugue as an unfolding process.

Considering all of Pound's statements, I can only endorse the view of Daniel
Pearlman in his superb study of the *Cantos:*

> In comparing his scheme to the organization of a fugue, Pound seems clearly
> to be limiting his discussion of structure to an explanation of his local tech-
> nique, the varied juxtaposition and repetition of themes that will remain his
> consistent method of organizing image-complexes throughout the whole of
> the *Cantos.* He is making no conscious attempt here to display a "main
> scheme" in terms of the overall plan of progressive development that would de-
> fine the poem's major form.[17]

Pound used other analogies for describing the *Cantos* (the Cosimo Tura fresco
described in the same passage from Yeats, for example), and other analogies for
his technique of juxtaposition–the Chinese ideogram, for one, or the film "cut,"
a less widely discussed parallel:

> The life of a village is narrative; you have not been there three weeks before
> you know that in the revolution et cetera, and when M. le Comte et cetera,
> and so forth. In a city the visual impressions succeed each other, overlap, over-
> cross, they are "cinematographic," but they are not a simple linear sequence.
> They are often a flood of nouns without verbal relations.[18]

The abstract, rhythmic episodes of Fernand Léger's film *Ballet mécanique,* with
George Antheil's music, provided Pound with a fair analogy. Yeats may not
have known "a fugue from a frog," but his explanation of the fugal idea seems
reasonably accurate. Pound was perhaps annoyed that Yeats laid so much stress
on architecture. Surely he was not pleased with the talk of Cézanne and art
which "thrusts itself without edges," although this description too is not devoid
of meaning. In any event, it should be apparent now, if it wasn't in 1929, that
very little can be gained from comparing the *Cantos* taken as a whole to the
structure of a musical form which rarely lasts longer than a few minutes.

At the time when Pound began writing cantos, his notion of fugue was bound with the generalized conception of "musical form" in his vorticist writings:

> One uses form as a musician uses sound. One does not imitate the wood-dove, or at least one does not confine oneself to the imitation of wood-doves, one combines and arranges one's sound or one's forms into Bach fugues or into arrangements of colour, or into "planes of relation."[19]

He describes one of Gaudier's pieces in terms of fugue, meaning no more than that the abstract triangles and circles create a self-consistent whole as in a piece of music:

> We have the triangle and circle asserted, *labled* almost, upon the face and right breast. Into these so-called "abstractions" life flows, the circle moves and elongates into the oval, it increases and takes volume in the sphere or hemisphere of the breast. . . . These two developed motifs work as themes in a fugue. We have the whole series of spherical triangles, as in the arm over the head, all combining and culminating in the great sweep of the back of the shoulders, as fine as any surface in all sculpture.[20]

Pound chooses the word "fugue" in these passages for its intellectual prestige and for its quality of "mathematical" abstractness, but he could have substituted any other musical form. In his article on Joyce for *Mercure de France,* in fact, Pound uses an analogy with sonata form in much the same way:

> Qu'est-ce que l'*Ulysses* de James Joyce? Ce roman appartient à la grande classe de romans en forme de sonate, c'est-à-dire, dans la forme: thème, contrethème, rencontre, développement, finale. Et à la subdivision: roman père-et-fils. . . .[21]

Pound might have used a dictionary to advantage here, since he has confused "finale" with "coda" and uses the word "contrethème," which is more appropriate to fugue than to sonata. The order of his terms, too, is perhaps more suitable to Joyce's novel than to musical realities. At the time when Pound was setting down his first cantos, then, his idea of musical analogies with poetry took a very general form of expression, and he does not seem to have arrived at any comparison between his techniques of juxtaposition and fugal counterpoint.

Pound did use the term "counterpoint," however, in one other way which may be considered appropriate not to poetic structure but to melopoeia:

> One might call it a "sort of" counterpoint; if one can conceive a counterpoint which plays not against a sound newly struck, but against the residuum and residua of sounds which hang in the auditory memory.
>
> In the two cases, Arabian music and Provençal verse, where there was no musical "harmony" and no counterpoint in Bach's sense of the word, this elaboration of echo has attained great complexity, and *can* give great delight to ears which are either "trained" to it or which have a natural aptitude for perceiving it.[22]

Pound concedes that his analogy is inexact:

I am inclined to think that the horizontal merits faded from music, and from the rhythm of poetry, with the gradual separation of the two arts. A man thinking with mathematical fractions is not impelled toward such variety of *raga* [sc. *tala*] as a man working with the necessary inequalities of words. But the verbal rhythm is monolinear. It can form contrapunto only against its own echo, or against a developed expectancy.[23]

This conception of a monolinear rhythm which hangs in the auditory memory may be extended to the Poundian juxtaposition recognized as a consecutive rather than a simultaneous pattern, but it refers first of all to the monolinear "contrapunto" of word sounds, for which Pound habitually produces the example of Arnaut Daniel's rhyme technique. One goes to Arnaut, he says, "for a sort of contrappunto of line terminations, rhyme in its most developed arrangement."[24] The intellectual contrivances of Arnaut's stanzaic structures may well seem on a level with Bach's counterpoint, but the analogy here concerns melopoeia, rhyme sounds and word sounds in general resonating in the ear. "The term harmony," Pound says (and he would have to include counterpoint as well),

is misapplied in poetry; it refers to simultaneous sounds of different pitch. There is, however, in the best verse a sort of residue of sound which remains in the ear of the hearer and acts more or less as an organ-base [*sic*].[25]

Hugh Kenner, in his recent study *The Pound Era*, expands on Pound's comparisons between rhyme and counterpoint. Pound's juxtapositions, he says, his so-called ideogrammatic technique, is a system of "subject-rhyme" and therefore a counterpoint: "there are subject rhymes, two sensibilities may rhyme, there are culture rhymes."[26] True enough. But push an analogy too far and it collapses. Worse, it may act as a smoke screen to conceal what is on the page. Nevertheless, critics cannot be blamed for introducing these analogies, nor can Pound, even if exhaustive pursuit must prove futile. These comparisons are so attractive, so needed, because they help explain phenomena in Pound's poetry which are new and strange, which must be brought closer to the familiar. Having served their purpose, however, they should be discarded. Pound is even now charged sometimes with a lack of originality, but the truth is he has invented techniques which have not got names.

Notes

1.   See, for example, Ezra Pound, *Guide to Kulchur* (New York: New Directions, 1952), p. 49.

2.   D. D. Paige, ed., *The Letters of Ezra Pound 1907–41* (New York: Harcourt, 1950), p. 321 (letter dated February 1939).

3.   Ibid., p. 293.

4.   T. S. Eliot, ed., *Literary Essays of Ezra Pound* (London: Faber, 1954), p. 27.

5. Forrest Read, ed., *Pound/Joyce: The Letters of Ezra Pound to James Joyce* (New York: New Directions, 1967), p. 102.

6. See, for example, D. G. Bridson, "An Interview with Ezra Pound," *New Directions in Prose and Poetry* 17 (1961):172.

7. "Harmony," for example, meant to Pound simply "chords that can be struck simultaneously," with little reference to tonality. See Ezra Pound, *Antheil and the Treatise on Harmony* (Chicago: Pascal Covici, 1927), pp. 12–13; full discussion may be found in my doctoral dissertation, "Ezra Pound and Music" (Toronto: University of Toronto, 1974), ch. 2.

8. Eliot, p. 434.

9. Ezra Pound, "Vorticism," *New Age* 16 (1915):277.

10. Pound, *Antheil,* p. 11; and Ezra Pound, "Muzik, as Mistaught," *Townsman* 1 (1938):8.

11. Ezra Pound, "Vortex," *Blast* 1 (1914):153–54.

12. Pound, *Antheil,* p. 44.

13. William Butler Yeats, *A Vision* (New York: Macmillan, 1956), pp. 4–5.

14. Paige, p. 293. Blackmur was the editor of *Hound & Horn,* which had printed Dudley Fitts's "Music Fit for the Odes," 4 (1931):278–89.

15. Paige, p. 210.

16. Ibid., p. 294.

17. Daniel Pearlman, *The Barb of Time* (New York: Oxford, 1969), p. 11.

18. Jean Cocteau, *Poésies 1917–20,* review in *Dial* 70 (1920):110.

19. Ezra Pound, *Gaudier-Brzeska: A Memoir* (Hessle, Eng.: Marvell Press, 1960), p. 125.

20. Ibid., pp. 137–38.

21. Read, p. 205.

22. Pound, *Antheil,* pp. 123–24.

23. Ibid., p. 47.

24. "The Island of Paris: A Letter," *Dial* 69 (1920):636.

25. Eliot, pp. 6–7.

26. Hugh Kenner, *The Pound Era* (Berkeley: University of California Press, 1971), p. 92.

Verbal Music in Theory and Practice

Patricia Haas Stanley

Of course it is impossible to reproduce in words either a simple musical chord or a complex counterpoint progression. It is possible, however, to approximate musical structures—a fugue, for example, or a toccata—and techniques—tonality, modulation, the leitmotiv, and even counterpoint. Verbal music, Steven Paul Scher's designation[1] for "structural phenomena ... artistic arrangement in musiclike sequence,"[2] is the literary evocation of a particular form of music by means of syntax, imagery, rhetorical devices, and/or technical vocabulary. It may be the evocation of a specific composition, for instance, *Die Meistersinger von Nürnberg* in Thomas Mann's *Doktor Faustus;* or a particular performance, such as Heinrich Heine's representation of a Paganini recital in *Florentinische Nächte I;* or an original creation, the "Symphonie" introduction to Ludwig Tieck's comedy, *Die verkehrte Welt.*[3]

In his 1965 novel, *Tynset,* whose external framework is a literary adaptation of the musical rondo,[4] Wolfgang Hildesheimer presents four episodes of verbal music: literary evocations of a toccata, a fugue, and two cadenzas. Hildesheimer's musicianship in these instances is influenced by his study of J. S. Bach and Mozart,[5] but the literary evocations were not inspired by any specific composition.[6] The rhetorical-technical practices examined in the following structural and stylistic analysis of the toccata are paradigmatic of Hildesheimer's technique in the other verbal music segments of *Tynset.* His goal is twofold: (1) to intensify the musicality and therefore the modernistic[7] orientation of *Tynset;* (2) to create a uniquely dramatic, visual, even tactile art form by adapting certain musical practices to literature.

The musical toccata, which originated at the beginning of the seventeenth century, is a highly idiomatic keyboard piece in free style intended to exhibit the touch (*toccare*) and execution of the performer. It has, therefore, an air of showy improvisation, usually with a good deal of repetition of similar figures. It may contain full chords, running passages, and rhapsodic or contrapuntal sections. J. S. Bach composed seven toccatas for clavier that feature short movements of

Originally published in *Germanic Review* 52 (1977):217–25.

markedly different tempo and style. His Toccata in G, BWV 915, for example, consists of an introduction, arioso, fugue, interlude, fugue, and coda.

The Hildesheimer literary evocation of a toccata, which is in four parts with a coda, recounts the narrator's participation in a pre-dawn concert by the roosters of Athens.[8] Standing in the Acropolis, where he had purposely spent the night, the narrator initiates the performance by crying out "Kikeriki" as loud as he can through his cupped hands. He hears a faint answer and repeats the cry. A second rooster crows and then others respond until finally "das Konzert breitete sich aus wie ein Brand."[9] At dawn the roosters gradually subside. The story ends with an anecdote about the Duke of Wellington, who slept through a decisive battle.

The literary toccata, on pages 63 to 70 of *Tynset,* simulates a musical performance consisting of the following sections:

I – Introduction (63:16 to 64:2)
II – Allegretto (64:3 to 67:3)
III – Fugato (67:3, last two words, to 69:6)
IV – Andante (69:7 to 70:10)
V – Coda (70:11 to 70:21)

Structurally this verbal music begins and ends on the initial idea of sleep. "Nun hatte ich eine lange Nacht vor mir, aber das schreckte mich nicht, ich war schon damals kein rechter Schläfer, und alle meine Nächte sind lang" (63–64) is the main point of the introduction. Following narrative pyrotechnics this idea, which thus resembles the tonic chord in music, returns: "Während einer solchen Nacht möchte ich kein Schlafsucher sein" (70). The coda is an amplification of the basic statement. To round off a toccata by recapitulation of the opening statement is one of several possibilities; Bach employed it in the Toccata in G.

Toccatas customarily pause between sections, and there is a paragraph pause between the introduction and Part II. This literary allegretto, a short piece in a lively tempo, is so designated because its thematic material, the narrator's initial cries followed by a series of descriptive passages locating the position and tonal quality of several roosters, is stated with a precise, unadorned vocabulary of vivid imagery that promotes rapid reading: "Und kaum hatte er noch einmal gerufen, da rief auch schon ein weiterer Hahn, der dritte, er rief tief und dröhnend, war aber weit weg, vielleicht am Fusse des Hymettos, jedenfalls in dieser Richtung, und gleichzeitig mit ihm rief einer unten in der alten Stadt, rief mit dem kühnen Ton eines Kämpfers, ein Nachbar des Hinterhofhahnes" (66).

"Darauf entstand eine kurze Pause, wie eine Pause der Überraschung, als hätten die drei keinen vierten erwartet" (67) constitutes the pause between Parts II and III. The simulation of a fugato section, a fuguelike passage within a non-fugal composition, is a miniature of the fugue that appears later[10] and consists of a short exposition, a lengthier development, and a coda. There are seven individual voices and an indeterminate number of similar but not specifically identified voices. Because it is the effect of this mass of sound that is important, the exposition is brief. Once the seven voices have been named, development begins.

The rapid shifting from one image to another that is the verbal equivalent of musical polyphony begins almost immediately after the verbal pause, noted above, that separates the allegretto from the fugato, and there is no time for periods or clauses; adjectives become nouns as the tempo increases, and images follow one another without amplification: "Und ein Fünfter kam hinzu, im Süden, und ein Sechster im Westen, beide weit, und ein Siebenter, diesmal wieder nah, sein Ruf warf ein Echo. Es klang aus, und sofort fielen die anderen wieder ein, der Dröhner, der Trompeter, der Kämpfer, und der Schmetterer, der Fünfte im Süden und der Sechste im Westen" (67).

Exposition is complete with the words "einzeln nicht mehr feststellbar" (67:19). At this time the voices have been introduced and development begins: "Es kam aus allen Richtungen, das Konzert breitete sich aus wie ein Brand" (67). Texture is still contrapuntal, that is, a rapid shifting from one image to another. A net of sounds becomes a carpet whose fringes extend to the sea, and when this farthest boundary has been reached the story's texture smoothes out into more elaborate descriptive passages: "Der Hahn von Kap Sunion, der krähte hinaus ins Wasser, wo ihn vielleicht nur ein früher Fischer hörte, nicht nur ihn, sondern er hörte eine ganze gezackte Küstenlinie voll von fernem und nahem Krähen" (68). The literary fugato moves gradually in this manner to a close on the initial statement of Part I, the narrator standing high above Athens.

After another paragraph break, Part IV begins with a melancholy tone: "Aber es endete, es erstarb. Die Nacht wurde dünner, wurde fadenscheinig" (69). This section is labeled andante, a moderately slow tempo, because it is noticeably periodic and contains more detail, thus slowing its reading time. However, there is a moment of spirited activity shortly before the close: "Und es begann, zaghaft zunächst, dann aber ansteigend und unaufhörlich, das Klappern und Poltern und Rufen des Athener Morgens" (70).

The andante also returns to the opening idea of Part I with the words "und während ich meinen Posten an der Mauer verliess, um mich vor den öffnenden Wächtern zu verstecken" (70); and the coda, Part V, follows this section without pause. While it elaborates on the introductory idea of sleep, it has a playful quality, because its story is that of a sound sleeper rather than "kein rechter Schläfer," and it concludes with the hearty declaration, "Das nenne ich mir einen Schläfer, einen begnadeten Schläfer" (70).

Hildesheimer's verbal music in the toccata relies on (a) a prose structure that combines syndetic and polysyndetic structures of hypotaxis with the more rapid motion of parataxis and a number of directional words ("hinzu," "hohe," "nahe," and so forth) to establish the range of sound and its movement within the landscape of the story; (b) extensive repetition of words to unify the thematic material within and among the sections; (c) landscape imagery (hills, plains, the sea) to create a setting in which the tones of the voices acquire an immediate acoustic quality; (d) a limited technical vocabulary to suggest specific sounds ("tenoralen Stimme," and so on) and in general a limited literary vocabulary in keeping with the simplicity of the story.

Prose structure, which is based on the principle of musical phrasing,[11] varies according to the tempo of each section.

Part I: "Die Hähne Attikas—: um sie krähen zu hören, stieg ich eines Abends zur Akropolis empor, versteckte mich vor Torschluss, als die Wärter ihren letzten Gang durch die Tempel und über das weite, steinige, steinerne Gelände taten, hinter einer dicken Säule dorischer Ordnung, ich rollte, nah an sie gepresst, wie ein Zahnrad quer über ihre Hohlkehlen, immer im Sichtschatten des gehenden Wärters, und liess mich einschliessen. Nun hatte ich eine lange Nacht vor mir, aber das schreckte mich nicht, ich war schon damals kein rechter Schläfer, und alle meine Nächte sind lang" (63–64).

This introduction consists of two sentences that (a) establish the position of the narrator, and (b) inform the reader of his insomnia, the only personal information given. In the first sentence a comma rather than a period is required after "Ordnung" in order to maintain the flow of the first half of the section.

The sentences of Part II progress smoothly and quickly, with an abundance of commas and paratactic constructions: "Aber nun war der Hahn unten wach und gespannt, er schüttelte nochmals die Flügel, ich hörte ein Scheppern von hohlem Blech, er hatte eine Büchse umgestossen, und plötzlich schien die Nacht auf prosaische Weise belebt" (65). The one-word sentence "Stille" (64.12) and the short "Ich rief nicht mehr" (65:16) create moments of dramatic expectancy within the flow of phrases.

Part III begins immediately after the literary indication of a pause (67:1–3):

> dann aber ertönten alle vier verschieden gestimmten Rufe in schneller Folge, und sofort darauf noch einmal in einer anderen Folge, als habe die erste die Rufer nicht befriedigt, und ein Fünfter kam hinzu, im Süden, und ein Sechster im Westen, beide weit, und ein Siebenter, diesmal wieder nah, sein Ruf warf ein Echo. Es klang aus, und sofort fielen die anderen wieder ein, der Dröhner, der Trompeter, der Kämpfer und der Schmetterer, der Fünfte im Süden und der Sechste im Westen und dann wieder der Siebente und dann das Echo, das diesmal nicht ausklang, denn die anderen fielen schneller ein, und es kamen neue hinzu, nahe und ferne, tiefe und hohe und heisere und klare, andere Schmetterer und Trompeter, Kämpfer, Dröhner, Fanfaren und Kastraten, einzeln nicht mehr feststellbar. (67)

This literary exposition features polysyndetic constructions, a somewhat static succession of clauses and phrases beginning with "und" that introduce the seven principal figures (voices) and a host of others. Increasing density of voices is simulated by the layering effect of the conjunction, which, at the height of the exposition from line 9 in the quotation above, simply links individual descriptive terms.

The developmental segment of Part III begins immediately after the last word of the quoted material:

> es kam aus allen Richtungen, das Konzert breitete sich aus wie ein Brand, es zog sich zwischen den Bergen entlang, sein Echo prallte an den Hängen ab, es erstreckte sich durch die Ebene, drang in die Täler, für mich und die Hähne meiner Umgebung nur noch zum Teil hörbar, auch waren die Hähne meiner Nähe schon heiser oder verstummt, aber sie waren mehrfach ersetzt durch andere Stimmen, alle Tonlagen waren besetzt und alle männlichen Stimmfächer bis zum Falsett. Und so zog sich das grosse attische Konzert durch das Land, überkreuz und in die Quere, ein Netz, das sich vergrössert, während seine Maschen enger werden, denn zwischen den Hähnen tauchten neue Hähne auf, als seien sie soeben erst erwacht. (67–68)

The parataxis of these opening lines produces a rapid flow of sound, a crescendo effect that subsides with "aber" in line 2 above. Syndetic and polysyndetic constructions dominate the remainder of the segment, which ends with a reference to the figure of the narrator (69:2–6). There are only four full stops in the entire section.

Part IV, the andante, moves in a steady flow of parataxis and periodic stops, seven in all. The last sentence (70:5–10) is a hypotactic construction that stretches over four lines of print in much the same way that the narrator might have stretched his cramped limbs in the cold dawn air. The direct, undramatic narrative quality of this last sentence carries over into Part V, the coda, which is both an unmusical anecdote with four periodic stops in only eleven lines of text and a tonal game of sibilants: "Schlafsucher . . . sagen . . . Schläfer . . . Schlacht . . . seiner entscheidenden Schlachten . . . Schokolade . . . seine Schlacht . . . Schläfer . . . Schläfer" (70).

Directional prefixes ("hinzu," "ab," "hinaus," "zurück") and adjectives ("ferne," "nahe," "tiefe," "hohe") create the dynamic effects of verbal crescendo and decrescendo within the continual motion of phrases and clauses that amplify and modify the toccata's narrative content. For example, the amplifying phrases in "er rief tief und dröhnend, war aber weit weg, vielleicht am Fusse des Hymettos, jedenfalls in dieser Richtung" (66) and the appositional "ein Vierter kam hinzu, ein Trompeter, er war sehr weit entfernt, in der Ebene, die sich nach Kap Sunion erstreckt" (66) maintain a driving energy as if in answer to a questioner who is never satisfied with the response he receives.

In the allegretto and andante sections, which are slower and more pictorial than the fugato, Hildesheimer ornaments his phrases with clusters of past participles: "Der Ruf hatte einen alten, ausgedienten Hahn geweckt, der nun in einer verbrauchten, heiser krächzenden Stimme antwortete" (65); "und schliesslich ertönte . . . ein vereinzelter, noch nicht ermüdeter, unermüdlicher Hahn" (69). Thematic texture is enhanced by these participles, but their static quality makes them unsuitable for sections where motion must be swift, and Hildesheimer does not use descriptive clusters in the fugato section.

Inverted word order begins each section of the literary toccata except for the andante, and it is a noticeable feature of every section except the coda where, after the opening line, inversion occurs only once more: "Und als er am nächsten Morgen . . . erwachte" (70). Inverted word order usually emphasizes adverbs of time or place: "Am frühen Morgen" (64), "und diesmal," "aber nun," "und irgendwo," all on page 65. The immediacy produced by these inversions is both narratively and musically efficacious. The scene is vivid; the reader knows immediately exactly when or where the action is taking place; and the adverb, with its decisive tone, approximates a strong downbeat and therefore varies the rhythmic flow.

The opening of the andante is deliberately regular word order to set in motion a quiet, calm flow of sound. Compare the effect of the weak upbeat opening of "Die Nacht wurde dünner" (69:7–8) and the strong downbeat of "Bald waren die Inseln . . ." (69:17),[12] which begins the second and somewhat more lively segment of the andante, when a rooster crows again. Inversion has different functions in the verbal music episodes, but its main purpose is to vary the stress in the rhythmic pattern of phrases.

Repetition and variation of words also vary stress and unite the sections. For example, "rufen" recurs sixteen times in past and perfect tenses and noun form in the allegretto, three times at the beginning and once at the end of the fugato, and then once in the andante. The noun "Fransen" in the fugato (68) becomes "verfranste sich" at the beginning of the andante (69). "Krähen" and "hören," the verbs that begin this evocation of a toccata, are most conspicuous as they alternate in the development segment of the fugato (68), but they also appear throughout the toccata (with the exception of "hören," which does not return after the fugato). Several simple and explicit verbs recur frequently: "Antworten," "erwachen," "horchen," "ertönen," "kommen"–with various directional prefixes.

The rhetorical scheme of anaphora defines the repetition of impersonal "es" constructions at the beginning of the fugato: "Es klang aus ... es kamen ... es kam ... es zog ... es erstreckte sich" (67). Epanalepsis appears once in this section: "Und jeder von ihnen krähte und horchte und krähte wieder" (68). More extensive use of the scheme would have had the same static effect as the polysyndeton. Instead, Hildesheimer varies the material between his repeated words as a composer would vary the tones around an important musical idea; and fugal texture is, after all, a limited number of musical ideas in various guises.

One of the dangers of verbal music is the monotony that may result from repetition. In the toccata the use of repetitive schemes (anaphora, epanalepsis) is minimal; rather, the author/composer manipulates his limited vocabulary by changing verbs to nouns or modifying the meaning of a word with the echo effect of assonance. "Krähte" becomes "bekrähte," "noch nicht ermüdeter" changes to "unermüdlicher," "steinige" becomes "steinerne."

The natural landscape in which the motion of the toccata takes place is acoustically important. In the solo voice introduction the narrator stands behind a pillar in a confining position so that he will not be seen. At the beginning of the allegretto he steps to the edge of the east wall of the Acropolis; his cry and the answers of the roosters spread over the city in an ever-widening arc during the fugato. Snatches of sound varying in timbre come from different directions, as if from different sections of an orchestra ("er rief tief und dröhnend ... rief mit dem kühnen Ton eines Kämpfers ... ein Vierter kam hinzu, ein Trompeter, er war sehr weit entfernt" on 66). At the moment of greatest tension during the fugato the sound spreads like a fire and echoes ricochet from the surrounding mountains. The landscape imagery encompasses first the coastline and then the sea itself, where a fisherman might be able to hear the coastline roosters. Sound travels out to sea and back to Athens and then up "in alle Himmelsrichtungen" (69) and down again to the narrator.

Special acoustic effects are created in the fugato's development segment by the verbs "prallte ... ab" (67), "tauchten ... auf" (68), "verhallte" (68). By contrast, the repetition of "stille" and the adjectives "dünner," "fadenscheinig," "vereinzelter," emphasize the softer, comparatively calm rise and fall of sound in the more limited landscape of the andante, which is articulated with chiasmus: "und in der Ferne bildeten sich Inseln aus Stille über Wellen aus Laut," and "Bald waren die Inseln Inseln aus Laut inmitten Ebenen aus Stille" (both on 69). Near the end of the andante there is a brief crescendo that takes in the entire city below: "und es begann, zaghaft zunächst, dann aber ansteigend und unaufhörlich, das Klappern und Poltern und Rufen des Athener Morgens" (70).

The landscape imagery is precise ("Meer," "Landzungen"), only infrequently adorned with adjectives or modified by descriptive phrases. For example, "eine ganze gezackte Küstenlinie" (68) is exceptionally elaborate in the body of the toccata; the first sentence of the introduction, however, contains two elaborate images. In the development segment of the fugato (68:4-5) the net imagery is modified by two succeeding phrases in present tense, the only exception to the past-tense structure of the toccata: "Und so zog sich das grosse attische Konzert durch das Land ... ein Netz, das sich vergrössert, während seine Maschen enger werden, denn zwischen den Hähnen tauchten neue Hähne auf" (68). The only reason for the foregrounding of this particular image is dynamic contrast. The net becomes for an instant a vivid entity.

Technical terminology in the literary fugato consists mainly of nouns: "Schmettern," "Trompeter," "Fanfaren," "Kastraten," "Konzert," "tenoralen Stimme," "Tonlagen," "Stimmfächer," "Falsett," "Dröhner." Like the landscape imagery the terms are precise. There are no indications within the verbal music itself to identify its form beyond the ambiguous mention of a "Pause" between the allegretto and fugato sections.

Onomatopoeic effects are achieved by the "Kikeriki" of the narrator and the first rooster, the verb "krähen" that echoes throughout the toccata and "Dröhner," "krächzenden" and "Klappern."

Hildesheimer's literary evocation of a toccata is otherwise distinguished, especially in the choice of verbs, by a relative simplicity and "Exaktheit." The overlapping and mingling of specific tones in a natural landscape (the "score" of this verbal music) is created with a minimum but expressive vocabulary frequently intensified with the acoustic ornamentation of assonance ("weite, steinige, steinerne," on 63; "leergefegt" on 64; "ganze gezackte" on 68; "Herzog aller Hähne" on 69) and alliteration (see 64:16-17, 65:21-22, 68:6-7). Individual words, like the individual tones of the roosters, are of utmost importance. The roosters' notes are brilliant but staccato, in fact, a monotone; the entire literary toccata, therefore, concentrates on the play of a somewhat narrow range of sounds.

There are three similes, one in the opening sentence ("ich rollte ... wie ein Zahnrad" on 63), one at the beginning of the fugato development ("das Konzert breitete sich aus wie ein Brand" on 67), and one at the end of the fugato ("hinauf zu mir ... still und wie ein Herzog aller Hähne" on 69). The metaphors of the net, carpet and designations for the roosters together with these similes represent simple pictorial or aural aspects of the verbal music and permit the reader to see and hear more clearly the mingling of the verbal toccata tones. Although "Netz" and "Teppich" are impressionistic tropes, they offer the reader uncomplicated, daily-life visualizations of a musical effect. The first simile, too, is related to the everyday world, though it is less common. These visualizations, however, reflect Hildesheimer's training in stagecraft and architecture.[13] He creates simple stage props to suggest the fugato's texture and, in order to illustrate the narrator's progress around the column, which he identifies as Doric with an architect's eye for detail, he uses a comparison with a bit of machinery that might be found at a building site or backstage in a theater.

The four verbal music episodes of *Tynset*, each a brilliant display of Hildesheimer's creative genius, are independent entities and could be extracted from

Tynset without detriment to its theme of alienation; but they are also externally linked to the overall rondo framework by means of motivic reference from the preceding refrain, and thus they partake, to some degree, in the narrator's reflective search for insight. The toccata's relation to alienation is based on the narrator's "Kontaktarmut"[14] and his positive response to nature. His desire and ability to become part of a natural phenomenon of the Athens pre-dawn is a variation of other attempts in the novel at communion with nature rather than interaction with people.

Notes

1.   See Steven Paul Scher, *Verbal Music in German Literature* (New Haven, Conn.: Yale University Press, 1968).

2.   Steven Paul Scher, "How Meaningful is 'Musical' in Literary Criticism?" in *Yearbook of Comparative and General Literature* 21 (1972):56.

3.   See Scher, pp. 13–142, for analysis of these works.

4.   Rondo form is an extension of sonata or ternary (a-b-a) form; it consists of a theme, called "refrain," which begins the work and returns in an alternating pattern with passages called "episodes." Episodes may contain new melodies or simply figurations of some kind. Rondo length is indeterminate, but the work as a whole is symmetrical (a-b-a-c-a-d-a, for example). In *Tynset,* which consists of fourteen refrains and thirteen episodes, each refrain is distinguished by a reflective, often lyrical, tone; episodes are impersonal stories.

5.   Hildesheimer is presently completing a biography of Mozart, and he recently published a collection of Mozart letters. Wolfgang Hildesheimer, ed., *Mozart Briefe,* (Insel Taschenbuch 128, Frankfurt am Main: Insel Verlag, vertrieb durch Suhrkamp, 1975). He told me during a visit with him in 1974 of his interest in Bach.

6.   Although Hildesheimer listened to Bach's "Kunst der Fuge" nearly every day while he was writing his literary fugue (which is Bachian in complexity), he did not purposely intend to evoke any specific composition.

7.   Modernists turn to music because of its abstract independence. A work of music is a self-contained universe without moral or empirical implications for the reality outside itself; the modernist utilizes principles of musical composition to produce a literary unit of words without moral or empirical implications for the reality outside itself. This literary universe of formal relationships exemplifies the modernist's belief that there is no meaning in the universe outside man, "and indeed not outside the self." See Walter H. Sokel, *The Writer in Extremis: Expressionism in Twentieth-Century German Literature* (Stanford, Calif.: Stanford University Press, 1968), p. 26.

8.   The toccata is based on a letter from Lawrence Durrell to Henry Miller dated August 10, 1940, and appended to Miller's book *The Colossus of Maroussi* (San Francisco: The Colt Press, 1941). Hildesheimer first heard about the Durrell letter in 1944, but he did not read Miller's book and the letter until sometime after 1952, when he became interested in the story of the Athens roosters.

9.   Wolfgang Hildesheimer, *Tynset* (Frankfurt am Main: Suhrkamp Verlag, 1966), p. 67. References to this work are by page and line number in the text. Page 26, line 7, for example, are indicated as 26:7.

10.   The "Bett-Fuge" of *Tynset* appears on pp. 191–214; ibid.

11. A musical "phrase" is a "division or section of a musical line, somewhat comparable to a clause or a sentence in language." Willi Apel and Ralph T. Daniel, eds., *Harvard Brief Dictionary of Music,* (Cambridge, Mass.: Harvard University Press, 1961), p. 224.

12. For a musical example, compare the upbeat opening of the first movement of Mozart's Symphony no. 40, K. 550, with the strong downbeat opening of the first movement of Sergei Prokofiev's *Classical* Symphony, op. 25.

13. Hildesheimer studied stage design, art, and architecture from 1934 to 1939 in Salzburg, Jerusalem, and London.

14. Hildesheimer described the narrator to me as "kontaktarm," and in an interview in *Die Zeit* [Hamburg] (13 April 1973) he said, "In *Tynset* war das Hauptthema die Resignation und die Kontaktarmut."

Two

The Theme and Variation Form in Poetry

Wallace Stevens and the Variation Form

Northrop Frye

We cannot read far in Wallace Stevens's poetry without finding examples of
a form that reminds us of the variation form in music, in which a theme is presented in a sequence of analogous but differing settings. Thus in "Sea Surface
Full of Clouds" the same type of stanza is repeated five times, each with just
enough variation to indicate that the same landscape is being seen through five
different emotional moods. Another type of variation form appears in "Thirteen
Ways of Looking at a Blackbird," where a series of thirteen little imagist poems
are related by the common theme of the blackbird, and which, to pursue the
musical analogy perhaps further than it will go, gives more the effect of a chaconne or passacaglia. Sometimes the explicit theme is missing and only the variations appear, as in "Like Decorations in a Nigger Cemetery."

We notice also that in the titles of Stevens's poems the image of variation
frequently turns up, either literally, as in "Variations on a Summer Day," or
metaphorically, as in "Nuances of a Theme by Williams," "Analysis of a
Theme," and, perhaps, "Repetitions of a Young Captain." "The Man with the
Blue Guitar" also gives us a strong sense of reading through a set of thirty-three
variations, or related imaginative presentations, of a single theme. Then again,
the long meditative theoretical poems written in a blank tercet form, "Notes toward a Supreme Fiction," "The Auroras of Autumn," "An Ordinary Evening in
New Haven," "The Pure Good of Theory," are all divided into sections of the
same length. "An Ordinary Evening" has thirty-one sections of six tercets each;
the "Supreme Fiction," three parts of ten sections each, thirty sections in all,
each of seven tercets; and similarly with the others. This curious formal symmetry, which cannot be an accident, also reminds us of the classical variation form
in which each variation has the same periodic structure and harmonic sequence.
Even the numbers that often turn up remind us of the thirty Goldberg variations, the thirty-three Diabelli waltz variations, and so on.

Reprinted by permission of Yale University Press from *Literary Theory and Structure: Essays in Honor of William K. Wimsatt,* edited by Frank Brady, John Palmer, and Martin
Price, Copyright (c) 1973, 395–414.

The variation form in Stevens is a generic application of the principle that every image in a poem is a variation of the theme or subject of that poem. This principle is the first of three "effects of analogy" mentioned in Stevens's essay of that title. There are two other "effects." One is that "every image is a restatement of the subject of the image in the terms of an attitude."[1] This is practically the same thing as Eliot's objective correlative and is illustrated in "Sea Surface Full of Clouds," where five different moods are unified by the fact that they all have the same correlative. Stevens also says, "In order to avoid abstractness, in writing, I search out instinctively things that express the abstract and yet are not in themselves abstractions."[2] His example is the statue in "Owl's Clover," which he also calls a "variable" symbol.[3] The implication is that such images are variations on the idea of the poem which is within the poem of words, the true as distinct from the nominal subject or theme.[4] We note that the correlative in Stevens may pair with a concept as well as with an emotion, which helps to explain why his commentaries on his own poems in the letters are so often woodenly allegorical.

The third "effect of analogy" is that "every image is an intervention on the part of the image-maker."[5] This principle takes us deep into Stevens's central notion of poetry as the result of a struggle, or balance, or compromise, or tension, between the two forces that he calls imagination and reality. We notice that in the musical theme with variations the theme is frequently a composition by someone else or comes from a different musical context. Similarly the poet works with imagination, which is what he has, and reality, which is given him. So, from Stevens's point of view, poems could be described as the variations that imagination makes on the theme of reality. In "Sea Surface Full of Clouds" a question is asked in each variation about who or what created the picture in front of us, and the answer, given each time in French, defines a distinctive mood of the imagination.

In a letter Stevens says, "Sometimes I believe most in the imagination for a long time, and then, without reasoning about it, turn to reality and believe in that and that alone. But both of these things project themselves endlessly and I want them to do just that."[6] This somewhat helpless remark indicates the strength of the sense of polarity in his poetic world. Stevens often speaks of the intense pressure that the sense of external reality exerts on the modern mind. One of the "Adagia" says, "In the presence of extraordinary actuality, consciousness takes the place of imagination."[7] Consciousness, by itself, is simple awareness of the external world. It sees; it may even select what it sees, but it does not fight back. The consciousness fighting back, with a subjective violence corresponding to the objective violence of external pressure, is the consciousness rising to imagination.[8]

The imagination confronts a reality which reflects itself but is not itself. If it is weak, it may either surrender to reality or run away from it. If it surrenders, we have what is usually called realism, which, as Stevens often makes clear, is almost the opposite of what he means by reality. He says, for instance, in connection with the painting of Jack Yeats, that "the purely realistic mind never experiences any passion for reality."[9] This maxim would also apply to the "social realism" demanded in Marxist countries, for which Stevens never expresses anything but contempt. The imagination that runs away retreats from the genuinely imaginative world into a merely imaginary one, for, Stevens says, "If poetry is limited to the vaticinations of the imagination, it soon becomes worthless."[10] Certain recurring symbols in Stevens represent the kind of facile pseudoconquest of reality which the imagination pretends to make whenever reality is not there: one of them is the moon. Such imaginary triumphs take place in a self-contained world of words which is one of the things that Stevens means by false rhetoric, or "Rodomontade."[11] The world of false rhetoric is a world where the imagination encounters no resistance from anything material, where the loneliness and alienation of the mind, about which Stevens speaks so eloquently, has consoled itself with pure solipsism.

Stevens says that it is a fundamental principle about the imagination that "it does not create except as it transforms."[12] It is the function of reality to set free the imagination and not to inhibit it. Reality is at its most inhibiting when it is most externalized, as it is in our own time. In "Two or Three Ideas" Stevens speaks of the way in which the pressure of externality today has created a culture of what he calls "detached styles," and which he characterizes as "the unsuccessful, the ineffective, the arbitrary, the literary, the non-umbilical, that which in its highest degree would still be words."[13] In one prophetic flash, which sums up the essence of the world we have been living through for the past few years, he speaks of this world of false imagination as the product of "irrationality provoked by prayer, whiskey, fasting, opium, or the hope of publicity."[14] It follows that Stevens does not accept the mystique of the unconscious and has nothing of Yeats's or Joyce's feeling for the dreamworld as having a peculiarly close relation to the creative process. He always associates creativity with cognition, with consciousness, even with calculation. "Writing poetry is a conscious activity. While poems may very well occur, they had very much better be caused."[15]

Stevens associates his word "reality" with the phrase "things as they are," which implies that for him reality has a close relation to the external physical world as we perceive it. The imagination contemplates "things as they are," seeing its own unreality mirrored in them, and its principle of contemplation Stevens calls resemblance or analogy. He also calls it, quite logically, "Narcissism."[16] This word points to the danger of uncontrolled imagination and the ease with which it can assume that there is another reality on the other side of things as they are. Traditional religious poetry, for instance, projects heavens and hells as objective and hidden realities, though it can construct them only out of the material of things as they are. Crispin, the hero of one of Stevens's most elaborate variation poems, soon comes to a point at which he can say, "Here was the veritable ding an sich, at last."[17] But this is a Kantian phrase, and Stevens is not Kantian: reality for him is always phenomenal, something that "seems" as well as is, and there is no alternative version of it that the poet should be trying to reach.[18] Hidden realities always turn out to be unreal and therefore simply mirrors of the imagination itself. Similarly, "poetry will always be a phenomenal thing."[19]

Stevens's arguments are poetic and not philosophical, and like many poetic arguments they turn on a verbal trick. The trick in this case consists in using the special-pleading term "reality" for the external physical world, which means that conceptions set over against this "reality" have to be called, or associated with, the unreal. Stevens is not unaware of this by any means, but his use of the word "reality," which becomes almost obsessive in the letters, indicates that, like his spiritual sister Emily Dickinson, he has a puritanic distrust of all self-transcending mental efforts, especially mysticism. More particularly, he feels that, as the poet's language is the language of sense experience and concrete imagery, any poet who bypasses things as they are, however subtly, is dodging the central difficulty of poetry. Such poets, who look for some shortcut or secret passage through reality to something else, and regard poetry as a kind of verbal magic, have what Stevens calls a "marginal" imagination; and he associates this marginal imagination, which explores itself to find its own analogue in reality, with, among others, Valéry, Eliot, and Mallarmé.

Stevens goes even further in suggesting that the conquest of reality made by the reason is also somewhat facile compared to that of the imagination, because it is possible for reason, in some degree, to live in a self-contained world and shut its gates in the face of reality. One of the products of reason is the theological belief in reality as a creation, a product of the infinite imagination of God. Such a belief is repugnant to Stevens: this would mean that reality is analogous to the imagination. The poet is a Jacob who has to wrestle with the necessary angel of reality; and if reality is itself ultimately a "supreme fiction," or something made out of nothing, then all his agonized efforts and struggles are a put-up job, something fixed or rigged, as so many wrestling matches are. Stevens says:

> The arrangement contains the desire of
> The artist. But one confides in what has no
> Concealed creator. One walks easily
>
> The unpainted shore, accepts the world
> As anything but sculpture.[20]

So whatever the imagination may do to reality, reality continues to present something residually external, some donkey's carrot pulling us on, something sticking through everything we construct within it. Even in the moment of death (or what appears to be death, on the last page of the *Collected Poems*), we confront something "outside" giving us the sense of "a new knowledge of reality." Or, as Stevens says in prose, "Poetry has to do with reality in that concrete and individual aspect of it which the mind can never tackle altogether on its own terms, with matter that is foreign and alien in a way in which abstract systems, ideas in which we detect an inherent pattern, a structure that belongs to the ideas themselves, can never be."[21] The imagination is driven by a "rage for order,"[22] but it works toward, not the complete ordering of existence, but rather a sense of equipoise or balance between itself and what is not itself.

We soon come to understand that for Stevens there are different levels or degrees of reality, arranged in a ladder or mountain or winding stair in which the poet has to undertake what he calls an "ascent through illusion."[23] In his essay "A Collect of Philosophy" Stevens attempts to list a few philosophical conceptions which seem to him to be inherently poetic, meaning by that, presumably, conceptions that particularly appeal to him as a poet. Among these, the theme of anabasis or ascent, the theme of Dante, looms up prominently.[24] At the bottom of the ladder is the sense of reality as an undifferentiated external world, or what Stevens calls a *Lumpenwelt*.[25] Such a world, Stevens says, is "all one color,"[26] a "basic slate,"[27] a sinister or scowling "pediment of appearance."[28] As such, it forces the imagination to define itself as its opposite, or nothingness. At this point a construct emerges which is rather similar to the construct of being and nothingness in Sartre. The *Lumpenwelt* is reality on the minimum imaginative basis; the imagination on the same basis is merely the unreal: reality is everything; the imagination is nothing. The imagination never brings anything into the world, Stevens says in an unconscious echo of the burial service, though it is not quite so true for him that it can take nothing out.[29] This confrontation of being and nothingness, the starting point of imaginative energy, is the vision of the listener in "The Snow Man," who,

> nothing himself, beholds
> Nothing that is not there and the nothing that is.[30]

Traditionally, the world of becoming has always been regarded as the product of being and nothingness. For Stevens there is no reality of being in the traditional sense of something that does not change. Whenever we try to imagine an unchanging ideal, we get involved in the hopeless paradox of Keats's Grecian urn, where the little town on the hidden side of the urn will never be inhabited to all eternity. The woman in "Sunday Morning" asks resentfully, "Why should she give her bounty to the dead?" but soon comes to realize that she cannot have any alternative without change, and therefore death, at the heart of it. Reality is phenomenal and belongs to the world of becoming. In the very late poem "Of Mere Being" the only unchanging thing about being is that it remains external, "at the end of the mind," "beyond the last thought."[31]

Two of the requirements of the "supreme fiction" are that it must change and that it must give pleasure, and it is clear that for Stevens these two things are much the same thing, change being the only real source of pleasure. Over and over Stevens returns to what he calls "the motive for metaphor," the fact that what is change in reality is also pleasure in the imagination. The imagination, the principle of the unreal, breaks up and breaks down the tyranny of what is there by unifying itself with what is not there and so suggesting the principle of variety in its existence. This is the point of identity on which all art is founded: in the imaginations of Cézanne and Klee, Stevens says, reality is transmuted from substance into subtlety.[32] We get the idea of unchanging being from the thereness of the physical world, the fact that it doesn't go away. What does go away, and is to that extent unreal, is what the unreality of the imagination builds on. The imagination, in short, "skims the real for its unreal."[33]

This kind of activity gives us a relatively simple type of variation form, the kind represented by the "Blackbird" poem. Here the variations are what Stevens calls the "casual exfoliations" of an imagination contemplating a real thing.[34] The recipe for this type of variation form is given in the poem "Someone Puts a Pineapple Together," one of "Three Academic Pieces" in *The Necessary Angel:*

> Divest reality
> Of its propriety. Admit the shaft
> Of that third planet to the table and then:

The third planet, he has explained, is the imagination; and there follow a series of twelve numbered variations on the pineapple. It is clear that such a

conception of imagination and reality has much to do with the affinity to the
pictorial in Stevens, with his fondness for subjects analogous to still life or landscape painting, where the real object and the imaginative variation of it are most
dramatically exhibited. Such variation poems are fanciful in Coleridge's sense of
the term: Stevens was familiar with Coleridge's distinction, which he acquired
through his reading of I. A. Richards.[35] They are, so to speak, cyclical poems,
where the variations simply surround the theme. As such, they are not the most
serious kind of writing. Stevens speaks of the almost total exclusion of "thinking" from such a poem as "Variations on a Summer Day" and says also, "I have
no doubt that supreme poetry can be produced only on the highest possible level
of the cognitive."[36] Again one thinks of the musical parallel. The greatest examples of the variation form, such as the last movement of Beethoven's Opus 111,
do not merely diversify the theme: they are sequential and progressive forms as
well, and we feel at the end that they have, so to speak, exhausted the theme,
done what there is to be done with it. We have now to see if we can discover a
sequential and progressive aspect to Stevens's variation form also.

We began with a confrontation between imagination and reality, in which
the former is a negation, the opposite of reality. Then we found that the imagination can intensify reality by seizing on the "unreal" aspect of it, the aspect that
changes and therefore gives pleasure. Stevens says, "A sense of reality keen
enough to be in excess of the normal sense of reality creates a reality of its
own."[37] As he goes on to say, this is a somewhat circular statement, and one
would expect it to lead to some such principle as Blake's "As the Eye, such the
Object," the principle that the degree of reality depends on the energy of the
imagination. Stevens resists this implication, because of his constant fear that the
imagination will simply replace reality and thereby deprive itself of its own material cause. For him the imagination is rather an informing principle of reality,
transmuting its uniformity into variety, its "heavy scowl" into lightness and
pleasure.[38] Still, it seems clear that we cannot go on indefinitely thinking of the
imagination merely as a negation or nothingness.

The fact that the imagination seizes on the changing aspect of reality means
that it lives in a continuous present. This means not only that "the imperfect is
our paradise," but that the imagination is always beginning.[39] The only reason
for finishing anything is that we can then be rid of it and can come around to
the point at which we can begin again. The shoddiness of being fixated on the
past, of refusing to discard what he calls the "hieratic," meets us everywhere in
Stevens.[40] The imagination in the sunlit world of reality is like food in hot
weather: whatever is kept spoils. Hence "one of the motives in writing is renew-
al."[41] This emphasis on constant fresh beginnings is connected, naturally, with
the steadfast resistance to anything resembling an echo or an influence from
other poets in Stevens, in striking contrast to the absorption of echoes and influences that we find in, for instance, Eliot.

What is true of the past is also true of the future, the desire to use the imagination to make over reality that we find in so many romantics, revolutionaries,
and spokesmen of the irrational. Stevens speaks of this desire with a good deal of
sympathy and understanding, for instance, in his essay on the irrational in poetry,
where he links the irrational, once again, with the pressure of external fact on

the modern poet and his consequent sense of claustrophobia and desire for freedom.[42] "Owl's Clover" is a carefully considered effort to come to terms with the
revolutionary desire for freedom and equality on a vast social scale. But when the
imagination is used as part of an attempt to make over reality, it imposes its own
unreality on it. The result is that perversion of belief which we see in all reli-
gions, including the contemporary atheistic ones. Belief derives from the imaginative unreal: what we really believe in is a fiction, something we have made up
ourselves. But all beliefs, when they become institutionalized, tend to ascribe
some hidden reality to themselves, a projection of the imagination which can
end only in disillusionment or self-hypnotism. The "romantic" of this type
(Stevens uses the word romantic in several senses, but this one is pejorative[43]) is
"incapable of abstraction," abstraction being among other things the ability to
hold a belief as a "supreme fiction" without projecting it to the other side of
reality.[44]

At the same time Stevens holds to an intensely social conception of poetry
and its function, though a deeply conservative one. The poet, he says, should try
to reach the "centre," and by this he means first of all a social center. The poet
expresses among other things "that ultimate good sense which we term civilization."[45] For him reality includes human society as well. As such, the imagination defines the style of a culture or civilization: it is whatever it is that makes
everything in Spain look Spanish and makes every cultural product of Spain a
variation on a Spanish theme. Stevens uses the phrase "variations on a theme" in
connection with a closely related aspect of culture: the predominance and per-
sistence of a convention, as in medieval or Chinese painting.[46]

If we ask what the characteristics of such imaginative penetration of reality
are in human life, the words "nobility" and "elegance" come fairly close, though
Stevens admits that they are dangerous words. The quality in literature that we
recognize as heroic, the power of the imagination to make things look more intensely real, is a quality of illusion in reality that is at the same time a growth in
reality. The imagination is thus socially aristocratic, though not necessarily in a
class sense. The more power it gains, the more freedom and privilege it enjoys,
and the more confident society becomes about its culture. In a time like ours the
imagination is more preoccupied in fighting its environment, which presses in
on it much harder. In the poem "Mrs. Alfred Uruguay," Mrs. Uruguay herself
rides up a mountain in the state of the snow man, looking at her world honestly
but reductively, as totally without illusion. She meets going down the mountain
a "capable man" who recalls the noble rider of Stevens's earliest prose essay,
whose imagination is of the same kind as her own but is more emancipated, and
hence to some extent its fulfillment. It is he who creates

> out of the martyrs' bones
> The ultimate elegance: the imagined land.[47]

So our confrontation between a negative imagination and a positive reality
has reached the point where this negation has informed human civilization and
produced a style of living. This process, considered in an individual context, is
the theme of the sequential variation form "The Comedian as the Letter C."
Crispin, the hero of the poem, begins with the principle: "Nota: Man is the intelligence of his soil," a strictly Cartesian principle in which man is the "sover-

eign ghost." This first variation is headed "The World without Imagination."
The fourth variation brings us to "The Idea of a Colony," which begins:

> Nota: his soil is man's intelligence.
> That's better. That's worth crossing seas to find.[48]

Stevens calls Crispin a "profitless philosopher," says that he never discovers the
meaning of life, that social contact would have been a catastrophe for him, that
he is an everyday man whose life has not the slightest adventure, and symbolizes
him by the one letter of the alphabet which has no distinctive sound of its
own.[49] Nevertheless, Crispin works very hard to achieve his own kind of reality;
and if he is not a poet he is at least a colonizer, someone who achieves a life-style
out of a pilgrimage and a settlement in new surroundings. The poem as a whole
goes around in an ironic circle; and Crispin ends much where he began, using
his imagination as so many people do, to select and exclude rather than create: a
realist who rejects reality. Hence the final line of the poem, "so may the relation
of each man be clipped." Stevens may also have Crispin partly in mind when he
says, "the man who has been brought up in an artificial school becomes intem-
perately real. The Mallarmiste becomes the proletarian novelist."[50] Still, Crispin
represents something of the historical process that produced the culture and the
tradition out of which Stevens himself developed, moving from baroque Europe
to realistic New England.

We have next to see how a negation can be an informing principle in reality. This brings us to Stevens's conception of the "supreme fiction." The imagination informs reality through fictions or myths (the word "fictive" in Stevens
means mythical), which are the elements of a model world. This model world is
not "reality," because it does not exist—it is not "there"; but it is an unborn or,
perhaps, potential reality which becomes a growth out of reality itself. Stevens
quotes Simone Weil, obviously with approval, on the subject of "decreation," a
moving from the created to the uncreated, going in the opposite direction from
destruction, which moves from the created to nothingness.[51] The conception is
Stevens's, though the terms are not. The first law of the supreme fiction is that
it must be abstract. It is abstract for the same reason that a god is not reducible
to his image. The supreme fiction is not a thing, something to be pointed to or
contemplated or thought of as achieved. In its totality, the supreme fiction is poetry or the work of the imagination as a whole, but this totality never separates
from the perceiving subject or becomes external. Stevens says, "the abstract does
not exist, but . . . the fictive abstract is as immanent in the mind of the poet, as
the idea of God is immanent in the mind of the theologian."[52] This last indicates that God is one of the supreme fictions. God for Stevens, whatever he
may be in himself, must be for man an unreality of the imagination, not a reality, and his creative power can manifest itself only in the creations of man. The
explicit statement that God and the imagination are one is made by the "interior
paramour," an anima-figure working under the direction of the imagination.

According to Stevens, "The wonder and mystery of art, as indeed of religion
in the last resort, is the revelation of something 'wholly other' by which the inexpressible loneliness of thinking is broken and enriched."[53] The phrase "wholly
other," which is in quotation marks, suggests the existential theology of Karl

Barth, as relayed through a poet who calls himself a "dried-up Presbyterian."[54] In Barth, of course, the otherness of God and the alienation of man are conditions of man's unregenerate state. God does not remain wholly other for two reasons: first, he has created and redeemed man; and second, he has revealed himself. Let us see what reality in Stevens can do along parallel lines.

When Crispin discovers that the Cartesian principle "Man is the intelligence of his soil" is less true than its reverse, that "his soil is man's intelligence," Stevens is saying that the antithesis of imagination and reality did not begin as such. Man grew out of "reality," and the consciousness which enables him also to draw away from it is a recent development. The human is "alien," but it is also "the non-human making choice of a human self."[55] The imagination is a product of reality—its Adam, so to speak, or exiled son. Just as, in Dante's *Purgatorio,* the poet makes his way back to the Eden which is his own original home, so the imagination contemplates the "rock," the dead inert reality before it, and realizes that it is itself the rock come to life. "I am what is around me," the poet says, and he continually returns to the sense of the "wholly other" as not only the object but the origin of the sense of identity.[56]

The rock is not dead, because it has never died; death is a process, not a condition. It represents rather the unconscious and undifferentiated external world at the bottom of the imaginative ladder, where the sense of thereness is overpowering and the imagination is simply its negation. In the course of time leaves cover the rock: life emerges from the inanimate, breaks up and diversifies the heavy *Lumpenwelt.* Life, then, if Stevens's general argument still applies, is the negation of the inanimate, the unreal at work in the real. The imagination does with "things as they are" what life does with the rock, and the poet's imagination is inseparably attached to the articulating of life in the rest of the world. The "howl" of the doves,[57] the "cry" of the leaves,[58] the sea in "The Idea of Order at Key West," the "Bantams in Pine-Woods," who are praising themselves and not a divine bantam in the rising sun, are all part of the symphony of life in which the poet has his own voice. We speak of a will to live, and similarly "imagination is the will of things."[59]

The poem "Oak Leaves Are Hands" describes a "Lady Lowzen," who is also the goddess Flora and who continues to "skim the real for its unreal" in human imagination as formerly in the vegetable world. Lady Lowzen is "chromatic," and the delight of vegetable nature in color supplies Stevens with his chief image for the imagination, which he thinks of as, so to speak, the coloring principle of reality. The basis of nature is metamorphosis, the basis of poetry is metaphor, and metaphor and metamorphosis are for Stevens interchangeable terms. Stevens completes the identification by saying "in metaphor the imagination is life."[60] In this context the variations which the imagination makes on reality join the Darwinian theme with variations in which every variety is a mutation thrown out toward the environment, the "reality" it has to struggle with, until a successful mutation blends and identifies with that reality.

The limit of poetry, as Stevens himself frequently remarks, has always been the imaginatively conceivable, not what is or "things as they are," and any poet deeply impressed by things as they are is apt to suffer from imaginative claustrophobia. Stevens has relegated God to the imaginative unreal, a fiction the human mind creates. He has made an uncompromising bourgeois rejection of all politically revolutionary values. He dismisses Nietzsche and his doctrine of the self-transcendence of man as being "as perfect a means of getting out of focus as a little bit too much to drink."[61] What is left? How much further can a "harmonious skeptic" carry his rage for order?[62] Even things as they are present themes which the poet cannot avoid and yet can hardly deal with on their terms. For instance, a surprising number of Stevens's poems are about death, and death is one subject where the imagination, like Good Deeds in *Everyman,* may be prevailed on to accompany the poet as his guide, while "reality," in whatever form or disguise, will always mutter some excuse and slope off. When Stevens gets to the point of saying that "Life and Nature are one," he has left very little room for any reality which he has not in some other context called unreal.[63]

In Stevens's cultural situation about the only consistent "position" left is that of a secular humanism. But, he says, the more he sees of humanism the less he likes it, and, more briefly and explicitly, "humanism is not enough."[64] He also says, "Between humanism and something else, it might be possible to create an acceptable fiction" and that "there are fictions that are extensions of reality."[65] This last concession means that Stevens is capable, at least in his poetry, of sweeping "reality" out of the way as a superego symbol and of reducing it to its proper role as the material cause of poetry.

In reality, man is a social being, and society is partly an aggregate, a mass of men, often dominated by, and expressing their will through, some kind of hero or leader. The hero in this sense is a fiction which has been, like so many other fictions, misapplied and misunderstood by society. In two poems particularly, "Examination of the Hero in a Time of War" and "Life on a Battleship," Stevens shows us how the dictatorial hero or charismatic leader is a false projection of the imagination, like the heavens and hells that are created by the imagination and are then asserted to be actual places in the world which is there. The genuine form of this fiction is the conception of all men as a single man, where the difference between the individual and the mass has ceased to exist. Or, as Stevens puts it, in commenting on a passage in "Notes toward a Supreme Fiction" which contains the phrase "leaner being,"[66] "The trouble with humanism is that man as God remains man, but there is an extension of man, the leaner being, in fiction, a possibly more than human human, a composite human. The act of recognizing him is the act of this leaner being moving in on us."[67] This "leaner being" is the "central man" or "man of glass" who is all men, and whom Stevens portrays as a titanic being striding the skies.[68] Even Crispin reaches an apotheosis of identity with this being.[69]

In this conception of a "general being or human universe,"[70] we are still in the area of fictions; but by now we understand that the poet "gives to life the supreme fictions without which we are unable to conceive of it."[71] Whatever unreal grows out of reality becomes real, like the graft of art on nature which Polixenes urges on Perdita in *The Winter's Tale.* The human universe is still a fiction and to that extent is not strictly true, but, as Abraham Cowley said of the philosophy of Thomas Hobbes, "'Tis so like Truth 'twill serve our turn as well." In any case, on this level of fiction we can understand how poetry can be called "a transcendent analogue composed of the particulars of reality," the word "transcendent" here being used, I think, quite carefully in its philosophical sense as going beyond sense experience but not beyond the mental organization of that experience.[72] Certain sentences in *The Necessary Angel* which Stevens mutters out of the corner of his mouth when he thinks his censor is not listening take on a new and illuminating significance. One such sentence is this one from "Imagination as Value": "The imagination that is satisfied by politics, whatever the nature of the politics, has not the same value as the imagination that seeks to satisfy, say, the universal mind, which, in the case of a poet, would be the imagination that tries to penetrate to basic images, basic emotions, and so to compose a fundamental poetry even older than the ancient world."[73] This universal mind is the mind that has produced "the essential poem at the centre of things," which is *the* supreme fiction as such.[74] In this perspective, "reality" becomes the stabilizing principle which enables us, even as we outgrow our gods, to recognize, even in the act of coming around to the beginning again, that the creative faculties are always the same faculties and that "the things created are always the same things."[75] In all the variations of what might be we can still hear the theme of what is there.

The supreme fiction of the "central," which is the total form of both man and the human imagination, takes us into a very different context of variability, a context less Darwinian than Thomist. It would be easy, but simplistic, to say that ultimately what is real in Stevens is the universal, the universal being the theme of which the individual is the variation—easy, because one could quote a good many passages from the later poems, at least, in support of it; but simplistic, because the traditional context of the real universal is a kind of essential world that Stevens never at any point accepts. "Logically," says Stevens, "I ought to believe in essential imagination, but that has its difficulties."[76] In the early "Peter Quince at the Clavier" we have the line "the body dies; the body's beauty lives." Considering the number of poets, in English literature and elsewhere, who would have drawn a Platonic inference from that statement, it comes as a deliberate and calculated shock for Stevens to say:

> Beauty is momentary in the mind,
> The fitful tracing of a portal,
> But in the flesh it is immortal.

"A Collect of Philosophy" has nothing of medieval realism, though it reflects Stevens's fascination with Plato; but it does express a keen interest in such conceptions as Alexander's "compresence" of mind and existence, and, more particularly, in the great passage in Whitehead's *Science and the Modern World* in which Whitehead rejects the conception of "simple location" in space and announces the doctrine of interpenetration, the doctrine that everything is everywhere at once. Stevens's comment on this passage is, "These words are pretty obviously words from a level where everything is poetic, as if the statement that every location involves an aspect of itself in every other location produced in the imagination a universal iridescence, a dithering of presences and, say, a complex of differences."[77] This last phrase shows that Stevens is still thinking within the metaphor of a theme and variations.

Stevens often refers to Eliot as a poet who represents the exact opposite of everything he stood for himself, and perhaps we are now beginning to understand why. The fifth way of looking at a blackbird, for example, is a way that Eliot constantly refuses to look at it:

I do not know which to prefer,
The beauty of inflections
Or the beauty of innuendoes,
The blackbird whistling
Or just after.

"A Collect for Philosophy" assumes in passing that all knowledge is knowledge after the experience of the knowledge.[78] For Eliot, the fact that there is a split second between an experience and the awareness of having had the experience is a memento of the Fall of Man. All three dimensions of time for Eliot are categories of unreality: the no longer, the not yet, and the never quite. Our ordinary existence in this time is the fallen shadow of the life we might have lived if there had been no Fall, in which experience and consciousness would be the same thing, and in which the present moment would be a real moment, an eternal now. Eliot's imagination revolves around the figure of Percival in the Grail castle, who, in the words of "The Dry Salvages," "had the experience but missed the meaning," because he was afraid to put the question that would have unified experience and meaning. In this sense we are all Prufrocks, vaguely aware that there is an "overwhelming question" to be asked, and wasting our lives in various devices for not asking it.

Stevens has nothing of Eliot's sense of the phenomenal world as a riddle, to be solved by some kind of conscious experience that annihilates it. When we start climbing the Ash-Wednesday staircase, we have to regard such things as "a slotted window bellied like the fig's fruit" as a distraction. This is because at the top of Eliot's staircase is a total unification and an absorption of reality into the infinite being of God. Like Dante whom he is following, Eliot wants his pilgrimage to pass beyond the categories of time and space and the cycle of nature that revolves within these categories. The slotted window is an image of that cycle, the vegetable cycle of flower and fruit, the cycle of human life that begins with birth from a womb. Stevens does not resemble Yeats any more closely than he resembles Eliot; but, like Yeats, he sides with the "self" in the "Dialogue of Self and Soul." For his Mrs. Uruguay, as for Yeats, the top of the mountain or staircase or whatever has to be climbed is the top of the natural cycle, and the fulfillment of climbing it is in coming down again. In Stevens, the imagination is life, and the only way to kill it is to take it outside nature, into a world where it has swallowed nature and become a total periphery or circumference, instead of remaining "central." So for Stevens, as in a very different way for Joyce in *Finnegans Wake*, the cycle of nature is the only possible image of whatever is beyond the cycle, "the same anew."

There is an elaborate imagery of the seasons of the year in Stevens, where summer represents the expanded and fulfilled imagination, autumn the more restricted and realistic imagination, and winter the reduction to a black-and-white world where reality is "there" and the imagination set over against it is simply unreal. The emotional focus of this imagery comes at the moment in spring when the first blush of color enters the world with "an access of color, a new and unobserved, slight dithering,"[79] or when a bird's cry "at the earliest ending of winter" signals "a new knowledge of reality,"[80] or at Easter. "On Easter," says Stevens, "the great ghost of what we call the next world invades and vivifies this present world, so that Easter seems like a day of two lights, one the sunlight of the bare and physical end of winter, the other the double light."[81] What Easter symbolizes to Stevens is that we are constantly trying to close up our world on the model of our own death, to become an "owl in the sarcophagus." As long as some reality is still outside us we are still alive, and what is still external in that reality is what has a renewing power for us. This vision is the point at which "dazzle yields to a clarity and we observe," when we see the world as total process, extending over both death and life, always new, always just beginning, always full of hope, and possessed by the innocence of an uncreated world which is unreal only because it has never been fixed in death.[82] This is also the point at which the paradox of reality and imagination comes into focus for the poet and he understands that

> We make, although inside an egg,
> Variations on the words spread sail.[83]

Notes

1. Wallace Stevens, *The Necessary Angel: Essays on Reality and the Imagination* (New York: Knopf, 1951), p. 128.

2. Holly Stevens, *Letters of Wallace Stevens*, ed. Wallace Stevens (New York: Knopf, 1967), p. 290.

3. Ibid., p. 311.

4. Samuel French Morse, *Opus Posthumous*, ed. Wallace Stevens (New York: Knopf, 1957), p. 223.

5. Stevens, *Necessary Angel*, p. 128.

6. Stevens, *Letters*, p. 710.

7. Morse, p. 165.

8. Cf. Stevens, *Necessary Angel*, p. 36.

9. Stevens, *Letters*, p. 597.

10. Ibid., p. 500.

11. Stevens, *Necessary Angel*, p. 61.

12. Stevens, *Letters*, p. 364.

13. Morse, p. 212.

14. Ibid., p. 218.

15. Stevens, *Letters*, p. 274.

16. Stevens, *Necessary Angel*, p. 80.

17.   Wallace Stevens, *The Collected Poems of Wallace Stevens* (New York: Knopf, 1954), p. 29.

18.   Cf. ibid., p. 339.

19.   Stevens, *Letters,* p. 300.

20.   Stevens, *Collected Poems,* p. 296.

21.   Morse, p. 236.

22.   Stevens, *Collected Poems,* p. 130.

23.   Stevens, *Necessary Angel,* pp. 7, 81.

24.   Morse, p. 193.

25.   Stevens, *Necessary Angel,* p. 174.

26.   Ibid., p. 26.

27.   Stevens, *Collected Poems,* p. 15.

28.   Ibid., p. 361.

29.   Stevens, *Necessary Angel,* p. 59.

30.   Stevens, *Collected Poems,* p. 9.

31.   Morse, p. 117.

32.   Stevens, *Necessary Angel,* p. 174.

33.   Stevens, *Collected Poems,* p. 272.

34.   Stevens, *Necessary Angel,* p. 86.

35.   Ibid., p. 10.

36.   Stevens, *Letters,* pp. 346, 500.

37.   Stevens, *Necessary Angel,* p. 79.

38.   Stevens, *Collected Poems,* p. 362.

39.   Ibid., p. 194.

40.   Stevens, *Necessary Angel,* p. 58.

41.   Ibid., p. 220.

42.   Morse, p. 216.

43.   Stevens, *Letters,* p. 277.

44.   Stevens, *Necessary Angel,* p. 139.

45.   Ibid., p. 116.

46.   Ibid., p. 73.

47.   Stevens, *Collected Poems,* p. 250.

48.   Ibid., p. 36.

49.   Stevens, *Letters,* pp. 293, 295, 778.

50.   Morse, p. 221.

51.   Stevens, *Necessary Angel,* p. 174.

52. Stevens, *Letters,* p. 434.

53. Morse, p. 237.

54. Stevens, *Letters,* p. 792.

55. Stevens, *Necessary Angel,* p. 89.

56. Stevens, *Collected Poems,* p. 86.

57. Morse, p. 97.

58. Ibid., p. 96.

59. Stevens, *Collected Poems,* p. 84.

60. Stevens, *Necessary Angel,* p. 73.

61. Stevens, *Letters,* p. 432.

62. Stevens, *Collected Poems,* p. 122.

63. Stevens, *Letters,* p. 533.

64. Ibid., p. 489.

65. Ibid., pp. 430, 449.

66. Stevens, *Collected Poems,* p. 387.

67. Stevens, *Letters,* p. 434.

68. Stevens, *Collected Poems,* pp. 212, 250.

69. Morse, p. 24.

70. Stevens, *Collected Poems,* p. 378.

71. Stevens, *Necessary Angel,* p. 31.

72. Ibid., p. 130.

73. Ibid., p. 145.

74. Stevens, *Collected Poems,* p. 440.

75. Morse, p. 211.

76. Stevens, *Letters,* p. 370.

77. Morse, p. 192.

78. Ibid., p. 190.

79. Stevens, *Collected Poems,* p. 517. The last word echoes the comment on Whitehead already quoted.

80. Ibid., p. 534.

81. Morse, p. 239.

82. Stevens, *Collected Poems,* p. 341.

83. Ibid., p. 490.

Theme and Variations as a Literary Form

Calvin S. Brown

Many problems in the interrelationship of the arts tend to be frustrating because the relationships are so tenuous, the media are so different, and the technical terms needed for the analysis are so inadequate that everything remains in the state of loose analogy, mere guesswork, or even, sometimes, pretentious humbug. Such a problem, for example, would be the relationship between perspective in painting and literature. Others are unmanageable because they simply go off in all directions at once, being actually clusters of quite different and essentially unrelated problems. I once devoted a good deal of time to a projected study of Wagner's influence on literature, only to realize at last that it is a problem of this type. The connection between the leitmotiv and the stream of consciousness, the use of Wagner as a literary character, the writing of works based on his operas (like Thomas Mann's *Tristan* and d'Annunzio's *Trionfo della morte*), and the literary manifestations of and satire against the fashionable Wagner craze are only a few of the essentially unrelated aspects of the topic, which turns out to be a whole set of subjects having little in common except the name of Wagner.

There are, however, topics in the interrelationships of the arts which are clearly circumscribed, readily definable, and amenable to reasonably brief and concise treatment. The literary use of the musical theme and variations is such a topic. I suppose Browning might despise me for not trying to outreach my grasp, but the procedure does have distinct practical advantages.

As a basic structural principle, repetition and variation run through practically every aspect of both literature and music and are of equal importance to both arts. All meters depend on short-range repetition and variation, and any extended passage in four-four time consisting entirely of four quarter notes in each measure would be as deadly as an extended passage of blank verse with five iambs in each line. At the other end of the scale, Wagner's *Ring* is built on the varied repetition of leitmotives, just as Cervantes's *Don Quixote* is built on various episodes each of which is a different manifestation of the same general idea.

Reprinted with permission from the *Yearbook of Comparative and General Literature* 27 (1978):35–42.

Music went beyond the general principle of repetition and variation to establish the theme and variations as a standard form. This development took place more or less simultaneously in Spain, Italy, and England; but our present knowledge indicates that Spain took the lead. In the second quarter of the sixteenth century Luis de Narváez and Antonio de Cabezón wrote full-fledged sets of variations; and the *Fitzwilliam Virginal Book,* with a terminal date around 1600, contains a number of mature and brilliant examples of the form by such composers as Giles Farnaby, William Byrd, and John Bull. From about 1550 to the present, then, the set of variations has been one of the principal musical forms. It might seem, offhand, that its use declined precipitously early in our century, but only until we note the fact that, no matter what it may call itself, any work using the techniques of serialism is necessarily a theme with variations.

During the four and a half centuries of its history the form has not, of course, remained static. One authoritative study distinguishes seven distinct kinds of sets of variations falling into a rough historical sequence in which several kinds may exist simultaneously.[1] For our present purposes it is not necessary to list or distinguish these species. It will be sufficient to indicate those characteristics of the genus which are important for its literary adaptations. Such a brief listing will necessarily imply a good deal of rather broad generalizing, and it should be understood that there are exceptions, though the generalizations seem to me perfectly sound.

The basic structure consists of a theme followed by a set of variations on it, normally falling into a distinct section for each variation. Anything in the original theme may be varied, and anything may be left unchanged. Thus the variation may be in the accompaniment, counterpoint, harmony, melodic line, meter, mode, tempo, orchestration, or any combination of these and various other musical elements. For example, Mozart's Piano Sonata in A (K. 331) has a theme for variation which is in six-eight time, andante. But the last variation is in four-four, allegro. The very first variation of the set in Beethoven's *Archduke* Trio is almost entirely arpeggios in the distinctive harmonic pattern of the theme, with hardly a trace of the melodic line. The only real limitation on what can be done in a variation is that it should be recognizable as one.

Each variation is a *consistently different* version of the theme. As a result, it can be roughly characterized in a few words, as by saying that it shifts the theme to the cello and runs a high obbligato against it in the first violin, while the second violin and viola are silent, or that it is simply a fugato passage based on the opening phrase of the theme. Beethoven's *Diabelli* Variations consist of thirty-three variations on a thirty-two-measure theme. If one were to play the first measure of the first variation, the second of the second, and so on through, he would have enough variations to complete the experiment, with one to spare; however, the result would not be another variation but rather a grotesque musical hash because the method of variation, instead of being consistent, would change with each measure.

The general tendency of a set of variations is from the simple and obvious to the elaborate and recondite. That is why incompetent pianists like me start out cheerfully on them but bog down about the third or fourth variation when the composer starts making technical demands that they cannot meet. The principle seems to be that each variation makes a hearer more familiar with the theme, so that he can then grasp and enjoy progressively more disguised or tenuous versions of it.

Finally, there is a clear problem as to how to end a set of variations. The mind gets accustomed to separate variations, each coming to a full stop and then being followed by another. How is the composer to bring it to an obvious conclusion instead of merely stopping and leaving his audience waiting for another variation that never comes?

In general, there are two ways of doing this. The first is to have the last variation return to a form far closer to the original theme than those immediately preceding it. Schubert's *Trout* Quintet, for example, is so called because it uses the melody of his song "The Trout" ("Die Forelle") for the theme of a set of variations. After increasingly greater departures from the theme, plus a passage extending a variation by sequences on its final phrase, Schubert has a final variation which is very similar to the first statement, but actually even antedates it by using the rippling triplet accompaniment figure of the song itself, which had not been included in the first statement in the quintet. The second way of concluding is to have a final section (often a formal coda) which the listener immediately senses to be something so unlike what has preceded that it cannot be another beginning and hence must be a conclusion. The variations in the vast set that ends Beethoven's last piano sonata have become more and more tenuous, until finally the music moves into scale passages in parallel motion. These are utterly different from anything in the variations, and hence can be used to signal the approaching end.—To put all this into a couple of simple metaphors, the composer can end a set of variations either by closing the circle or by flying off at a tangent.

From a literary point of view, these are the essential characteristics of the variation form. The poet who wants to use the form in literature can succeed only if he meets these specifications and solves the problems inherent in them.

A considerable number of poets have actually made such attempts. As in music, the principle of variation was extensively applied before the actual variation form was attempted. The delight in the extended use of synonyms in Old English and Old Norse poetry was probably conditioned by the technical requirements of alliterative versification, but it became an attraction in itself. The same sort of thing could happen from time to time with figurative language. When the basic idea is expressed by imagery drawn from different metaphors, the result can be a set of variations. Shakespeare's sonnet, "That time of year thou mayest in me behold" (no. 73), is a perfect example. The basic idea of each of the three quatrains is "I am growing old," but each one uses a different metaphor. The first describes old age, with appropriate imagery, as the autumn and winter of life. The second makes it the twilight of life. The third represents it as the burning out of life's embers. And the result is inevitably a little set of three variations, though I doubt if Shakespeare intended the musical analogy.

The first example I know which I believe deliberately follows the example of music is not a set of variations but simply a pair. In Eve's morning song to Adam in *Paradise Lost,* Milton has a positive statement followed immediately by a negative variation:

Sweet is the breath of morn, her rising sweet
With charm of earliest birds; pleasant the Sun
When first on this delightful Land he spreads
His orient Beams, on herb, tree, fruit, and flour,
Glistring with dew; fragrant the fertil earth
After soft showers; and sweet the coming on
Of grateful Eevening milde, then silent Night
With this her solemn Bird and this fair Moon,
And these the Gemms of Heav'n, her starrie train:
But neither breath of Morn when she ascends
With charm of earliest Birds, nor herb, fruit, floure,
Glistring with dew, nor fragrance after showers,
Nor grateful Eevning mild, nor silent Night
With this her solemn Bird, nor walk by Moon
Or glittering Starr-light without thee is sweet.

[4:641–56]

Considering Milton's musical interests and competence, we can reasonably assume that this passage was written under direct musical influence.

It is considerably later, however, that attempts to adapt the full variation form to literary use made their appearance. The first clear example that I have been able to find is in 1799, in Ludwig Tieck's zany play *Die verkehrte Welt (The Topsy-Turvy World)*. The play is provided with a verbal prelude and entr'actes, all given musical labels and designed to supply the place of a theater orchestra. The last of these is a "Menuetto con Variazioni" consisting of a prose statement of about eighty words, followed by three very loose variations on it. The variations are not too convincing, but the intent is clearly shown by things like the fact that each of the four sections consists of two paragraphs, the first one about four times as long as the second, and that each of the second paragraphs begins, "Je nun."

This general example has been followed repeatedly in the nineteenth and twentieth centuries. Or, to speak more precisely, the same idea that occurred to Tieck has occurred to many other writers. In the age of Wagner's *Gesamtkunstwerk,* the *transposition d'art,* and Baudelaire's "Correspondances" such things were in the air, but it is significant that there is absolutely no tradition of the literary set of variations. Every poet who has attempted it seems to have hit on the idea independently and to have gone directly to music for his model. This has happened more often than one might guess, though most of the attempts have been made by very minor poets indeed, and it is pointless to cite names that are bound to be unfamiliar and meaningless. Only rarely do we encounter even minor recognized poets like John Gould Fletcher, Théophile Gautier, Sacheverell Sitwell, and Josef Weinheber.

The poets who attempt to adapt the theme and variations to literary use are confronted by a number of technical problems. The first of these is simply a question of the length of the theme and the individual variations. In music, the composer of variations often uses what the Elizabethans used to call "divisions": he divides his basic beat into notes of smaller and smaller time values. That is the whole principle of Handel's "Harmonious Blacksmith" variations, and it is the main one of the variations in the Andante of Beethoven's Fifth Symphony.

By decreasing the time-values of his notes, the composer can add more elaboration and detail to his treatment of a theme without increasing its actual length, or duration. The poet, however, cannot do this. There is far less variability in the speed of syllables than in that of notes, and what variability there is is entirely out of the poet's control. This is the rock on which Sacheverell Sitwell is wrecked. He has several sets of variations on themes taken from other poets—a standard musical practice—using Herrick, Pope, Milton, and Peele for this purpose. But his theme from Peele, for example, is only two lines in length, whereas each of his three variations on it runs to about a page. If anything resembling the musical effect is to be achieved, variations on a two-line theme must be approximately two lines each, and the stretching of two lines into a page produces something that bears little resemblance to the musical form.

Another problem lies in getting the effect of novelty in a variation instead of mere redundancy. This problem seems to arise from the fact that we remember the actual notes of a theme, so that we can reproduce it, but we remember the content of language rather than the words in which it is presented. This difference may be due to the general ability to read words, but not notes. As Emerson observed, "Our notebooks impair our memories." Whatever the cause, the fact is that a literary variation runs the risk of appearing to be mere pointless repetition because the reader does not remember the wording of the original statement. The total inseparability of form and content in music keeps this problem from plaguing the composer. As a general rule, in literature some fairly striking alteration is required if the effect of variation is to be achieved.

One way of getting around this difficulty is to change the imagery, as Shakespeare did in the sonnet on old age. The abstract intellectual content, "I am growing old," remains the same in all three quatrains; but the shift from winter to twilight to a dying fire is an alteration of content, not merely a change of words, and consequently the reader perceives it as a variation rather than a mere repetition.

There is another interesting possibility in the use of imagery. The imagery can be symbolic and unchanging, but a series of interpretations of its significance can constitute a set of variations. I know of only one use of this technique, in a poetic "sonata" by E. H. W. Meyerstein.[2] The theme is a baldly stated fairy-tale sort of account of a king who lived in a glass house and had a magic ring. Each of the seven variations is a different interpretation of the obviously symbolic theme. The result is not very successful, but the technique is ingenious and offers distinct possibilities. It is interesting to note that, except for the fact that Browning's story is not symbolic, this is really the method of *The Ring and the Book,* to which I shall return later.

Changing the imagery or the interpretation of it also automatically solves the problem of making each variation a consistent alteration of the original. Failure to achieve this is the greatest weakness of most literary attempts. John Gould Fletcher's "Steamers,"[3] for example, consists of three eight-line stanzas (the theme and two variations?), each stanza beginning

Like black plunging dolphins with red bellies,
The steamers. . . .

But the three descriptions do not deal with three aspects, or views, or points of view, nor are they clearly differentiated in tone or technique. As a result, the true variation effect is entirely missing.

Making the variations consistently different really should be no great problem, and I suspect that this is so seldom effectively done in literary variations simply because the writers are not aware that it has to be done if they are to follow their musical prototypes or to keep the interest of their readers. Even the most obvious technical devices, such as the use of different meters or verse-forms, are seldom employed. It is also possible, of course, to vary overall sound-patterns, general content, tone, point of view, diction, and a number of other elements, singly or in combination. But these possibilities are seldom exploited. I believe that the fact that each poet has hit on the idea of literary variations independently is to blame. The poet seems to think that what he considers to be the originality of his idea is sufficient to carry it off without much real thought or effort. But, as Mallarmé told Degas, you do not make a poem out of ideas, but out of words.[4] I am quite aware, of course, that the same stricture applies to the ideas I am now advancing about how literary variations should or might be written.

However they may be written, the main problem remains: The average person learns and remembers a tune far better than he does a poem. This fact is attested by the universal experience of knowing the tune perfectly but having only a spotty recollection (if any) of the words, even with the tune as a crutch to lean on. Because of this difference it is necessary for literary variations to depart more conspicuously from their theme than musical ones must, for otherwise they will not be *recognized as variations,* but will simply produce an effect of prolixity and repetition. And since the words are not likely to be remembered with any usable accuracy, the variation has to be something that readers *will* remember, such as rhythm, tone, imagery, or pure intellectual content.

One very interesting attempt along these lines is worth looking at in some detail. It is a highly successful use of formal literary variation, though it is not a theme and variations because the variations are not in sequence but are equally spaced throughout the work.

Zola's *Une Page d'amour* is a novel of about 350 pages written in a subdued tone and employing a very small cast of characters. After serial publication, it appeared in book form in 1878. Zola liked a change of pace, and this novel, with its general restraint and formal art, supplies such a change from the tumultuous world of the Parisian working class in *L'Assommoir* (probably his greatest work), which was published the year before. Zola himself pointed out the exact symmetry of *Une Page d'amour*—"like a ·checkerboard"—with its division into five parts, each consisting of five chapters.[5]

The principal characters, a widow (Hélène), her daughter (Jeanne), and the widow's lover, live in a suburb on a hill overlooking Paris, which is always there as a visible presence but which Hélène has visited only a few times and does not know at all. In fact, when Jeanne asks about some of the major landmarks of the city, Hélène cannot identify them. To both mother and daughter, Paris is only a spectacle seen from afar, and this fact points up the seclusion and isolation of their lives.

Each of the five sections of the novel closes with a chapter of ten or twelve pages dominated by a description of the view of Paris. These chapters are not mere descriptions because the thoughts and talk of the characters enter into them, but they are set pieces nevertheless and are designed to be recognized and to function as such.

These descriptions of Paris are variations because each time the city appears under–literally–a different light. But the fact that they are variations of the same theme is emphasized by a group of about a dozen landmarks–the Champ de Mars, Notre-Dame, the Opéra, the Panthéon, Sainte Clotilde, the Seine wind-ing across the whole scene–most of which recur in each of the descriptions. The first one shows Paris on a morning in February, with a touch of spring in the air, as the sun gradually burns through the drifting mists of the early morning. Then we have a late afternoon view as the sky clears after a rain. Then there is a strik-ing account of a September twilight as it moves into night, with the first lights appearing in isolation and then extending into lines as the lamplighters move down the streets. The fourth account shows the city during the varied intervals of a blinding thunderstorm. In the final description Hélène, just before moving away, visits the grave of her daughter in a small cemetery on the same suburban hill. It is December and Paris is shrouded and silent under a light fall of snow. After her departure, in the final sentence of the novel, "Jeanne, morte, restait seule en face de Paris, à jamais."

These variations seem to present a highly complex interrelationship of the arts in that they are, in effect, a literary work taking its form from music and its contents and effects from painting. It is a striking fact that the publication of *Une Page d'amour* preceded by eighteen to twenty years Monet's *Cathedrals,* a set of paintings of the façade of the cathedral of Rouen seen under different circum-stances and lightings; otherwise we might think that Zola was following Mon-et's example, especially since he was much more at home in painting than in mu-sic. But there is evidence to show that Zola found his model for these passages in music. His notes and plans for his novels almost always indicate models and sources, and in his notes for this one he chooses for his setting "un coin particu-lier de Paris, assez retiré, et permettant des descriptions poétiques, *revenant comme un chant*" (Zola's italics).[6] Thus it seems that musical repetition with variation was the model for his varied descriptions of Paris.

Interesting and striking though they are, these descriptions do not constitute a set of variations in the musical sense. I propose now to examine, in some de-tail, two such literary sets. These are the two most successful attempts that I know of to domesticate the variation form in literature, and they offer an inter-esting contrast because the imitation of the musical form is about the only thing they have in common. Beyond this, they are conspicuously different, if not dia-metrically opposite, in almost all respects.

The first of these is Josef Weinheber's "Variationen auf eine hölderlinische Ode" (1934).[7] Weinheber is an interesting figure little known in this country, an Austrian poet of great verbal virtuosity, though without a great deal of poetic imagination. He enjoyed setting himself difficult technical problems and solving them triumphantly, and it is significant that he liked to call himself not a *Dich-ter,* but a *Wortkünstler.* He had a great interest in music and a good knowledge of it, and his Hölderlin variations are a serious attempt to reproduce in literature as faithfully as possible both the structure and techniques and the effects of the musical variation form. In my opinion, he succeeds far better than anyone else who has made the attempt.

Weinheber uses a theme by another poet, just as many composers have used other people's themes. Brahms's Variations on a Theme of Haydn is a familiar example. Weinheber's theme is Hölderlin's ode "An die Parzen," a twelve-line poem as familiar in German literature as, say, Shelley's "Ozymandias" is in English. It is written in a classical meter, in three Alcaic strophes, and is consequently unrhymed. It is a poet's appeal to the Fates to spare him for one more summer and one more fall; after that, when he has finished his work and secured his earthly fame, he will welcome the peace of the world of shades. Weinheber's set of variations consists of 11 sections and adds up to 187 lines. The first section is, quite properly, simply Hölderlin's ode, exactly as he wrote it. Then Weinheber follows the frequent practice of changing, in the early variations, not the theme itself, but its surroundings (in music, often the accompaniment or orchestration). What he changes is the meter. The theme is in Alcaics. The first variation is another classical meter, the Sapphic strophe, which is also an unrhymed four-line stanza. The second variation, also metrical, is in a modern form: a dactylic stanza of eight short lines which departs from the classical norm by being rhymed.

These first three sections, then, form a block in which the variation is entirely a matter of versification. Weinheber alters the wording only enough to fit the new meter and, in the third section, the demands of rhyme. Hölderlin's ode begins, "Nur *einen* Sommer gönnt, ihr Gewaltigen!/Und einen Herbst zu reifem Gesange mir." The Sapphic variation opens: "Einen Sommer, gönnt, ihr Gewaltgen. Einen / Herbst mir nur zu reifem Gesange. . . ." And the dactylic variation begins: "Mir einen Sommer nur, / voll und gedrang, / und einen Herbst mir / zu reifem Gesang / gönnt, ihr Gewaltigen."

As in music, these close variants serve the purpose of getting an audience thoroughly steeped in the basic theme before moving on to less obvious variations. In this case, the familiarization involves not only the central idea, but the vocabulary as well. Hölderlin's ode contains a number of words which seem to set the tone of the poem, such as *Gewaltigen, gesättig(e)t, Orkus, Schattenwelt,* and *Saitenspiel,* and the reader comes to recognize them and expect their return. This fact is important later in the poem.

The next three sections are labeled "Variations of Content," and they form a block parallel to the first three. This sort of arrangement of the single units into larger sections also happens in musical variations. For example, the passacaglia of Bach's Passacaglia and Fugue in C Minor consists of the theme and twenty variations, and the variations are laid out, by similarities of treatment, into four blocks of five each. In the third block, for example, the theme moves from the bass to the upper voices. Weinheber's three variations of content consider the question of artistic achievement, death, and posthumous fame from the three points of view of the man whose thoughts are set on this world, the dead, otherworldly man, and the dead man reincarnated. It is important to note that these variations of content do not replace metrical variation, but are added to it, and that this principle holds for all the variations: No two of them (including the theme itself) are in the same meter.

The next three variations form another block in which single phrases from the theme are elaborated to form independent poems. This also is a common musical practice. In earlier musical sets of variations it was commonly done by taking a part of the theme (usually its opening phrase) as the subject for a fugato passage: the exposition section *only* of a fugue. By the late nineteenth century, however, the elaboration of single phrases was a very common method of writing all sorts of free variations. Weinheber's three variations of this type are designated as a nocturne, a scherzo, and a rondo. The first two are, of course, not musical *forms,* but musical genres determined by their general tone. The rondo is a genuine form, or, strictly speaking, a complex of forms all having the principle of recurring material alternating with new materials. Weinheber's rondo does not conform to the exact specifications of any of the musical types, but it does have repeated lines that conform to the general principle of the rondo.

Some of this set offers interesting methods of variation. For example, in Hölderlin's ode the poet says that if he is allowed to finish his work he will gladly die, "vom süssen Spiele gesättiget." *Spiele* refers here to the playing of a musical instrument, in the age-old tradition that metaphorically equates poetry with music. If we translate the phrase as "sated with sweet playing," we will be prepared for the nocturne variation. It begins with the identical phrase, but the metaphor is shifted from the musical realm to the erotic: "Sated with sweet playing, the lovers rest."

After these three blocks, each of three variations, Weinheber concludes his set with two more variations, each of which stands by itself and serves its own individual purpose. As is very often the case in music, the first of these (next to the last in the set) is the point of furthest departure from the original theme. Its technique, however, has no analogy in music. It might be described as a verbal anagram. What Weinheber does here is to take all the words of Hölderlin's ode—no more and no less—and rearrange them into an entirely new poem in free verse. The job is done strictly and accurately, not even allowing the substitution of different grammatical forms of the same word. In the process, some compound words are split up, and some originally separate ones are combined. A variation of this sort is no easy task. Having translated this set of variations, I know whereof I speak.[8] But it does work in that it gives the desired effect of a very free variation, primarily because of the expected recurrence of the striking words. Weinheber once said that he usually first conceived a poem as a rhythm and a "Wort Urmasse"—the same term that he uses in his heading for this variation to designate the original vocabulary.

He ends his set by closing the circle. The final variation is, like the first one, in the four-line strophes of a different classical meter (the fourth asclepiad), and it stays as close to the words of Hölderlin's ode as the new meter will permit: "Einen Sommer nur, einen Herbst / gönnt zu reifem Gesang mir, ihr Gewaltigen!"

Weinheber's set of literary variations is not only far more faithful to the structure and techniques of the musical genre than any other such attempt that I have found, but (probably because of this faithfulness) it also succeeds better than any other in producing in its reader's mind the same effect. Unfortunately I must in honesty add the comment that it is not a great poem, though it is an interesting and brilliant tour de force.

The only things that Weinheber's poem and Browning's *The Ring and the Book* have in common are that both are literary sets of variations and both were written by men who knew and understood music. Browning's poem appeared sixty-five years earlier, in 1869. It is a vast work of nearly twenty-one thousand lines—112 times as long as Weinheber's—and the whole thing is in a single meter, blank verse. Weinheber's poem is simply a theme and variations; Browning's is a prelude, theme and variations, and coda. Weinheber's title and headings stress the musical parallel, but Browning has only one slight allusion to it, at the very end. It is safe to assume that few of Browning's readers have been aware of it; and there have even been studies of Browning and music which miss the connection, obvious though it is.

The Ring and the Book is divided into twelve books. The first of these contains the prelude and theme; the next ten give the ten variations; and the final one is the coda. The whole structure is symmetrical, even to the fact that Book 1 is entitled "The Ring and the Book" and Book 12 is "the Book and the Ring." These titles refer to an extended simile in which the making of a ring—alloying the gold with baser metal to make it workable and durable, etc.—is compared to the composition of the poem. After developing this figure of speech, Browning goes on to tell how he bought in Florence an old book containing the accounts and records of a murder trial in Rome nearly two centuries earlier.

The established facts of the crime constitute the theme. Pompilia, the very young and beautiful putative daughter of a comfortably fixed old couple in Rome, was married to Count Guido Franceschini, a much older, impoverished scion of an ancient and proud family. She and her parents went to live with him in Arezzo. Then the parents returned to Rome. Some months later, Pompilia fled to Rome in the company of a young priest. And some months after that, after she had borne a son, Guido and some accomplices went to Rome, killed her parents, and mortally wounded her, though she lived long enough to make her deposition on the events. These, then, the undisputed facts of the case, are Browning's theme.

The case made a great commotion and excited such wild partisanship that it is difficult to state the facts. For example, I had to call Pompilia the "putative daughter" because one faction contended that she was the daughter of a whore and the old couple had palmed her off on Guido as their own child. Was she actually their child? Was the priest her saintly savior or her accepted lover? Was her murder an act of vicious depravity or of outraged and commendable retribution? These and a host of similar questions are the basis of Browning's variations.

Before he begins the variations proper, however, Browning gives a summary of them as a sort of prospectus. Here he devotes something like thirty to fifty lines to each of the books which will follow, indicating the main lines of a variation that will eventually be developed at several hundred times this length. I know of no musical parallel for this procedure and cannot even think how one could be devised. Browning's purpose here is to make the reader aware, in advance, of the wide variations in the interpretation of the simple facts which will confront him later, and the device works very effectively. The "posy" of the ring, a lyrical apostrophe to the poet's dead wife, ends the first book.

The structure of the next ten books is simple enough. Each one is a variation presenting the events, characters, and motives as they are interpreted by one group or person. This procedure brilliantly solves the problems of distinguishing the variations and keeping the reader's interest. We might say that in each version the events are the same, but the story is a different one, conforming to the interests and character of the interpreter. Thus Browning's set falls neatly into the classification of the nineteenth-century "character variation" in music.[9]

The first three variations are gossip and represent the ill-informed partisanship and prejudices of the Roman populace. "Half-Rome" is fanatically on the side of the outraged and long-suffering husband. "The Other Half Rome" is just as fanatically on the side of the innocent, pure, and martyred wife. "Tertium Quid" represents the viewpoint of a small group of more judicious and intellectual Romans who weigh the evidence carefully and subtly, are not on either side, and are, in fact, inclined to say (as François Villon said about himself and La Grosse Margot) that it is a case of a bad cat for a bad rat.

The next three books give the testimony of the three principals in the case. "Count Guido Franceschini" presents the husband's claim to be a tricked, defrauded, cuckolded, long-suffering victim finally driven to an act of violent justice. "Giuseppi Caponsacchi" gives the priest's denial not only of any amorous involvement with Pompilia but of any personal knowledge of her at all until she appealed to him to help her escape and he did so because he saw that continuing to live with Guido would corrupt and endanger her immortal soul. Pompilia gives the dying wife's moving and, on the whole, convincing deposition as she defends herself and forgives her enemies.

The next three books are official legal considerations of the case. "Dominus Hyacinthus de Archangelis" argues the case for the defense, and "Juris Doctor Johannes Baptista Bottinus" speaks for the prosecution. Both lawyers are pompous asses thinking primarily of their own advancement, but they have some endearing human traits, and each has his own distinctive sort of asininity. "The Pope" presents the interior monologue of the pontiff when he, as the court of last resort, weighs all the circumstances and evidence carefully and responsibly, and condemns Guido and his confederates to death.

"Guido," the last of the variations, gives Guido's bitterness, meanness, and cynicism as he awaits execution and descends to groveling and to mounting terror. It ends with his sublime outcry:

Abate,—Cardinal,—Christ,—Maria,—God, . . .
Pompilia, will you let them murder me?
[11:2426-27]

The final book is a coda containing its own little set of variations balancing those of the preview in the first book. This set consists of four different eyewitness accounts of the execution. At the end of the poem Browning returns to the metaphor of the ring and the posy, but just before that he explains that he has chosen to tell his story in this way because it offers the only way of getting at the whole truth. If you merely tell the truth as you see it, you can only offend those who see it differently and produce dissension rather than conviction—

. . . but here's the plague
That all this trouble comes of telling truth,

> Which truth, by when it reaches him, looks false,
> Seems to be just the thing it would supplant,
> Not recognizable by whom it left:
> While falsehood would have done the work of truth.
> But Art,—wherein man nowise speaks to men,
> Only to mankind,—Art may tell a truth
> Obliquely, do the thing shall breed the thought,
> Nor wrong the thought, missing the mediate word.
> So may you paint your picture, twice show truth,
> Beyond mere imagery on the wall,—
> So, note by note, bring music from your mind
> Deeper than ever e'en Beethoven dived,—
> So write a book shall mean beyond the facts,
> Suffice the eye and save the soul beside.
>
>   [12:852–67]

As the poem was originally published, Browning had the third-from-last line of this passage "Deeper than ever the Andante dived," but in his final version he dropped "the Andante" and substituted "e'en Beethoven."[10] Thus we can safely say that his model was one or more of Beethoven's numerous andante variation movements.

A comparison of Weinheber's and Browning's uses of literary variations reveals two interesting facts. First, by a strange coincidence—for it can be nothing more—in spite of the tremendous difference in scale, the structures are remarkably similar. Each contains three groups of three each, followed by an isolated different segment which leads finally to a return to the beginning.

More significant is the final judgment which the two poems elicit. Weinheber set out to transfer the musical form and its techniques to literature as accurately as possible, and he succeeded brilliantly in doing exactly that, but not a great deal beyond it. Browning set out to make a significant poetic comment on human life, and he hit on a form borrowed from music as the best way of handling his material. He used this form seriously and, on the whole, accurately, but he did not emphasize its musical source. In fact, his variations are on a scale so much larger than that of any musical set that they have generally gone unrecognized. By concentrating on the poem rather than the technique, Browning produced a work of far greater significance and power than Weinheber's verbal fireworks, brilliant though they are.

Perhaps this comparison can be extended to the general question of the interrelationships of the arts. It would seem to be best for each art to mind its own business, not hesitating to steal from the other arts anything that will actually serve its own purposes, but not making an issue or a virtue of it. Browning simply borrowed a tool that would help him to do his job, but Weinheber took over a form that would enable him to exhibit his verbal virtuosity. An artist should borrow from another art as a man borrows a neighbor's lawn mower, not as an acrobat dances on a tightrope.

Notes

1. Robert U. Nelson, *The Technique of Variation* (Berkeley & Los Angeles: University of California Press, 1948), p. 3.

2. E. H. W. Meyerstein, *Three Sonatas* (n.p., 1948), pp. 16–19.

3. John Gould Fletcher, *Preludes and Symphonies* (New York: Macmillan Company, 1930), pp. 50–51.

4. Paul Valéry, *The Collected Works,* ed. Jackson Matthews (New York: Pantheon Books, 1956–75), vol. 12, *Degas, Manet, Morisot,* p. 62.

5. Zola called it "une symétrie de damier." Paul Alexis, *Emile Zola: Notes d'un ami* (Paris: G. Charpentier, 1882), p. 113.

6. Emile Zola, *Les Œuvres Complètes,* ed. Maurice Le Blond (Paris: F. Bernouard, n.d.), vol. 9, *Une Page d'amour,* pp. 363–64.

7. Josef Weinheber, *Sämtliche Werke* (Salzburg: O. Müller, 1954), 2:35–42.

8. Calvin S. Brown, "Josef Weinheber's Hölderlin–Variations: A Comment and Translation," *Southern Humanities Review* 2 (1968):463–79. (I am not responsible for the many typographical errors in the German text.)

9. See Nelson, pp. 90–111.

10. A. K. Cook, *A Commentary upon Browning's "The Ring and the Book"* (Oxford: Oxford University Press, 1920), p. 326.

Three

The Sonata Form in Poetry

The Music of *The Waste Land*

Paul Chancellor

... ce n'est pas de sonorités élémentaires par les cuivres, les cordes, les bois, indéniablement mais de l'intellectuelle parole à son apogée que doit avec plénitude et évidence, resuiter, en tant que l'ensemble des rapports existants dans tout, la Musique.

Stéphane Mallarmé, Crise de Vers

With *Four Quartets* Eliot extended an open invitation to consider his work as poetry in which two dreams cross—a dream in words and a dream in music. Without benefit of such a beckoning title, the crossing was of course evident in earlier works, notably in long poems like "The Hollow Men" and "Ash Wednesday." And shortly after *The Waste Land* appeared, Professor I. A. Richards wrote of it as "a music of ideas," a very apt phrase but tantalizing because it is not too specific about the nature of the music. Indefiniteness (not to mention inaccuracy) has always plagued discussion of the music of poetry. Many literary critics have known little or nothing of music as an art. Some have been content to account for verbal music only in terms of rhetorical adornment; worst of all, some seem to have been completely insensitive to music. But failure to read with musical sensitivity and understanding may quickly reduce much poetry to a play of the intellect rather than the complete artistic experience it should be. To such a reduction *The Waste Land* may easily succumb, and currently it seems to have so succumbed among many of the professors and critics. One must certainly come to all of Eliot's poems with the intellect alert and, very often, with a learned background. *The Waste Land* is, indeed, an all-too-learned poem, yet upon it still more intellection and learning have been piled. It has been used as the grounds for academic hunting parties in hot pursuit of allusions and sources and opportunities for heady escalations to higher and higher levels of meaning. Too often, it has been taken from the humanities classroom to the anatomy clinic, where, after the most subtle dissection, it has been left etherized upon the laboratory table. Certainly, some exegesis of *The Waste Land* is necessary, but after such exegesis, what poetry? Or what music?

Reprinted by permission from *Comparative Literature Studies* 6 (1969):21–32.

In *The Music of Poetry* Eliot showed clearly the nature and value of musicality and in that essay was certainly speaking of his own poetic practice, of the music of his own poetry. In one key passage he wrote:

> A "musical poem" is a poem which has a musical pattern of sound and a musical pattern of the secondary meanings of the words which compose it, and . . . those two patterns are indissoluble and one. And if you object that it is only the pure sound, apart from the sense, to which the adjective "musical" can be applied, I can only reaffirm my previous assertion that the sound is as much an abstraction of it as the sense.

One could hardly imagine a statement more positively emphasizing the value of the music of poetry and particularly its relation to meaning. And it should be noted that *two* "indissoluble" types of musicality are mentioned: one, "a musical pattern of sound"; the other, "a musical pattern of the secondary meaning of the words." The first type speaks of a familiar quality of poetry; the second, however, presents a more novel idea that warrants fuller examination.

Consideration of the purely aural qualities of poetry—those actually apprehended by the ear or the auditory imagination—is as old as criticism of poetry, and there is no occasion here to enter into any lengthy discussion of such verbal music and its components: rhythm, consonance, dissonance, tone color, sonority, and the rest. These terms are, of course, a part of the vocabulary of music as well as poetry, and it might be mentioned in passing that careful use of other musical concepts and terms would clarify and enhance discussion of the music of poetry. *Orchestration,* for instance, is a useful term, since it refers to musical qualities of tone color and resonance. *Pitch, tempo,* and *dynamics* are considerations when one reads poetry aloud. All these qualities and more are woven into the "musical pattern of sound" of poetry that Eliot mentioned. Such patterns are evident in *The Waste Land* from beginning to end, but one section alone, "A Game of Chess," may be taken as an illustration of the poem's aural music and its relation to meaning. Thus, to evoke with subtle irony the Didoesque figure first presented in this section, Eliot uses the heroic line of Marlowe and Shakespeare. The words move in a grand melodic line, *tempo maestoso;* rich color and sonority give full orchestration to the passage.[1] When this queenly figure begins to speak and changes, almost magically, to become a bored and pampered modern socialite, she speaks in quickened tempo and broken rhythm and with a more shrill sonority. The replies of the husband are much more deliberate in speed, more controlled in rhythm, and of fuller sonority. This whole passage has the effect of a tense opera-dialogue in *recitativo.* One can imagine the line of the woman's voice sparsely harmonized with abrupt chords; that of the man's with sustained chords on the strings. In the final passage of "A Game of Chess," pitiable Lil is evoked by lines in which speech rhythm is dominant; the flat word-music is that of Cockney dialect; the tone color is as dull and hollow as Lil's own existence. The general aural effect is that of *senza vibrato,* except for the urgent leitmotif of the bartender, "HURRY UP PLEASE ITS TIME," with its insistent rhythm and brassy sonority, and for the closing lines in which we hear with poignant irony the delicate, broken music of Ophelia's voice.

Such an attempt to give a sort of musical scoring to poetry is suggestive, not definitive; for any musical reading of the poem must be in part subjective. Yet such a reading and analysis may serve not only to demonstrate the innate expressiveness of the poem's aural qualities but to show as well their link to its sense. For although aural qualities may be as old as poetry itself, the *conscious* use of "a musical pattern of the secondary meaning of the words" is distinctly a modern phenomenon, dating from the French symbolists. This is a kind of musicality, moreover, about which there has been the greatest confusion. Eliot's statement about it is not entirely clear, because his term "secondary meanings" is somewhat ambiguous. In another part of *The Music of Poetry,* he speaks of "a music of imagery," with specific reference to G. Wilson Knight's studies of the image patterns discoverable in Shakespeare's plays. Are we to read then, "a musical pattern of the secondary meaning of images"? It is true that images may be patterned in some "musical way." There is, however, a difference between images used descriptively or as metaphor and images used as symbols. The image "The stern was formed / A gilded shell / Red and gold" carries its prose meaning with it, but "Here is Belladonna, the Lady of the Rocks, / The lady of situations" has limited meaning in isolation. Belladonna's full significance—or rather, plural significance—must be intuited from contexts in which she later appears. And the image of "the man with three staves" represents the Fisher King only by Eliot's arbitrary designation. Both Belladonna and the man with three staves are true symbols, and *The Waste Land* is a symbolist poem. Its basic Grail myth is in itself symbolic, its leading ideas are presented through symbols, and its structure is very significantly determined by their patterning.

And symbols give the poem a kind of musicality not heard by the ear. It is literally unheard music, but not like Keats's "ditties of no tone," which are an ideal music heard in the imagination. Rather, it is a kind of music found in the poems of the archpriest of symbolism, Stéphane Mallarmé, and described by him in his writings on the aesthetics of poetry. For some reason Eliot always seemed to shy away from a full discussion of symbolism—by that name. The omission would seem ingratitude to one of his masters had he not acknowledged his debt in "Little Gidding." For Mallarmé is certainly a part of that "familiar compound ghost" whom the poet-warden met during the terrible night of the fire raid. The dead master, surprised to be summoned up and to be in England again, could well tell the poet: "I am not eager to rehearse / My thought and theory which you have forgotten." The writer of *Four Quartets* had indeed by then "forgotten" a great deal of the master's teaching: In those poems of his maturity he spoke with his own voice and through his own art. In *The Waste Land,* on the contrary, he spoke with many voices: It is a polyvocal poem, and it speaks with the art of many poets; but at its heart is the "thought and method" derived from the dead French master, for although Mallarmé had little or no technical knowledge of music, he was endowed with an exquisite musical sensibility. As a poet, his lifelong obeisance went to language (even, as he said, to "les vingt-quatre lettres" of the French alphabet). But after the word, he, like Verlaine, wanted his poems to have "de la musique avant toute chose" and incorporated music in a much more intellectual way than Verlaine.

Mallarmé's own master, Baudelaire, had opened the way to a developed symbolist art when, in *Les Correspondences,* he had described the world as "une forêt de symboles" which give off "confuses paroles" like fragrances from "des parfumes." In the esoteric metaphysic which Mallarmé fashioned, as well as in his highly intellectualized aesthetic, the world is still seen and known through symbols, but for him the idea corresponding to a symbol does not arise like a perfume; rather, "musicalement se lève." That is to say, from the symbol the thought arises *as it does when one listens to music*. His use of music as an analogy instead of Baudelaire's perfumes is more than the substitution of sound for smell, of one metaphor for another. Rather, it is the substitution of a developed, disciplined art, one with syntax and form, for vague and amorphous impressions created by fragrances. (Unfortunately, the perfume metaphor persists, to give the notion that a symbol may "mean anything.")

For Mallarmé, bringing music into his symbolist art also offered a way of moving toward that impossible goal of *la poésie pure*. Music has been the envy of many poets because in its abstract form at least—in a Bach toccata or a Mozart chamber work—it conveys meaning by the pure stuff of its own art. Melody, harmony, and rhythm alone can be fashioned into significance without the intrusion of explicitly verbalized ideas. Music may, as many feel, even express thought beyond the power of words. And so the seeker for *la poésie pure* strives to use the very stuff of his own art—images, rhythms, sonorities, and perhaps symbols—to suggest ideas while minimizing the use of flat prose statement. Also, as with musical melodies or motifs, verbal symbols can undergo almost magical metamorphoses of significance as they appear in changed contexts. It is this magic metamorphosis of symbol in *The Waste Land* that Eliot asks us to follow when he notes that "all the women are one and the two sexes meet in Tiresias."

Poems may be built around one symbol or many. If upon many, the poet may pattern them to reveal the meaning of his complete poem; that is, in a successful long poem using many symbols, the symbols are a structural element. We cannot, in fact, arrive at the total meaning of such a poem until we have sensed the ideas corresponding to the symbols, observed their transformation, and followed their pattern. We sense the poem's structure through the play of its symbols; and indeed, the full meaning of individual symbols is often not revealed until we have experienced their use throughout the poem. Thus, reading a long symbolist poem resembles the experience of listening to one of the extended forms of music—to sonata form, for instance. In that form at its simplest, two or more melodic subjects—tonal symbols—are first presented in an exposition section. These subject symbols are then developed; that is, transformed by changes of key, rhythm, or harmony, by fragmentation, by contrapuntal treatment, or by other techniques the composer has to express changed dramatic or lyric implications of his basic themes. Following this development section, the themes originally heard reappear in a recapitulation, basically in their original form, but most often with altered context or even some little development to give them somewhat changed implications. Finally, to complete the movement there is the coda, a section giving a sense of conclusion, perhaps of triumph, of happy peace, or of resignation. This brief description of sonata form, no doubt tedious to anyone with a rudimentary knowledge of music, is given here chiefly to make one point: No matter how lovely or stirring (or relatively uninteresting) the basic melodies of the movement may be, their full significance can be known only after the entire movement has been heard. The form both directs and limits the implications of the themes. So it is with any long, successful symbolist poem. No matter how richly ambiguous the individual symbols may be, or how much metamorphosis they may undergo, their implications are controlled and limited by the complete structure of the poem.

The power of abstract music to be at the same time so richly ambiguous yet so clear in intent is, of course, limited in program music—in, for instance, a symphonic poem by Liszt or Richard Strauss. Even though the latter's *Till Eulenspiegel* purports to be a work "in rondo form" and may be followed as such (or as sonata form), the complete intent of the composer is not realized until the listener attaches specific ideas to the two themes—musical symbols—on which the work is built: one symbolizing Till the lover of adventures, and the other, Till the incorrigible prankster. Nor can we fully relish the humor of the work until we know that transformations of those themes illustrate the rogue hero's wild escapades which ultimately lead him to court trial and hanging, as well as to apotheosis in legend.

Since forms of music, whether abstract or programmatic, are built on the controlled use of musical symbols—themes or motifs—it is easy to see why symbolist poets or writers of prose fiction have been attracted to the patterning of verbal symbols in some musical form. *Four Quartets* directly suggests an analogy to a form of abstract music: the string quartet, a form with no "story" structure. But symbolist writers have also been attracted to the use of myth as a way of "ordering experience"; and often myth and musical patterning have been combined, notably by Thomas Mann, James Joyce, and by Eliot in *The Waste Land.* Insofar as Eliot's poem is patterned by the Grail myth, it has a narrative order; and so any analogy to musical form sought for it should be in a form of program music such as the symphonic poem. Before pursuing that analogy further, however, we might make a relevant digression suggested by mention of the Grail myth, which readily recalls *Parsifal* and Richard Wagner.

Little attention seems to have been paid to the Wagner references in *The Waste Land;* yet it is at least unusual to find an English poet quoting the libretto of *Tristan und Isolde,* turning the Rhine Maidens of the *Ring* into Thames maidens, and quoting from Verlaine's sonnet *Parsifal.* And whether by design or not,[2] *The Waste Land* is an anti-*Parsifal.* In Eliot's mythical land there is no majestic Monsalvat, no nobility in suffering, no healing Grail, no redemption. In place of these are vulgarity, boredom, lust, fear, and spiritual death, and the Grail quester is incompetent to redeem the land. However sketchy and shadowy the narrative element of *The Waste Land* may be, it is still, like Wagner's music drama, the medieval Grail myth. It has a quester, a waste land, a fisher king, quite a few temptresses, a chapel perilous, and perhaps other features of Wolfram von Eschenbach's story. The notes to the poem suggest, of course, that we turn to *The Golden Bough* and *From Ritual to Romance;* and these books do, so to speak, open the back door of the Christian myth to a vista going back to ancient fertility myths. The latter are certainly evident in the poem, yet its framework is no tale of Attis or Adonis. It is essentially the Christian myth, and by it the symbols of the poem are in part patterned to reveal its ultimate meaning.

But however far into the past the *myth* may be carried, the symbolist *art* of the poem goes back no farther than the great years of conscious symbolist art, the years of Mallarmé and Wagner. One feature of the latter's art which has influenced symbolist writers (notably Thomas Mann) is the leitmotif, an ungainly term for what is merely a musical symbol. The hundreds of leitmotifs that

Wagner used in his later music dramas are, moreover, symbols with fixed correspondence and are used generally for simple reference or recall. A certain leitmotif represents the Rhine (and only that); another, Walhalla; another, Siegfried;
and so on. All are woven into the vast musical web of the work as consciously
placed points of reference. The literary allusions of *The Waste Land* are remarkably like Wagner's leitmotifs in that respect. They too establish definite points
of reference (and like the musical motifs are often of lyric interest in themselves). They differ from Wagner's use of leitmotifs, however, in that they are
introduced mostly for ironic or mocking contrast. Thus in "The Fire Sermon"
Spenser's line, "Sweet Thames run softly till I end my song," recalls the *Pro-
thalamion,* a celebration of happy and fruitful marriage. There is sharp irony in
the reference because the Thames of *The Waste Land,* far from being "sweet," is
a dirty, littered stream, and the loves recently celebrated on it were no more than
sordid, lustful, and sterile affairs. Thus the literary allusions, by carrying the reader to the spirit of their sources, become powerfully expressive devices, often creating some of the sharpest dissonance in the poem. Moreover, since almost all of
the allusions are introduced by the Quester himself and are drawn from so many
sources, they give him polyvocality and even polytonality. And woven into the
poem as they are, like Wagner's leitmotifs they are also an integral part of its
musical structure.

But even though Eliot patterned *The Waste Land* on the Grail myth, he
notoriously fractured normal narrative presentation of it. No doubt readers coming to it for the first time find only "subdivisions prismatiques de l'idée," a collection of flashing gems strung only on broken bits of the silver wire of logic.
Even its five sections and their titles are only of small help in revealing its meaning. Since a myth is itself composed of symbolic people, places, and events, all in
themselves variable but set in a fixed pattern, it is to the chief symbols of the
poem, as well as to their transformation and patterning, that we must turn to
find the ultimate meaning of *The Waste Land.* When Mallarmé spoke of "subdivisions prismatiques," he was speaking of a strength and not of a weakness of
symbolist poetry. As noted above, symbolism offers a method of minimizing
prose statement, including explicit exposition and transition. What is retained is
something closer to the pure, self-sufficient stuff of poetry—something therefore
closer to the nature of music and musical structure. Accordingly, the reader of
The Waste Land will move more readily toward its meaning if he approaches it
musicalement—as he would listen to music and follow it. It is by such "listening"
to the poem that we arrive at the "secondary meaning" of its words and their
pattern.

One final question about the musical quality of *The Waste Land* remains to
be considered. Is the entire work cast in a form analogous to any form of music,
such as the symphony or the symphonic poem? Helen Gardner, one of Eliot's
most sensitive and appreciative critics, has found that the five "movements" of
The Waste Land, along with certain structural patterns within each movement,
give it a form similar to that of *Four Quartets.* No doubt such similarities may be
seen, but stylistic and structural differences between the two poems are even
more evident. *Four Quartets* has justifiably evoked comparison with the late
string quartets of Beethoven; but Eliot's sensibility as it is felt in *The Waste
Land* is not Beethoven's—early, middle, or late. It is as distinctly a twentieth-

century sensibility as Stravinsky's or Schoenberg's and, in 1922 at least, as new and startling. Moreover, in any attempt to find some musical pattern of ideas from the structural components of the poem—the myth, the symbols, and the allusions—it is better to ignore its five sections and consider it as a whole, following the method by which one may discern a musical pattern in *King Lear* by ignoring its divisions into acts. It should be noted too that *The Waste Land* is not poised and meditative like chamber music; it is declamatory and dramatic. It unfolds the tale of a quester's visit to a waste land, and in doing that it is like program music. Again, it is not the music of four strings but of the full orchestra with all its variety and richness of color and its range of power. To suggest a full analogy of the form of *The Waste Land* to some musical form is a bold venture, but its structure may be seen as that of a symphonic poem in sonata form using the chief symbols as its themes, and with a declaiming voice woven with it, partly to supply related but dissonant leitmotifs.

Such a musical work has never been written and may never be, though it is scarcely beyond possibility in this century of adventurous composers. At all events, tentative acceptance of such an analogy may be useful as a "musical" approach to the meaning of the poem. Thus, assuming sonata form for it, most of "The Burial of the Dead" would serve as the exposition section, in which the basic themes of sterility and fear of rebirth are set forth, along with the derived themes of Madame Sosostris's tarot cards: the Quester, the Fisher King, Belladonna, the Wheel, and the rest. The final passage of "The Burial of the Dead," beginning with the evocation of the "Unreal City," is transitional. Although it ends with a terrifying reiteration of the fear-of-rebirth theme, it also initiates the journey through the waste land with the picture of the London crowd, the first development of the wheel theme. The journey continues through the next three parts of the poem, "A Game of Chess," "The Fire Sermon," and "Death by Water," which form the development section in which the tarot themes especially appear, transformed into new dramatic guises, in different "melodic" forms, rhythms, and orchestration. As the development section ends quietly with the death of Phlebas the Phoenician sailor, the recapitulation begins with "What the Thunder Said." The initial themes heard in "The Burial of the Dead" return with even greater intensity of expressiveness and with different orchestration. There are reminiscences too of the tarot themes, with that of the Hanged Man heard fully for the first time. The music has the tension and vividness of hallucination as the Quester reaches the Chapel Perilous. Here the theme of sterility rises mockingly, for while the chapel seems to offer little active peril, the Quester cannot even rise to meet what test it offers. The journey and the recapitulation end with the derisive cock crow. At the first "DA" of the thunder, the coda begins; for this final passage is clearly an epilogue to the whole poem and not merely a part of its fifth section. The coda is different too in that it is dominated by the voice of the Quester. It rises above the more subdued, transmuted sterility and tarot themes as he introduces new motifs suggesting at least some possibilities of salvation. At the end, however, the themes of sterility and spiritual death persist. His last motifs are of desolation and exasperation, and only the thought of Arnaut Daniel's purgation by fire seems to offer a hope before the poem ends with the three quiet, solemn chords of "Shantih."

What has just been described is no musical composition; it is a composition in the music of poetry. Any analogy between forms of poetry and music must be imperfect. There is always the inexorable fact that language has one syntax and music another; and form is, in a sense, a larger extension of syntax. Still it can be said that the theory and method of symbolism offer one of the most viable means of bringing the two arts together, of achieving musicality in poetry. When the unheard music of symbol play is combined with a sensitively corresponding aural music of words, each confirms the other to make them "indissoluble and one." It is this doubly rich music that is the essence of the poetry of *The Waste Land.*

Music offers a constant example and reminder to readers—and shall we add, teachers—of poetry: that only by *experiencing* it as complete sentient, imaginative human beings can we arrive at its meaning. Music does not live in printed scores; it is totally ours only in performance. The subtlest verbal analysis of a Beethoven piano sonata fumbles as it comes to the threshold of the essential mystery of music. Such analysis, moreover, can never make that sonata one's own, nor can any exegesis of *The Waste Land.* Musicology, which is devoted to such analysis, has been called "words without song," and much criticism of Eliot's poetry has been just that—score analysis.

One of Mallarmé's best statements, about the music of poetry and the part played by the symbol in evoking it, is found in a passage of *Sur l'évolution littéraire* in which he is expressing his reaction to the hard precision of the Parnassian poets:

> In the contemplation of things—in the image arising from reveries evoked by them—in these lie true poetic song. The Parnassians take an object in its entirety and display it to us. In so doing, they fail to attain mystery; they deprive our minds of that exquisite joy of believing that we are creating something. Merely to *name* an object is to cut off three-fourths of poetic pleasure. To *suggest* the object is the ideal. The use of symbol constitutes the perfect practise of this mystery.[3]

Perhaps the most arresting thought in this passage is that of the "joy of believing that we are creating something." There is no doubt that a certain excitement can be experienced by exploring *The Waste Land* in the *lumen siccum* of the intellect. But to miss the music of its poetry—its heard music and its unheard music of symbols and their patterned play—is to miss not only much of the pleasure it offers but also a clear approach to its meaning, especially a personal meaning. Exegesis and criticism lead to consensus of meaning; the music of poetry gives meaning a latitude which enables each reader to make Eliot's waste land one of his own experience or imagination.

Notes

1. The more complex phenomenon of synesthesia is evident here, as it is in many places throughout the poem. The rich color in the visual imagery here enhances—even seems to transfer to—the sound as it is read.

2.   Speaker A in T. S. Eliot's *A Dialogue on Poetic Drama* (1928) has this to say: "I have also heard you railing at Wagner as 'pernicious.' But you would not willingly resign your experience of Wagner either. Which seems to show that a world in which there was no art that was not morally edifying would be a very poor world indeed."

3.   My own translation of this passage.

The Music of *Four Quartets*

Helen Gardner

> And thou, sweet Music, Dancing's only life,
> The ear's sole happiness, the Air's best speech,
> Loadstone of fellowship, Charming rod of strife,
> The soft mind's Paradise, the sick mind's Leech.
> Sir John Davies, Orchestra

By calling his poem *Four Quartets,* T. S. Eliot has made it necessary for any critic, even though as ignorant as he confesses himself to be of "a technical knowledge of musical form," to discuss the debt he owes to the art of music in his solution of the problem of finding a form for the long poem. He has given some indications of what that debt is in his lecture on *The Music of Poetry.*

> I think that a poet may gain much from the study of music: how much technical knowledge of musical form is desirable I do not know, for I have not that technical knowledge myself. But I believe that the properties in which music concerns the poet most nearly, are the sense of rhythm and the sense of structure. I think that it might be possible for a poet to work too closely to musical analogies: the result might be an effect of artificiality; but I know that a poem, or a passage of a poem, may tend to realize itself first as a particular rhythm before it reaches expression in words, and that this rhythm may bring to birth the idea and the image, and I do not believe that this is an experience peculiar to myself. The use of recurrent themes is as natural to poetry as to music. There are possibilities for verse which bear some analogy to the development of a theme by different groups of instruments; there are possibilities of transitions in a poem comparable to the different movements of a symphony or a quartet; there are possibilities of contrapuntal arrangement of subject-matter. It is in the concert room, rather than in the opera house, that the germ of a poem may be quickened.

As the title shows, each poem is structurally a poetic equivalent of the classical symphony, or quartet, or sonata, as distinct from the suite. This structure is

Reprinted, by permission of the author, from her book *The Art of T. S. Eliot* (London: The Cresset Press, 1949), pp. 36–56.

clear when all four poems are read, as they are intended to be, together, and is essentially the same as the structure of *The Waste Land*. It is far more rigid than would be suspected from reading any one of the poems separately, but it is sufficiently flexible to allow of various arrangements and modifications of its essential features. It is capable of the symphonic richness of *The Waste Land* or the chamber-music beauty of "Burnt Norton." The form seems perfectly adapted to its creator's way of thinking and feeling—to his desire to submit to the discipline of strict poetic laws and at the same time to have liberty in the development of a verse capable of extremes of variation and in the bringing together of ideas and experiences often divorced. The combination of apparent license with actual strictness corresponds to the necessities of his temperament.

Each poem contains what are best described as five "movements," each with its own inner necessary structure. The first movement suggests at once a musical analogy. In each poem it contains statement and counter-statement, or two contrasted but related themes, like the first and second subjects of a movement in strict sonata form. The analogy must not be taken too literally. Eliot is not imitating sonata form, and in each poem the treatment or development of the two subjects is slightly different. The simplest is the treatment of the river and sea images in "The Dry Salvages," the symbols for two different kinds of time: the time we feel in our pulses, in our personal lives, and the time we become aware of through our imagination, stretching behind us, beyond the record of the historian, and continuing after we have gone. The two subjects are presented successively, in contrast. The first movement of "Burnt Norton" shows a similar division into two statements. Here the contrast is between abstract speculation and an experience in a garden, a meditation on consciousness and a presentation of consciousness. But in "East Coker" the first movement falls into four parts. The first theme of the time of the years and the seasons—the rhythm of birth, growth, and death—is resumed in the third paragraph; and the second theme— the experience of being outside time, of time having stopped—is briefly restated at the close. While in "Little Gidding," the most brilliantly musical of the four poems, the third paragraph is a development of the first two, weaving together phrases taken up from both in a kind of counterpointing. In general, however, it is true to say that the first movement is built on contradictions which the poem is to reconcile.

The second movement is constructed on the opposite principle of a single subject handled in two boldly contrasted ways. The effect is like that of hearing the same melody played on a different group of instruments, or differently harmonized, or hearing it syncopated, or elaborated in variations, which cannot disguise the fact that it is the same. The movement opens with a highly poetical lyric passage, in a traditional metrical form: irregularly rhyming octosyllabics in "Burnt Norton" and "East Coker," a simplified sestina[1] in "The Dry Salvages," and three lyric stanzas in "Little Gidding." This is followed immediately by an extremely colloquial passage, in which the idea which had been treated in metaphor and symbol in the first half of the movement is expanded and developed in a conversational manner. In the first three poems the meter used is the same as the meter of the first movement, though in each case here the passage begins with the long line; in "Little Gidding" a modification of terza rima is employed. In "Burnt Norton," the highly obscure, richly symbolic presentation of the "flux of life" perceived as a unity in the consciousness turns to a bare statement in philosophic language of the relation of stillness and movement, past, present, and future. At the close there is a return to imagery, when after the abstract discussion three concrete moments are mentioned:

> . . . the moment in the rose-garden,
> The moment in the arbour where the rain beat,
> The moment in the draughty church at smokefall.

In "East Coker" we have first a confusion in the seasons and the constellations. This turns to a flat statement of the same confusion in the lives of individual men, where the settled wisdom of old age is dismissed as a deception. Imagery returns here also, in the expansion of Dante's "selva oscura":

> In the middle, not only in the middle of the way
> But all the way, in a dark wood, in a bramble,
> On the edge of a grimpen, where is no secure foothold,
> And menaced by monsters, fancy lights,
> Risking enchantment.

Again, in the last two lines,

> The houses are all gone under the sea.
> The dancers are all gone under the hill,

we have a faint recalling of the whole of the first movement, the briefest possible evocation of what was there said. In "The Dry Salvages" the beautiful lament for the anonymous, the endless sum of whose lives adds up to no figure we can name and leaves little trace but wrecks and wastage on time's ocean, hints in its last stanza where meaning can be found, and the hint is then developed directly, at first with little metaphor, but at the close with a full and splendid return to the original images of the river and the sea. This return to imagery in "The Dry Salvages" comes with wonderful power and force after the purging of our minds by the colloquial and discursive passage in which the poet has deliberately deprived himself of the assistance of imagery. It is a poetic effect comparable to the moment when, after a long and difficult passage of musical development, the original melody returns with all its beauty. The particular treatment of the second movement in "The Dry Salvages" is the poetic expression of its subject:

> We had the experience but missed the meaning,
> And approach to the meaning restores the experience.

The effort to find meaning restores the original imaginative vision of the river and the sea; the images return with power. In "Little Gidding" the exquisite lyric on the decay of our mortal world changes to the colloquy with the "dead master," after the air raid, when human fame and the achievement of the poet are likewise shown to be vanity. The second part of the movement, though metrically distinct from the first, is metrically formal and imagery runs through it.[2] This is in keeping with the whole tenor of "Little Gidding" in which the stylistic contrasts are less violent than in the two middle poems and one is more conscious of the counterpointing of themes. As in the first movement, then, the relation between the two parts varies with the character of each poem. We can say generally that the first part is traditional in its meter, symbolic, romantic in its imagery, and lyrical; and the second part discursive, colloquial, meditative. But in "Burnt Norton" the second part is philosophic and abstract, in "East Coker" and "The Dry Salvages" it is personal and reflective—more immediately personal in "East Coker" and more generally reflective in "The Dry Salvages"—and in "Little Gidding" it is particular, and the reflection arises out of a firmly established situation.

In the third movement one is less conscious of musical analogies. The third movement is the core of each poem, out of which reconcilement grows: It is an exploration with a twist of the ideas of the first two movements. At the close of these center movements, particularly in "East Coker" and "Little Gidding," the ear is prepared for the lyric fourth movement. The repetitive circling passage in "East Coker," in particular, where we seem to be standing still, waiting for something to happen, for a rhythm to break out, reminds one of the bridge passages and leading passages between two movements which Beethoven loved. The effect of suspense here is comparable to the sensation with which we listen to the second movement of Beethoven's Violin Concerto finding its way toward the rhythm of the rondo. But the organization of the movement itself is not fixed. In "Burnt Norton" it falls into two equal parts, divided by a change of mind, with no change of meter. In "East Coker" the change of feeling is not represented by a break. The break in the meter occurs after the change the movement records has occurred. The change is one that "comes upon" the mind: "the darkness shall be the light, and the stillness the dancing." There is a change in the rhythm, not a break, from the six-stress line to the four-stress. Then, after a pause there comes the "bridge passage," in which we wait for the moment when its "requiring" is answered by the firm rhythm of the great passion lyric. In "The Dry Salvages" there is no real break; but there is a change in temper from the reflective to the hortatory, represented by a similar change of rhythm from the tentative six-stress line to the firm handling of the line of four stresses. In "Little Gidding" there is a very definite break as the poet changes from the personal to the historic. The poet here turns to the beautiful three-stress line which before this was reserved for the close of the last movement.

After the brief lyrical movement, the fifth recapitulates the themes of the poem with personal and topical applications and makes a resolution of the contradictions of the first. It falls into two parts in each poem; but the change is slighter than in the second movement, and it is reversed. Here the colloquial passage comes first, and then—without a feeling of sharp break, for the meter remains fundamentally the same—the base of the line contracts and images return in quick succession. In various ways the last lines echo the beginning of the whole poem or employ images from the other poems in a conclusion of tender gravity, touched at times by a lyric sweetness.

The Waste Land, if one allows for its much wider scope, its essentially dramatic method of presentation, and its hosts of characters, follows the same main pattern. "The Burial of the Dead" contains far more than two statements, but formally it is a series of contrasts of feeling toward persons and experiences, which are related by a common note of fear. "The Game of Chess" opens with the elaborate, highly poetic description of the lady at her dressing table, a passage like a set-piece of description in a late Elizabethan play. This contrasts with the talk of Lou and her friends in the public house at closing time. But the violence of the stylistic contrast only makes clearer the underlying similarity of emotion: boredom and panic, and the common theme of sterility. There is something comparable to the return of images at the close of this section in the *Quartets* in the use made of Ophelia's words: "Good night, sweet ladies, good night," though here the effect is ironical. "The Fire Sermon," the poem's heart, has moments when the oppression lifts, and a feeling of release and purification floods in. This twist is given by the evocations of another world than the appalling world of the twining serpents which Tiresias sees. The reference to the Buddha, the "collocation of western and eastern asceticism," to which attention is drawn in the notes, anticipates the use of the *Bhagavad-Gita* in the same movement of "The Dry Salvages." "Death by Water," the fourth movement, is again a brief lyric, and the fifth section, "What the Thunder Said," while being naturally far more complex than the final movements of the *Quartets,* performs the same function of resolution. It returns also to many of the themes of the first movement, recalling its crowds, as well as the separate figures of the second and third movements, and treating again of its theme of birth and death.

It is obvious, however, that, in spite of the basic similarity of structure, the form is far more highly developed in *Four Quartets* and that both the whole poem and the separate poems depend upon the form in a way that *The Waste Land* does not. In *The Waste Land* Eliot took the Grail myth, as interpreted by Weston, for his ostensible subject, or starting point. *The Waste Land* is given coherence not by its form, but by this underlying myth, to which constant reference can be made and of which all the varied incidents and the many personages are illustrative. But in *Four Quartets* the title of the whole poem tells us nothing of its subject, and the titles of the separate poems tell us very little. The poems are not about places though their subjects are bound up with particular places.[3] There are no books to which we can direct an inquirer. The works of St. John of the Cross, though relevant, will not help a reader in the same way as *The Golden Bough* or *From Ritual to Romance* will, in Eliot's own words, "elucidate the difficulties" of *The Waste Land.* We might begin a description of *Four Quartets* by saying that it presents a series of meditations upon existence in time, which, beginning from a place and a point in time and coming back to another place and another point, attempts to discover in these points and places what is the meaning and content of an experience, what leads to it, what follows from it, what we bring to it, and what it brings to us. But any such description will be brief and abstract; we have to use words like "time," "memory," "consciousness"— words whose meaning we do not really grasp, abstractions from sensation. We shall find we are leaving out all that makes the poem memorable, whereas if we told the story of the Fisher King we should be leading a reader toward the poetry of *The Waste Land.* It is better to abandon these abstractions and return to a consideration of the form, to which the meditation owes its coherence. The form is inspired by the composer's power to explore and define, by continual departures from and returns to very simple thematic material. The thematic material of the poem is not an idea or a myth, but partly certain common symbols. The basic symbols are the four elements, taken as the material of mortal life; and another way of describing *Four Quartets,* and a less misleading one, would be to say that "Burnt Norton" is a poem about air, on which whispers are borne, intangible itself, but the medium of communication;[4] "East Coker" is a poem about earth, the dust of which we are made and into which we shall return; it tells of "dung and death," and the sickness of the flesh; "The Dry Salvages" is a poem about water, which some Greek thinkers thought was the primitive material out of which the world arose and which man has always thought of as surrounding and embracing the land, limiting the land and encroaching on it, itself illimitable;[5] "Little Gidding" is a poem about fire, the purest of the elements, by which some have thought the world would end—fire which consumes and purifies. We could then say that the whole poem is about the four elements whose mysterious union makes life, pointing out that in each of the separate poems all four are present and perhaps adding that some have thought that there is a fifth element, unnamed but latent in all things—the quintessence, the true principle of life—and that this unnamed principle is the subject of the whole poem.

By relying on form and these simple underlying symbols, Eliot has found not only a personal solution of his personal problems as a poet, but a solution, which may greatly influence later writers, of the problem of the long poem. He has freed it from its dependence on a subject that can be expressed in nonpoetic terms. In lyric poetry, particularly in brief lyrics and songs, it is often true to say that the subject cannot be separated from the poem; but the longer meditative poem has usually to find a subject which is separable from the poetry, though often of little interest in itself when so separated. One can, for instance, "summarize the argument" of the "De Rerum Natura"; one can give a factual account of Wordsworth's life from "The Prelude"; one can "trace the development of the thought" in "In Memoriam." But with *Four Quartets* we cannot summarize the argument, nor can we say "what happens." Eliot has not given us a poem of philosophic argument, though his poem includes philosophic argument. He would probably assent to Keats's confession: "I have never yet been able to perceive how anything can be known for truth by consequitive reasoning." He has not related to us in autobiographical narrative "the growth of a poet's mind," though this would be one possible subtitle for *Four Quartets.* The difficulty of employing an autobiographical framework is that the present is always ahead. The Red Queen and *Tristram Shandy* both show us how hard one has to run to keep in the same place. The poet who sets out to tell us what brought him "to this place and hour" has passed on to another place and hour by the time he comes to finish. There cannot be a true conclusion. By rejecting autobiography, Eliot has been able to include without difficulty, and with perfect relevance, experience that was in the future when the poem was planned. The poem has grown with the poet and changed with changing circumstances, without outgrowing its original plan. "Burnt Norton" was published in the *Collected Poems* (1936) and it was announced then that it was the first of a series of four quartets. The scheme appears to have been laid aside while *The Family Reunion* was written. "East Coker" was not published until Good Friday, 1940, and came with extraordinary appropriateness. Its words, "And that, to be restored, our sickness must grow worse," seemed prophetic at that time of waiting, the period of war that was not war. When "The Dry Salvages" appeared the war at sea was at its height, and "Little Gidding" includes without any distortion of its original

purpose a fire raid on London and a warden's patrol in Kensington. But while
Four Quartets shares with a spiritual diary such as "In Memoriam" the power to
include present experience without irrelevance, it escapes the diary's defect of dif-
fuseness and lack of concentration. The diary can give us a sense of progress and
development, but not the sense of the end implicit in the beginning, of necessary
development; it has the interest of narrative, not the deeper delight of plot. In
the long poem that depends on the day-to-day development of a mind, the parts
will seem greater than the whole, and even Tennyson's powers of variation can
hardly save "In Memoriam" as a whole from the monotony of life and give it
the coherence of art. The form of *Four Quartets* transforms living into art, not
thought, and gives us a sense of beginning and ending, of the theme having
been fully worked out, which is rare in the long poem. The separate parts combine in a way that the sonnets of a sonnet sequence or a series of repeated stanzas
cannot. The strict limitations of the form make possible the freedom of the treatment. The poet can say what he wishes because he must say it in this way. The
nearest analogy I can suggest is the Greek Pindaric ode, and Eliot might be said
to have succeeded in finding what earlier English poets had tried to find: a proper English equivalent for the formal ode. Here again, as in his metrical experiments, he has found a way suited to the genius of the English language, which
has formed and been formed by the English ear, impatient of the kind of elaborate pattern that the Greeks and Italians enjoyed. He has not in any sense imitated the Pindaric ode, but he has found a kind of equivalent: an original form
supplying the same need and giving something of the same delight. The strict
Pindaric has never seemed more than a feat of virtuosity in English, while the
loose Pindaric has too little formal organization to give pleasure; it arouses no
expectancy, and so cannot delight by satisfying or surprising. The quartet form,
though capable of almost unlimited variations, has a secure formal basis by
which we recognize the variations as variations.

The more familiar we become with *Four Quartets,* however, the more we realize that the analogy with music goes much deeper than a comparison of the
sections with the movements of a quartet, or than an identification of the four
elements as thematic material. One is constantly reminded of music by the treatment of images, which recur with constant modifications, from their context, or
from their combination with other recurring images, as a phrase recurs with
modifications in music. These recurring images, like the basic symbols, are common, obvious, and familiar when we first meet them. As they recur they alter, as
a phrase does when we hear it on a different instrument, or in another key, or
when it is blended and combined with another phrase, or in some way turned
around or inverted. A simple example is the phrase "a shaft of sunlight" at the
close of "Burnt Norton." This image occurs in a rudimentary form in "The Hollow Men," along with a moving tree and voices heard in the wind:

> There, the eyes are
> Sunlight on a broken column
> There, is a tree swinging
> And voices are
> In the wind's singing
> More distant and more solemn
> Than a fading star.

At the close of "Burnt Norton" a "moment of happiness," defined in "The Dry Salvages" as a "sudden illumination," is made concrete by the image of a shaft of sunlight which transfigures the world:

> Sudden in a shaft of sunlight
> Even while the dust moves
> There rises the hidden laughter
> Of children in the foliage
> Quick now, here, now, always—
> Ridiculous the waste sad time
> Stretching before and after.

This is the final concrete statement of what "Burnt Norton" is about; but it re-calls the experience we have been given in a different rhythm and with different descriptive accompaniments in the second half of the first movement, as the sun for a moment shines from the cloud and the whole deserted garden seems to be-come alive:

> Dry the pool, dry concrete, brown edged,
> And the pool was filled with water out of sunlight,
> And the lotos rose, quietly, quietly,
> The surface glittered out of heart of light,
> And they were behind us, reflected in the pool.
> Then a cloud passed, and the pool was empty.

The image repeated, but with such a difference, at the close establishes the valid-ity of the first experience. Brief and illusory as it appears in the first movement, it has not been dismissed. It has remained in thought and it returns. Though

> Time and the bell have buried the day
> The black cloud carries the sun away,

when the "sudden shaft" falls, it is time that seems the illusion.

But this image of "a shaft of sunlight" seems to have a rather different meaning when we meet it at the close of "The Dry Salvages," united with the images of "East Coker": the "wild thyme unseen" and "winter lightning," and deprived of "suddenness."

> For most of us, there is only the unattended
> Moment, the moment in and out of time,
> The distraction fit, lost in a shaft of sunlight,
> The wild thyme unseen, or the winter lightning
> Or the waterfall, or music heard so deeply
> That it is not heard at all, but you are the music
> While the music lasts. These are only hints and guesses,
> Hints followed by guesses; and the rest
> Is prayer, observance, discipline, thought and action.

Here the poet seems to suggest by his tone, and by the natural images which he associates with his "shaft of sunlight," and by the phrase "distraction fit," and by the whole slow, rather dreamy rhythm, that these moments must not be relied on or indeed hoped for very much, but received in thankfulness as gifts when

they occur. "The Dry Salvages" is a poem about ordinary people; its annunciations are the common annunciations of danger, calamity, and death. It is not
about special people with special gifts; it mentions the saint, only to turn back
to "most of us" who are given no special revelation but the one Annunciation
which is for all men. The image occurs here lightly and beautifully; no weight
of meaning is put onto it.[6]

At the opening of "Little Gidding" this image of sunlight is totally transformed; it is made highly particular, linked with a particular season, and worked
out with great descriptive detail. It is also made impersonal. The flash of winter
sunlight which creates "midwinter spring" is not a hint or a guess, or a hint followed by guesses, nor is it an almost indefinable moment of happiness, so brief
that it seems perhaps an illusion; it is a revelation, apocalyptic in its intensity
and brilliance:

> The brief sun flames the ice, on ponds and ditches,
> In windless cold that is the heart's heat,
> Reflecting in a watery mirror
> A glare that is blindness in the early afternoon.
> And glow more intense than blaze of branch, or brazier,
> Stirs the dumb spirit: no wind, but pentecostal fire
> In the dark time of the year.

The sunlight of the earlier poems has become "frost and fire" and turns to
"flame of incandescent terror."

The more one reads *Four Quartets* the more these recurring images fix themselves in the mind; and through them and the changes in them we can apprehend the changing, developing subject. The yew-tree, for instance, used many
times in the last three poems of *Ash Wednesday,* occurs only three times in *Four
Quartets,* but each time with great and different significance. In the second verse
of the lyric in "Burnt Norton," the "chill fingers of yew"—the touch of death
hardly brushing the cheek—give us a vague sense of foreboding; at the close of
"The Dry Salvages," on the other hand, the phrase "not too far from the yew-
tree" gives a sense of security. This is the familiar yew of the churchyard, symbol
both of mortality and immortality, beneath whose shade we may rest in peace.
At the end of "Little Gidding," "the moment of the rose and the moment of the
yew-tree"—the apprehension of love and the apprehension of death—are linked
together, so that each seems of equal validity, an apprehension of life.

In the same way as images and symbols recur, certain words are used again
and again, their meaning deepened or expanded by each fresh use. Indeed, another way of describing *Four Quartets* would be to say that the poem is an exploration of the meaning of certain words. Like the images and symbols just referred
to, they are common words, words we take for granted. Perhaps the words that
first strike us in this way as recurring with a special and changing emphasis are
the pair "end" and "beginning," sometimes occurring together, sometimes apart
from each other. The word "end" occurs first, by itself, in the opening lines of
"Burnt Norton":

> What might have been and what has been
> Point to one end, which is always present.

Here, "end" has plainly some meaning beyond that of "termination"; but we are not quite certain how much meaning to give it. Even when these two lines are repeated at the end of the first movement, the word "end" remains vague. It is only in the fifth movement—when the word is linked with "beginning" in the context of ideas about form and pattern and we have apparently paradoxical statements—that we begin to think of end as meaning "completion," "purpose," or even "final cause":

> Or say that the end precedes the beginning,
> And the end and the beginning were always there
> Before the beginning and after the end.
> And all is always now.

In "East Coker," the opening inversion of Mary Stuart's motto throws the stress on the word "beginning" and the whole poem ends with the word. If in "Burnt Norton" it is "end" we are thinking of, and the word "beginning" seems used mainly to give meaning to "end," in "East Coker" the opposite is true. It is a poem about beginning. On the other hand, in "The Dry Salvages" the word "beginning" does not occur at all, and the word "end" is only used to be negated. At the close of the first movement we hear of women lying awake

> Between midnight and dawn, when the past is all deception,
> The future futureless, before the morning watch
> When time stops and time is never ending.

To stop is not to end: there is no more meaning in time stopping than in time going on. For there to be an end there must be a beginning, and there is no beginning without an end. In the sestina the word "end" is repeated again and again, but only in questions and negative replies: "Where is there an end of it?" and "There is no end"; until the last line points us to where both Beginning and End are to be sought. "Little Gidding" not merely uses the words again and again, but is full of synonyms for both, picking up one or other of the various meanings, and it constantly translates the words into images. The refusal to speak of "beginning" and the consequent denial of "end" in "The Dry Salvages" make the restoration of both words to us in the last poem particularly moving. The tentative paradoxes of "Burnt Norton" return with confident certainty:

> What we call the beginning is often the end
> And to make an end is to make a beginning.
> The end is where we start from.

Read in this way, with a mind alert to recognize recurrences—not only of words like "end" and "beginning," "movement" and "stillness," "past," "present," and "future," but recurrences of the common prepositions and adverbs: "before" and "after," "here," "there," "now"—the poem seems to have for its "thematic material" not only symbols and images, but certain words in common use, which bring with them no images, though they can be associated with various images. These words receive the same kind of development as the images do. The line from the close of "Burnt Norton"—"Quick now, here, now, always—" is as meaningless and unpoetic by itself, on a page, without any context as

Shakespeare's "Never, never, never, never, never." When it is repeated, right at
the close of "Little Gidding," it gives us one of the most intense poetic experiences of the whole poem. After all the variation and turning, the discussion
and development, the subject is once more, for the last time, given us. It is given
in the briefest possible way, with all adornment stripped away. For a moment, it
is just as simple as that, and we knew it all the time. It is the end, and we are
back at the beginning; we have had this answer before, and we recognize it as
the only answer.

This musical treatment of the image, the phrase, and the word to bring out
latent meanings and different significances should prevent any reader from trying
to fix the symbols in *Four Quartets*. The poem must not be read as if it were allegory, in which one finds values for x, y, and z and then can make the whole
work out. Here one must not hunt for meanings and precise correspondences,
and, because an image seems to mean something definite in one context, force
the same meaning on it whenever it occurs. It is obvious that the sea of "East
Coker" holds a different meaning from the sea of "The Dry Salvages." It is better in reading poetry of this kind to trouble too little about the meaning than to
trouble too much. If there are passages whose meaning seems elusive, where we
feel we are missing the point, we should read on, preferably aloud; for the music
and the meaning arise at a point of intersection, in the changes and movement
of the whole. We must find meaning in the reading, rather than in any key
which tells us what the rose or the yew stands for, or in any summary of systems
of thought, whether pre-Socratic or Christian. Reading in this way we may miss
detailed significances; but the whole rhythm of the poems will not be lost, and
gradually the parts will become easier for us to understand. In fact, to read *Four
Quartets* one must have some sense of the whole before one attempts to make
very much of the parts. The sources are completely unimportant. No knowledge
of the original context is required to give force to the new context. In *The Waste
Land* the poet showed that it was necessary to pay some regard to his sources by
himself directing us to them. But we do not need to remember Tennyson's "Ma-
riana" when we read in "East Coker" of

> . . . a time for the wind to break the loosened pane
> And to shake the wainscot where the field-mouse trots
> And to shake the tattered arras woven with a silent motto.

If we recognize that Eliot is drawing on this favorite poem, we have pleasure in
the recognition; we are not helped toward understanding what a house falling
into ruin and decay is going to mean within the poem. Again, in "Little Gidding," the initial capital and the archaic form in "Behovely" tell us that the
words "Sin is Behovely, but all shall be well, and all manner of thing shall be
well" are a quotation, and we need to realize that they have the authority of a
maxim. The poet is speaking in words that are not his own, because these words
are more expressive than anything he could say. We do not gain any particular
help in the understanding of "Little Gidding" from knowing that the sentence
comes from Julian of Norwich.

When we read *Four Quartets* in this way, attentive to this "music of meaning," which arises at the point of intersection where word relates to word, phrase
to phrase, and image to image, we realize that though Eliot may have given to

other poets a form they can use for their own purposes, and though his treatment of the image and the word may suggest to his successors methods of developing poetic themes, *Four Quartets* is unique and essentially inimitable. In it the form is the perfect expression of the subject, so much so that one can hardly in the end distinguish subject from form. The whole poem in its unity declares more eloquently than any single line or passage that truth is not the final answer to a calculation, nor the last stage of an argument, nor something told us once and for all which we spend the rest of our life proving by examples. The subject of *Four Quartets* is the truth which is inseparable from the way and the life in which we find it.

Notes

1.   The *sestina* is a poem of six six-line stanzas, each stanza repeating the rhyme words of the first but rearranging them. There is often a coda of three lines with the rhyme words in their original order in the middle and end of each line. Spenser adopted a simpler form of rearrangement of the rhymes than the Italian sestina shows in his August Eclogue, no doubt to suit our duller ears. Eliot does not rearrange his rhymes, as he wishes to give the effect of repetition without progression, a wavelike rise and fall. He also does not confine himself to the repetition of the six rhyme words of the first stanza, employing other rhymes and sometimes assonance and only returning to the original rhyme words in his last stanza.

2.   The meter is an original modification of terza rima. The want of like terminations in an uninflected language such as English involves most translators and imitators of Dante in a loss of his colloquial terseness and austere nobility in an effort to preserve the rhyme. Eliot has sacrificed rhyme and, by substituting for it alternate masculine and feminine endings, he has preserved the essential forward movement of the meter without loss of directness of speech and naturalness.

3.   When a resident of East Coker, justly enthusiastic over its beauty, said to me: "Personally, I don't think Eliot has done justice to the village," it was difficult to do anything but agree, without wounding local pride by the suggestion that he had not really tried to.

On the other hand, failure to recognize that the titles are place-names may mislead. "Je suppose que le quatrième quatuor, *Little Gidding,* porte le nom d'un petit garçon cher à T. S. Eliot," writes a Belgian critic, Pierre Messiaen, "Le sens de l'oeuvre poétique de T. S. Eliot," *Etudes* 259 (December 1948):382–85. But his summary of the poem's "message" does not suggest that a mere understanding of the title would have helped him very much: "A ce petit garçon, l'auteur veut léguer trois pensées: que la vie est dure, qu'elle est composée d'échecs et qu'elle est sans cesse un recommencement. Ce qui compte, c'est que le feu brûle et la rose fleurisse."

4.   Donne speaks of air in this way, as a necessary medium, in "The Extasie":

> On man heavens influence workes not so,
> But that it first imprints the ayre.

In Sir John Davies's *Orchestra,* in the passage from which I have taken the epigraph for this chapter, there is a disquisition on Air also:

> For what are breath, speech, echoes, music, winds
> But Dancings of the Air, in sundry kinds?

5.   A glance at a collection of early maps shows how man instinctively conceives the sea as "the land's edge."

6.   When Walter Hilton, at the end of the fourteenth century, a time of much mystical enthusiasm, wrote his tract *Of Angels' Song,* he did not deny that some men might truly hear wonderful sounds, though he plainly thought that a good many more thought they did and were deceived; but he concluded with some words which have the same humility as this closing section of "The Dry Salvages": "It sufficeth me for to live in truth principally and not in feeling."

T. S. Eliot: "The Music of Ideas"

D. Bosley Brotman

Any line, if drawn without deviation, is simply carried farther away from its origin and ultimately loses itself, or loses at least its connection with its beginning and source. If, however, this line is led back to the starting point, as in the circle, it describes a satisfying and perfect figure; it perfects by enclosing space. This principle is fundamental to any classic unity in art.

That the poetry of T. S. Eliot has tended to become more classical in form, that the poet has been evolving toward the kind of unity just described, can be seen from a chronological study of his work. That he has been aware of musical forms and the possible analogies between them and the forms of poetry is also apparent in the poems themselves and by the poet's own statement in various essays, from *Ezra Pound, His Metric and Poetry* (1917) to *The Music of Poetry* (1942). Thus it is not startling to find that in *Four Quartets* he has achieved a structure analogous to that of the classical sonata form at its apogee as exemplified in the last quartets of Beethoven. To what extent the musical structure has been consciously contrived by the poet is not known by this writer; but that lack of information does not detract from an understanding or enjoyment of the poetry. For the unity is an organic one: The form is implied in the kind of thing the poet is saying and the way in which it must be said.

The implication here is not that poetry and music are in any way the *same thing*. The fogginess of some of Mallarmé's attempts to equate the two gives evidence (if it is needed) that they are not. And Eliot is well aware that words, besides expressing "visual beauty and beauty of sound ... [must communicate] a grammatical statement."[1] But poetry can at least approach the condition of music, and in *Four Quartets* the poet has, through particular kinds of rhythm and structure, suggested meaningfully both definite ideas and emotions and the forms which they must take. These forms, suggested by the nature of the ideas presented, are implicit in the poetic structure and in the kind of musical composition already suggested.

Reprinted from *University of Toronto Quarterly* 18 (1948):20–29 by permission of *University of Toronto Quarterly*.

I realize that too close an analogy of this sort can become procrustean and unprofitable; for the ultimate value of this, as of any work of art, lies in the effect of the whole, to which the strategy of composition of any of its parts is subordinate. On this point Eliot has noted: "In a perfect sonnet, what you admire is not so much the author's skill in adapting himself to the pattern as the skill and power with which he makes the pattern comply with what he has to say. Without this fitness, which is contingent upon period as well as individual genius, the rest is at best virtuosity."[2] Also, formal relationships are by no means an end in themselves; they can be completely meaningless. On the other hand amorphousness in a certain context can be meaningful, can be a form.

Eliot has characterized the aims of a poet (or a period in poetry) as including first of all the search for a "modern colloquial idiom." When this idiom has been stabilized, however, "a period of musical elaboration can follow," a period in which the poet is concerned with further polishing the actual form and refining "visual beauty and beauty of sound" within his idiom. He continues:

> I think that a poet may gain much from the study of music: how much technical knowledge of musical form is desirable I do not know, for I have not that technical knowledge myself. But I believe that the properties in which music concerns the poet most nearly, are the sense of rhythm and the sense of structure. I think that it might be possible for a poet to work too closely to musical analogies: the result might be an effect of artificiality; but I know that a poem, or a passage of a poem may tend to realize itself first as a particular rhythm before it reaches expression in words, and that this rhythm may bring to birth the idea and the image; and I do not believe that this is an experience peculiar to myself. The use of recurrent themes is as natural to poetry as to music. There are possibilities for verse which bear some analogy to the development of a theme by different groups of instruments; there are possibilities of transitions in a poem comparable to the different movements of a symphony or a quartet; there are possibilities of contrapuntal arrangement of subject matter.

In his early poetry Eliot carried on the struggle for a "modern colloquial idiom," a struggle the resolution of which at that time was probably most complete in *The Waste Land*. But even through this period there is a musical richness in the rhythms and repetitions of the poetry, and a consciousness of relationships between two art forms sometimes even in titles, as "Preludes" and "Rhapsody on a Windy Night." In some poems there is even a suggestion of the hypnotic quality of pure sound apart from meaning, as in lines from "Marina":

What seas what shores what grey rocks and what islands
What water lapping the bow. . . .

But through all this early poetry there is little stress laid on the perfecting of a technical form: the initial search is for an idiom.

By the time of *Four Quartets,* however, the idiom has been stabilized, and the poet's concern is primarily for elaboration and refinement of that idiom. He is also engaging in a much larger projected work than any previous, so that there is additional concern for a theme which will satisfy the demands of a complex abstract form.[3] The themes of the four poems in this cycle are essentially one, insofar as the parts are related to and clarify each other, and become finally different aspects of the same point of view. The spiritual condition of man, the aspects and the paradoxes of time within eternity, and man's concern with them— this is the material of all the poems. In each one the point of view is elaborated, a dialectic further developed. The material of each of the poems works to construct a unified whole, but each poem is itself complete and describes its own circle.

It is apparent upon casual reading that each of these four poems has in a large sense the basic structure of a string quartet. What is further interesting, however, is that under analysis this poetry can be seen to follow in rather surprisingly close fashion the principles of construction of its musical counterpart, and the principle of *return* in musical composition. The general statement and the pattern of development in each of these poems are essentially the same, although each is individual in its particular kind of statement and development. The variations and deviations, however, are not different from nor greater than those in any two musical quartets. Within the larger orthodox framework numerous variations are possible. What is described below as a basic musical structure in *East Coker* does not hold up explicitly for the other three poems in the cycle any more than the technical analysis of any one sonata, symphony, or quartet can be carried over completely to another. What does carry over, however, is the large framework within which the individual possibilities operate, and certain basic abstract principles of construction peculiar to the form as a whole.

The three-part song form, which in its third part provides for and executes a return to the beginning (*a-b-a*), is the basic design of the sonata form, which is utilized in the opening passages of *East Coker*. In an allegro mood the principal theme, time, is stated:

> In my beginning is my end. In succession
> Houses rise and fall, crumble, are extended. . . .

The mood is one of change, flux, impermanence. There is living and dying in quick succession. Time passes, and fires become ashes, pass into the earth, "Which is already flesh, fur and faeces. . . ."

The subordinate theme, eternity, follows. Here is an opposition to the principal theme. The mood is slower, in a different key. Time has stopped, and there is silence. Description replaces the positive statement of the first section:

> . . . the deep lane insists on the direction
> Into the village, in the electric heat
> Hypnotised. In a warm haze the sultry light
> Is absorbed, not refracted, by grey stone.
> The dahlias sleep in the empty silence.
> Wait for the early owl.

These two, time and eternity, are the themes for the poem. Following the idea of musical themes, they become independent "sentences," distinct from each other in style and character. They are broad in concept and significant enough in idea to offer potentialities for the wide and varied development demanded in this kind of form. Time for Eliot is impermanent. There is continuous flux, mobility. Against this is eternity, containing a paradox of movement through time, yet itself motionless and still.

Following the ternary design, the material comprising *b* of the *a-b-a* structure (lines 24–47) approximates the length of the initial exposition (1–23). Each of the themes is developed alternately, in a sort of poetic scherzo of alternating metres. In time,

> On a summer midnight, you can hear the music
> Of the weak pipe and the little drum
> And see them dancing around the bonfire. . . .

Then a transition appears from time to eternity, for the mirth of the earth feet dancing is the

> Mirth of those long since under earth
> Nourishing the corn.

And time in eternity is merely repetition of event:

> Feet rising and falling.
> Eating and drinking. Dung and death.

Here a rhetorical pause occurs,[4] linking the material to a recapitulation which, though merely started, is sufficient.

> Dawn points, and another day
> Prepares for heat and silence. Out at sea the dawn wind
> Wrinkles and slides. I am here
> Or there, or elsewhere. In my beginning.

The da capo is obvious. The beginning theme has merely to be stated for identification. We are at the start of the poem again; a circle is completed.

The first movement of the poem is analogous to the sonata form except for one noticeable stop (in the form of paragraphing) between the statement of the two themes at the beginning of the poem. Such a stop is not ordinarily found in this form of musical composition. Transitional devices, such as modulating passages, are customary; but complete stops, unless demanded by the material, defeat the essential idea of movement through a complete exposition—which continuous flow is fundamental to a highly developed sonata form. However, this break may be necessary: by their natures the formal patterns of one art form cannot be carried over completely into another, and in the final analysis of any work the material must be seen to dictate the particular form and its variations. In a musical work the composer would have the advantage of definite changes of key as vehicles for presenting contrasting material. In poetry such breaks in mood and tonality may be effected by period and paragraph.

The second movement of "East Coker" follows the rondo form (couplet, refrain, couplet). The themes are the same but are developed this time on a more cosmic scale; the material is more deeply analysed. The passage of time is visualized in the contrast of young and old:

> What is the late November doing
> With the disturbance of the spring

And creatures of the summer heat,
And snowdrops writhing under feet. . . .

The two-part song form pattern (*a-b*) of this first couplet of the movement splits in the middle with a perfect cadence. No transitional material is used; from the earth—its roses and its early snows—we are transported suddenly to the heavens:

Thunder rolled by the rolling stars
Simulates triumphal cars
Deployed in constellated wars
Scorpion fights against the Sun
Until the Sun and Moon go down. . . .

War in time continues—change and impermanence, death and rebirth:

Comets weep and Leonids fly
Hunt the heavens and the plains
Whirled in a vortex that shall bring
The world to that destructive fire
Which burns before the ice-cap reigns.

Science has disclosed these things: time, the earth, the sun are impermanent. As for man, he must realize his insignificance before the terrible facts of science. One is reminded of Bloom's astronomical cerebrations: "Gasballs spinning about, crossing each other, passing. . . . Same old ding-dong always. Gas, then solid, then world, then cold. . . ." Beginning to end to beginning continues without cessation.

The refrain, eternity, is next developed in a subdued, contrasting tone:

That was a way of putting it—not very satisfactory:
A periphrastic study in a worn-out poetical fashion. . . .

The abrupt change of tone is astonishing, but a relief to the ear and the senses following as it does the excitement and violence in the cosmic view. Eliot's shift to the prosaic would seem to be an intentional one; the intensity of the celestial display can be sustained for just so long, after which a passage of less intensity is necessary as contrast.[5]

The poem continues to elaborate the refrain. Explanations in time will not suffice; one is left still

. . . with the intolerable wrestle
With words and meanings. The poetry does not matter.

The "elders" had killed religion, put man rather than God in the center of things. From their point of view man in time would achieve a long-hoped-for serenity, and the wisdom of age. But what value could this have in an eternity?

Had they deceived us
Or deceived themselves, the quiet-voiced elders,
Bequeathing us merely a receipt for deceit?

The serenity only a deliberate hebetude,
The wisdom only the knowledge of dead secrets. . . .

Following the *a-b-a* return to the beginning, the second couplet begins, using the material of the first couplet (time) but with new exposition, here a discussion of the Bergsonian concept:

There is, it seems to us,
At best, only a limited value
In the knowledge derived from experience.
The knowledge imposes a pattern, and falsifies,
For the pattern is new in every moment
And every moment is a new and shocking
Valuation of all we have been.

And as in the constellated wars in which heat and cold oppose until both are ex-
tinguished, as "Leonids fly" wildly and blindly "whirled in a vortex," so man is
in darkness, knowing not where he is going:

. . . in a dark wood, in a bramble,
On the edge of a grimpen, where is no secure foothold.
And menaced by monsters, fancy lights,
Risking enchantment.

In the face of this, only one condition can sustain man through time:

The only wisdom we can hope to acquire
Is the wisdom of humility: humility is endless.

The second movement concludes with a coda utilizing material from the
first couplet in a repeated-cadence formula:

The houses are all gone under the sea.

The dancers are all gone under the hill.

A coda at this point was optional. If used, it might have included material from
either of the themes or from transitional passages, or have been completely new
material. In music it is very often presented in a repeated-cadence formula (domi-
nant-tonic), as suggested in the lines above.

The third movement is a theme with variations. Here is a continuation of
the subordinate theme of the first movement, an expansion of the initial suggestion of eternity, hypnotized in stillness, the "wait for the early owl" which is the
beginning of darkness. In this movement we have come full upon it:

O dark dark dark. They all go into the dark,
The vacant interstellar spaces, the vacant into the vacant. . . .

The theme of darkness and eternity is developed with its variations. Here the
imaginative composer presents his material in every conceivable aspect. The first
variation is a series of phrases enumerating those who will go into the darkness.
In the final reckoning,

... we all go with them, into the silent funeral,
Nobody's funeral, for there is no one to bury.

The second variation, beginning

I said to my soul, be still, and let the dark come upon you
Which shall be the darkness of God,

follows the circle of three-part song form (*a-b-a*). The theme is stated: Man must submit to what is taking place in time, in eternity—without fear, without love, without hope—only aware of what is taking place. This is followed by a contrasting description of emotion and darkness:

... an underground train, in the tube, stops too long between stations
And the conversation rises and slowly fades into silence
And you see behind every face the mental emptiness deepen
Leaving only the growing terror of nothing to think about. . . .

In return, the reiteration—the expansion of the idea of danger in emotion:

I said to my soul, be still, and wait without hope
For hope would be hope for the wrong thing; wait without love
For love would be love of the wrong thing. . . .

There is feeling, and thought, in eternity, but we cannot yet comprehend it. Perhaps, as in Rilke's *Prodigal Son,* God is not yet willing to have us perceive and love him. Added paradox is established: that of movement in the stillness of eternity. God's dark, if we let it come upon us, will become the light: "So the darkness shall be the light, and the stillness the dancing."

A third variation appears, a series of musical phrases, enumerations in time—light, laughter, and ecstasy, but "pointing to the agony / Of death and birth."

Variation four is a series of complete musical periods (that is, sentences) utilizing further the material of paradox. Each period is an entity in itself, but as each new one is stated the momentum is increased, the intensity deepened:

In order to arrive at what you do not know
   You must go by a way which is the way of ignorance.
In order to possess what you do not possess
   You must go by the way of dispossession.
In order to arrive at what you are not
   You must go through the way in which you are not.
And what you do not know is the only thing you know
And what you own is what you do not own
And where you are is where you are not.

The fourth movement is a pure transitional device, a relief from the heavy-falling cadences and abstractions, a lead-up to the summation of the fifth movement. This fourth part is a complete form in itself, but in a sense not a real movement at all. It is a bridgelike form, in mood and length a transition between two larger, more completely elaborated movements. For a comparative structure in musical composition one may cite Beethoven's Quartet no. 15 in A

Minor opus 132, fourth movement, the forty-six measures of which serve as a transition to the following movement.

In this movement the poet is reworking the same material, elaborating further his paradoxes, this time in a series of five regular double-periods in 2/4 time (iambic tetrameter). A four-measure phrase is added to each double-period, which contains a deceptive cadence leading into the extra phrase, i.e.:

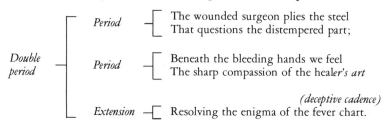

The double-period in music finds a common poetic analogy in almost any stanza of four fairly long lines, that being a design in which one can expect unity of meaning, uniformity of metric structure, the progressive evolution of one continuous thought, corroboration of rhyme, and at the same time some degree and kind of contrast. All of these materials are utilized in this structure, and the total effect is one of tautness and tenseness, a temporary holding back of the kind of elaboration and intensity pursued in the third section.

The last movement is the summation of all the suggestions touched on in the preceding movements. The same thematic material is used, but now the instruments are muted, the mood is less immediately intense. The emotion has been clarified and refined, and the summation is presented quietly, for "what there is ... has ... been. . . ." There is nothing new; the vast circle continues.

This section can be interpreted as the real fourth movement of the quartet, the final summation and recapitulation of themes. Musical feeling has been clearly achieved here in the intrinsic mood of summation and realization, the "mood of resurrection" common to the last movement of many symphonies. The poet has realized fully his own state in time. After the five uniform stanzas of the preceding movement, there is a break, and the last section begins:

> So here I am, in the middle way, . . .
> Trying to learn to use words, and every attempt
> Is a wholly new start, and a different kind of failure
> Because one has only learnt to get the better of words
> For the thing one no longer has to say, or the way in which
> One is no longer disposed to say it.

And, in spite of knowledge, the danger of becoming ensnared in false feeling is eternally imminent:

> And so each venture
> Is a new beginning, a raid on the inarticulate
> With shabby equipment always deteriorating
> In the general mess of imprecision of feeling,
> Undisciplined squads of emotion.

Time passes fleetingly, bringing with it change. One begins in childhood, living "the intense moment," feeling each event isolated and significant. As maturity is approached, one realizes progressively the strangeness of the world, the complex pattern of existence. There are echoes from the first movement:

> There is a time for the evening under starlight
> A time for the evening under lamplight. . . .

But time continues, and man must continue with it, accepting his role in humility. For we do not know, there is

> . . . perhaps neither gain nor loss.
> For us there is only the trying. The rest is not our business.

But,

> We must be still and still moving
> Into another intensity
> For a further union, a deeper communion
> Through the dark cold and the empty desolation. . . .

The quartet ends with the ultimate paradox, the mirror-inversion of the principal statement at the opening of the first movement: "In my end is my beginning." The circle has been completed, the themes resolved satisfactorily within a classical framework.

It is interesting to see here that the poet has been able to carry through this form without suggesting a poetic or musical pastiche, or in any other way producing an effect of artificiality. This effect of freshness of technique is largely the result of a particular combination of contemporary and traditional material, in structure, idiom, diction, and allusion. Part of that intention can be evinced from Eliot's previously discussed statement of the need, and the search for, a "proper modern colloquial idiom." In calling for that idiom, Eliot is of course only repeating what any age of revolution in poetry may announce, what Wordsworth called for in his prefaces. "And he was right," Eliot observes, "but the same revolution had been carried out a century before by Oldham, Waller, Denham, and Dryden; and the same revolution was due again something over a century later." But Eliot has been concerned on the whole not merely with the contemporary idiom, nor even with the immediate form the use of that idiom is to take, but with the way the complete work will fit into a continuing tradition in poetry, will make use of a living past as well as a living present, and of "tradition" as well as the "individual talent." That he is one of the most conscious artists of our time is a conclusion that can be fairly drawn. Certainly his stated theories of poetic content and structure are well illustrated in his own poetry. His critical theories, too, are of the same cloth.

In a certain sense this illustrates nothing more than consistency within the poet-critic. And this kind of critic may be, as Eliot remarks, not so much a judge as an advocate. But the final relevance of both the consciousness and the various kinds of consistency in the artist lies in the degree to which he has been able to effect a unity of ideas and form through his own art; and in the overall oneness of vision (or purpose) with which he has evolved from his earliest to his latest work. In the light of this, it is not surprising that Eliot, in his long double concern for both the traditional and the modern, should have arrived in *Four Quartets* at a point where he has been able successfully to combine both elements; he has achieved to a very great extent a modern range within classical limitations.

Notes

1.   T. S. Elliot, *Ezra Pound, His Metric and Poetry* (New York: Alfred A. Knopf, 1917), p. 14.

2.   T. S. Eliot,"The Music of Poetry," reprinted in T. S. Eliot, *On Poetry and Poets* (New York: The Noonday Press, 1943). All following quotations in prose by Eliot are to be found in this essay, unless otherwise noted.

3.   The converse of this suggestion is of course also true. A poet may begin with a definite theme, or with the idea of working within a given large form.

4.   The rhetorical pause is a musical, as well as literary, device. Cf. Haydn, Symphony no. 101, bar 218, where the development ends on the dominant of the following recapitulation.

5.   Whether this kind of prosaic transition may have been intentional here can be considered in the light of a general statement by Eliot that "in a poem of any length, there must be transitions between passages of greater and less intensity, to give rhythm of fluctuating emotion essential to the musical structure of the whole; and the passages of less intensity will be, in relation to the level on which the total poem operates, prosaic. . . ."

Eliot, Beethoven, and J. W. N. Sullivan

Herbert Howarth

Eliot, who is fond of detective stories, has planted clues for his biographers in almost every one of his critical articles and lectures. A capital clue to the origins of *Four Quartets* was rescued by the late F. O. Matthiessen from an unpublished lecture given by the poet at New Haven in the winter of 1933. It showed that at that time he was concerned with the idea of writing poetry that would be transparent and thus beyond poetry, and that he had in mind as his model Beethoven's late quartets where the music is beyond music. At a date only a little later than the New Haven statement, Stephen Spender wrote the chapter of *The Destructive Element* in which he compares *Ash Wednesday* with Beethoven's A Minor Quartet opus 132. Stanley Edgar Hyman subsequently pointed out confusions in Spender's study but suggested that *Four Quartets* clearly asked by their five-movement structure to be correlated with the A Minor Quartet.

A comparison between the five movements of the Beethoven masterpiece and the five sections into which each of Eliot's quartets is divided is rewarding. Beethoven's first movement is an allegro; his second a scherzo with a markedly contrasting trio; the third a slow movement of "unearthly beauty," with a contrasting section at a rather quicker, more animated pace; the fourth a very short alla marcia; the fifth an allegro appassionato in rondo design leading to "an extended coda, breathless, brilliant, fully-scored, yet airy." (These quotations are from the H. M. V. program notes available in England in the 1930s.)

In "Burnt Norton," which appeared in 1936 as the last of the poems dated 1909-35, Eliot reproduced this formal scheme. In addition he attempted, notably in the first and fifth sections, to find a verbal equivalent for the elusive gusts of the strings by choosing images and rhythms that imply quickness and elusiveness. The allegro of "Burnt Norton" tries to catch music's motion by the use of time and the bird and the echo, the sudden flowering of the lotus, leaves and laughter, and time again. His second section candidly attempts the three-four impetus of a late Beethoven scherzo, and his "trilling wire" image is a grasp at the excited pitch of the music. For the contrasting trio he changes to long lines in his special introspective idiom. By an act of poetic intuition he saw that he

Reprinted by permission from *Comparative Literature* 9 (1957):322–32.

could thus adapt Beethoven's contrast to his needs; this was the first of several such acts of intuition which occur in the later quartets and make all four fascinating to the student of poetic form. The slow movement opens like Beethoven's with an exploration, in slow lines, of a place of disaffection: then it proceeds to a second section which does not quicken with new life as Beethoven's does, but instead goes deeper and slower "into the world of perpetual solitude." For Beethoven's alla marcia, Eliot writes a short rhyming lyric, pivoting on two questions and so leading—"attacca subito"—to the last movement which, after discussing the differences between words and music, tentatively answers the questions by saying that "the detail of the pattern is movement" and that love is the cause and the end of movement.

The other quartets retain this scheme; they have the same sections in the same order, and within the sections the equivalent subsections. But there are certain changes. There is a gradual extension of thought through the four quartets. It seems that the thought progresses through the struggle with the form and that the form is capable of sudden successful modification when the thought moves.

Perhaps I should state here that these notes are not an attempt to interpret the *Four Quartets* (although I hope they may provide material relevant to an interpretation), nor can they take account of the whole range of allusions. They are concerned mainly with Eliot's choice of form—the reasons that influenced it, and the consequences of it. This being said, I would like to face two preliminary questions: Why, of the late Beethoven quartets, did Eliot choose opus 132 as his model? And why did he retain it for four poems? He might have attempted to write an equivalent for each of the late Beethoven quartets in turn, and it is possible to imagine that in 1933 he played with that idea; but in the end he preferred to labor at opus 132, marvelously exploiting its resources.

My supposition is that Eliot's attention was compelled to the A Minor Quartet by the description which Beethoven wrote above the slow movement: "Heiliger Dankgesang eines Genesenen an die Gottheit . . ." On the occasion of the Braille Centenary Eliot gave, as an act of generosity, an informal talk before a small audience at the National Book League in London. A blind reader recited from *The Rock,* Eliot commented that for two or three years preceding the composition of that pageant he had gone through a barren and difficult period; there had been moments when he doubted whether he had any more poetry to write. The London churches then asked him to undertake *The Rock* and he responded, composing the choruses by an act of the will. The result was (I *think* he meant after that work, not in it) a release of his blocked poetical powers. In fact we know that a rich phase opened after *The Rock;* the second half of his creative life opened and yielded all his full-length plays and the *Quartets.*

Eliot did not touch in that talk on the sources of his new creative power. Personally I feel, as Matthiessen evidently felt, that his return to America after eighteen years' absence had radical effects; perhaps the metaphorical family reunion that began with the Harvard lectures of 1932–33 played a double role in the crisis and the emergence from crisis, first completing the dislocation of his forces, then providing the sustenance out of which they were to be reorganized. The consideration of that process is not the purpose of these notes. In relation to the form of *Four Quartets* the point is that Eliot felt from 1933, or a little later, that he had passed through severe difficulties, through a state like illness, that demanded a confrontation with himself at the profoundest level, and desired to write poetry that recorded and examined and offered an understanding of the experience. Such poetry would be his sacred song of thanks to the Godhead for recovery. As he reflected on Beethoven's final style, to which he had been drawn by the theory that an artistic medium ultimately becomes transparent in the hands of a master, Eliot realized that he must attempt that transparency on the model of the A Minor Quartet for that was also the highest example of a hymn of thanks for safe passage through the dark. If he wrote to that pattern, the form would show that he was writing a sacred song.

"Burnt Norton" was only a half-success. Eliot diminished the impact of the poem by the procedure which he hoped would convey the aural effect of music, the dependence on rhythms and imagery meant to suggest the *elusive*. The scherzo-lyric of the second section is in its way a triumph of equivalence for the Beethoven scherzo, but even that is too insubstantial to be the most satisfactory poetry. The opening movement is much too elusive; and so is the close of the last, though the twenty-two lines that begin "Words move, music moves" overcome the difficulties and take on force as they report the poet's experience with words. How does he succeed with the central and formally most significant slow movement? He writes a convincing personal waste-land version of the state of illness with which Beethoven is initially concerned, but he does not go on to attempt a version of the contrasting section which the composer marked "Neue Kraft fuehlend." I would guess that the reason for this omission is that in 1935, even though beginning to use his new strength, he did not yet feel sufficiently sure of it to dare to speak of it or write as its interpreter; possibly he was not yet wholly, not umbilically, detached from the state of illness.

There is no more exacting critic of his own work than Eliot, and he knew that while he had written a poem fine enough to print he had not solved his problems. That is why he returned to the same pattern, determined to solve them. The success of the renewed experiments can be gauged according to his success in writing the "Neue Kraft fuehlend" section. In "East Coker" there is the first trace of new power realized. Though he tells himself

> I said to my soul, be still, and wait without hope
> For hope would be hope for the wrong thing; wait without love
> For love would be love of the wrong thing . . .

there is already a trace of the hope and the love in the animating lift of the lines. In "The Dry Salvages" he alters the form of the slow movement because the story of the journey into illness has changed into a study of the transatlantic journey which itself is a symbol of the journey of the soul through life and death; the division into contrasting sections has to be let go in favor of this thematic requirement. In the last quartet, "Little Gidding," the first section has ceased to be a brooding on illness and has become a statement of adaptation to life. Eliot is sure of himself now, completely confident; and the second section is a full realization of Beethoven's animated andante section, beginning with a promise of such transfiguring that

> All shall be well, and
> All manner of thing shall be well. . . .

Perhaps the closest formal reproduction of Beethoven's pattern is in "East Coker." The first, second, and fifth sections follow the procedure set in "Burnt Norton," but do it better with a firmer hold. The third section, as we have seen, does not completely represent Beethoven's slow movement, but it does feel in that direction and closes with the famous mystical statement of the contraries which are the key to health. This in turn suggests a function for the alla marcia passage, which in "Burnt Norton" had been only an interposed question; Eliot now makes it a metaphysical lyric imaging the world in terms of sickness, a sickness which can be understood by analogy with the function of an individual's sickness in the Jungian psychology: as the opportunity for salvation.

Five years elapsed between "Burnt Norton" and "East Coker." It took Eliot that long to advance in his control of the pattern. Then, having controlled it, he was able in the next two quartets to use it with an appearance of superb ease, and to pass to virtuoso modifications of it, which result in work of great technical beauty. In "The Dry Salvages" he drops his trilling-wire scherzo, because it has been leading him into "worn-out" periphrasis, and replaces it with the quasi sestina. To this piece of writing he probably looks with satisfaction when he applies to himself one of his favorite tests: "Have I in any way made useful technical innovations?" Through the six stanzas the six lines rhyme in unchanging order, and the rhyme words are sometimes new and always as if dictated by the sense, so that they become an undertow giving the depth and sea rhythm to the poem that it needs to state its meaning. It is an improvement on the previous scherzi, and it leaves them and the Beethoven shape behind, but it is only possible because these have been the stepping-stones to it. The earlier management of the trio through long probing introspective lines still operates. In "Little Gidding," however, Eliot reverses the plan: Once more he writes a rhymed lyric to open the section, only now he has squeezed the periphrasis out of it, or at any rate has substituted his own kind of periphrasis for the outworn kind; but for the trio he suddenly builds, by a compelled passionate insight, a tense new formal structure.

Using Canto XV of the *Inferno* as a frame of reference, he describes a meeting with a "compound ghost" (inclusive of Mallarmé, Babbitt, Pound, Whitman, Owen, and his younger self). This ancestor meets him in the empty streets of blitzed London—a land consumed by fire. For Brunetto Latini's foretelling of Dante's future he substitutes a prophecy of Eliot's success, which, inseparable from misunderstanding and approval for the wrong reasons, must be the profoundest source of dissatisfaction to the poet. For this episode Eliot writes lines that look as if they are Dante's terza rima, but in fact they do not rhyme; they are held together by interlocking masculine and feminine endings. This form lends them a higher austerity than the usual imitations of Dante's terza rima can give. It has a dignity outstanding even amid Eliot's dignified poetry; it has an awful dignity, and at the end a bitter dignity (which is actually out of keeping with the reconciliation towards which the *Quartets* are by this stage quickly moving—but nonetheless the lines are supreme). Now if we consider this section in relation to the "trio" of the three preceding quartets, we see, as before, that the astonishingly triumphant development has been made possible by the struggle to meet the demands of the section quartet by quartet; the preceding attempts are the basis from which this makes its upward spring.

The gradual evolving and modifying of the five-movement pattern was a process spread over seven years. Helen Gardner has written that the four quartets were conceived from the outset as a unity. I have never been able to satisfy myself that this was the case. The Faber catalogue which eventually announced the gathering of all four together for the autumn of 1944 certainly says that "the author ... has always intended them to be published as one volume, and to be judged as a single work." But in 1940 the autumn catalogue which had announced "East Coker" had shown the author as a little less definite in intention: "This is a poem of the same length and in the same form—described by the author as a 'quartet'—as 'Burnt Norton.' These two poems, and at least one yet unwritten, are intended to form a kind of sequence." What this blurb fixes is that Eliot was determined, by the time "East Coker" was finished, to persist in the *A Minor* pattern, proper to his theme and proving so challenging technically, and to continue, with the help of it, to explore his quadrilateral of themes: the themes of illness and its values and the nature of healing; the theme of exploration itself, and of migration, expatriation, and repatriation; the theme of history, arising alike from the study of society's illness and of exploration, and made urgent in "Little Gidding" by the circumstances of the war; and the theme of the artist's struggle with his medium. The last theme is a curious consequence of the struggle to emulate Beethoven. At the beginning of the fifth section of "Burnt Norton," he had reflected on the difficulties and opportunities of that struggle, contrasting the potentialities of words and music. Thus, as he treated a related problem in the same place in each quartet, he made a series of disquisitions on the mastery of the medium a leading feature of his experiment in mastering the medium.

To master the medium and make it transparent was not an aim of Eliot alone. Among his English friends in Bloomsbury, Roger Fry had long spoken of it. Fry had praised Derain for outsoaring his medium so that the painting was forgotten in the immediacy of the result. Eliot, so closely associated with Bloomsbury, must have been aware of Fry's dicta and perhaps impressed by them. But it is not surprising that, when he consciously formulated his attempt at poetry beyond the medium, he did so in emulation of a musical precedent rather than a precedent from painting. There is imagery from the visual arts in his poems, but it is, I think, slight compared with his references to music. In his earliest verse he wrote preludes and rhapsodies. He alluded to ariettes. He satirized the Chopin cult. In *The Waste Land* he used Wagner as his frame of reference (like so many other writers of the time), leading through a verse from *Tristan,* an imitation of the Rhinemaidens, and evocations of *Parsifal* to a conflagratory collapse of London recalling *The Dusk of the Gods.* From passages in his prose we know that in his early London days he was an enthusiast for Stravinsky, whose music he defended against sceptical friends at the point of an umbrella. He was a connoisseur of the ballet. When he launched *The Criterion,* he very early appointed J. B. Trend his music critic, and issue by issue Trend contributed papers which make the files of that defunct periodical still valuable reading for the musical amateur. Probably his musical knowledge, at once many-sided and discriminating, was a gift of St. Louis. Dreiser, who arrived in the city in 1892 when Eliot was four years old, has described it as confident and exacting in its musical culture.

I do not know whether or not Eliot usually read books on music and musicians. But there is evidence, external and internal, that he was acquainted with a study of Beethoven which appeared in London in 1927: *Beethoven – His Spiritual Development* by J. W. N. Sullivan. Sullivan was a largely self-educated Londoner of considerable capacity and passionate convictions. He had been encouraged in his literary work by Middleton Murry, who had linked him with Eliot, Conrad Aiken, Aldous Huxley, and others in his band of brilliant contributors to *The Athenaeum* between 1919 and 1921. In *Ushant* Aiken has told how he was present at a four-cornered luncheon in the early 1920s with Huxley, Sullivan, and Eliot. When J. B. Trend wrote in *The Criterion* for March 1928 on appropriate and inappropriate literary approaches to music, he singled out Sullivan's *Beethoven* as one of the few recent instances of a really useful study. Eliot was an editor who conscientiously read all the contributions to his periodical; the periodical and his own writings alike show, again and again, the impact of previous contributions on his thought; to analyze *The Criterion* is to be impressed by the dynamic developments that can occur when a poet-editor takes his editorial duties seriously. I believe that either Eliot had looked through Sullivan's book already, out of an interest in both the man and his subject, and was confirmed in a positive response to it by Trend's remarks; or that Trend's remarks sent him to the book. It is striking that, when Spender writes about Eliot and Beethoven in *The Destructive Element,* he quotes from Sullivan to characterize the late music. I am inclined to speculate that Eliot himself had mentioned Sullivan to Spender. Perhaps at a *Criterion* lunch or a Bloomsbury-set encounter Eliot told Spender that he was desirous of creating poetry of the late-Beethoven transparency and referred him to Sullivan's work of interpretation. Whereupon Spender, wrongly thinking that Eliot had already attempted an equivalent to Beethoven, sat down and read Sullivan and forcibly correlated what he found with *Ash Wednesday.*

Eliot was actually describing something still fermenting. He was turning over and over in his mind the story of Beethoven's last period as Sullivan told it. Some of Sullivan's phrases can be heard in *Four Quartets.* Here is a list:

(1) Sullivan quotes from Beethoven's journal: "Submission, absolute submission to your fate ... O hard struggle! Turn everything which remains to be done to planning the long journey." This spiritual journey of Beethoven gives Eliot one of his themes—which he pursues both in the terminology of a journey into the dark and through a study of his ancestors' journey to America and his own journey back to Europe, which become symbols of the inner migration. Eliot thinks of Beethoven's "submission," which made the journey possible for the composer, in the lines in "East Coker":

> ... what there is to conquer
> By strength and submission, has already been discovered
> Once or twice, or several times, by men whom one cannot hope
> To emulate. ...

(2) Three times Sullivan refers to "Beethoven the explorer." In the last section of "East Coker" Eliot says, "Old men ought to be explorers." We can read this line as an endorsement and extension of Sullivan's words, and inflect it "Old men *ought* to be explorers."

(3) Sullivan has a quick, poignant discussion of Beethoven's intense but mishandled affection for his nephew. Eliot writes:

> Do not let me hear
> Of the wisdom of old men, but rather of their folly . . .

(4) The "East Coker" lyric imaging Christ as the wounded surgeon may have grown from reflections on the letter written by Beethoven's physician, quoted by Sullivan, pp. 257–58: ". . . When I promised him alleviation of his suffering with the coming of the vitalizing weather of spring he answered with a smile, 'My day's work is finished. If there were a physician could help me his name should be called Wonderful.' This pathetic allusion to Handel's 'Messiah' touched me deeply. . . ."

(5) Sullivan tells how Beethoven finished the B-flat Quartet, Opus 135, at Gneixendorf: " 'The name sounds like the breaking of an axle-tree,' said Beethoven." The memory of this vivid simile filtered into the "Burnt Norton" scherzo:

> Garlic and sapphires in the mud
> Clot the bedded axle-tree.

Matthiessen, at the suggestion of John L. Sweeney, related these lines to Mallarmé's "tonnerre et rubis aux moyeux," but was not, I think, able to show their relevance to the poem. If we hear the verse as a late Beethoven scherzo and realize that the axle-tree that is breaking is Beethoven's mind and that accordingly it carries suggestions of the danger to the mind of the artist exploring a frontier, then it takes on significance. Also, the point of the borrowing from Mallarmé, with which the image is fused, grows clear; it is a borrowing from "M'introduire dans ton histoire," and what Eliot is doing is making a montage, superimposing himself on Beethoven's history, as he is fully aware.

(6) The first movement ends, says Sullivan, "as only Beethoven would end with what sounds like a startling and celestial trumpet call." Eliot does not attempt to equal this effect in "Burnt Norton"; but in "East Coker" there is a hint of it, and in "The Dry Salvages" he superbly transposes it with "Clangs / The bell." Professor Grover Smith has surmised, in his recent book on Eliot, that the triple "Resign" in *Coriolan* may be a reminiscence of the heartbeat figure in Beethoven's Coriolan overture.[1] If that is so, Eliot had already experimented with equivalents for the kind of dramatic musical stroke that he now in "The Dry Salvages" is able to incorporate perfectly into his own material. His incomplete *Coriolan* might be analyzed as a first encounter with Beethoven.

(7) Sullivan tells how Beethoven copies "mystical sentences from Eastern literature." Eliot also is fond of Eastern mystical literature; he might in any case have written his passage on Krishna and Arjuna in "The Dry Salvages," but it is just possible that his natural tendency was prompted and sanctioned by Sullivan's reference.

(8) Eliot's theme of illness and suffering and sterile hiatus in creation is of course implicit in the whole Beethoven biography. But there is one passage that sounds particularly relevant. Writing of the Grosse Fuge "in which the apparently opposing elements of life are seen as necessary and no longer in opposition,"

Sullivan goes on: "Beethoven had come to realize that his creative energy, which he at one time opposed to his destiny, in reality owed its very life to that destiny. It is not merely that he believed that the price was worth paying; he came to see it as necessary that a price should be paid. To be willing to suffer in order to create is one thing; to realize that one's creation necessitates one's suffering, that suffering is one of the greatest of God's gifts, is almost to reach a mystical solution of the problem of evil. . . ." From this point Eliot starts his own exploration of illness and suffering; in the course of it he makes his own mystical reconciliation of opposites; and in the closing lines of the whole sequence he offers

> A condition of complete simplicity
> (Costing not less than everything). . . .

(9) There is one further connection of considerable thematic importance. Sullivan describes Beethoven's special lack of the "language mentality": "It is not only that he was untrained and clumsy in the use of language; his most important states of consciousness, what he would have called his 'thoughts,' were not of the kind that can be expressed in language." Perhaps this prompts Eliot's inquiry, pressed through each of the quartets, into the difference between words and music, the precarious availability of words for the expression of difficult thoughts, the poet's struggle "trying to learn to use words."

Did Eliot succeed in writing poetry beyond poetry? Not in *Four Quartets*. He wrote a searching, moving sequence on the subject of trying to do so. Sometimes there are lines and even passages of several lines that make statements so intently and effectively that they are almost beyond poetry, but then the voice alters—yielding poetry that is often outstandingly beautiful but that is, for that reason, not what Eliot was seeking. Instances of this evident poetry are "the salt is on the briar rose," and the celebrated image of the train halted in the subway tunnel, or "Out at sea the dawn wind / Wrinkles and slides."

But though the *Quartets* did not produce the result for which Eliot was working, they showed him, in the contest with the material, more about the result than he had known before. He was then able to proceed to it in *The Cocktail Party* and *The Confidential Clerk*.

He had told himself that the result was necessary in the highest interests of writing at the supreme level where truth burns away ornament. But the impulsion to it was finally provided by a strictly practical need. For thirty years he had been speculating on how to make poetry which would cross the boards of the theater and be received without prejudice by the large, regular theater audience. He had worked for the style of *Four Quartets* with incomplete success; but writing for the stage afterwards, and challenging himself to find a style not so much beyond poetry as beyond prejudice, he found himself capable of something new. Exercised by Beethoven and Sullivan, he was sufficiently master of words to obtain the half-colloquial rhythms, the natural idiom and accentuations, and the distillation of flavor and feeling from them, that carry the late popular plays.

The final dramatic style is certainly transparent. Perhaps one could quibble at the description of it as "beyond poetry." It is not supra-poetry. Detractors might call it infra-poetry. It is really para-poetry. That means that it is on the same level as what is commonly called in our tradition poetry, but apart from it and kept distinct from it to avoid confusion.

Toward the end of *The Cocktail Party* there is a moment when Eliot invites us to see the proof of his success. Harcourt-Reilly asks: "Do you mind if I quote poetry?" Edward and Lavinia are polite enough, and cowed enough, to encourage him, and he quotes—since Eliot, whose reading of poetry began, after Omar, with Shelley, is returning to Shelley at the last—a magnificent archetypal passage from *Prometheus Unbound.* It is a crucial moment of the play and completely serious, and thus Shelley is apt for it; but I fancy that the humorist in Eliot is also active in the formulation of it, and so is the technical critic. For he wants us to note that traditional poetry sounds unmistakably different from the new poetry, the transparent medium, that he has invented after a lifetime of discipline.

The surprise in the result is that, while Beethoven's journey took him beyond the common ear, Eliot's immersion of himself in Beethoven and his struggle to emulate Beethoven ultimately produced poetry to which the common ear has opened. Eliot probably regards this as right. Though he is the most aloof of men, his inner self is fired by socioreligious convictions; and such convictions require the mending of the channels of communication between the poet and the public. It is part of the characteristic Eliot paradox that he took the most private way in company with the most individual genius to this collective end. And, if the end differentiates him from the musical ancestor, Beethoven, it also separates him from a literary forebear, Mallarmé. Mallarmé honored the word, but Eliot, while respecting Mallarmé so much, honors what the word signifies and is intent that the word be forgotten in favor of its significance.

Note

1. Throughout this paper I am writing without comment on the difficult question of analogies between musical and poetic idiom. This much is clear, however: the exceptional, dramatic strokes in music—which are already, in a sense, nonmusical—are easier for a poet to equate than music's normal effects, which depend so much on flow and interflow. A poet can more easily write, and a reader can more easily pick up, equivalents for the strikingly exceptional.

Music and the Analogue of Feeling:
Notes on Eliot and Beethoven[1]

Harvey Gross

Artistic practice and critical speculation in the nineteenth century effected close connections between music and literature. From Schumann to Mahler, composers wrote program music or music with distinct literary affinities. Mallarmé in France and Whitman in America were forging new prosodies out of a "language, retempered and purified by the flight of song."[2] Pater formulated his doctrine that *all art constantly aspires toward the condition of music.* Although neither Pater nor Mallarmé propounded any substantial aesthetic theory – Pater is prophetic but scarcely explanatory, while Mallarmé has a precise way of almost saying something – those interested in searching the grounds of comparison between poetry and music can find much that is provocative in their scattered ideas.

Pater believed that the essence of poetry is in "an inventive handling of rhythmical language," and that music represents an art in which form and idea are perfectly mingled. In music form *is* idea, and poetry is excellent as it approaches the purity of music. Agreeing with Pater, Mallarmé also sees music as the norm for an ideal poetry in which the distinction between form and idea would be obliterated. More importantly, Mallarmé recognized that the music of poetry is not "the elemental sound of brasses, strings, or wood-winds, but the intellectual and written word in all its glory – music of perfect fulness and clarity, the totality of universal relationships."[3] The music of poetry is not a matter of sound effects. Alliteration or such pseudo-onomatopoeia as "Forlorn! the very word is like a bell" is not the essential music of poetry; it lies in "the totality of universal relationships."

These relationships are established and articulated in the structures of language; the significant music of poetry is heard in the forms of grammar, the order of words, and the patterns of stress and quantity. Syntax, the order of words as they arrange themselves into patterns of meaning, is the analogue to harmony in music. Like harmony, syntax generates tension and relaxation, the feelings of

Reprinted from *The Centennial Review of Arts and Science* 3 (1959):269–79 with permission of author and publisher.

expectation and fulfillment which make up the dynamics of poetic life. As Susanne Langer puts it:

> The tension which music achieves through dissonance, and the reorientation in
> each new resolution to harmony, find their equivalents in the suspensions and
> periodic decisions of propositional sense in poetry. Literal sense, not euphony,
> is the "harmonic structure" of poetry; word melody in literature is more akin
> to tone-color in music.[4]

Syntax gives us the arc of "propositional sense," the articulations of meaning.
Like harmony in music, syntax makes connections, strengthens ideas, and relates
thematic material.

Closely related to syntax, and sometimes inseparable from it, is prosody. I
identify, perhaps arbitrarily, a poet's prosody with his metrics. While there are
probably nonmetrical prosodies (Blake in the *Prophetic Books* and Whitman in
many poems), meter commonly defines a poet's prosody. Meter in poetry has, of
course, its counterpart in music. The connections between musical and poetic
meter are often obvious, though the failure of prosodists to successfully adapt
musical notation for scanning English verse indicates many thorny problems. On
the whole, however, there exists an easy commerce between the musical theorists
and the prosodists. It makes sense to talk of the dactylic movement in the
scherzo of Beethoven's Ninth Symphony; it makes equally good sense to recognize the fourth foot here as syncopated:

To be or not to be—that is the question.

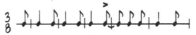

Meter in poetry and measure in music have similar and familiar functions: like
syntax and harmony, they create expectation and promise fulfillment. In poetry,
meter and its variations are involved with referential meanings; metrical uniformity or irregularity serves to stress, suspend, and sometimes demolish "propositional sense."

An examination of syntax and prosody demonstrates basic relationships between poetry and music. Such an examination is more than an account of certain
musical techniques used in poetry. These techniques may be consciously or unconsciously employed. In certain poems the development of thematic material
parallels sonata or fugue form. We can also find in poetry such devices as diminution and augmentation, ostinato effects, and inversion. But the deepest affinities between the arts of poetry and music lie at yet an unexamined level—where
the basic musical and poetic discourse can be expressed in such terms as tension,
ambiguity, expectation, and fulfillment. At this level spiritual affinities between
certain musical works and poems prove more than fanciful recognitions.

II

Eliot had been using musical techniques long before he composed *Four
Quartets*. *The Waste Land* was an experiment in the use of repeated thematic material as well as being orchestral in its elaborate handling of contrasting sonorities. Eliot's method in the *Quartets* is more formally musical: in addition to handling his material thematically, he employs the devices of theme and variation,

inversion, and diminution. He uses a five-movement form where long sections of philosophic density are contrasted to shorter lyrical sections. The first movement of each quartet develops a pair of themes in what can be roughly called sonata form. If *The Waste Land* is orchestral, designed for public hearing in a large hall, the *Four Quartets* are chamber music and must be heard in a small room.

But Eliot goes beyond the techniques of musical composition. He does a job of transmutation, of reproducing in the articulations of language the articulations of music. Through a deliberate and idiosyncratic use of syntax, Eliot gives us qualities common to both music and poetry—the feelings of arrest and motion, of beginnings and endings, of striving and stillness. This use of syntax is so much Eliot's own that I feel the "Eliotic style" is formed on it.

The syntax of Eliot's lines in "Burnt Norton" is a musical arrangement:

> Time present and time past
> Are both perhaps present in time future,
> And time future contained in time past.
> If all time is eternally present
> All time is unredeemable.
> What might have been is an abstraction
> Remaining a perpetual possibility
> Only in a world of speculation.
> What might have been and what has been
> Point to one end, which is always present.[5]

We hear the echoing repetitions of individual words and phrases: we hear the more subtle repetitions of syntactical structure, the persistently unvarying grammatical forms. The syntax is static: the noun *Time,* the modifiers *past, present, future,* the copulatives *is* or *are,* all follow in strict order. Grammar is repeated in a way that makes us realize syntax is working as harmonic structures work in music: to produce tension and relaxation, the very curve of feeling. We hear how propositional sense is modified by each repetition of word and phrase; we also hear how the repetitions of syntax produce musical meaning.

Note the grammatical marking-time in these lines: "If all time is eternally present/ All time is unredeemable." Eliot tells us how time can be immovable, without direction. But there is a point where Eliot must resolve his meaning, where a composer would introduce a cadence to tell us where his music is going, harmonically speaking. Then Eliot changes his syntax; he drops the copulatives and allows the movement of the preceding lines to pivot on the active verb *point:* "What might have been and what has been/ Point to one end, which is always present." Eliot has suspended syntactical movement by using only the verbs *is* and *are* for nine lines running. The verb *point* releases us into a new idea, and we modulate into a new syntactical unit:

> Footfalls echo in the memory
> Down the passage which we did not take
> Towards the door we never opened
> Into the rose-garden. My words echo
> Thus, in your mind.[6]

Here the verbs are active; the repeated *echo* emphasizes the music of "Footfalls echo in the memory . . . My words echo/ Thus, in your mind." The same music is heard, a haunting syntactical melody, as it were: "Down the passage ... Towards the door ... Into the rose-garden. ..."

Another kind of music is heard in the lyrical fourth section of "Burnt Norton":

> Time and the bell have buried the day,
> The black cloud carries the sun away.
> Will the sunflower turn to us, will the clematis
> Stray down, bend to us: tendril and spray
> Clutch and cling?
> Chill
> Fingers of yew be curled
> Down on us? After the kingfisher's wing
> Has answered light to light, and is silent, the light is still
> At the still point of the turning world.[7]

We hear the insistent repetitions as in the first section: "turn to us ... bend to us ... Down on us." These are the melodies. We have, however, an effect which, to quote Langer again, involves "the suspense of literal meaning by a sustained ambiguity resolved in a long-awaited key word."[8] Reading the penultimate line, we briefly poise on the word *still*. Since the usual tendency is to pause slightly at the end of the line, the mind first understands *still* as an adjective modifying *light*. When we complete our reading, we understand that *still* is more exactly an adverb whose effect is strong enough to modify the sense of both lines. The light is *even yet* at the still point of the turning world.

We realize the ambiguity here, and how the word functions as a grammatical pivot on which the movement and meaning of the lines turn. The effect is exactly like an ambiguous harmonic structure which hovers between tonalities, a structure which might take any of a number of possible directions but which is suddenly resolved by an unexpected cadence.

We note in "East Coker" another effect of harmony which might be called "the illusion of tonality." The poem opens in this "key":

> In my beginning is my end. In succession
> Houses rise and fall, crumble, are extended,
> Are removed, destroyed, restored, or in their place
> Is an open field, or a factory, or a by-pass.[9]

At the end of the first section we have:

> Dawn points, and another day
> Prepares for heat and silence. Out at sea the dawn wind
> Wrinkles and slides. I am here
> Or there, or elsewhere. In my beginning.[10]

Again Eliot builds tension through repeated syntax: "... or in their place ... or a factory ... or a by-pass." This syntactical pattern is repeated, in diminution, just before Eliot restates his theme: "I am here/ Or there, or elsewhere. In my beginning." The familiar, almost expected, syntax acts as a return section, preparing us for the new entrance of the theme in its proper "tonality." We stress this musical preparation through syntax. Many have recognized Eliot's use of repeated thematic material without realizing how complex Eliot's musical procedures actually are. At the end of "East Coker" we hear the same broken, hesitant syntax announcing the return of the theme, in inversion:

> The wave cry, the wind cry, the vast waters
> Of the petrel and the porpoise. In my end is my beginning.

The striking effect created by each return of the theme is not achieved through simple verbal repetition or even through verbal modifications. It is achieved through the manipulation of syntax which gives this "illusion of tonality." Eliot's procedure parallels sonata form where the principal tonality is reestablished at the end of a movement and the main theme makes its final appearance.

The musical qualities of Eliot's syntax are reinforced by the prosody. Like syntax, prosody is responsible for the movement of words and contributes toward the dynamics of feeling. More than syntax, prosody produces affective states below the level of explicit meaning. Syntax is concerned with literal sense; but prosody retards, speeds up, or emphasizes literal sense by directly physical means. A particular rhythm may communicate an emotion far more vividly than a statement about that emotion.

I distinguish between rhythmic effects and basic metrical patterns in the *Quartets*. These rhythmic effects occur within the context of a formal metric; however, the ordinary symbols of scansion—which can adequately outline meter—do not reveal the more subtly musical aspects of Eliot's rhythms. By applying some of the methods of musical analysis, we can hear how Eliot develops a rhythmic idea and how, through rhythmic expansion, an idea accumulates emotional power. If we assign note-values to Eliot's word groups, we get something like this:[11]

time present	♩ ♫
time past	♩ ♩
time future	♩ ♫
time is eternally	♪♪♪ ♪♪♪
time is unredeemable	♫♪♪ ♪♪♪

The rhythm (♩ ♫) is speeded up as the idea evolves and emotion intensifies. The rhythm persists in our memories, modifying meaning and feeling: as the units of the phrase quicken and expand, we feel the arc of "propositional sense" tighten. The rather slack statements about the nature of time in the first three lines are followed by the taut proposition of lines four and five: "if all time is eternally present,/ All time is unredeemable." This is awesome; the notion challenges the imagination. We accept the opening statements as curious or teasing, the speculations of a poet with a taste for conundrums. But lines four and five have accumulated the tension (through repeated syntax as well as rhythmic expansion) appropriate to the idea: that everything we have done is still *doing,* that everything we *shall do* is already taking place. Metaphysics is implicit in the paradigms of verbs: The possibilities of human action (what might have been; what has been) are conjugated in Eliot's syntax. And all grows to thought in the expanding rhythms of Eliot's language.

The formal prosody of *Four Quartets* is extremely varied, yet Eliot maintains an overall consistency in metrical tone. Eliot allows a contrasting metric to beat against the basic iambic meter of English speech. The opening of "Little Gidding" provides a good example of this:

> Midwinter spring is its own season
> Sempiternal though sodden towards sundown,
> Suspended in time, between pole and tropic.
> When the short day is brightest, with frost and fire,
> The brief sun flames the ice, on pond and ditches,
> In windless cold that is the heart's heat,
> Reflecting in a watery mirror
> A glare that is blindness in early afternoon.[12]

Eliot is writing a four-stress alliterative line, not unlike the line of *Piers Plowman*. Despite the thumping consonants and the hesitation of each caesura, Eliot keeps a sense of iambic movement. At least one of the lines can be scanned, without undue equivocation, as blank verse: "The brief sun flames the ice on pond and ditches." The opening of "The Dry Salvages" moves in almost regular trisyllabic feet, anapests and dactyls; but there is none of the solemn torpor of *Evangeline* or the galloping boredom of *The Destruction of Sennacherib:*

> I do not know much about gods; but I think that the river
> Is a strong brown god—sullen, untamed and intractable,
> Patient to some degree, at first recognised as a frontier;
> Useful, untrustworthy, as a conveyer of commerce:
> Then only a problem confronting the builder of bridges.[13]

Each line has five principal stresses and a strongly felt caesura; the meter is anapestic pentameter with dactylic and spondaic substitutions. But the ear does not hear anapests and dactyls; it hears the slow and primitive music of the Mississippi as it flows through past and present, recalling Eliot to childhood memories. What the ear hears are the inflections of the human voice, the infinitely subtle music of feeling.

III

Further analysis would show more precisely the musicality of *Four Quartets.* The point I wish to establish is that Eliot, through syntax and prosody, evokes a complexity of feeling in ways that music evokes analogous states in the minds of sensitive listeners. Eliot is attempting to extend the limitations of language by entering the domain of another art. He uses syntax and prosody like music to enlarge the available means of expression. But he is not approaching the condition of music because he wishes to lose his ideas in his form, or to create mere patterns of pleasing sounds. He is striving to evoke states of consciousness which cannot be expressed by the purely cognitive aspects of language.

Beethoven struggled with the reverse of this problem: the inability of purely instrumental music to express specific ideas. The finale of the Ninth Symphony begins with a recapitulation of all the abstractly musical possiblities of the preceding three movements. These are rejected, and we hear the double-basses struggling to become articulate, to transform the forms of feelings into the forms of statements. Beethoven has to supplement his instruments with human speech, and the baritone cries—as if he knows that the unaided orchestra could not tell us what Beethoven means to tell us—"O Freunde, nicht diese Töne!" Music itself for Beethoven was not enough, as poetry was not enough for Eliot:

> Words strain.
> Crack and sometimes break, under the burden,
> Under the tension, slip, slide, perish,
> Decay with imprecision, will not stay in place,
> Will not stay still.[14]

But there is stillness in the movement of music; for in music there is no concern with the burden of cognition, of fixing meanings in place. Rather, as Langer eloquently puts it:

> The imagination that responds to music is personal and associative and logical, tinged with affect, tinged with bodily rhythm, tinged with dream, but concerned with a wealth of formulations for its wealth of wordless knowledge, its whole knowledge of emotional and organic experience, of vital impulse, balance, confict, the ways of living and dying and feeling. Because no assignment of meaning is conventional, none is permanent beyond the sound that passes; yet the brief association was a flash of understanding. The lasting effect is, like the first effect of speech on the development of the mind, to make things conceivable rather than to store up propositions. Not communication but insight is the gift of music; in a very naive phrase, a knowledge of "how feelings go."[15]

The significance of music is "with the ways of living and dying and feeling"; its meaning is "a knowledge of how feelings go." Music, Langer continues, is a real semantic: a language which has no fixed signs, but which has a syntax of feeling as the language of words has the logical forms which relate the parts of speech. To clinch Langer's argument, I quote from J. W. N. Sullivan. Sullivan's remarks on significance in music clearly anticipate her chapter in Philosophy in a New Key. Here Sullivan is commenting on music as an expressive language, capable of rendering states of consciousness:

> Beethoven most certainly regarded his music as expressing states of consciousness which might conceivably have been expressed by some other art. Indeed, he seems to have regarded music not only as a medium for the presentation of "beauty," but as a language with which he was more familiar than any other.... Beethoven ... considered that his music had an extra-musical content, that is to say, a content that could be ... expressed in some other medium.... Music, as an expressive art, evokes states of consciousness in the hearer which are analogous to states that may be produced by extra-musical means.[16]

Like Langer, Sullivan denies that the meaning of music lies within a context of purely abstract musical relationships: he believes that music refers to the human world of gesture, action, and feeling.

We can test this theory against our own experience with a musical work. In listening to the *Pastoral* Symphony, we do not experience nature; nor do we necessarily form mental images of the walk in the country, the flowing brook, or the shepherd playing on his flute. The bucolic opening theme of the symphony is bucolic only if we want to think it so. The significance of this music lies in the complex emotional states which the melody induces: feelings of undisturbed ease, relaxation, quiet movement punctuated by periods of rest. We might possibly have exactly these feelings when we walk in the country; most of us will have similar ones.

There is, however, no direct correspondence between music and the emotions; nor is music itself emotion. Music is an analogue to feeling in the same way that words symbolize objects and abstractions. Words are arbitrary designations; there is nothing in the word *apple* that is intrinsically applelike. Music is also an arbitrary designation, not for objects or ideas but for feelings. Thus Langer uses the term *symbolic* to describe the way music communicates its content of emotion, and she argues that the structures of music are indeed *symbolic forms.* She is arguing against the notion that music is a set of emotional signs: a woman's cry over a sick child, a drowning man's cry for help. Under these conditions the designation of emotion requires a particular action: sympathy for the woman, rescue for the man.

Music requires no action on the listener's part. The *marcia funebre* of the *Eroica* tells of grief and consolation, but we need console no mourners nor show any sympathy. We apprehend grief in its deepest and most painful aspects; we know more about grief than language could possibly communicate. We are allowed to experience not this particular grief and that actual sorrow: We are given a universal knowledge "of how grief goes."

IV

Eliot uses his poetic resources in ways that music operates: to give us the knowledge of how certain feelings "go." In a real sense we have a musical experience when we read or, better yet, listen to Eliot read the *Quartets.* We might ask now whether we can find analogues to Eliot's world of feeling in a particular musical work. Can we demonstrate spiritual affinities between the quartets of Eliot and those last quartets of Beethoven, from which Eliot seems to derive "his title, much of his form, elements of his tone and content"?[17] Can we demonstrate that such affinities are more than "literary" recognitions made in the mind of a poetizing listener?

A description of certain sections of Beethoven's Quartet in C-sharp Minor opus 131 may suggest what Eliot heard in Beethoven. My selection of this quartet is arbitrary; the same points can be made by examining the Quartet in B-flat opus 130 or the Quartet in A Minor opus 132. Eliot was certainly not influenced by a specific musical work, and we cannot find literal resemblances. Rather, the musical gestures of Beethoven's late quartets evoke responses relevant to Eliot's poetry: We respond to ambiguity, surprise, contradiction, unexpected delay; we experience a world of stress, of exultation, of resignation, and of final affirmation. I choose the Quartet in C-sharp Minor because of its great variety in mood and technical effect, and because its vast musical scheme offers a rich context of contrasting feeling.

The deepest affinity between Beethoven and Eliot is that the Quartet in C-sharp Minor and the *Four Quartets* are cyclical structures; they develop organically out of a single controlling idea. In the C-sharp Minor Quartet everything starts with the opening fugue and its seminal motto, G#, B#, C#, A. From these notes Beethoven builds a musical structure in which all elements are closely unified; in which technical device serves the expression of a single spiritual fact. Each of the *Four Quartets* elaborates a central theme; each radiates out from a proposition on the nature of time, on the meaning of history, on the flow of the great river, and on the paradox of the seasons. These themes are finally resolved in the last *Quartet,* "Little Gidding." Every theme contains its opposite, its musical inversion. Man, alienated from self and society, finds reconciliation in God; despair becomes the way to joy; time and history become ways leading out of time and beyond history.

To express such a context of opposition and contradiction, Eliot came, almost by necessity, to employing the form and method of music. For music has the striking ability to express *simultaneously* opposite states of feeling. In the opening fugue of the C-sharp Minor Quartet, Beethoven states a theme which contains polar extremes of feeling. The first four notes [A] generate extreme tension; the *sforzando* on A is a cry of pain. The second half of the theme [B] is suave and conciliatory, offering resolution to the tension of the first four notes. These two motifs make up the basic material of the first movement:

A second theme, derived from motif B, introduces a mood of repose and quiet:

At bar 91 something extraordinary happens. The quiet second theme is played by the first violin and imitated below at the sixth by the second violin. At the same time the viola enters with the four-note motto:

It is toward the expressiveness of the above passage—where the first motif, agonized and unresolved, is set against its own emotional opposite—that Eliot is striving. We know that poetry can never achieve such absolute expressiveness; the sounds of language cannot combine in the way that musical tones unite or oppose. Yet we must remember that Eliot is searching for a poetic medium which transcends the limitations of language, and that the forms and structures of music can provide patterns to reach into the mystical silence where opposites are reconciled:

> ... words or music reach
> The stillness, as a Chinese jar still
> Moves perpetually in its stillness.
> Not the stillness of the violin, while the note lasts,
> Not that only, but the co-existence,
> Or say that the end precedes the beginning,
> And the end and the beginning were always there
> Before the beginning and after the end.[18]

The second movement of the C-sharp Minor Quartet is an intermezzo, lyrical and urgent in mood. There is a sudden change in tonality, accomplished by simple and surprising means. At the end of the fugue, the texture thins out to a bare C# played by all four instruments; then the instruments quietly move up a semitone to D, establishing the tonality of D major. The first violin swings into an iambic tune:

The instrumental color is more various than in the first movement; the melodies move in octaves and unisons. The movement hesitates; the tune hurries along, then slows down, then picks itself up again. The meaning seems full of human concern. We hear fevered haste and a sense of indirection. It is one of those incomplete moments in life when we temporarily lose our sense of purpose. It is also a moment of descent; from the lonely contemplation of the first movement, we return to middle earth—where we hear

> ... upon the sodden floor
> Below, the boarhound and the boar
> Pursue their pattern as before ...[19]

The great center of the quartet is the fourth movement. This world is inhabited and populous. We find in the theme and its six variations a wealth of possibility and development:

The variations encompass a great variety of expression. We hear how certain less exalted but more comfortable emotions "go": pathos, regret, nostalgia, even sentimentality. Toward the end of the movement, the variations become freer; we sense impending dissolution and chaos. The theme returns, disappears, then returns again. It is finally repeated in a hesitant, almost timid statement:

We should note the long pauses between each phrase. Beethoven exploits the expressive possibilities of silence: Where we expect another repetition of the phrase, we get a bar-long rest. The phrase echoes silently in our minds. Eliot, too, knows the place of silence in metrical schemes, and the expressive value of a significant pause:

> The only wisdom we can hope to acquire
> Is the wisdom of humility: humility is endless.
>
> The houses are all gone under the sea.
>
> The dancers are all gone under the hill.[20]

What Eliot may have learned from Beethoven can only be conjectured, but it is undeniable that their use of silences is often strikingly similar.

The fifth movement is in mood and movement a scherzo, although it is written in double and quadruple time. We can hear

> Earth feet, loam feet, lifted in country mirth
> Mirth of those long since under earth
> Nourishing the corn. Keeping time,
> Keeping the rhythm in their dancing
> As in their living in the living seasons.[21]

We hear the joy of continuous movement in energetic dance. There are pauses to catch our breath (marked in the score *molto poco adagio*); then the dance rushes on. A contrasting theme appears; it is marked in the score *piacevole,* agreeable:

The entire movement is in good humor. After extensive repeats the fifth movement ends on three repeated E's.

Between the fifth movement and the finale is another intermezzo—improvisatory, brief, and pregnant with expectation. It consists of a single melody, played first by the viola, then an octave higher by the first violin. This melody is almost indescribably piercing in its melancholy. It recalls the loneliness and pain of the first movement; it looks forward to the inexorable march of the finale:

The finale opens with a powerful rhythmic motif which is an anagrammatic arrangement of the motto phrase: the G#, B#, C#, A of the first movement is now C#, G#, A, B#:

The first violin immediately plays a march rhythm which controls the whole last movement. Another theme appears, "pathetic" in quality and also based on the motto phrase:

This material is developed in sonata form. The tonality of D major returns in the recapitulation like a threat. This remote key has the effect not of destroying, but of strengthening the C# tonality. It is affirmation by negation; it is reaching a desired conclusion by indirection, or by what might at first seem the wrong direction:

> In order to arrive at what you are not
>   You must go through the way in which you are not.
> And what you do not know is the only thing you know
> And what you own is what you do not own
> And where you are is where you are not.[22]

Beethoven leads us along harmonic paths which seem far from the main road. At first there seems no apparent connection between the intrusive sections in D major and the final assertions of C# tonality. Historically this harmonic relationship, appearing usually as the Neapolitan sixth, was a colorful and decisive type of cadence. It became a mannerism in the work of Alessandro Scarlatti and certain of his contemporaries. Beethoven enlarges what was actually a musical cliché into a pole or antipole. Thus the harmonic connection is made through contradiction, as love is sometimes reached through hate. When we examine the whole quartet, we understand that this D major is an element of almost symbolic significance. We might call it the "destructive element" which carries the threat of chaos. The quartet struggles with and overcomes this threat; in the last bars we hear again the motto theme, a welcome call to order, and the work closes in major tonality.

Polarity and dramatic conflict are the essence of the Quartet in C-sharp Minor; its meanings are completeness and unity. We understand completeness in the variety of its forms and the exploitation of every technical means. We understand its unity not only as a function of its related and contradictory themes and harmonies, but as the musical expression of a world in which defiance and resignation, joy and pain, abstract existence and warm humanity, find their reconcilation.

V

What I have heard in Beethoven is what I feel to be the significance of his music: "A knowledge of emotional and organic experience, of vital impulse, balance, conflict, the *ways* of living and dying and feeling." I have tried to suggest the relevance of Beethoven's music to *Four Quartets*. I also suggest that Beethoven's music "means" what Eliot's poetry means. Eliot starts with aspects of Beethoven's external form in the overall organization of his poems. More importantly, Eliot handles his syntax and prosody like musical sequences. Most importantly, Beethoven and Eliot work with a root experience: To see and understand an ordered universe as the inevitable expression of its conflicts and tensions, and to see disorder as the very patent of order.

Notes

1.   A shorter version of this paper was read before members of the Modern Language Association at its annual convention, December 27, 1958. I wish to acknowledge the help of Professor Jan La Rue of New York University. Many of his ideas have been incorporated in this paper, and his stimulating interest has made me aware of the possibilities inherent in this subject.

2.   Stéphane Mallarmé, *Selected Prose Poems, Essays, and Letters,* trans. Bradford Cook (Baltimore: The Johns Hopkins Press, 1956), p. 49.

3.   Ibid., p. 42.

4.   Susanne K. Langer, *Philosophy in a New Key* (Cambridge: Harvard University Press, 1942), p. 261.

5.   T. S. Eliot, "Burnt Norton," in *Four Quartets* (New York: Harcourt, Brace, and Company, 1943). Reprinted by permission of Harcourt, Brace and Company, Inc.

6.   Ibid.

7.   Ibid.

8.   Ibid., p. 261.

9.   Ibid.

10.   Ibid.

11.   My notation of the rhythms may be compared with Eliot's reading on H. M. V. Record C, 3598. Any attempt to note precisely a particular reading is necessarily mechanical. What I wish to show is the changes in tempo and movement. This can be done only by musical notation.

12.   Ibid.

13.   Ibid.

14.   Eliot, "Burnt Norton."

15.   Langer, p. 244.

16.   J. W. N. Sullivan, *Beethoven: His Spiritual Development* (New York: Mentor, 1949), pp. 32–33.

17.   I quote here from *Time* 41 (7 June 1943):96. The Beethoven-Eliot parallels have been recognized by many, including Stephen Spender, Stanley Edgar Hyman, and more recently, by Herbert Howarth. See Herbert Howarth, "Eliot, Beethoven, and J. W. N. Sullivan," *Comparative Literature* 9 (1957):322–32.

18.   Eliot, "Burnt Norton."

19.   Ibid.

20.   Eliot, "East Coker," *Four Quartets.*

21.   Ibid.

22.   Ibid.

The Orchestration of Meaning in T. S. Eliot's *Four Quartets*

Thomas R. Rees

Many critics and students have come dangerously close to subscribing to the tenuous proposition that a nearly exact formal analogy exists between the structure of T. S. Eliot's *Four Quartets* and that of Beethoven's late string quartets. Despite the obvious musicality of Eliot's poem and the immense value of musicological studies of its structure, I intend to prove that attempts to establish a strict correlation between the quartets and specific musical compositions, without considering other musical influences, can lead to confusing and inaccurate oversimplifications. I would also like to identify and assess some of the more important musical as well as literary and philosophical influences on the structure of the quartets, and to demonstrate Eliot's skill in using a variety of musical and literary devices to bring out his meanings.

Certain commentators, whose contributions to the study of the quartets have been otherwise sound and perceptive, have gone so far as to identify definite string quartets as models for Eliot's poem. Herbert Howarth traces the origin of the *Four Quartets* to one of Eliot's Yale lectures in 1933, in which Eliot expressed his concern with "the idea of writing poetry that would be beyond poetry, and that he had in mind as his model Beethoven's late quartets where the music is beyond music." Howarth identifies Eliot's model here as Beethoven's A Minor Quartet op. 132.[1] The poet's interest in Beethoven was evidently aroused by reading J. W. N. Sullivan's *Beethoven—His Spiritual Development* (1927). In this work Sullivan describes the musician's feelings as he composes the Quartet in A Minor: Beethoven is grateful to his physician for alleviating his suffering with the coming of spring (hence Eliot's symbolic image of Christ as the wounded surgeon). Sullivan also refers to Beethoven as "the explorer" (hence Eliot's "Old men ought to be explorers."). Beethoven's submission to fate, his interest in oriental literature, his self-doubts over his creative abilities, his artistic struggles with his medium—all of these things, according to Howarth, are treated thematically in Eliot's poem.[2]

From *The Journal of Aesthetics and Art Criticism* 28 (1969-70):63–69. Copyright 1970 by The American Society for Aesthetics. Reprinted by permission of the Society.

Harvey Gross perceives a number of formal similarities between the *Four Quartets* and Beethoven's C-sharp Minor Quartet op. 131 because of that composition's "great variety in mood and technical effect, and because its vast musical scheme offers a rich context of contrasting feeling." Both Eliot's poem and Beethoven's quartet, Gross asserts, are composed in cyclical form with a "seminal motto"; they "develop organically out of a single controlling idea": Man, who is estranged both from himself and from society, "finds reconciliation in God; despair becomes the way to joy; time and history become ways leading out of time and beyond history."[3]

Certain other critics have been more general in identifying the musical models for Eliot's poem. Hugh Kenner says that Eliot is "reported to have said that he was paying attention chiefly to Bartok's quartets Nos. 2–6 . . . ,"[4] while Dorothy E. Rambo relies on the fact that the "central experience" dominating each of Beethoven's quartets corresponds to Eliot's "still point" or "Logos," which represents "an all powerful force which permeates the texture" of the poem.[5] D. Bosley Brotman, on the other hand, notes that each of Eliot's quartets has "the basic structure" of a string quartet providing a "large framework" for the systematic development of the poet's ideas.[6]

Each of these critics, despite a slight tendency toward overgeneralization, has made some extremely valuable contributions to our understanding of the musicological format of the *Four Quartets.* Nor can it be denied that the composition of the quartets has been influenced by a variety of musical forms.

Indeed, from the time of his earliest compositions Eliot has continually exploited the musical idiom as a source of formal organization in his verse. In "Portrait of a Lady" and "The Love Song of J. Alfred Prufrock," the unity and progression of images is based on interlocking patterns of repeated words and symbols, which approximate the progression of interweaving motifs in the impressionistic music of Debussy and Ravel. The numerous false starts and broken phrases of Prufrock's dialogue follow an incremental development pattern similar to Chopin's deferred resolutions. The confused and fragmentary development of themes in *The Waste Land,* combined with the use of recurrent patterns in the dominant image-groups, reflect the fused influences of Stravinski and the Wagnerian leitmotif. Finally, in the composition of the *Four Quartets,* Eliot molds his deepest religious feelings into a broader format for thematic organization suggested by the sonata-allegro form of Beethoven's string quartets. It is a format ideally suited to the orderly and sustained development of contrasting themes.

An examination of the standard sonata-allegro form might help us to understand more clearly the analogy existing between the form of the *Four Quartets* and that of a musical quartet. In the first movement of a conventional quartet there are three principal sections: (1) the exposition section, which introduces the two contrasting themes or subjects; (2) the development section, in which these two themes are subjected to manifold variations, extensions, inversions, and counterpointing; and (3) the recapitulation section, where the original themes are restated in final form, having been resolved and transfigured in the development section. This fruitful form also constitutes the structural base for the composition of sonatas, quartets, overtures, concertos, and symphonies.

The basic subject, or thematic idea, of the *Four Quartets* is the poet's search, through mortal time, for eternal reality. In adapting his material to the sonata-allegro form Eliot arranges the subject into two contrasting but related themes—the main theme of eternity versus the countertheme of temporal mutability. In each of the quartets these themes are introduced, developed, and recapitulated in such a way that the poet's ideas, as he moves closer to his moment of ultimate reality, are expanded in an amplifying pattern from quartet to quartet. The two opposing themes are synthesized in the idea that the poet can perceive eternity only through his experiences in the temporal world.

The themes, in turn, are projected in terms of dominant images which either vary or are reiterated in expanded form from one quartet to the next. The main theme of eternity most often recurs as the still point in the garden in which the poet catches glimmerings of ultimate reality. The subdominant theme of temporal mutability manifests itself in a variety of forms: The joyful village dancers in "East Coker" whose end is death, the eternal confusion of human desires and neurotic preoccupations, the Heraclitan flux in mind and nature.

Although treatments of the two major themes run alternately all the way through the quartets, the specific subjects change from section to section. The moment in the garden, the recurring patterns of earthly and planetary motions, the poet's difficulties with words and music, deaths at sea, journeys by ship and rail—these passing subjects might be considered as subthemes or incidental themes which support the two main themes. Each subject is a frame enclosing the poet's images and ideas, and as such it forms a solid, recognizable base for the projection of thematic materials.

"Dry Salvages" provides an excellent illustration of how Eliot presents his two related but contrasted themes in the form of dominant images. The river, in symbolizing the mortal time which we feel within ourselves, represents the temporal mutability theme, while the sea around us represents the eternity theme in that it makes us aware of the vast time that stretches before and after us. The two themes are first presented consecutively, then they are developed together as contrasting modes, and finally the sea-theme of eternity asserts its dominance as a preserver and destroyer of mortal life and time.

The formal resemblance of the *Four Quartets* to a musical quartet, however, must not be exaggerated. In reality the exterior structure of the poem stands merely as a rough approximation of the form of Beethoven's quartets. Nor does Eliot's poem, as a literary adaptation of musical form, have a strict formal correspondence to any other quartets or symphonies.

First of all, the reading time for all four of Eliot's quartets is about the same as the playing time for a string quartet or classical symphony. The four poems of the *Quartets*, moreover, correspond to the four movements of a conventional quartet or symphony, except for the fact that the sonata-allegro form is repeated in all four movements of Eliot's poem. It might be preferable, therefore, to consider the entire work as *one quartet,* for all of the poems are united by interlocking patterns of dominant images which project the two themes of eternity and temporal mutability.

A single movement of a musical quartet constitutes a separate, autonomous composition with its own distinctive themes and style. Similarly, each of Eliot's quartets conforms generally to the principle of autonomy and stylistic distinctness. Furthermore, like a movement in a musical quartet, each of Eliot's poems contains a full exposition, development, and recapitulation of themes. For these reasons each of the four quartets should perhaps be treated as a *movement* within the quartets as a whole.

The five divisions within each of Eliot's quartets have been called "movements" by several commentators. Since none of these divisions is formally complete (as a musical movement should certainly be), they must be analyzed simply as segments or sections within the movement which represent progressive phases of thematic development.

A parallel mode of thematic treatment informs each of the quartets. As the comments on the jacket of Eliot's recording indicate, the first section of each quartet presents "two or more subjects which are to be interwoven and eventually resolved." The second section treats one of the subjects in "two contrasting ways, and the ideas are expanded and developed." In the third section we encounter further explorations of the ideas presented in the first two sections. The brief fourth section represents a "purely lyrical" development of one of the subjects, while the fifth "recapitulates the earlier themes and resolves the contradiction" propounded in the opening section.[7] In a word, in each quartet "themes and counter-themes are modulated and interwoven," and "all four poems employ a recapitulation or coda with the last four lines of 'Little Gidding' as a thematic coda of the whole poem. . . ."[8] This pattern of development might be typical for a *single movement within a musical quartet,* but not for an entire quartet.

Despite the fact that a different set of leading images dominates each of the poems, most of the important image patterns occur in two or more of the poems. The motto-image of the garden, representing the eternity theme, is found in all four poems; that of the sea appears predominantly in "Dry Salvages," although it receives light treatment in both "East Coker" and "Little Gidding." The subordinate image of water (rivers, pools, ponds, and rain, as distinguished from sea-water) appears in all of the poems except "East Coker," where it appears to be absorbed, as it were, by the dominant earth-image of that poem. The interweaving and overlapping of these and other images from poem to poem suggest a pattern of structural organization which departs radically from Beethoven's sonata-allegro form inasmuch as Beethoven selected different subjects and styles for each of the movements within his quartets and symphonies.

Because of the recurrence of dominant image patterns throughout the four poems, the true form of the *Four Quartets* in many respects resembles the format of Hector Berlioz's *Symphonie Fantastique,* which represents an elaboration on the traditional sonata-allegro form. In addition to the regular introduction, development, and recapitulation of themes, Berlioz introduces a *motto-theme* to unite all the movements of his symphony and, owing to the recurrence of this theme in each movement, the form is called *cyclical.*

Either by coincidence or by the author's intention, the structural organization of the *Four Quartets* bears at least as much resemblance to Berlioz's cyclical form as it does to the form of Beethoven's string quartets. For whatever reason, Eliot exploits the motto-theme device, for all of the poems are threaded together by means of motto-images. These images, in projecting the two themes of eternity and temporal mutability, create a highly integrated thematic texture.

But whether the external structure of the *Four Quartets* is more like the form of Beethoven's quartets or the cyclical organization of Berlioz's symphonies, the important thing to remember, according to Marcello Pagnini, is that Eliot's poetic dialect conforms to the dialect of musical discourse. Besides that part of the poetic discourse involving the interweaving of opposing themes, the quartets also allow for a dialect of opposing voices. Eliot varies his voices like instruments used in a musical quartet; and in "Burnt Norton," for example, one can distinguish two voices; the lyric and the didactic.[9] These voices, however, are variant manifestations of a single voice in different moods. Hence the quartets lack the complexity of *The Waste Land* with its multiplicity of dramatic voices. As B. H. Fussell remarks, the poem is a dialogue that reveals the profoundly subjective experiences of "a single consciousness in the act of thinking and feeling . . ."; it is an interior dialogue involving the fusion of opposing voices.[10]

The tension created by these oppositions in voice and theme is reinforced by tensions arising from the flow of meaning. Tense moments are often followed by sudden resolutions and resolutions dissolve into conflicts, with lyric smoothness alternating with the roughness of unresolved dilemmas. This flow of tensions and resolutions resembles the changing harmonic progressions in a musical composition in which dissonances resolve into harmonies.

Since the structural organization of the *Four Quartets* does not conform exactly to any recognized musical format, Eliot's poem must be judged ultimately by standards which are primarily literary. And regardless of Eliot's success in exploiting the musical idiom, the musical influences must be weighed carefully against the complexly varied influences deriving from literature, philosophy, and religion.

Chief among the literary influences are the medieval theological notions and concrete symbolic imagery of Dante. The rendering of such concise visual images as that of the fire and the rose with their multiple symbolic connotations is traceable to Dante's influence. Despite the final glimpse of paradise in "Little Gidding," the predominant coloring of Eliot's poem is purgatorial, and with Eliot as with Dante the image of fire often symbolizes spiritual purgation and divine suffering as well as the burning away of carnal desires. From the point of view of "overall structural framework," the quartets appear to be arranged according to "an ordered scale of emotions" such as one finds in the *Inferno*. This scale provides a scaffold for the progression of purgatorial effects in Eliot's poem.[11]

Reinforcing the emotional and religious scaffolding of the *Four Quartets* is Eliot's symbolic use of Heraclitus' four basic elements—air, earth, water, and fire. Each element represents the dominant symbolism for each of the quartets. "Burnt Norton" is dominated by the symbol of air, which signifies the breath of life, spiritual resuscitation, the destruction of earthly things; it is "the wind that sweeps the gloomy hills of London. . . ." "East Coker" is elemented by earth and is characterized by the earthly village dancers. In "Dry Salvages," dominated by water imagery, symbolic manifestations of river and sea are presented. The last of the poems, "Little Gidding," is symbolized by fire, progressing from the image of the sun flaming on ice to the "crowned knot of fire" at the poem's climactic ending.

The philosophy of Heraclitus also thickens the poem's thematic structure. In order to underscore the temporal mutability theme with firm philosophical concepts, Eliot borrows Heraclitus's notion that everything is in a state of eternal flux; that is, everything is in the process of becoming, nothing is complete, and nothing is permanent except change itself. But for this ceaseless change not to become chaos, "it must conform to fixed patterns under the control of a divine intelligence," which is the Logos or still point around which the wheel of flux turns;[12] it is the unmoving spiritual force which governs the endless Heraclitan movement. The wheel of flux, then, is a symbolic projection of the temporal mutability theme while the still point symbolizes the theme of eternity. Both themes are synthesized in the image of the wheel of flux turning around the still point.

Even the images of the poem seem to exist in a state of Heraclitan flux. The idea of eternal recurrence is echoed in the recurrence of leading symbols—the sea, the rose-garden, the fire. These occur in all or most of the poems, reflecting a world of changing appearances. In moving from quartet to quartet the reader is aware of a sort of shadowy dance of returning images of recurring thematic components that flit in and out of the poem's ideological structure illuminating the principal themes. This dance of leading images is governed or "timed" by a firm metrical structure which varies according to subject and mood yet consistently reflects the poets' changing voices.

The metrical structure of the *Four Quartets* reveals Eliot's musicological perception of poetic rhythm. In choosing the four-stress accentual line as his norm for the poem, Eliot settled on a type of metrical sequence which approximates the measured sequence of a melodic line in music: While the number of unaccented notes or syllables may vary within each beat, the accents tend to fall with some degree of regularity; metrical unity here derives from the preponderance of recurring rhythmical units within a given sequence. In music these rhythmical units might be duplets, triplets, quadruplets, or multiples thereof; in poetry they are iambs, trochees, anapests, and so on.

As the metrical norm for all of the quartets, the four-stress accentual line recurs frequently throughout the poem. In its more regular and strongly accented form this line usually gives firm support to the eternity theme as illustrated in the beginning lines of "Burnt Norton":

> Time present and time past
> Are both perhaps present in time future . . .

When its metrical structure is somewhat more dense and heavy, yet tending to be regular in the disposition of accents, the labored cadence reflects the struggles of the artist in expressing difficult ideas—

> Midwinter spring is its own season
> Sempiternal though sodden towards sundown,
> Suspended in time between pole and tropic.

The accentual tetrameter with its strong medial pause, according to Helen Gardner, provides Eliot with a flexible metrical base enabling him to shift at will into "the evenness of duple or the ripple of triple rhythm," depending on the desired effect.[13]

The flexibility of the accentual tetrameter is such that it permits the poet to develop his ideas through rhythmic expansion. Harvey Gross illustrates Eliot's exploitation of this device with the following notations:

time present	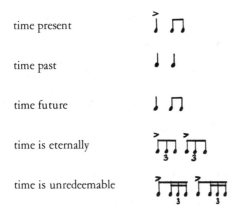
time past	
time future	
time is eternally	
time is unredeemable	

Here the rhythmic texture is thickened as the idea accumulates emotional power.[14] The rhythmic expansion device, incidentally, is often used by Beethoven in the opening sections of his quartets and symphonies.

Although Eliot's control of accentual sequences is assuredly refined and intensified by his musicological perceptions, the influence here is still primarily literary as it derives from such diverse sources as the Anglo-Saxon poets, Swinburne, and Ezra Pound. Eliot's use of conventional devices of versification, however, reflects influences that are more obviously literary in character.

Counterpointed against the accentual norm are sequences of rhymed and conventional syllabic verse, occurring principally in the second and fourth sections of each quartet. Here we find iambic tetrameters closely but irregularly rhymed; a sequence of rhymed accentual tetrameters (as a variant on the earlier syllabic tetrameters); a variation on the sestina form; a sequence containing internal rhymes; a succession of five stanzas in a fixed rhyme scheme; and so on. In each instance the regular meter and rhyme emphasize the lyric parts of the poem and are accompanied by imagery of unusual symbolic richness.

In the lines beginning "If you came this way in may time . . . ," Eliot uses a combination of rich Tennysonian assonance and internal rhyme to underscore the sensuous beauty and heavy voluptuousness of the scene. Such luxuriant effects, however, are sporadic and rare in the poem. As in Eliot's use of rhyme and traditional English metric, they serve chiefly to intensify the lyrical episodes of the poem in contrast to the discursive passages.

In opposition to the many highly rhythmical and imagistic passages in the quartets are several sustained passages which seem utterly lacking in rhythmical character. Indeed, if one subscribes to the principle of regularity in the succession of accents as well as to that of dominant and subordinate rhythmical figurations as being fundamental requirements of verse, then certain parts of the poem cannot be considered verse at all. A case in point might be the following lines from "The Dry Salvages":

I sometimes wonder if that is what Krishna meant
—Among other things—or one way of putting the
same thing . . .

Here one perceives the irregular rhythms and unsteady tempos of English prose discourse. There are no predominating rhythmical figurations, no subordinate variants, no regular beats—only a hodgepodge of heterogeneous rhythmical units.

Yet many of these prosaic passages serve a particular function. Like the Cockney scene in *The Waste Land* but lacking its racy, repetitive colloquial rhythms, these passages are pieces of prose collage introduced into what is primarily a verse medium. At their worst they seem like awkward and digressive interpolations. At their best, however, they heighten the realism of the poem and paradoxically expand the sphere of poetry by adding a nonpoetic dimension to the quartets. Within the stricter context of the poem itself they exist in dynamic opposition to the lyrical passages and seem appropriate to the discursive purposes of the poet.

At all events, the *Four Quartets* abundantly illustrate Eliot's skill in adapting a variety of formal devices, both musical and literary, to the changing flow of meaning. Although the earlier verse also reflects Eliot's adaptive skills, the modified sonata-allegro form of the quartets provides the poet with a more orderly mode of thematic development than do the forms of his earlier work. Hence, in comparison with "Gerontion" or *The Waste Land*, the progression of stylistic effects in the quartets is more regularized, with easier transitions and more sustained patterns of development.

The fruitfulness of the sonata-allegro form notwithstanding, Eliot was too much a master of eclectic synthesis to rely heavily on any one musical form, or even on a number of musical formats. By syncretically fusing several important musical and literary influences in the composition of his poem, he was able to produce something that seems to go beyond poetry—that is, a species of writing which expands the dimensions of poetry by exploiting nonpoetic devices.

As the last great masterpiece of T. S. Eliot, the *Four Quartets* crown the poet's lifelong struggles with artistic form. In addition, Eliot's masterpiece resolves a lifetime of spiritual conflict and wrestling with difficult metaphysical and philosophical ideas. As a literary work of art the poem predominantly reflects the efforts, not of a musician, but of a sensitive literary craftsman, albeit with refined musical tastes, who has succeeded in exploiting certain musicological and literary devices in an effort to articulate a new kind of poetry. Perhaps Eliot's last great performance is indeed "a poetry beyond poetry."

Notes

1.   Herbet Howarth, "Eliot, Beethoven, and J. W. N. Sullivan," *Comparative Literature* 9 (1957):322.

2.   Ibid., pp. 327–30.

3.   Harvey Gross, "Music and the Analogue of Feeling: Notes on Eliot and Beethoven," *The Centennial Review of Arts and Science* 3 (1959):282.

4.   Hugh Kenner, *The Invisible Poet: T. S. Eliot* (New York: Harcourt, Brace & World, 1959), p. 306.

5.   Dorothy E. Rambo, "An Analysis of *Four Quartets* by Eliot with Particular Respect to Its Prosody," (Ph.D. diss., Northwestern University, 1958), pp. 72–73.

6.   D. Bosley Brotman, "T. S. Eliot: 'The Music of Ideas,' " *University of Toronto Quarterly* 18: (1948):22.

7.   "Four Quartets," Angel 45012, Electric and Musical Industries (U.S.) Ltd. (phonograph recording).

8.   Gordon Kay Grigsby, "The Modern Long Poem: Studies in Thematic Form," (Ph.D. diss., University of Wisconsin, 1960), p. 422.

9.   Marcello Pagnini, "La Musicalità dei 'Four Quartets,' " *Belfagor* 13 (1958):435–36.

10.   B. H. Fussell, "Structural Methods in *Four Quartets,*" *Journal of English Literary History* 22 (1955):212–14.

11.   Rambo, pp. 34–35.

12.   Ibid., pp. 51–53.

13.   Helen Gardner, *The Art of T. S. Eliot* (London: The Cresset Press, 1949), p. 29.

14.   Gross, p. 276. [Editor's note: see p. 130 of Gross's article in this volume for his depiction of the same metrical patterns, noting that Rees's citations do not agree in all cases.]

Four

The Sonata Form in Short Fiction

Thomas Mann's Use of Musical Structure and Techniques in *Tonio Kröger*

H. A. Basilius

I

The relations of the individual arts to each other and to art in general became a serious object of interest and study in the western world around 1800
through the work of the romantic aestheticians, critics, and artists. With them
the primacy of art in the hierarchy of human achievements received its first em-
phatic assertion since classical antiquity. The implications of their point of view
left its mark on the development of aesthetic theory in the nineteenth century
and also exerted important influences on the artistic creations of the century. As
a matter of fact the evidence warrants the conclusion that, after approximately a
century of ripening, these "new" ideas of the romantics culminated in the artistic
theories and creations of the symbolists and have continued to enrich Western
literature ever since.

In the first half of the century "synaesthesia" became the watchword of
many romantic artists and critics. Beginning with the now famous concept of architecture as frozen music, first cited by Schelling in his Jena-Würzburg lectures
on the philosophy of art[1] and later broadcast all over Europe by Mme de Staël
and Lord Byron,[2] they developed and applied the related metaphorical concepts
of "word music," "tone painting," and "orchestral color." These concepts were
later extended by the symbolists and impressionists of the second half of the century to include "color orchestration" and "planes of sound."[3] The goal of the romantics was the union of the arts which would abolish the differences between
painting, poetry, and music—especially the latter two.

This type of thinking led to such well-known phenomena as the "liter-
arization" of painting and music throughout the nineteenth century. Conversely,
as regards literature, it was responsible for the vogue of the visual arts in the
writings of Tieck, E. T. A. Hoffmann, the pre-Raphaelites, and others. More extensive and deeply rooted, however, was the impact of music on literature. And
by this I do not mean merely the adoption of the musician and musical subjects
as literary motifs or themes.[4] Rather, the sensuous materials of word-art—that is,

Originally published by *Germanic Review* 19 (1944):284-308.

the tonal properties of sounds, syllables, words, and phrases—and the rhythmic properties of word-clusters came to be appreciated more and more as essentially musical phenomena. What more natural than that writers should therefore begin to think as "music thinks,"[5] and as a consequence we witness the spectacle of celebrated *litterateurs* adapting, for example, the fugue to literature as in the case of De Quincy[6] and James Joyce.[7]

Tieck's famous pun, which is today virtually a commonplace, expressed the new point of view perfectly, viz., why should mere content constitute the content of a poem?

The musicologist Láng puts it thus:

> They (Mendelssohn, Schumann, Chopin) proved that the soul of romanticism is music, that music, the art of pure sentiment, is the crowning of poetry, of lyricism. And romanticism appreciated the fact that music and lyricism are inseparable; with all its senses, with all its thoughts, poetry, experience, and faith, romanticism longed for music, it wanted to become music. This it hoped to achieve in the *Gesamtkunstwerk*.[8]

One might add that the whole history of *Lied* composition from Mendelssohn and Schubert to Hugo Wolf is corollary to this proposition: The "total meaning" of a poem is obfuscated by the conceptual meanings of the various words and phrases that make up the poem; hence, it is necessary to translate the entire complex of "meaning" into an accompanying musical idiom.[9]

What the romantics started, the symbolists finished, as Edmund Wilson has shown in *Axel's Castle*. "To approximate the indefiniteness of music was to become one of the principal aims of Symbolism," he says, after having quoted Edgar Allan Poe, the spiritual godfather of the symbolists, on the indefiniteness of the true music of poetry, and after having pointed out the tremendous impact of Richard Wagner's theory and music upon the symbolists.[10]

In Germany it remained for the spiritual godfathers of Thomas Mann, his triple constellation (*Dreigestirn*) of Schopenhauer, Wagner, and Nietzsche, to weld this preoccupation with music into a metaphysical and critical whole. Although Wagner failed in the attempt to create the *Gesamtkunstwerk,* he succeeded in making Schopenhauer's thesis that music was the immediate expression of the Will more plausible; in any case he created a music of the kind the romantics longed for, which the symbolists worshipped, and which will continue to outlive his critical theories. In the writings of Nietzsche music placed its indelible stamp upon the development of German prose—a fact, incidentally, which is completely missed by all who read him only in English translations. Nor should the musicality of the prose of Schopenhauer himself be neglected in this connection. The greatest potentialities of the romantic-symbolist complex of music, poetry for prose, seem to me, however, to have been reserved for realization in the writing of Thomas Mann.

Mann's preoccupation with music and his debt to it are common knowledge. His creative works abound in musical motifs and allusions, and in his critical works he has often and at length taken occasion to express himself on the various aspects of the subject.[11] One of his most pregnant and pointed statements is the following:

> Here [in *Tonio Kröger*] probably I first learned to employ music as a shap-
> ing influence in my art. The conception of epic prose-composition as a weaving
> of themes, as a musical complex of associations, I later on largely employed in
> *The Magic Mountain*. Only that there the verbal leitmotiv is no longer, as in
> *Buddenbrooks*, employed in the representation of form alone, but has taken on a
> less mechanical, more musical character, and endeavors to mirror the emotion
> and the idea.[12]

I shall have occasion to return later to significant parts of this passage.

But although Mann himself has so often discussed his relations to music and
musical techniques and structures, both European and American criticism have
failed to make much of it. The most obvious thing, Mann's delight in allusion
to musical personages and works, has, to be sure, often been noted.[13] Much has
also been written about Mann's "musical style" but practically all of this is quite
general and, with specific reference to music, metaphorical. The sole specific in
these discussions is the poet's use of the leitmotiv. One of the many cases in
point is the Englishman James Cleugh's account of the "symphonic" structure of
Buddenbrooks, of which a few excerpts will illustrate the point:

> With the accession of the young Thomas Buddenbrook to the headship of
> the firm the Wagnerian overture, containing the fundamental *motifs* of what is
> to follow, concludes. The development of the main theme of decadence now
> gathers force and complexity. [p. 81] . . . The second movement of the sym-
> phony is over [p. 83] . . . The resolution of the theme, the third movement of
> the symphony, ends in a fugal lament for the cruel war of destruction waged
> by life. [p. 86] . . . The *Leitmotif,* the device invented by the author of the Iliad
> and patented by Wagner, is a prominent feature of the style of Buddenbrooks.
> [p. 89][14]

In Germany the critical situation is little better. Marriott Morris has summarized the consensus of German criticism of Mann from 1900 to 1930 as follows:

> In the first period [first decade of twentieth century] there was much spec-
> ulation over, but little real understanding of Thomas Mann's style. We have
> noticed that in all three periods [first three decades of twentieth century] many
> of the same stylistic peculiarities were noticed, for instance the cold, abstract,
> intellectual manner as well as the psychological penetration, and the con-
> ciseness and pregnancy of expression [which several critics found comparable
> only to music]. Yet the *Leitmotif,* mistaken for lack of coherence in the first pe-
> riod and only accepted in the second on the authority of Wagner, was given
> little attention in the third; it had become identified to such an extent with
> Mann's personal style that it was no longer felt as a specific feature of it.[15]

Here, too, we note an absence of critical penetration beyond the fact that
Mann's style is "musical," whatever that might mean in addition to his employment of a kind of Wagnerian leitmotiv.

II

Oskar Walzel has recently recalled the fact that it was Friedrich Schiller who
in the modern period first wrote with discrimination concerning the musical

character of poetry.[16] He points out that it is obvious from Schiller's discussions that the musical character of poetry involves three considerations, namely (1) the purely tonal aspect of poetry; (2) music as the immediate, direct, and exclusive expression of emotion; and (3) the structure, i.e., the artistic ordering of the temporal succession in a musical structure.

European criticism doubtless had the first of these in mind when discussing Mann's leitmotiv, and the second was probably meant by "the pregnancy of expression" in his style. The leitmotiv has since received exhaustive scholarly treatment.[17] H. A. Peter's book, which I have cited several times, is to my knowledge the only systematic attempt to get an analysis of Mann's "pregnancy of expression" as it relates to the development of character. Ronald Peacock gives a critical summary of the literature on the leitmotiv and an exhaustive and enlightening analysis of the Mannian leitmotiv. He also attempts a solution of the question of the musical nature of Mann's art which seems to me, however, to be biased and deficient. I shall take occasion to discuss some aspects of his argument later in this paper.

The third aspect of the musical character of poetry, namely the artistic ordering of the temporal succession as in a musical structure, has gone almost unnoticed by critics. And this despite Mann's studied allusion to the fact that already in *Tonio Kröger* (1903) he had learned to use music as a formative element and that the musical structure of *Tonio* was later on repeated on a larger scale in *The Magic Mountain*.[18]

The American school edition of *Tonio* comes closest to the heart of the matter. It senses the tripartite structural pattern of the story, though it fails to see it clearly, and also notes the deliberate restatement of the leitmotivs in the final part. But even these observations fail to suggest a specifically musical form. Instead *Tonio* is described as a "triptych" in the following words:

> The story is an admirable specimen of narrative "economy." It is, like most
> of the creations of Heinrich Heine, whom Mann always admired, a perfect trip-
> tych. We have first the exposition, Tonio's youth, then, preceded by a lyric-
> philosophic intermezzo (conversation with Lisaweta), the crisis, the hero's un-
> happy visit to his old home—*à la recherche du temps perdu;* another transition,
> the storm, and finally the dénouement, his awakening in Denmark. The paral-
> lels between the last part and the first are many and striking.[19]

It has, however, been the merit of an American critic to sense the musical structure in another of Mann's short stories. Vernon Venable, in what is one of the finest pieces of critical writing in the entire Mann literature, experiences the *Death in Venice* as a *passacaglia* form—that is, "a ground bass repeating the same theme over and over again for progressive variations in the upper register, occasionally emerging into the treble itself, with the effect of affirming emphatically the singleness of the thematic material in both registers."[20] The death-motif is, of course, heard as the ground bass. Venable's fine insight into the art structure of this *Novelle* is without doubt due to the fact that, as he himself states, he approaches Mann as being an artist. Most critics come to the works of Mann and most other word-artists as to the products of social critics, philosophers, statesmen—in short, as the work of anyone but an artist. This single fact is probably responsible for the singular worthlessness of much literary criticism.[21]

III

Mann once ascribed to himself a quotation from a short story of Grillparzer: "... Was ich machte, meine Kunstarbeiten, urteilt darüber wie ihr wollt, aber *gute Partituren waren sie immer,* eine wie die andere." (*Betrachtungen eines Unpolitischen* [Berlin, 1929], p. 306. The italics are Mann's.) And it is precisely a good score which one "hears" in the reading of most of Mann's stories, as, for example, his favorite *Tonio Kröger.* The core of the novelle is the opposition of the two themes "I am artist," i.e., "I love my fiddle, my verses, and my Bohemian mother," and "I am bourgeois," i.e., "I love Lübeck, Hans Hansen and Inge Holm, and I respect my father's sense of propriety." After the thorough exploitation of these ideas, the opposition is resolved on the basis of that love without which men remain as sounding brass and tinkling cymbals even though they speak with the tongues of men and of angels. That is to say, an artist is great only in proportion to his capacity for loving his fellowmen and life. One "hears" the opposition and eventual resolution of these two themes presented in terms of a statement, followed by a digression, followed in turn by a restatement of the original statement. This tripartite sequence of statement-digression-restatement is the essence of most musical structure and, as Mann manipulates it, it assumes the character of the most highly developed of the ternary forms, that of the sonata-allegro with its sequence of exposition-development-recapitulation.

The fable of *Tonio* is readily ordered according to the conventionally accepted pattern of this form, as follows:

Introduction: Winter setting, dismissal of school.
I. Exposition.
Principal theme: (in the form of a three-part song which revolves about the literary motiv of Schiller's *Don Carlos*)
The happy-sad love of Tonio Kröger, who plays the violin and writes verses and is introspective, for Hans Hansen, the athletically inclined boy of action, the leader whom everyone likes.
A: Tonio, the exact opposite of Hans in every respect, loves Hans precisely because Hans is his counterpart. Hans reciprocates this love to a certain extent because he senses something "superior"[22] in Tonio.
Tonio's love is an unhappy one, however, because of his innate tendency to introspection, in this case the observation that "he who loves the more is the inferior and must suffer." Such introspection was to him equal in importance to his violin playing and verse making about Lübeck (though not specifically so stated, it is common knowledge that Tonio's home is the birthplace of Mann, namely Lübeck) and the sea, and far superior to the routine requirements of his teachers at school. His consequent low standing in class brought upon him the disapproval of his stern, ultra-respectable father, whom Tonio respected highly; but it remained a matter of complete indifference to his mother, whom Tonio could not respect because of her unconventional attitudes but whom he loved with passion.
All the complexities of the relationship between Tonio and Hans are summarized and illustrated in the episode of Schiller's *Don Carlos,* which Hans promises to read as a result of Tonio's urging. The

poignancy of the relationship receives final and perfect expression by allusion to the fact that "the king [in *Don Carlos*] has been crying because the marquis betrayed him."

B: Erwin Jimmerthal disrupts the happy rapprochement taking place between Hans and Tonio—and the king (Tonio) again weeps because the marquis (Hans) betrays him by calling him Kröger instead of the more intimate Tonio in the presence of a third person.

C: Hans reaffirms his desire and intent to read *Don Carlos* and he and Tonio part as the best of friends and with Tonio supremely happy.

The principal theme is concluded with the following perfect cadence:

"Damals lebte sein Herz; Sehnsucht war darin und schwermütiger Neid und ein klein wenig Verachtung und eine ganze keusche Seligkeit."

["His heart beat richly: longing was awake in it, and a gentle envy; a faint contempt, and no little innocent bliss."]

Subordinate theme: (which revolves about the literary motiv of Storm's
                                              Hyazinthen)

Tonio falls in love with Inge one evening at dancing school. [Episode: The conduct of the dancing school by the asinine François Knaak.] But Inge looks with appreciation and pleasure upon Knaak whereas she hardly notices Tonio, who disgraces himself in attempting to dance a quadrille. Magdalena Vermehren, who always falls down when dancing, is on the other hand attracted to Tonio because he writes verses. Tonio, however, loves only Inge and waits for her but she never comes to him.

The conclusion of the subordinate theme is a perfect cadence which parallels with variations the cadence concluding the principal theme.

1st Codetta:

Tonio's introspection with regard to the observation that happiness is not in being loved but in loving. (Return to the material of the principal theme.)

2nd Codetta:

Tonio's sad observation that being true to his love for Inge is as impossible as in the case of his love for Hans; for loyalty of any kind is humanly impossible. And so he shrugs his shoulders and departs.

3rd Codetta: (Transition to the Development)

Following a brief return to the principal theme for repetition of various thematic material, particularly that relating to his father and mother and Lübeck, we hear that Tonio goes the way he must go as artist. He leaves home and becomes a seeker after form, a very diligent virtuoso in the knowledge that "good work comes out only under pressure of a bad life."

II. Development (in sectional form):

The antiphony between Tonio Kröger and Lisaweta Iwanowna of the "lilting intonation." [The antiphonal mood is consistently sustained by virtue of the fact that the sections are a series of contrasts.] The antiphony begins with the observation by Lisaweta that Tonio has come to her *geladen,* that is "loaded" with problems which he has to "unload" by discussion.

Section One: (revolves about the literary figure of Adalbert and the café)
                              The contrast between art and nature, i.e., between the smell of paint and fixative within the studio and spring outside.

The motif of Adalbert the novelist who flees to the neutral terri-
tory of the café, that typical analogue of art, in the face of disturbing spring, and to whom, since he lacks love, "only the irri-
tations and icy ecstasies of the artist's corrupted nervous system
are artistic." But Tonio cannot flee because he is ashamed of his
"artfulness" in the face of the purity and naturalness, the con-
quering youthfulness of spring. He is ashamed of "the spring of
his art" that is its artificiality, particularly when "the innocent"
praise it.

Art is not a calling, a profession. It is a curse. The artist wears
the sign of Cain from early youth. If his heart is loving enough,
he suffers excruciating tortures from his fate.

Section Two: (revolves about the literary figure of the banker-novelist and
Wagner and his *Tristan*)

The contrast between the popular notion about artists and what
the latter actually are.

Human lethargy and convenience have never been more effective
than over and against the answer to the question: What is an
artist?

The "innocent," the people, believe the artist to be merely a personality with extraordinary talent for expression, and hence
something essentially good. Tonio, however, regards the artist as
a kind of sleight-of-hand charlatan, whom his forebears had already looked upon with distrust. To Tonio the talent of the artist is exactly comparable to that of the banker who while serving
a prison term for embezzlement finds an outlet for his thwarted
criminal instincts by writing short stories. That is, the creative
urge has something in common with the criminal impulse.

Tonio supports his contention by citing Richard Wagner's *Tristan und Isolde,* which to him is deeply ambiguous and morbid,
but which effects only elevation, strengthening and warm and
just inspiration in the "innocent."

Section Three: (revolves about the literary figure of Hamlet, so dear to the
symbolists)

The contrast between knowledge and life.

Lisaweta defends art, specifically literature, by citing its cathartic
effect on the emotions through knowledge [*Erkenntnis*]. Tonio
concedes this with particular reference to "the awe-inspiring,
holy Russian literature," but in contrast he mantains that artists
also suffer from a nauseating surfeit of knowledge [*Erkenntnise-
kel*], as exemplified by Hamlet. Literature, he says, is less a salvation or catharsis through the Word than it is a cooling and putting on ice of the emotions.

Literature—that is, art—never understands that life insists upon
continuing to live even after it has been "saved"—that is, sublimated in art. All activity, everything dynamic is, in the eyes of
the spirit, sin.

But Tonio confesses that he nevertheless loves life, as in the exposition he had confessed his love for Hans and Inge and
Lübeck. And so he finds himself overcome with longing for "the
bliss of the commonplace." But unfortunately he is able to win
as his friends only people with fine souls, but who are always fall-

ing down. Never can he win the blond and the blue-eyed. The latter should never be seduced by art – that is, poetry – for it spoils them as it made ludicrous the lieutenant who wrote verses.

Section Four: The contrast of art and nature, of life and knowledge in Tonio's soul is resolved by Lisaweta's observation that he is a bourgeois gone astray in art.

Lisaweta resolves the discussion in this way after Tonio has again identified himself and his problems with Hamlet and Hamlet's question. For all of which Tonio thanks her and departs, saying that he is "expressed" [*erledigt*] – that is, "unloaded."

Codetta: (retransition to the recapitulation)

Tonio decides to return to the north again after an absence of thirteen years. He does not wish to go to the south, to the cult of the *bellezza* (mother-motif), but only to the north (father-motif, sea-motif), to Denmark (Hamlet-motif). From Tonio's embarrassment, when questioned by Lisaweta, it is perfectly obvious that he is really returning to Lübeck, his home town.

III. Recapitulation.

   Principal theme: (in the form of a three-part song which as in the exposition revolves about a literary figure, only that now the literary figure is the successful artist Tonio)

Tonio's short but extraordinary visit home is portrayed entirely by variation of the thematic material of the exposition.

A: Tonio returns to Lübeck filled with the excitement of anticipation. He walks to the hotel, where he is received with the curiosity and suspicion usually accorded new guests. He orders supper served in his room, but his troubled spirits have stolen his appetite. Scarcely touching his supper, he goes to bed and to strange, longing dreams.

B: Next morning he fares forth into the town and, impelled by magnetic attraction as it were, to the market place, to the house where Inge had once lived, then to the old Hansen villa, and finally to the ancestral manse. But the old homestead had become a public library. He goes through it, perusing various books, among them his own, but finally leaves under the obvious suspicion of the librarian and returns to his hotel, prepared to depart from the city at once.

C: His departure is delayed by a policeman with a warrant for a fugitive from Munich with a curious name like that of Tonio Kröger and the suspicion that Tonio may be that fugitive. Tonio's only identification is a manuscript on which he has been working and this evidence of artistic attainment is sufficient grounds for his release; for, as stated in the development, the public regards artists as being "good" people. He goes down to the harbor and boards ship for Denmark.

"And such was the manner of Tonio Kröger's visit to his ancestral home" serves as a perfect cadence to close the principal theme.

Episode: Transition to the subordinate theme: The journey by boat and coach to Aalsgard. This lyric-comic passage contains a magnificent description of the sea and revolves about episodic material dealing with a merchant from Hamburg.[23]

The Hamburg merchant is reminiscent of the lieutenant in the development who writes verse, for Mann says of him: "Surely this man writes verse."
(S, p. 120)

Subordinate Theme: (combines the main and subordinate themes of the exposition, but the scene is at Kronborg and thus a connection is made with the Hamlet-motiv in the development)

The reappearance of Hans Hansen and Ingeborg Holm in the form of a brother and sister who "were Hans and Inge not so much by virtue of individual traits and similarity of costume as by similarity of race and type."

At a ball at Tonio's hotel an almost exact replica of the François Knaak episode of the exposition takes place. Again Tonio looks in from without upon beautiful Inge who "must dance" while he "would sleep." Inge scarcely sees him, but, just as formerly, the double of Magdalena Vermehren, the girl who always falls down when dancing, does. And this time, as she dances, she actually does fall and it is Tonio who goes to her rescue.

With a last look at Hans and Inge, Tonio goes to his room to reflect and to weep about the two souls within him, the one which loves life, simple and beautiful as are Hans and Inge, and the other which makes him an artist, that is a man with soul and intellect and beset by the creative urge.

The theme concludes with the following perfect cadence:

"Here in his room all was still and dark. But from below life's lulling, trivial waltz-rhythm came faintly to his ears."

Coda: In a letter to Lisaweta from away up north, thus complementing and completing the development as well as connecting with the exposition, Tonio decides "to state things in general terms (rather) than go on telling stories."

The entire problem which appears in the story is resolved into an explanation or reinterpretation of Lisaweta's remark that Tonio was a bourgeois gone astray in art. Returning to the principal theme of the exposition, Tonio reaffirms his love of life and argues that it is precisely this love of life and of men, like unto the love of First Corinthians, chapter thirteen, which makes him a genuine artist.

The movement and hence the whole piece concludes with a restatement of the beautiful perfect cadence which closed the principal theme of the exposition.

It must be obvious that the mere mechanical ordering of the incidents of a fable according to the ternary form, or the mere allusion to musical works, personages, or events, or the mere use of a repetitive linguistic formula are insufficient grounds for attributing "musical style" to a poet. We can allege such style for a literary artist only if his works possess the immediacy of emotional expression that is peculiar to the art of music over and against the other arts. I borrow a quotation from Ronald Peacock to illustrate the point. He quotes the following apt analogy from Georg Simmel's essay on Böcklin's landscapes:

In this—at least for the immediate emotion—complete cessation of all reference to all externals Böcklin's art approaches music. . . . Never probably except in music has mood so completely used up its substance. Wherever a feeling of graphic forms is present, these latter retain some sort of character, they still have a comprehensible existence and meaning beyond the mood which comes to us from out of them. Only for music has this independence of the material disappeared. In music it no longer expresses anything separable from itself, beside which it might have an (independent) existence, even if only as a remnant. Music has overcome this duality; it is no longer both the expresser and the expressed but it is completely and entirely only the expression, only sense, only mood. And as little as one may therefore, in the sense of the other arts, inquire after the truth of music, so little may one direct this inquiry to Böcklin's landscapes. For these springs and rocks, these groves and meadows, even these animals, fauns and people have no being, no reality other than as vehicles of a mood. They have become completely identified with the latter.[24]

Peacock concedes that parts of *Tonio Kröger* measure up to this criterion of musical expressiveness but denies that *Tonio* as a whole has the emotional intensity of a musical composition. If I understand him correctly, he holds generally that the arts are comparable to each other in only very general terms and that one wastes time in seeking musical analogies in literature. Some of Mann's leitmotivs, he maintains, do express the mood of the whole piece with the immediacy of music–for example, "Damals lebte sein Herz, etc." in *Tonio*,[25] but the literary artist is not able as such to sustain this immediacy and consequently his piece lacks the intensity of emotional expression which is so characteristic of music. Peacock points out further that the exact imitation of musical counterpoint, alleged by some for Mann's works, is impossible in literature inasmuch as musical counterpoint consists of the synchronous sounding of two contrasting "points" whereas in prose the sounding is sequential.[26]

In general Peacock's criticism is much too disparaging in regard to the musical analogies in Mann's work. He completely misses the fact, for example, that musical form encompasses not only the vertical principle (counterpoint) but also the horizontal (fugue), and that musical expressiveness may be achieved by the sequential contrasting of themes as well as by the vertical or contrapuntal. He has completely failed to sense the tremendous musical expressiveness of the form of *Tonio Kröger,* as is quite clear from his following statement:

> In the first place let it be noted that he who seeks musical analogies at all costs will perhaps experience a certain disappointment here (that is in the analysis of *Tonio Kröger*) when he compares this *Novelle* with *Tristan:* for the former lacks what is so conspicuously present in the latter–a "prelude." The story begins at once; not until the unfolding of the narrative is underway does Thomas Mann introduce his leitmotivs.[27]

One is led to conclude from this statement that a "prelude" is a sine qua non of musical form. I believe that Peacock has also overlooked several other important musical analogies in his otherwise fine analysis.

In *Tonio Kröger* I find at least four types of musical analogy which I should like to exemplify and discuss, namely: (1) the allusion to a work of musical art in such a way that the allusion is expressive of the same conative-affective complex as the musical work itself; (2) the conscious and consistent exploitation of the tonal and rhythmic properties of words and word-clusters for the expression of the feel-quality of an experience which the words already attempt to express conceptually; (3) the use of literary leitmotiv (a) to intensify by repetition the feel-quality of an experience, (b) to unify the individual parts of a composition, and (c) to relate the various parts into a single unified whole; and (4) the manipulation of all the above devices according to the principles of the ternary form—that is, according to a fugue pattern in which theme alternates with countertheme, is "developed," and is finally restated.

Undoubtedly irrelevant to the precise point under discussion but significant nevertheless as expression is Mann's frequently noted allusions to musical personages and works in both his critical and creative writing. Think, for example, of the title, fable, and "meaning" of *Tristan,* to mention but one obvious example among literally hundreds. Mention of Richard Wagner and *Tristan und Isolde* is also made in *Tonio* and other works. Indeed the lion's share of these musical allusions in Mann's works go to Richard Wagner.[28] In general, music comes off best when compared with the other arts. So, for example, when Tonio Kröger in his musings formulates his hierarchy of the arts he begins with Beethoven and then lets Schopenhauer and Michelangelo follow in order: "Even if I in my own person had written the nine symphonies and *The World as Will and Idea* and painted the Last Judgment, you would still be eternally right to laugh." (S, p. 130).

Such allusions contribute greatly to the feel of all Mann's work, if only by way of preparing one's mood for what is to come. When constantly immersed in things musical, the reader is indirectly but effectively prepared for the artistic expression in the peculiar way in which one receives musical expression.

These allusions do not, however, constitute a musical analogy. Poets have from the beginning of time made allusions to musicians and musical events and compositions but they have also made similar allusions to the spheres of architecture, literature, painting, sculpture, and other arts. In *Tonio,* for example, Mann makes pointed allusion to Schiller's *Don Carlos,* Storm's *Hyazinthen,* Shakespeare's *Hamlet,* Schopenhauer's *Die Welt als Wille und Vorstellung,* Michelangelo's *The Last Judgment,* and Wagner's *Tristan und Isolde,* and makes several other less direct allusions to the world of art and thought. Conversely, painters and sculptors and musicians make frequent allusion to works, personages, and events in the literary world. The purpose of such allusions is usually, if not always, to evoke either a train of thought or an emotional response in some way related to the subject of the allusion. Obviously when this happens, the painter, for example, does not become "literary" any more than the literary artist becomes "musical" or "graphic" or "pictorial." One would hardly maintain that Mendelssohn's style was "literary" because he composed *A Midsummer Night's Dream.* True, the knowledge that he composed to Shakespeare's play adds significance of a kind to his composition. This is, however, something extraneous to his music as music. In the same way Mann's allusions to musical personages and works in no wise change the fact that he is a word-artist, albeit one with a definite and great penchant for music.

But on the other hand, when the manner of presenting the musical allusion is such that it expresses the same conative-affective complex in words and word-rhythms as were expressed in a musical composition, then I believe that we may legitimately speak of a musical analogy. I have in mind, for example, the relation

of Hans Castorp's favorites among the phonograph recordings to his basic formative experiences (*Urerlebnisse*).[29] One of these recordings, it will be remembered,
is that of Schubert's *Der Lindenbaum,* the "haunting song of loyalty and death."
It is curious and revealing to note how Mann used this motiv many years prior
to the composition of the *Magic Mountain* in *Tonio Kröger,* in a much less obvious but no less effective manner. One of the most beautiful leitmotivs which
sings its way through Tonio is that of Lübeck. The first statement of the motiv
occurs in the opening pages, as follows:

> The fountain, the old walnut tree, his fiddle, and away in the distance the
> North Sea, within sound of whose summer murmurings he spent his holi-
> days—these were the things he loved, within these he enfolded his spirit,
> among these things his inner life took its course. And they were all things
> whose names were effective in verse and occurred pretty frequently in the lines
> Tonio Kröger sometimes wrote. (S, p. 87)

Whether one is conscious of it or not, the image of the fountain and the
walnut tree in combination attune one's mood to Schubert's music and one's
subconscious echoes the words and melody "Am Brunnen vor dem Tore, da
steht ein Lindenbaum." And as the fountain–walnut tree motiv is repeated and
varied throughout the story, Schubert's "haunting song of loyalty and death" is
vicariously expressed over and over again, although no specific mention of the
song has been made. It becomes indeed expressive of "a fruit, sound and splendid enough for the instant or so, yet extraordinarily prone to decay; the purest
refreshment of the spirit, if enjoyed at the right moment, but the next, capable
of spreading decay and corruption among men. It was the fruit of life, conceived
of death, pregnant of dissolution." (*Magic Mountain,* transl. by Lowe-Porter, p.
821) The imagery and rhythm of the motiv is expressive of the conative-affective
complex of loyalty and death in the same immediate way that the music-words
are expressive of it in the song.

More obviously musical and the obvious continuation of the tradition of the
romantics and symbolists is Mann's conscious exploitation of the tonal and
rhythmic properties of words and word groups. The Ingeborg Holm motiv
which introduces the subordinate theme of the exposition is reminiscent and illustrative of Edgar Allan Poe's aesthetic theorizing with respect to "The Raven"
and the entire "Lenore" vogue which began with Bürger's ballad of that name.

> Die blonde Inge, Ingeborg Holm, Doktor Holms Tochter, der am Markte
> wohnte, dort, wo hoch, spitzig und vielfach der gotische Brunnen stand, sie
> war's, die Tonio Kröger liebte, als er sechzehn Jahre alt war.[30]

The sonorous resonance of the *o*-vowels coupled with liquids and nasals, the
contrasting *a*-vowels at the end of the figure, the threefold identification of Inge
based on sonorous *o*'s which climaxes in the assonant juxtaposition *Doktor: Toch-
ter,* the staccato allegro rhythm, which gradually develops into a more sedate ral-
lantando—these are the media through which Mann introduces the feel-quality of
nostalgia in connection with the Inge episode which will be fully developed and
related to the entire composition by means of the repetitive leitmotiv. The fact
that Tonio fell in love with a girl by the name of Ingeborg Holm when he was
sixteen years old is not the essential thing here. What is important is the feel-

quality of the experience, and this is expressed entirely by the tonal and rhythmic properties of the words which then attain their full effect through repetition. This is, of course, the significance of those later passages (once in the codetta concluding the development and again at the end of the subordinate theme in the recapitulation) in which the author makes specific allusion to the feel-quality (for him) of names like Ingeborg:

> Nehmen Sie auch nur die Namen, die Vornamen, mit denen die Leute dort oben geschmückt sind und von denen es ebenfalls schon viele bei mir zu Hause gibt, einen Laut wie "Ingeborg," ein Harfenschlag makellosester Poesie. (N, p. 48)
> Er flüsterte zwei Namen in das Kissen hinein, diese paar keuschen, nordischen Silben, die ihm seine eigentliche und ursprüngliche Liebes-, Leides- und Glücksart, das Leben, das simple und innige Gefühl, die Heimat bezeichneten. (N, p. 85)

The well-known motiv beginning "Damals lebte sein Herz," which serves as a perfect cadence for the principal theme of the exposition as well as for the entire composition, shows similar characteristics. Its first statement is the following: "Damals lebte sein Herz; Sehnsucht war darin und schwermütiger Neid und ein klein wenig Verachtung und eine ganze keusche Seligkeit." (N, p. 16; S, p. 92)

We observe here the bright quality of the *e*-vowels and the jumpy character of the trochaic-dactylic rhythm, later contrasted with the soft dragging effect of the accumulated sibilants which in turn culminate crescendo in the phrase "ganze keusche Seligkeit." Note also the expressive effect of the chiasm *Sehnsucht-Neid: Verachtung-Seligkeit* which is bound together by the alliterating *s*'s of the first and last members.

This motiv occurs four times (N, pp. 16, 24, 85, 88, with a casual but incomplete fifth allusion, p. 83, and an "inverted" allusion, p. 27; *Stories*, pp. 92, 97, 131, 132, 131, 99 respectively), twice in full and twice in only partial statement and is iconically expressive of the feel-quality of that dualism of art-bourgeoisie, spirit-life in Tonio Kröger which it is the purpose of the whole composition to express. The function of the motiv as perfect cadence for both principal theme and for the whole gives it a prominence which adds to its expressiveness.[31]

As a third illustration I should like to cite one of the loveliest instances of tonal and rhythmic onomatopoeia in the entire story, namely the perfect cadence which concludes the recapitulation: "Aber von unten tönte gedämpft und wiegend des Lebens süsser, trivialer Dreitakt zu ihm herauf." (N, p. 86; S, p. 131)

I am thinking particularly of the lilting, liquid quality of the phrase "des Lebens süsser, trivialer Dreitakt" which is effected by the predominating high-front vowels interspersed with two *a*-sounds, the undulating rhythm and ascending stress of the sequence of iambs, anapests, and amphibrachs [u-|u-u|uu-|u-u], and the alliterated sequence of alveolars (*d, t*) contrasting with the liquids.

The most obvious musical analogy in Mann's works is, to be sure, the oft-noted use of the literary leitmotiv, all or most of which are, incidentally, characterized by tonal and rhythmic properties of the type which I have just illustrated and discussed. The atechtonic leitmotiv[32] was already quite noticeable in *Budden-brooks* and the earlier *Novellen* of Mann and is present in quantity in *Tonio Kröger*. Various critics such as Jethro Bithell have, however, taken exception to "the wearisome repetition of facial and personal peculiarities and tricks of diction and gesture"[33] in *Buddenbrooks,* and Mann himself has discussed the difference in application of the technique in *Tonio Kröger* as compared with *Buddenbrooks*.[34]

A single example will perhaps illustrate the difference. Mann's ability to create names which are iconically expressive of the characters to which they are attached is apparent in *Buddenbrooks*. The reader is not likely to forget Bendix Grünlich, Alois Permaneder, the Kistenmakers, Pfiffi and Gerda Buddenbrook, to mention only a few. By contrast, however, the names of Tonio Kröger, Hans Hansen, and Ingeborg Holm are of the web and woof of *Tonio Kröger*. The latter two sing of the healthy humanity of the North historically, tonally, and rhythmically whereas Tonio's dual personality, the artist and the bourgeois, are iconically expressed by his hybrid name, half romanic, half nordic. The poet does not state this to be the case explicitly until the unfolding of the story is well underway. But the feel-quality of the distinctions is present in the opening pages and becomes cumulative. Hans tells his schoolmates that he has promised to take a walk with Kröger; when the two are alone, he calls the latter Tonio. The reader then learns of the contrasting characters of the two boys and the polar attraction between the opposites, but he "hears" it more than he reads it through the poet's manipulation of the names. The matter culminates in the Jimmerthal[35] episode in which the poet has Hans become explicit regarding his failure to call Tonio by his given name. Actually, of course, Hans calls Tonio by his family name before the other boys because he is secretly ashamed of his attraction for the "abnormal" Tonio. He explains his action to himself and to Tonio, however, on the grounds that Tonio's name is such a "crazy" one. In short, Mann introduces this name material as a musician uses a musical figure. It is stated and restated in various combinations until it finally receives full and adequate development. The important thing from the point of view of expression is, however, that the manipulation of the name material "tells the story" as much as the narrative of events and the exposition of the significance of the names. And the poet often sustains the feel-quality of a name developed in this manner throughout an entire story or novel. Note, for example, the magnificent effect he gets with the restatement of the full name Tonio Kröger in the development where it is used "contrapuntally" with Lisaweta Iwanowna for the expression of the feel of the north-south and the east-west axes which constitute so important a part of Mann's problematics and hence also of Tonio Kröger's.

In precisely the same manner the author uses the Ingeborg Holm. We "hear" the entire character of Inge and Tonio's relation to her in the opening paragraph of the subordinate theme which I quoted and discussed above. We also saw how the author eventually made the significance of the name explicit as he had done in the case of Tonio's name.

In the light of the above the significance of the François Knaak material in both exposition and recapitulation—Knaak as counterpart and foil to Tonio—is likewise completely contained and perfectly "heard" in the name François Knaak ("*Mon nom est Knaak.*").

Several other atechtonic leitmotivs and leitmotiv-symbols, not usually noted in the commentaries on *Tonio* but equally striking in their musical effect, might be pointed out here.

Of the former perhaps the best known is the delightful alliterated "Wonnen der Gewöhnlichkeit" (N, pp. 43, 87), the musical effect of which is lost in the translation "bliss of the commonplace" (*Stories*, pp. 108, 132). Another is "Pointe und Wirkung" (N, pp. 32, 33, 57, 61), which likewise loses some of its effect in the translation (*Stories*, p. 102 twice, and p. 118: "effect"; but p. 116, "certain climax and effect"). Still another is "Er pflegte es zu sagen (und hatte es auch bereits schon aufgeschrieben.)" (N, pp. 25, 27; *Stories*, pp. 98, 99) with its ironical parentheses. The student of Mann will also not miss the delicious effect of the locution "Bewandtnis haben" (N, pp. 26, 41) which was a favorite of E. T. A. Hoffmann from whom Mann may have learned its expressiveness inasmuch as Hoffmann is one of his favorite writers. In his autobiographical sketch Mann himself has called attention to the fact that the word "Beziehung" ("relation"), a synonym for "Bewandtnis," has always had an impressive ring for him.[36] The reason for this will be obvious to anyone acquainted with Mann's attitude toward life on the basis of his writings.

Of leitmotiv symbols the use of the color "black" in the recapitulation is striking, for example the black cabs (N, p. 49), the black lions (pp. 50, 53, 62), the majordomo in black (pp. 51, 53, 58 twice), the black sea (p. 69), the black eyes (p. 82). Further, the well-known frustration motivs of the "Jalousie" (N, pp. 22, 24; S, "blind," pp. 96 and 97), the "grünen Fensterläden" (N, p. 69; S, "green blinds," p. 122) and the "Glastür" (N, pp. 58, 72, 73, 77; S, pp. 116, 124 twice, 126). The mythological statues (N, p. 49; S, p. 111), the two lions (N, pp. 50, 53, 62; S, pp. 112, 113, 118), and the two lamps (N, p. 77; S, p. 126) appear to be still another concatenation of symbols expressive of frustration and suggest a connection with the "candles on the mantle-shelf" (N, p. 19; S, p. 94).

More subtly musical is the use of the techtonic leitmotiv. The culmination of the story and the resolution of the problem by Tonio's identification of his love for the bliss of the commonplace with the love (charity) of the thirteenth chapter of Paul's first letter to the Corinthians is the logically and artistically perfect crowning of a carefully prepared structure. The love[37] theme is stated in the opening pages and repeated periodically throughout the story. As a matter of fact the theme of the story might be summarized thus:

> Although I, Tonio Kröger, am an artist, that is an objectifier of life and not a liver of life, I nevertheless love life. I deny, however, that because I love life, I am a bourgeois gone astray in art rather than a legitimate artist. Indeed, I maintain the very contrary: No man can be a true artist unless he hath this love.

The following quotations will illustrate the frequency of restatement of this basic theme: "Tonio loved Hans Hansen" (S, p. 86). "He who loves the more ... must suffer" (p. 86). "The fountain, the old walnut tree, his fiddle, and away in the distance the North Sea ... these were the things he loved" (p. 87). "Tonio loved his dark, fiery mother" (p. 88). "Tonio's love for Hans Hansen. He loved him. . . ." (p. 88). "Hans Hansen should love him; and he wooed Hans Hansen. . . ." (p. 89). "The marquis did it only out of love for the prince" (p.

89). "Everybody loved him (Hans) as he was, and Tonio most of all" (p. 92). "Ingeborg Holm ... she it was Tonio Kröger loved" (p. 92). "Happiness is in loving" (p. 97). "I love life" (p. 107 twice). "My love of life" (p. 131). "My bourgeois love of the human, the living, the usual" (p. 132). "Do not chide this love, Lisaweta; it is good and fruitful" (p. 132).

To cite another example of the techtonic leitmotiv, most of the effect of which is unfortunately lost in the translation, I call attention to the thought-and word-complex *geladen: erledigt* about which the entire development revolves. Near the beginning of the section Lisaweta tells Tonio: "Denn das sehe ich genau, dass Sie heute *geladen* sind." (Italics my own both here and in the following quotations.) (S, p. 102: "For I can see perfectly well that you are *too full for utterance*").[38] A few lines on Tonio denies that he is "geladen" but with magnificent irony concludes the section with the remark that he is "erledigt," that is to say that his conversation with Lisaweta affords him the way out of his difficulty which is typical for the *Literat,* namely expression: "Ich danke Ihnen, Lisaweta Iwanowna; nun kann ich getrost nach Hause gehen. Ich bin *erledigt*" (N, p. 46). "Thank you, Lisaweta Iwanowna; now I can go home in peace. *I* am *expressed.*" (S, p. 110; Morgan translates with "finished," p. 218).

Between these two (or rather three) points in the section a conscious play on the contrast *geladen: erledigt* occurs four times more as a climax to the entire section in the paragraph beginning "Eine andere aber nicht minder liebenswürdige Seite der Sache. . . ." (N, p. 41). ["Then another and no less charming side of the thing. . . ." S, p. 107.], as follows:

> Im Ernst, es hat eine eisige und empörend anmassliche Bewandtnis mit dieser prompten und oberflächlichen *Erledigung* des Gefühls durch die literarische Sprache. ["Honestly, don't you think there's a good deal of cool cheek in the prompt and superficial way a writer can *get rid of* his feelings by turning them into literature?" (Morgan translates with "dispatching of emotions"; p. 214)].
>
> Er wird Ihnen Ihre Angelegenheit analysieren und formulieren, bei Namen nennen, aussprechen und zum Reden bringen, wird Ihnen das Ganze für alle Zeit *erledigen.* ["He will analyze and formulate your affair, label it and express it and discuss it and *polish it off.* . . . (Morgan translates with "relieve," p. 214.)]
>
> Was ausgesprochen ist, so lautet sein Glaubensbekenntnis, ist *erledigt.* ["What is uttered, so runs his *credo,* is *finished and done with.*" (Morgan translates with "settled," p. 214.)]
>
> Ist die ganze Welt ausgesprochen, so ist sie *erledigt,* erlöst, abgetan. ["If the whole world could be expressed, it would be saved, *finished* and done." (Note Lowe-Porter's change in the order of the adjectives. Morgan translates with "settled," p. 214.)]

To recapitulate, the developmental section is built up around the word-complex *geladen: erledigt.* These words (and their derivatives) occur in all seven times in the following sequence: "geladen, geladen, Erledigung, erledigen, erledigt, erledigt, erledigt." The sequence in the Lowe-Porter translation is: "too full for utterance, too full for utterance, get rid of, polish off, finished and done with, finished, expressed." The sequence of the Morgan translation is: "loaded, loaded, dispatching of emotions, relieve, settled, settled, finished." The German words are obviously related etymologically to each other. The imagery which they suggest is that of loading and unloading, which is particularly apt with reference to the disparaging picture of the literary artist which Mann has been at pains to develop. This deliberate and exceedingly expressive play on words, which is perhaps necessarily lost in any translation, gives a structural unity to the development and relates this section to the rest of the story in the same way that a composer establishes structural relationships. Any doubt about this is dispelled when one recalls from Mann's critical writing the doubly ironical statement: "Im Grunde hasse ich die erledigende Wirkung des kritischen Wortes." ["Basically I hate the cathartic effect of the critical word."] In short, the word-play *geladen: erledigt,* particularly when used as in this section of the story, has the immediacy of musical expression.

In concluding the discussion of techtonic leitmotivs, I should like to cite a complex of motivs which illustrates how difficult it is to make absolute distinctions between various types and kinds of leitmotivs. I have in mind the following four statements:

Tonio "ging seiner Wege." (N, p. 25; S, p. 98)
"Er ging den Weg, den er gehen musste." (N, p. 25; S, p. 98)
"Und Tonio fuhr gen Norden." (N, p. 48; S, p. 111)
"Tonio Kröger sass im Norden." (N, p. 86; S, p. 131)

The expressiveness of the complex lies partly in the feeling of ceaseless, weary, but inevitable pilgrimage resulting from the repetitions "seiner Wege gehen," "den Weg gehen, den er gehen musste" and "gen Norden fahren." These locutions have an almost biblical aroma and the repetitive element common to them is so complete an expression of Tonio's hopeless but never-ending quest for the "Wonnen der Gewöhnlichkeit." At the same time the complex serves a techtonic function which is equally expressive: The first two uses of the motiv serve to conclude the exposition and to make the transition to the development; the third, in turn, which begins the recapitulation, serves to connect this with both development and exposition and by that very function expresses the ironical fact that the way which it was necessary for Tonio to travel upon leaving his home is simply the road back home. The fourth use introduces the concluding coda whose function is the summation of the whole story-complex. Tonio Kröger now "sat up in the north" whence he had come and whither he returned and was about to write a letter to his eastern friend, before whom he had discoursed about his life-problem—a letter in which he would explain that he had finally succeeded in resolving the dualism which had beset him. He had resolved it in the north and on the basis of that very love of northern bliss of the commonplace which had been the more disturbing of the original antitheses.

It is variation rather than mechanical repetition that makes this motiv-complex. Note for example the effective contrast of *ging: fuhr: sass.* Note also the contrasting effect of *gen Norden* and *im Norden* with the first two statements which imply the peregrination away from the north and home. There is neither a mechanically repetitive linguistic formula nor a mechanically repeated symbol-image here, but rather a brief series of variations of both the linguistic pattern and the basic image. There can be no doubt, however, that the four statements constitute a leitmotiv-complex and that they function techtonically.

In my earlier analysis of the fable of *Tonio Kröger* I have shown how iconically expressive allusions and motivs are bound into a higher unity by the use of the ternary form. At the risk of stating the obvious, I should perhaps make explicit the fact that Mann has not arbitrarily and mechanically adapted a musical form here, but that his structure is based upon the inner necessity of a sequence of epic-lyric/dramatic-dialectic/epic-lyric sections. This sequence grew inevitably from the quality of the experience which he sought to express, namely the dialectic of feeling and thought. The character of each of the sections in turn is determined by and expressed through its respective style. The extraordinary popularity of *Tonio* not only with the reading public but also with its creator is doubtless due in no small measure to the powerful expression of the feel-quality of that awe-full experience of the Hamlet-question which all sensitive men and women undergo from time to time. It is doubtful whether any art other than the musical or musico-literary were capable of expressing the quality of that experience, which is not so much the reconciling of antitheses as it is the finding and maintaining of an equilibrium in a polar dualism. What means other than art could possibly express the feeling of the dynamic tension of this dualism? What art other than music or the musicoliterary possesses a technique for sustaining this feeling of tension which is comparable to the theme-countertheme technique and form which is peculiar to music?

IV

The foregoing analysis of Tonio Kröger as exemplifying the sonata-allegro form demonstrates that when Mann referred to (his) art as being "fugue and point-counterpoint," he was not using these and similar terms in the vaguely general and metaphorical sense in which his critics have used them. Scattered throughout his critical and journalistic writings are continuous hints that he has consciously sought to adapt the techniques of music to literature. However, even when he specifically says this, the statement remains quite broad; for example:

> Perhaps more than chance willed it that it was a musician and connoisseur
> of music (namely Oskar Bie) who performed this decisive function in my life
> (namely accepted *Der kleine Herr Friedemann* for publication in *Die Neue
> Deutsche Rundschau*), bringing to light a writer whose work was from the first
> marked by a deep inward affinity to the art and a tendency to apply its tech-
> nique in his own field.[39]

It is typical of Mann to wait until 1930 to say of *Tonio Kröger,* published in 1903, that he had here "first learned to employ music as a shaping influence" in his art, and that he conceived of epic prose-composition in general "as a weaving of themes, as a musical complex of associations" which he employed later on and on a larger scale in *The Magic Mountain.* (See quote above, page 155.) But it is not till 1941 in a personal interview that he states publicly for the first time that *The Magic Mountain* "is like a symphony" to him.[40] I have little doubt that it is a matter of simple analysis to demonstrate the symphonic structure of *The Magic Mountain* in technical terms, or for that matter to show the *Joseph*-tetralogy to be a symphonic poem. And unless one reads or rather "hears" them in that way, one misses much of their artistic message.

In thus successfully adapting the techniques and forms of music to word-art Mann achieves the romantic and symbolist ideal of "word-music." That the extent of such adaption from one sister-art to the other is necessarily limited goes almost without saying. As previously pointed out, for example, literary counterpoint is sometimes only an approximation of musical counterpoint. Similarly, there can be no exact equivalents of tonality or even modality in literature. If in *Tonio Kröger,* for example, one designated the principal theme, Tonio's happy love for Hans, as being in the major mode by contrast with the minor mode of the subordinate theme, Tonio's unhappy love for Inge, the observation would be entirely metaphorical though pertinent and enlightening.

The so-called Cult of Unintelligibility showed rather conclusively that literary art can only approximate music; it can never become music completely. As indicated above, music as music is distinguishable from the other arts by its immediacy of emotional expression. But in the literary art words and word-clusters can never be completely divested of their common connotations; they continue to express something beyond that which their sounds and rhythms alone express. The poetry of Gertrude Stein and the prose of James Joyce are well-known illustrations of the point.

When a word-artist such as Thomas Mann succeeds, however, in adapting musical techniques and forms to literature, he creates a kind of literary program music, or rather a musical program literature, in which the materials of his art—namely words—by virtue of their dual conceptual and iconic function constitute both the program and the music. This type of "word-music" which romantics and symbolists strove to attain lies midway betwen traditional prose and lyric and the "absolute" word-music of Stein and Joyce and probably represents the highest possible degree of fusion of the two arts of music and literature which a consensus will support. For Richard Wagner, who approached the problem in reverse by attempting to fuse literature with music, failed to gain an approving consensus for his *Gesamtkunst.*

Notes

1.   Oskar Walzel, "Wechselseitige Erhellung der Künste," *Philosophische Vorträge,* no. 15 (Berlin: Reuther & Richard, 1917), p. 6.

2.   Erika von Erhardt-Siebold, "Harmony of the Senses in English, German, and French Romanticism," *Publications of the Modern Language Association of America* 47 (1932):577–92.

3.   For an excellent summary of the history of the concept of synaesthesia see ibid. See also W. D. Allen, *Philosophies of Music History* (New York: American Book Co., 1939), p. 143.

4.   See in this connection Fr. von der Leyen, *Deutsche Dichtung in neuer Zeit* (Jena: E. Diederichs, 1927), pp. 309–10 (section "Verirrte Musik"), which disapproves of the *Musikalisierung* of literature, although it is never quite clear whether the author understands by this the adaptation of musical techniques to literature or merely the treatment of musicalia.

5.   Alfred Döblin, "The Use of Music in Literature," *This Quarter,* 3 (1930–31):248–51.

6.   C. S. Brown, Jr., "The Musical Structure of De Quincy's Dream-Fugue," *Musical Quarterly* 24 (1938):341–50.

7.   S. Gilbert, *James Joyce's Ulysses* (New York: Alfred A. Knopf, 1934), p. 29.

8.   Paul H. Láng, *Music in Western Civilization* (New York: W. W. Norton & Co., 1941), pp. 1011f.

9.   Ibid., p. 825.

10.   Edmund Wilson, *Axel's Castle* (New York: Charles Scribner's Sons, 1943), p. 13 and elsewhere.

11.   For summaries and references see, among others, Hans Armin Peter, *Thomas Mann und seine epische Charakterisierungskunst* (Bern: Paul Haupt, 1929); Ronald Peacock, *Das Leitmotiv bei Thomas Mann* (Bern: Paul Haupt, 1934); E. M. Martine, "The Phenomena of Sound in the Writings of Thomas Mann" (Ph.D. diss., Stanford University, 1936); and J. G. Brennan, *Thomas Mann's World* (New York: Russell & Russell, 1942).

12.   See Thomas Mann, *Stories of Three Decades,* trans. H. T. Lowe-Porter (New York: Alfred A. Knopf, 1938), p. vi. This is only an approximate translation of the original statement contained in Mann's "Lebensabriss," published in *Die Neue Rundschau* 41 (1930):746.

13.   See, for example, Martine. See also P. Bülow, "Musik und Musiker in der neueren deutschen Literatur," *Zeitschrift für Deutschkunde* 46 (1932):736–44.

14.   James Cleugh, *Thomas Mann: A Study* (New York: Russell & Russell, 1968), pages as indicated. See the German works of A. Eloesser and M. Havenstein on Thomas Mann for the same vague kind of allusion to musical characteristics.

15.   Marriott C. Morris, "A History of Thomas Mann Criticism in Germany, 1900–1930" (Ph.D. diss., University of Wisconsin, 1939), pp. 149–50. See also pp. 2, 44, 50, 104, 107, 113 for more detailed discussion of the same points.

16.   Oskar Walzel, *Gehalt und Gestalt im Kunstwerk des Dichters,* Handbuch der Literaturwissenschaft (Berlin: Akademische Verlagsgessellschaft Athenalon, 1923), pp. 347f.

17.   Walzel, Ibid., pp. 358–64. See also Walzel, *Das Wortkunstwerk* (Leipzig: Quelle & Meyer, 1926), pp. 152–81; Peter, pp. 197–212; Peacock.

18.   See above excerpt from p. vi of Mann, *Stories of Three Decades* (note 12).

19.   J. A. Kelly, ed., *Tonio Kröger,* by Thomas Mann (New York: Crofts, 1932), Introduction, pp. xiii–xiv.

20.   Vernon Venable, "Poetic Reason in Thomas Mann," *Virginia Quarterly Review* 14 (1938):65.

21.   See in this connection the critical review of American criticism of Mann by E. Ordon, "Thomas Mann's Joseph-cycle and the American Critic," *Monatshefte für Deutschen Unterricht* 35 (1943):286–96, 318–30.

22.   The text of Tonio Kröger which I quote is that of Thomas Mann, *Stories of Three Decades.* The German text is that of Thomas Mann, *Gesammelte Werke,* Vol. 2, *Novellen* (Oldenburg: S. Fischer Verlag, 1960).

23.   It has been conjectured that Heinrich Heine may have suggested this episodic material. See Kelly, p. 86.

24.   Quoted in Peacock, pp. 43–44. The translation is my own.

25.   See note 31 for reference.

26.   This same point has been made previously by Brown. It should be noted here, however, that precisely such synchronous literary counterpoint has been attempted in modern lyric poetry and drama—for example, O'Neil's *Strange Interlude.*

27.   Peacock, p. 31. The translation is mine.

28.   Martine, p. 22, has counted 124 allusions to Wagner and his works, which is more than to all other composers combined.

29.   Hermann John Weigand, *Thomas Mann's Novel "Der Zauberberg"* (New York: D. Appleton-Century Co., 1933), p. 166 (Notes, pt. III, no. 6).

30.   See Mann, *Novellen,* p. 16; and Mann, *Stories of Three Decades,* p. 92. It is obviously essential to quote the original here; for full duplication of tonal and rhythmic properties is necessarily limited, if possible at all, in a translation.

31.   For a more detailed analysis of the expressiveness of this motiv, see Peacock, pp. 38ff.

32.   See the references in notes 17 and 18 above for the literature on the literary leitmotiv. Walzel defines the literary leitmotiv as a purely formal means for adding something to the ordinary meanings of words and distinguishes between leitmotivs which help to determine the structural whole of a composition (techtonic) and those which have nothing to do with structure (atechtonic). He admits that where the formal-linguistic pattern is lacking, it is difficult to determine whether or not one is dealing with a leitmotiv. Peacock, on the other hand, who incidentally professes to deal only with the leitmotiv as used by Thomas Mann rather than with the subject in general, distinguishes between recurring linguistic formulae which express emotional content and serve as vehicles for the mood of the whole and as unifying structural elements (genuine leitmotivs) and mere repetition of linguistic formulae (alleged leitmotivs by popular usage). Where the strict linguistic formula is lacking, Peacock recognizes the "leitmotiv symbol" (*leitmotivisches Symbol*) but again distinguishes between those which have genuine symbolic value—that is, express emotional content—and those which are mere mechanical repetitions of ideas, facts, events, characteristics, and so forth. It is apparent that Walzel makes a purely formal distinction and leaves as a question whether one is properly dealing with a leitmotiv at all when the formal-linguistic element is absent. Peacock, however, makes a functional distinction between both recurring linguistic formulae and nonformulistic repetition which express emotional content and those which do not.
  I am inclined to regard the distinctions of both Walzel and Peacock as valid only in general terms, for I can, for example, conceive of Walzel's atechtonic leitmotiv as differing only in degree and not in kind from the techtonic. In the last analysis every repetitive linguistic formula, even the apparently most casual, must be techtonic in the sense that it has some effect upon the structural whole. Similarly in the case of Peacock, it seems to me that every repetitive sequence, whether linguistic formula or not, acquires a feel-value by virtue of the mere repetition even though it may not be a vehicle for the mood of the whole. His distinction is also one of degree rather than of kind. By combining the theoretical observations of both Walzel and Peacock we obtain a slightly more precise research instrument, as follows: By the term literary leitmotiv we understand (a) words or word-clusters which by repetition acquire a symbolic emotional value (repetitive linguistic formula); (b) allusions to things, ideas, facts, characteristics, events, and so on, which by repetition acquire a symbolic emotional value (leitmotiv symbol). We distinguish very generally between (c) leitmotivs which are primarily and obviously carriers of the mood of the whole composition and thus have a unifying formal structural value (techtonic leitmotiv); (d) leitmotivs which function primarily as mood-

carriers for individual characters, situations, events, and other parts less than the whole of the composition (atechtonic leitmotiv).

33.   J. Bithell, *Modern German Literature, 1880–1938* (London: Methuen & Co., 1939), p. 346.

34.   See page 155 for the quotation and note 12 for the documentation.

35.   Lowe-Porter's translation changes the original and exquisite Jimmerthal to Immerthal for reasons unknown and difficult to imagine unless it be for the alliterative effect. But no effect can equal the comic one produced by the obvious play on "Jammertal" by means of the tittering *i*-sound in Jimmerthal.

36.   See Mann, "Lebensabriss," p. 753.

37.   Note in this connection the rich connotativeness of the German *Liebe* and *lieben* in the classic treatment of the matter by Martin Luther in his *Sendbrief vom Dolmetschen.*

38.   It is interesting to compare the Lowe-Porter translations here with those of B. Q. Morgan in Kuno Francke, ed., *The German Classics: Masterpieces of German Literature* vol. 19 (New York: The German Publication Society, 1914). Morgan renders "geladen" with "loaded."

39.   See S, p. v.

40.   See Brennan, p. 104.

"The Murders in the Rue Morgue" and Sonata-Allegro Form

Robert K. Wallace

Music and literature, as Calvin S. Brown has pointed out, are in several ways unique among the arts. Essentially, they differ from painting, sculpture, and architecture in that they communicate through time and in sound (broadly defined).[1] Interesting critical comparisons have been made between music and poetry; less has been done with music and fiction—a field of equal promise. Near the end of *Aspects of the Novel,* E. M. Forster, a novelist with a keen appetite for music, wrote that "in music fiction is likely to find its nearest parallel."[2] Judging from the scant criticism on music and fiction, one would hardly tend to think Forster correct. But that criticism may come when it is realized how similar are *some* of the ways in which we "take in" prose fiction and classical music.

In one area of fiction such similarities have already gained critical recognition: novels and short stories by twentieth-century authors who deliberately followed musical models. Studies of the "Sirens" episode of *Ulysses* are in this category.[3] So are many of the investigations of Thomas Mann and music, including Harold Basilius's 1944 article on "Thomas Mann's Use of Musical Structure and Technique in *Tonio Kröger.*"[4] Basilius's piece is a model for those critics who wish to show how an author succeeded in designing a piece of fiction so it would approach—though not duplicate—the way music works on a listener.

The present study, however, deals with a different problem—one that has yet to be carefully explored. Its goal is to show how works of prose fiction and classical music can "work in the same way" even though neither author nor composer used the other art as a model. In this sense it parallels the kind of inquiry Leonard Bernstein pursued in his 1973 Norton Poetry Lectures. In those lectures, Bernstein pointed out fundamental similarities between musical and linguistic discourse and explored parallels between such concepts as musical and literary syntax and musical and literary ambiguity. There, as in this study, the goal was not to show how a specific author or composer was influenced by a figure or idea from the other discipline, but rather to explore deep structural and communicative patterns shared by both music and literature.[5] In this essay, the method

From *The Journal of Aesthetics and Art Criticism* 35 (1977):457–63. Copyright 1977 by The American Society for Aesthetics. Reprinted by permission of the Society.

for exploring a new kind of relation between music and literature will be to present a structural comparison of Edgar Allan Poe's "The Murders in the Rue Morgue" and the first movement of Beethoven's *Pathétique* Sonata op. 13.

Edgar Allan Poe was a literary man obsessed by music—or at least by the idea of music. He played the flute and perhaps the piano. Protagonists in his fiction are mesmerized by the sound of stringed instruments. His literary criticism points to Music as the Art to which all Poetry aspires. Poe's works have themselves inspired several hundred musical compositions. Yet there is no evidence that Poe had a technical knowledge of musical forms or that he consciously imitated musical models in his fiction.[6] This being so, the structural comparison offered here between one of his short stories and a movement of a Beethoven sonata is strictly coincidental. The point is not to show that Poe was directly influenced by Beethoven or by the concept of sonata-allegro form, but rather to show that music and prose fiction are potentially so similar in the way they work that the kind of "musical" effects a Mann or Joyce intentionally strove for can also be achieved unconsciously and unknowingly.

Essentially, my argument is that the structure of "The Murders in the Rue Morgue" is comparable to the first movement of Beethoven's *Pathétique* in that the story can meaningfully be said to possess an exposition, a development, and a recapitulation. For this reason, any sonata-allegro movement by Haydn or Mozart or Beethoven would have served for comparison. The first movement of Beethoven's *Pathétique* has been chosen for two reasons. Poe listened to piano music and during his lifetime the *Pathétique* was extremely popular among both professional and amateur players. The likelihood that Poe had heard the work many times (though irrelevant to the central argument here) makes the comparison of it with one of his stories appropriate. More important is the fact that the first movement of Beethoven's *Pathétique* is a sonata-allegro movement with "options." Before the exposition is an introduction; between the exposition and development is a transition; following the recapitulation is a coda. Each of these "options" has its parallel in the Poe story, as the following analysis will make clear.

I

The chart below forms the skeleton of a structural comparison between the first movement of *Pathétique* Sonata and "The Murders in the Rue Morgue." The numbers for the sonata indicate bars; for the story, paragraphs.

	Sonata	Story
Introduction	1–10	1–4
Exposition	11–120	5–50
Transition	121–132	51–57
Development	133–194	57–98
Recapitulation	195–285	99–122
Coda	286–310	123–124

The above schema for the short story's structure will have to be explained and defended, but that for the first movement of the sonata is based on Tovey and is universally acknowledged as accurate in its broad outlines.[7] The portentous grave introduction comprises the first ten bars, leading to the lively allegro di molto e con brio, which develops according to sonata-allegro form. The exposition, comprising bars 11-120, consists of the first group, or main theme, in C minor (11-50), and the second group in two sections (sometimes called the second and third theme) in E-flat minor (51-88) and E-flat (89-120). A short transition based on the main theme (bars 121-32) ushers in the development section. Beginning with a brief reference to the grave introduction (bars 133-37), the development takes materials from the main theme and introduction, fuses them into a single phrase, and runs them through several permutations (138-94), which vigorous activity leads back to the recapitulation. There the main theme appears again in C minor (195-221), the first section of the second group is heard in F minor (222-53), and the second section of that group is transposed into the tonic (254-85). Beethoven, not satisfied with a "simple" recapitulation, adds a coda based on the main theme (286-95), the introduction (296-99), and the main theme again (300-310).

No one, whether musical or literary, would deny that the first four paragraphs of "The Murders in the Rue Morgue" can rightly be called an introduction. The first sentence—"The mental features discoursed of as the analytical are, in themselves, but little susceptible of analysis"—establishes a pseudo-philosophical tone that is sustained throughout the narrator's ponderous comments on the various mental qualities called into play in such games as chess and whist.[8] The abstract introduction ends with the short fourth paragraph:

> The narrative which follows will appear to the reader somewhat in the light of a commentary upon the propositions just advanced.

The narrative proper, which is much livelier than the introduction, begins immediately with paragraph 5:

> Residing in Paris during the spring and part of the summer of 18–, I there became acquainted with a Monsieur C. Auguste Dupin. This young gentleman
> . . .

There follows a detailed description of where Dupin and the narrator lived and how they passed their time. This section concludes, importantly, with an extended account of how Dupin read the narrator's mind as they walked the street (a concrete demonstration of the abstract analytical qualities written of in the introduction). Immediately after Dupin's brilliant achievement, the narrative takes a new turn:

> Not long after this, we were looking over an evening edition of the "Gazette des Tribunaux," when the following paragraphs arrested our attention.
> "EXTRAORDINARY MURDERS. This morning, about three o'clock . . ."

Four newspaper paragraphs describe the horrible and inexplicable fate of Madame d'Espanaye and her daughter. The fifth paragraph from that evening's newspaper (and the thirty-first of Poe's story) reads:

> "To this horrible mystery there is not as yet, we believe, the slightest clew."

The story's next short paragraph is from the narrator.

The next day's paper had these additional particulars:

Seventeen newspaper paragraphs later the tabloid account of the murders ends again with the words, "There is not, however, the shadow of a clew." One more paragraph, the fiftieth in the story, summarizes (rather than quotes) what little new information the second day's evening edition contained.

These forty-five paragraphs that follow the short introduction correspond to the exposition in the sonata. Like that exposition, it is made up of what can be called a main theme followed by a second group in two sections. The main theme (paragraphs 5–25) is the description of the relationship between Dupin and the narrator, capped by the demonstration of Dupin's analytical abilities. The second group consists of the newspaper's two-part account of the murders— in the first day's edition (paragraphs 26–31) and in the second day's (32–50). At this point, to have imposed the structure of musical exposition on this part of the story may seem arbitrary. When what can be called the development and re-capitulation sections of the story have been discussed, however, the procedure might seem apt.

Before the development, though, comes a brief transition, just as there was in the sonata movement. The sonata's transition used material from the first theme. By coincidence (and coincidence only) so does the story. The seven paragraphs that connect the exposition with the development return to Dupin's relationship with the narrator. Dupin asks him his opinion respecting the murders. The narrator agrees "with all Paris" that the case is insoluble. Dupin tells him not to be so sure. They briefly visit the scene of the crime. Until noon of the next day, Dupin is silent. Then, in the middle of paragraph 57, the development begins—

... He then asked me, suddenly, if I had observed any thing *peculiar* at the scene of the atrocity.

The next forty-one paragraphs are pure cerebral activity, at the end of which Dupin has unravelled the entire puzzle. In more ways than one this section deserves to be called a development.

In the development section of a sonata-allegro movement, materials from the exposition (and often from the introduction, if there is one) are augmented, diminished, dissected, combined, or otherwise forced into new shapes. In the development section of Beethoven's opus 13, first movement, part of the introduction and part of the first theme of the exposition are combined and then "developed." In the Poe story a comparable process is at work. Dupin's analytical ability (part of the main theme of the exposition) and the seemingly contradictory newspaper facts (the second group of the exposition) are juxtaposed and, through the power of Dupin's mind, "developed." As in the musical example, no essential new material is presented. Dupin merely discovers truths that were latent but unseen in the raw materials of the newspaper accounts. From these materials alone he derives his theories about the language of the murderer(s), the means of entry, the means of escape, and the strength of the murderer(s). The development section concludes with paragraph 98, when Dupin's full theory has been spun out, including his speculations about an orangutan whose owner must be a seaman and the newspaper advertisement Dupin has placed in order to draw the owner to his dwelling.

Though Dupin is quite exhilarated about his theory, he cannot be sure of it until the sailor actually comes and confesses. With a musical schema in mind, there is no difficulty in seeing the one-sentence paragraph 99 as the beginning of the recapitulation: "At this moment we heard a step upon the stairs." For the next seventeen paragraphs, Dupin deftly manages to assure the sailor that he may tell his story without fear of punishment. His performance here is in effect a repetition of the first theme as it appeared in the exposition (that is, the theme of how Dupin is able to relate with people and to read their minds). This first section of the recapitulation ends with paragraph 116, where the sailor says, after a brief pause:

> "So help me God . . . I *will* tell you all I know about this affair; but I do not
> expect you to believe one half I say—I would be a fool indeed if I did. Still, I
> *am* innocent, and I will make a clean breast if I die for it."

The rest of the recapitulation is the narrator's summary of what the sailor admitted. It begins with the words, "What he stated was, in substance, this." It ends six paragraphs later with the full explanation of how the murders occurred. This short simple account straight from the source reconciles all that had seemed contradictory in the newspaper account of the murders (the second group of the story's exposition). And it resolves those contradictions in full agreement with the development section (Dupin's theorizing). The satisfaction gained by the resolution of seemingly contradictory material is comparable to the effect in the recapitulation of the classic sonata-allegro movement, where the second group of the exposition (there presented in a key contrasting to that of the first theme) is transposed into the tonic. The resolution achieved in paragraphs 117–22 of "The Murders in the Rue Morgue," then, is comparable to the resolution achieved in bars 222–85 of Beethoven's sonata.

As in the sonata movement, nothing needs to be added once the material presented in the exposition and processed in the development is "brought home," as it were, in the recapitulation. But Poe, too, adds a coda as a finishing touch. It comprises the two short paragraphs that complete the story, the first of which begins with the words, "I have scarcely anything to add." The coda concludes with Dupin, in full control of the situation, throwing a last light barb at the Paris Prefect of Police.

II

Now that the skeletal comparison has been fleshed out, what does the comparison mean?

The meaning is on two levels, one to be called surface structure, the other dynamic structure (the latter might have been called "deep structure" had not that term already more meanings than an M.I.R.V. has warheads). Surface structure refers to the fact that the sonata movement and the short story can be seen to correspond exactly to each other by bar groups and paragraph groups. The correspondence is even more detailed than the original skeletal comparison shows, for matching subgroups can be listed under both exposition and recapitulation:

	Sonata	Story
Exposition	11–120	5–50
First Theme	11–50	5–25
Second Group	51–120	26–50
First Part	51–88	26–31
Second Part	89–120	32–50
Recapitulation	195–285	99–122
First Theme	195–221	99–116
Second Group	222–285	117–122
First Part	222–253	(117–122)
Second Part	254–285	(117–122)

Comparable dynamic structure refers not to the fact that the sonata movement and the short story have measurable parts that can be seen as comparable to each other's but to the fact that in each separate case those measurable parts interact with one another in such a way as to produce comparable development, tension, and form.

At the level of surface structure, the comparison emphasizes those qualities music and literature have in common which are not shared by the other arts. It *is* possible to divide "The Murders in the Rue Morgue" into sections labeled introduction, exposition, transition, development, recapitulation, and coda. By no stretch of the imagination could a painting, a sculpture, or a work of architecture be so divided. That terminology is potentially applicable only to works of music and literature, where the artistic material develops through time and where the memory of the listener/reader is necessary in order to hold the work together. (Whether that terminology could be applied as successfully to a poem or a play as to a work of fiction is a question outside the scope of this inquiry.)

Still on the surface level, though shading into the dynamic, the comparison means something different than those which show how Mann's or Joyce's fiction imitates musical structures. The comparison shows that the two arts have enough potential similarities that they can parallel each other in structure accidentally and coincidentally. It also suggests that there are significant structural comparisons between fiction and music that have not yet been adequately investigated—both at the surface and at the dynamic level.

It might fairly be argued that an awareness of the surface structure discussed above is not necessary in enjoying either the sonata movement or the short story. Undoubtedly, one can "enjoy" the first movement of Beethoven's *Pathétique* without knowing a thing about introductions, expositions, first themes, second groups, developments, recapitulations, codas, and tonic and contrasting tonalities. Likewise, one can "enjoy" "The Murders in the Rue Morgue" without subjecting that work to structural analysis (whether with literary or musical terminology). But such analysis, while it may have very little to do with the first-time enjoyment of a work of art, can have very much to do with explaining the why and the how of that enjoyment. Furthermore, while "enjoying" a work of art does not require analyzing its surface structure, it does require some apprehension of what can be called its dynamic structure.

Take the untrained reader of "The Murders in the Rue Morgue," for example. He feels deep satisfaction when the seaman's story straightens out the seemingly contradictory newspaper facts and confirms Dupin's theorizing—though he would never resort to structural analysis to explain it. If he does not experience at least that level of satisfaction he has not experienced the story. Likewise, the attentive but untrained listener who hears the first movement of the sonata *Pathétique* feels satisfaction when the first theme returns in its original shape after passing through the perils of the development (he may also feel satisfaction when the second group of the exposition is transposed into the home key during the recapitulation, though probably not at the conscious level). At this basic level of dynamic structure, essential to a minimal apprehension of either work, the story and the sonata movement work in similar ways.

The point here is not that the sonata-allegro form can be imposed on "The Murders in the Rue Morgue" but that that form explains as well as any literary terms could the dynamics by which the story unfolds and by which it must be apprehended. The kind of tension felt by one who reads the story is comparable to the kind of tension felt by one who hears the sonata movement, for it is a tension that results from apprehending similar structural developments. This is not to say that the moods, or the affective effects, of the two works are comparable. What the listener and the reader are left with emotionally may very well be different. But whatever each gets he gets by apprehending comparable forms: in each case a slow introduction followed by a narrative of some speed; an exposition presenting materials of contrasting natures; a development of those materials in such a way as to lead toward their resolution; a recapitulation in which the original material is set forth in such a way as to resolve previous contradictions; and a coda which concludes the work and displays the composer's/writer's exhilaration, hopefully shared by the listener/reader, at having brought everything so nicely off.

The comparison of the Poe story and the Beethoven sonata movement at the level of what has been called dynamic structure brings us back to E. M. Forster's idea that "in music fiction is likely to find its nearest parallel." His statement deserves to be seen in context. Forster has been musing over similarities between music and fiction. He has successfully shown how both arts use types of repetition and variation and he turns to "the more difficult question."

> Is there any effect in novels comparable to the effect of [Beethoven's] Fifth Symphony as a whole, where, when the orchestra stops, we hear something that has never actually been played? The opening movement, the andante, and the trio-scherzo-trio-finale-trio-finale that composes the third block, all enter the mind at once, and extend one another into a common entity. This common entity, this new thing, is the symphony as a whole, and it has been achieved mainly (though not entirely) by the relation between the three big blocks of sound which the orchestra has been playing. I am calling this relation "rhythmic." If the correct musical term is something else, that does not matter; what we have now to ask ourselves is whether there is any analogy in fiction.
>
> I cannot find any analogy. Yet there may be one; in music fiction is likely to find its nearest parallel.[9]

What Forster called "rhythmic relation" I have called dynamic structure. My comparison between a short story and a sonata movement is different in scale from the one he sought between a novel and a symphony but it is identical in kind. It is *one* analogy, and it supports Forster's hunch about music and fiction.

In a final attempt to explain what my structural comparison means, I will address myself to three friendly objections that have been raised during the course of its development. When the basic comparison was first presented to a class, a student said, "Fine, but aren't Poe and Beethoven doing what you do when you tell a freshman to write his essays with an introduction, a body, and a conclusion?" A former teacher after hearing a short description of the comparison pointed out that historically musicians have followed writers and rhetoricians in finding ways to give shape to their art. And a literary man who heard a detailed presentation of the comparison said that to him the musical experience was smoother and more continuous than the literary one, that he felt less a sense of obstacles and compositional dangers having been overcome in the Beethoven than in the Poe.

As to whether the Poe story or the Beethoven sonata movement is smoother or more continuous, that probably depends on who is listening or reading. Just as the literary man found the Poe story loaded with compositional hazards deftly negotiated, so might a musicologist be likely to find the Beethoven sonata movement. To the nontechnical eye or ear each work can seem smooth and continuous. But whether the process seems smooth or not, to follow this sonata movement or this story requires a certain kind of awareness, a certain kind of eye or ear for development. The process of apprehending the two works, no matter how difficult or easy each seems, is comparable to the degree that their structures are comparable. To take them in the reader/listener must, whatever his conscious awareness of doing so, comprehend comparable forms.

The other objections can be addressed together. Most effective writing—like most effective rhetoric—has a beginning, a middle, and an end. The same can be said for music. But "The Murders in the Rue Morgue" does not work just as a freshman essay would, with an introduction, a body, and a conclusion. It presents us, rather, with an abstract introduction followed by a narrative that begins with two men and some seemingly contradictory facts. It then shows the mind of one of the men as it dissects those facts in such a way as to make them fit together in a meaningful way. It then shows us those materials after they have been perfectly resolved. This is not a formula that would apply to most essays, most rhetoric, or most fiction—though it may apply to most detective stories. "The Murders in the Rue Morgue" has a particular dynamic connecting its parts which other forms of writing do not necessarily share, and this is the quality it has in common with the Beethoven sonata movement.

The same is true of the musical example. The sonata-allegro form, like the *a-b-a* form, has a beginning, a middle, and an end. The amateur listener probably does not consciously distinguish one from the other. But whether consciously or not, he must apprehend them, if he does apprehend them, in different ways. In the *a-b-a* form the original theme returns after an interlude consisting of different material altogether: There is the given, the unfamiliar, the given again (as in Chopin's "Octave" Etude or the classic minuet-trio-minuet). With the sonata-allegro form the process is quite different. There the original material returns after itself having been run through a vigorous development section: There is the given, the given put through stress, then the given again. It is this latter quality, which in this context can be called the "development" quality, which the first movement of Beethoven's *Pathétique* Sonata has in common with Poe's "The Murders in the Rue Morgue."

Notes

1.   Calvin S. Brown, *Music and Literature: A Comparison of the Arts* (Athens: University of Georgia Press, 1948), pp. 8–10.

2.   E. M. Forster, *Aspects of the Novel* (New York: Harcourt, Brace, 1927), p. 168.

3.   Stuart Gilbert was one of the first to address this topic. David W. Cole, "Fugal Structure in the Sirens Episode of *Ulysses*," *Modern Language Studies* 19 (1973):221–26, is one of the more recent.

4.   H. A. Basilius, "Thomas Mann's Use of Structure and Techniques in *Tonio Kröger*," *Germanic Review* 19 (1944):284–308.

5.   Leonard Bernstein's Norton Poetry Lectures are available on videotape, on discs (Columbia Records), and in book form: *The Unanswered Question* (Cambridge, Mass.: Harvard University Press, 1975).

6.   Though Mary Garrettson Evans, in *Music and Edgar Allan Poe: A Bibliographic Study* (New York: Greenwood Press, 1968), p. 2, quotes Killis Campbell's *The Mind of Poe* (New York: Russell & Russell, 1962) in order to point out Poe's "acquaintance with technical terms in music," there is nothing in the sources drawn upon by Campbell to indicate that Poe was familiar with, say, the structure of a sonata-allegro movement.

7.   What Tovey calls the second group (in two parts) of the exposition of the first movement of opus 13 other musicologists have called the second and third theme, or the second theme and the closing theme. I follow Tovey because his terms fit so conveniently with the two-part "second group" in the Poe story. To do so, though, in terms of my basic argument, is not to load the dice. This particular parallel is one of the many in the comparison that is coincidental, not essential.

8.   Passages from "The Murders in the Rue Morgue" are taken from Edward D. Davidson, ed., *The Selected Works of Edgar Allan Poe* (Boston: Houghton Mifflin, 1956).

9.   Forster, pp. 240–41.

Research for this essay was aided by a summer grant from the National Endowment for the Humanities.

Five

The Sonata Form in the Novel

Great Circle: Conrad Aiken's Musico-Literary Technique

Robert Emerson Carlile

There is relatively little literary criticism regarding music and Conrad Aiken's prose. As early as 1919, Aiken begins making clear to the public that music and his conception of art are inextricably linked and that a meaningful if not necessary point of view for the intelligent reader to consider is music,[1] but even in the case of Aiken's poetry not much has been written. Then, in the twenties, Aiken begins adding novels and short stories to his already impressive body of poetry and literary criticism; and, in such novels as *Blue Voyage, Great Circle,* and *Ushant,* one wonders why Aiken's literary technique has not been the subject for more musico-literary discussion, especially as musical allusions and analogies are notably present.

Vance Mizelle comes closer than anyone to date in presenting a musical critique which, in some respects, points toward my critical analysis of *Great Circle.* With regard to *Ushant,* he tells us that

> ... Aiken has sought to create a work which is controlled by a thematic development and which has as its basic structure the simultaneous flowing of several distinct themes throughout the course of the work. If these themes be considered as analogous to musical themes, one can see the author's interest in the interplay of melodies and all the rich and evocative music which is thereby produced through conflict, contrast, and harmony of themes. If this belief is correct, then we may call *Ushant* a unique and significant attempt at literary counterpoint. And if the basic structure is analogous to that of musical counterpoint, then *Ushant* may be as long and deliberate an attempt at contrapuntal prose as we now have, and, in light of Aiken's views on the subject, this may be his largest symphonic work: a masterly effort culminating forty years of interest in the relationships between music and literature.[2]

To what extent this point of view can be taken toward *Great Circle* is questionable. Although there are the themes of infidelity and *gnothi seauton,* it is doubtful that they can be considered "as analogous to musical themes" any more than *gnothi seauton* can be safely considered a "musical" theme in *Ushant.* But the

Originally appeared in the Spring 1968 issue of *The Georgia Review,* copyright 1968 by the University of Georgia, and is reprinted by permission of *The Georgia Review.*

basic structure of *Great Circle* does have certain qualities about it which justify using the term "musical counterpoint." Furthermore, there are the convincing statements in Aiken's "Counterpoint and Implication" which, although said in reference to poetry, may be reasonably applied to our consideration of Aiken's prose. Aiken tells us that "I had from the outset been somewhat doubtfully hankering for ... some way of getting contrapuntal effects in poetry–the effects of contrasting and conflicting tones and themes, a kind of underlying simultaneity in dissimilarity"; and, somewhat later, "One must provide for one's symphony a sufficiently powerful and pervasive underlying idea–and, above all, make it sufficiently apparent."[3] Aiken himself reminds us that we are not "to press the musical analogies too closely," and it is quite possible that Mizelle may have gone too far in his musical critique of *Ushant.* The question then becomes: To what extent can and should musical analogies be linked to content and/or literary technique? The fact is that music and its terminology in *Great Circle,* if not *Ushant,* are most probably Aiken's way of talking about metaphor, and limited analogy is all that is justified. One is reminded of Mark Schorer's comment that "the analogy with music except as a metaphor, is inexact, and except as it points to techniques which fiction can employ as fiction, not very useful to our sense of craftsmanship."[4] But there is evidence from Aiken himself which justifies at least some kind of musical critique of *Great Circle,* and it is to this which we now turn.

Aiken makes emphatically clear in the author's preface to *3 Novels* that music is very much a part of *Great Circle:*

> *Great Circle,* written five years after *Blue Voyage,* is just as insistently psychological in its approach to its theme, but less closely tethered to my own personality than its predecessor. This permitted me greater freedom in the choice of form, and here it will be observed that as in the five symphonies of *The Divine Pilgrim* ... my early and continued preoccupation with musical form was allowed greater play. The novel is in fact constructed in four parts, like a symphony, each section with a different key and movement of its own. The first section is an account of Andrew Cather's return.... This is the "fast" movement, full of latent violences, and tragic-comic in tone–it has been likened (and so has the whole novel) to Jacobean tragedy.... Next comes a slow-motion, parenthetical flashback, to a memory of a summer in Andrew's childhood at Duxbury.... [There is] the third section, in which Andrew ... pours out his story.... And this catharsis of course leads quite naturally into the fourth and final section, again a slow movement, but now lighter and happier in tone–in fact, taking its key from Mozart's overture to *The Magic Flute,* which he listens to and paraphrases, while he looks down from the balcony at the concert, and sees his wife sitting down there alone, with his own empty seat beside her. The éclaircissement is now at last in sight, the great circle to a conclusion can now be completed.[5]

With Aiken's incisive remarks regarding *Great Circle* and music, it should now be understood that my paper is primarily an explicative enlargement of Aiken's statement by a close examination of musical allusions in the novel. By musical allusion, I mean those references to music which occur in the thought and dialogue of the characters or in other ways in the narrative. As will be seen, these references or allusions are frequent and become so pervasive as to be viewed as an essential part of Aiken's literary technique. I will examine particularly the extent to which Aiken's reference to Mozart's *The Magic Flute* in chapter 4 becomes a key to a greater understanding of the tone of the novel. By tone, I mean Aiken's attitude toward his subject and material and the attitude the protagonist, Andrew Cather, takes toward himself and other characters in the novel. I will demonstrate that musical thought is an important adjunct to the way in which Andrew Cather views himself and human experience.

In chapter 1, we discover that Andrew Cather is on the train hurrying back to Boston where he knows he will find his wife, Bertha, and his good friend, Tom Crapo, carrying on their adulterous affair in Andrew's flat. Andrew imagines the circumstances of the discovery and constructs in his mind what his response will be. Maybe he should get off the train before it reaches Boston. "Perhaps they were merely playing duets. Side by side on the long mahogany bench, leaning together, leaning apart, Tom the bass and Bertha the treble, the Haydn Surprise, the Drum-roll Symphony, his foot on the pedal, her hand on the page. Shall we take that again? We'll start at G in the second bar. Haydn duet, hide and do it." And what about Andy during this scene? Andy would be "a ghost behind the music." The entire scene is likened unto a musical presentation, a duet, with Andy nothing more than a ghost. A few pages later we learn that "it was a mere disinterested love of music that brought them together [Tom and Bertha] in the first place," and that "for years Tom and Bertha hadn't missed a night at the Sanders Theater concerts. No indeed. How they loved Haydn. How they adored Bach! What about a little Brandenburg tonight?" He pictures them at the piano when he walks in and wonders what they will say. Andrew thinks of himself as saying, "Don't stop playing–do go on–shall I turn the pages for you–or the sheets?" Andrew arrives in Boston and proceeds to Cambridge in a taxi. The narrative is still almost entirely Andrew's thoughts: "And the midnight operas, with Tom at the piano.... The first step toward Haydn, and a more refined appreciation of music." Trying to summon up evidence that Tom is not at Andrew's flat making love to Bertha, Andrew goes to Tom's apartment and buzzes. Tom doesn't answer, and Andrew speculates that he is probably at the Faculty Club, a burlesque show ... or "he is playing the grand piano at the Signet to an admiring audience of sophomores and a pederastic philogist" or that he is humming "the waltz from the 'Rosenkavalier,' feeling the chords tensing his fingers."

All these musical allusions occur in chapter 1 prior to Andrew's arriving home. As he walks into the flat, there is recapitulated a certain sequence of events which were envisioned by Andrew during his return trip. A brief exchange of dialogue occurs between Tom, Bertha, and Andrew. Tom leaves; there is a rather brief and awkward scene between Andrew and Bertha; and, somewhat later, Andrew thinks of his marriage as being rhythmic: the "inevitable approaches and retreats: love, indifference, hate–then over again, love, indifference, hate. Disgust, then renewed curiosity. Exploration, then renewed retreat." And finally, Bertha's crying is "one of her pianissimos, a soft whispering sound, persistent, uninterruptible, the kind that could go on for hours, for all night."

From this detailed account of musical allusion in chapter 1 several things can be noted. First, musical thought and associations are part of the complex mind of Andrew Cather which the reader comes to know through the limited third-person point of view from which the entire novel is constructed. Second, many of these musical allusions are linked to characters and events in the story in such a way that music becomes a key element in much of the action and development. Third, such frequency of musical references tends to become a clearly established part of Aiken's literary technique. Last and most important, the reader gets the impression that there is something like a musical performance being acted out and embellished by the dramatically minded and psychologically oriented protagonist, Andrew Cather.

Chapter 2 has very few direct allusions to music, and those which do occur are not an integral part of what is happening in the narrative. This almost total absence of musical allusions tends to call attention to the fact that the narrative is told through the eyes of a child whose aesthetic sensibilities are less fully realized than they are as he appears to us as an adult narrator in the other three chapters. But chapter 2 is most certainly an elaboration of the theme of infidelity initially stated and elaborated upon in chapter 1, and this in itself should not preclude the chapter from being "musical" in its relationship to the structure of the whole novel, if one recalls Aiken's comments cited from "Counterpoint and Implication" and the author's preface. However, perhaps what gives this chapter its essential musical quality is its reordering of time, its focus on the past (so significant to music as well as literature). The setting of chapter 2 is at the summer home on the coast, Duxbury, during a span of time in Andrew's childhood. Andrew is recalling, reliving that summer in his youth when he discovers the bodies of his mother and Uncle David in the latter's yacht after a terrible storm. The entire chapter is extremely important because Andrew's mother was having an affair with his uncle. And it is through the recollection of Andrew's childhood that we discover the extent to which Andrew Cather's wife's infidelity (and his response to it) is necessarily linked to his past. This vague childhood awareness of his mother's infidelity becomes the focal point for the psychological scrutiny which Andrew subjects himself to in chapter 3. The flashback narrative of chapter 2 and its preoccupation with past events represent a vivid contrast to chapter 1 where the present (Andrew's return trip to Boston) and future (the incidents as he imagines them on the return trip and which do happen) constitute the focus of time.

Chapter 3 has as its setting the apartment of Andrew's psychoanalyst friend, Bill. Musical references are not as numerous as in chapter 1, but they do occur frequently enough to warrant consideration and to remind us that Aiken's musical references are a deliberate part of his literary technique. By the second page of the chapter Andrew is talking to Bill and says, "Suddenly the snow is paper snow, one almost expects to hear an accompaniment of sob music on nicely ordered violins, or the whole world breaking into applause." Happiness becomes, according to Bill's definition, "Defeated pride. A highball with ice. Ignorance." Andrew has been betrayed and he says, "What's the use. Tea dance today. Novelty dance tonight. There will be charming favors, and saxophones will syncopate your livers." Somewhat later he describes his friend Tom Crapo as "frequenter of wrestling matches, lover of Beethoven, but also the lover of my wife." Logical discourse is thrust to the background, and Andrew becomes even more bizarre in his statements: "All his days he [Andrew frequently refers to himself in third person] will walk attended by an orchestra of Elizabethan worms." He then becomes more philosophical and decides that "the art of living is the art of exclusion or mitigation of the disagreeable," and music, painting, poetry, and psychoanalysis become part of that escape. Wallowing in self-pity, he decides that he will reappear to Tom and Bertha as "one of the bats that circle above the orchestra." He becomes a pig who, in his dying spasms, performs many kinds of acts of daring: The "dying pig will now play the Chinese whole-tone scale on an arrangement of coins, with his hoof. And instantly on a table . . . the pig tapped out rapidly with his hoof the Chinese whole-tone scale." Andrew somehow staggers to Bill's bed, leaving Bill fast asleep on the living room couch, and collapses, still in a state of Freudian self-examination.

Thus the first three chapters have given evidence of "the effects of contrasting and conflicting tones and themes," the themes of infidelity and *gnothi seauton*, and brought Andrew to the point where he can psychologically accept his wife's infidelity as well as his mother's. And, as a result of an examination of these three chapters from a musical point of view, the reader is now better prepared for the extensiveness of musical references in chapter 4.

The setting for most of chapter 4 is at the concert hall, where the first selection is the overture to Mozart's *The Magic Flute*. Andrew is in the balcony and sees Bertha seated downstairs next to an empty seat. Prior to this Bill had known that Bertha would be there, given Andrew his own ticket, and then called Bertha to tell her of Andrew's probable presence at the concert. The word "recapitulation," having recurred in various ways and places throughout the novel, now recurs with even more frequency: "The slow pang, recapitulative, rose in the darkness of his thought. . . . He poured himself a whiskey . . . as if for the pleasures of repeating, or re-enacting a lost attitude . . . he crumbled the paper napkin, as if to crush once again the recapitulative pang." What is happening in these few instances noted (necessarily given out of context) is that Andrew is "reliving" things he said, did, and thought, particularly during the psychological purging which he had subjected himself to the night before. And part of the reliving, the recapitulating, is to go to the concert where he will probably see Bertha and Tom. "Was he to go to the concert at all?" But he does. "Pull yourself together. Enter. Climb the stair. Ten minutes to eight. Take your seat and look about you."

At this point, except for the last few pages of the novel, the rest of the story takes place in the music hall. He has his program, the orchestra comes in, "and the squeakings and squawkings and runs and trills began, the grunts of the cellos, the tappings and listenings of the kettle drummer, and the delicious miscellany of tuning." Koussevitsky comes to the stage, and "at precisely that moment, Bertha [alone] entered from the door." The music starts and Aiken turns the reader's attention (in a montagelike fashion) from the program notes, to Andrew Cather, to Bertha, to the music, to the program notes, and then to Andrew, as Bertha looks up toward the balcony and understands Andrew's signals to meet him in the lobby after the overture to *The Magic Flute*. Andrew thinks of how she looks. Bertha becomes absorbed in the music, and Andrew becomes increasingly absorbed in watching her, simultaneously listening to the music and intermittently paraphrasing the program notes concerning the opera. Finally the overture is over, and Bertha leaves her seat to meet Andrew in the lobby. He tells her he is going to Duxbury, and she pleads to go with him. He refuses and leaves her "climbing the stairs, lifting her frock at the knees." He borrows Bill's car and starts out for Duxbury: "The strange and exciting mixture of astonishment and suffering with which—at a moment of discovery—one loses oneself in order to create oneself! The end that is still conscious of its beginnings. Birth that remembers death." He will recapitulate the Duxbury infidelity by returning to the scene of the trauma. "Life was good—life was going to be good." All that need be recapitulated has, is, and will be done. The conclusion, the circle is made.

It is impossible to recreate the mood in which the last chapter is presented. As Calvin Brown says, "Certain things can be communicated only by devious means, and . . . these happen to be precisely the things which Aiken wishes to communicate"[6] and which explication cannot possibly duplicate. But certainly it is clear that the musical setting and references have been an important part of what the reader experiences. And part of the setting and allusions has been *The Magic Flute*.

Aiken himself tells us that the fourth and final section of his novel is "now lighter and happier in tone—in fact, taking its key from Mozart's overture to *The Magic Flute*." Succinctly, then, it *is* this opera which becomes the key to the tone in which we are to accept the final chapter if not the entire novel. The story concerns the efforts of Prince Tamino and the humorous bird-catcher foil, Papageno, both of whom search for Pamina, the daughter of the Queen of the Night. Interspersed between the half-serious love affair between Tamino and Pamina there is Papageno who also longs for a woman. He is finally tricked into taking an old woman who, upon being accepted by Papageno, changes into a beautiful, female bird-catcher. Thus the tone of the opera is decidedly humorous, and certainly the overture is no less in that vein.

As recently as 1967, Marc Chagall's production of *The Magic Flute* prompted Irving Kolodin to point out that "as the late Bruno Walter wrote at the time of the Mozart bicentenary in 1956, Mozart's last opera is the epitome of the man himself—his nobility represented by Tamino, his relish for life and simple pleasures embodied in Papageno."[7] Likewise, it is apparent that there are two rather definite tones, serious and comic—tragicomic, if you will—to *Great Circle*. Indeed, there is the Tamino *and* Papageno in Andrew Cather himself, and the very tone of each of the chapters reinforces these two sides to Andrew Cather. Andrew is "cuckolded," and "one-eyed" Cather finds the domestic situation humorous in certain respects; but there is also the serious vein. Bertha's actions have forced upon him the circumstances of his past, which are anything but funny. By the end of the novel, then, if we are to know Cather as Aiken might have us know him, Cather is undoubtedly a very funny *and* a very serious creature.

Keeping in mind Aiken's comment regarding "the effects of contrasting and conflicting tones and themes, a kind of underlying simultaneity in dissimilarity," there is the song from *The Magic Flute* which is called to our attention in the program notes paraphrased by Cather in chapter 4. We are told in *Great Circle* that "the day before he [Mozart] died, he sang with his weak voice the opening measures of 'Der Vogelfanger bin ich ja' " (I catch the birds from dawn to dark). Papageno himself sings the song, but the tone of the novel, the "simultaneity in dissimilarity" becomes even richer and more subtle, if we consider the last verse of the song. "Papageno-Andrew" sings:

I would be pleased with all in life
If once I had a pretty wife.
From all the maids I would select
The fairest as my bride-elect.
I'd bring her sugar ev'ry day,
And she with kisses would repay.
A happier man could never be;
The world would then belong to me.[8]

Chapter 4 is important because it is the peak point in the novel. It is the clearing up of what Andrew Cather has been and is. The first chapter states the conflict, the theme of infidelity, in a frenzied, frantic fashion. But the conflict is not only Bertha's indiscretions but his mother's, which the reader vicariously experiences in chapter 2 by reliving that period of time in Cather's life. Chapters 2 and 3 are concerned with the penetrating and complex development of the two themes of infidelity and *gnothi seauton*. As in the development of, say, a Mozart symphony, the theme or themes are intricately worked and reworked until their significance is indelibly a part of the listener's experience. And chapter 4 represents Andrew's recapitulation of what has gone before and his coming to some sense of resolution with regard to his future status with Bertha. By the end of the novel Andrew already has, in a sense, gone to Duxbury and completed the circle. Bertha is paying the price of her suffering, and a reunion is possible. But it is unimportant whether a reunion occurs. Andrew has accepted it all.

There is a striking truth to Brown's observation with regard to Aiken that "music is a symbolic way of presenting the otherwise inexpressible complications of human thoughts, dreams, even relationships and daily lives,"[9] and perhaps this is no less true with respect to the musical allusions which have enabled us to become a part of the narrative and psychological growth of Andrew Cather. To view these musical allusions as anything less than a mode of thinking of Andrew Cather and a mode of literary technique of Conrad Aiken is to underestimate the significance of the novel and of Aiken as a musico-literary craftsman whose far-ranging musical mind has yet to be sufficiently explored.

Notes

1.   See Conrad Aiken, "Counterpoint and Implication," originally published in *Poetry* (1919). Reproduced in toto in Conrad Aiken, *The Divine Pilgrim* (Athens: University of Georgia Press, 1949), pp. 285–88.

2.   Vance Mizelle, "Conrad Aiken's Use of Music" (Master's thesis, University of Georgia, 1960), p. 96. His critique of *Ushant* is published in slightly modified form as "Conrad Aiken's 'Music Strangely Subtle,' " *The Georgia Review* 19 (Spring 1965):81–92.

3.   Aiken, "Counterpoint and Implication."

4.   Mark Schorer, "Technique as Discovery," in *Forms of Modern Fiction,* ed. William Van O'Connor (Minneapolis: University of Minnesota Press, 1948), p. 25.

5.   Conrad Aiken, *3 Novels* (New York: McGraw-Hill, 1965), p. 11–12. The author's preface and all quotations cited from *Great Circle* refer to the McGraw-Hill Paperback edition.

6.   Calvin Brown, *Music and Literature: A Comparison of the Arts* (Athens: Univeristy of Georgia Press, 1948), p. 201.

7.   Irving Kolodin, Review of *The Magic Flute, Saturday Review* 50 (4 March 1967):46.

8.   English version of *The Magic Flute* (New York: G. Schirmer, Inc., 1941), pp. 22–23.

9.   Brown, p. 204.

Hermann Hesse's *Steppenwolf:*
A Sonata in Prose

Theodore Ziolkowski

The critical and popular reception of Hesse's *Steppenwolf,* when it appeared in 1927, was so hostile that the author felt himself obliged to defend his book a good many times in letters to friends and readers. Again and again he protested that the novel is in no way a betrayal of the positive values which he had always expounded in his life and works, and he pointed out repeatedly that the book achieves a structural perfection which equals, if not surpasses, that of his other works.

Subsequent scholarship has substantiated Hesse's contention that the novel fits organically into the entire pattern of his thought and that it does not represent a defection from his earlier beliefs. But little or nothing has been done to demonstrate that his insistence upon the structural quality of his book is valid.

Among the many passages in which Hesse remonstrates against the criticism of formlessness in the novel, the following is one of the most interesting: "Rein, künstlerisch ist der 'Steppenwolf' mindestens so gut wie 'Goldmund', er ist um das Intermezzo des Traktats herum so streng und straff gebaut wie eine Sonate und greift sein Thema reinlich an."[1]

The present analysis of the structure of the novel can begin with Hesse's own analogy of the sonata, but for the moment it will be permissible to regard this analogy simply as a symbol of strict form in general. It will be our task to discover whether and, if so, precisely in what way Hesse was justified in comparing his novel to a form which represents the highest in musical structure.

I

Confusing upon first perusal is the apparent lack of external structure in *Steppenwolf:* for instance, the absence of the customary division into parts and chapters. Instead, we are presented with a running record of a phantasmagoria of events, interrupted toward the beginning by an apparently incongruous document called "Tractat vom Steppenwolf" and introduced by the remarks of a minor figure who appears in the story itself. But if we look for internal structure

Reprinted from *Modern Languages Quarterly* 19 (1958):115-33.

we see that the book falls naturally into three main sections: the preliminary material, the action, and the so-called "magic theater."

The preliminary material, in turn, has three subdivisions: the introduction, the opening passages of the book itself, and the "Tractat." These three subdivisions are not involved directly in the action or plot of the novel; they are all introductory in nature. This fact distinguishes them from the second and longest part of the book, which tells the story and which alone of the three main sections has a form analogous to the structure of the conventional novel. It relates action covering roughly a month, and it is essentially a straightforward narrative. The third section, finally, sets itself apart from the bulk of the novel by virtue of its fantastic elements: It belongs, properly speaking, to the action of the novel, for it depicts a situation which takes place in the early hours of the day following the final scene of the plot, and there is no technical division whatsoever. But the conscious divorce from all reality separates this section from the realistic narrative of the second part.

Beginning with this rough outline, we can proceed to bring some order into the work. The introduction is written by a young man who is revealed as a typical bourgeois both by his own words and by the brief mention he receives in the book itself. The function of this introduction is twofold: to explain the circumstances regarding the publication of the book and to portray the central figure through the eyes of a typical *Bürger*. The young man is the nephew of the lady from whom a certain Harry Haller rents an apartment upon his arrival in the (unnamed) city. The date of Haller's arrival in the house is given as several years prior to the writing of the introduction, and it is stated that Haller lived in the house for nine or ten months. For the most part the strange tenant lived quietly in his rooms, surrounded by books, empty wine bottles, and overflowing ashtrays. However, toward the end of his stay he underwent a profound change in conduct and appearance, followed then by a period of extreme depression. Shortly thereafter he departed without farewells, leaving behind nothing but a manuscript which the young man now chooses to publish as "ein Dokument der Zeit" (p. 205),[2] for in retrospect he discerns that the affliction which disturbed Haller was symptomatic of the times, and not simply the malady of an individual.

Yet more important than this external information is the view of Haller which we receive through the eyes of a young member of the bourgeoisie before we ever meet him in his own manuscript. The editor, by his own admission, is "ein bürgerlicher, regelmässig lebender Mensch, an Arbeit und genaue Zeiteinteilung gewohnt" (p. 196); he drinks nothing stronger than mineral water and abhors tobacco; he feels uncomfortable in the presence of illness, whether physical or mental; and he is inclined to be suspicious of anything which does not correspond to the facts of ordinary existence as he knows it. Haller offends all of these sensibilities and many others. He makes it clear that Haller was by no means a man congenial to his own temperament: "Ich . . . fühle mich durch ihn, durch die blosse Existenz eines solchen Wesens, im Grunde gestört und beunruhigt, obwohl er mir geradezu lieb geworden ist" (pp. 189–90).

Yet despite his bourgeois inhibitions the young man is portrayed as an intelligent and reliable observer. His affection and interest allow him to perceive the conflict which disturbs Haller:

In dieser Periode kam mir mehr und mehr zum Bewusstsein, dass die Krank-
heit dieses Leidenden nicht auf irgendwelchen Mängelu seiner Natur beruhe,
sondern im Gegenteil nur auf dem nicht zur Harmonie gelangten grossen
Reichtum seiner Gaben und Kräfte. [p. 193]

He reveals for the first time in the course of the book the arbitrary dichotomy
into Steppenwolf and Bürger, by which Haller chooses to designate the two polar aspects of his personality. The introduction, then, states the two conflicting
themes and, without full comprehension of their meaning, portrays Haller in
both capacities. The young man narrates the facts of Haller's life without ascrib-
ing to them the import which they assume in Haller's own mind.

The opening pages of the manuscript itself recount one typical evening in
the life of the forty-eight-year-old littérateur Harry Haller. In atrabilious words
he portrays his state of mind, his beliefs and goals, his erratic existence up to the
present date. His remarks actually parallel the comments of the introduction, and
in many cases the specific events mentioned are identical in both sections. But
Haller's remarks are on a different plane: Whereas the introduction depicted him
externally from the bourgeois standpoint, we now meet him psychologically as
he elects to think of himself, and we feel the full effect of his ambivalent attitude toward the bourgeoisie. He acknowledges that he is out of place in normal
society, and he leads the life of a lone wolf, always on the fringe of humanity.
Yet he is beset by a continual yearning for all that has been left behind:

Ich weiss nicht, wie das zugeht, aber ich, der heimatlose Steppenwolf und ein-
same Hasser der kleinbürgerlichen Welt, ich wohne immerzu in richtigen
Bürgerhäusern, das ist eine alte Sentimentalität von mir. Ich wohne weder in
Palästen noch in Proletarierhäusern, sondern ausgerechnet stets in diesen hoch-
anständigen, hochlangweiligen, tadellos gehaltenen Kleinbürgernestern.... Ich
liebe diese Atmosphäre ohne Zweifel aus meinen Kinderzeiten her, und meine
heimliche Sehnsucht nach so etwas wie Heimat führt mich, hoffnungslos, immer wieder diese alten dummen Wege. [p. 210]

The conflict is elucidated with many pertinent examples as Haller contemplates
his existence and its value in the course of an evening walk.

These speculations are interrupted by the interpolation of the "Tractat," a
document which Haller acquires on this walk and takes home to read. Since the
"Tractat" is of central importance in the novel, it is necessary to recall briefly
how it comes into Haller's hands. Wandering down a familiar alley that evening,
he perceives a previously unnoticed doorway in the wall. Above the door is af-
fixed a placard on which he is able to make out the fleeting, almost illegible
words:

Magisches Theater
Eintritt nicht für jedermann
—nicht für jedermann. [p. 215]

As he steps closer, the evanescent words vanish, but he glimpses a few letters
which seem to dance across the wet pavement: "Nur—für—Ver—rückte!" After a
time Haller proceeds to his restaurant, still musing over the significance of the
queer letters he had seen or imagined. Out of curiosity, he passes back through

the same alley later in the night and notes that the door and sign are no longer there. Suddenly a man emerges from a side street, trudging wearily and bearing a placard. Haller calls to him and asks to be shown the sign. Again he discerns "tanzende, taumelnde Buchstaben" [p. 222]:

Anarchistische Abendunterhaltung
Magisches Theater
Eintritt nicht für jed. . . . [p. 223]

But when he greets the bearer and seeks further information, the man mutters indifferently, hands him a small pamphlet, and disappears into a doorway. Upon his return home Haller sees that the pamphlet is entitled "Tractat vom Steppenwolf." At this point its text follows.

This "Tractat," as Haller reads to his astonishment, offers still a third description of Harry Haller, the Steppenwolf. Whereas the first represented the objective but superficial impressions of a typical *Bürger,* and the second the subjective interpretation of the subject himself, this third depiction is the observation of a higher intelligence which is able to view Haller perspectively *sub specie aeternitatis.*

The "Tractat," in essence, makes a distinction between three types of beings, differentiated relatively according to their degree of individuation. The remarkable cosmology which is developed here can best be visualized by the analogy of a sphere situated on an axis whose poles represent the opposite concepts of nature and spirit. The center of the sphere, as the point farthest removed from all extremes, is the bourgeois ego; the cosmic regions outside the sphere, on the other hand, are inhabited by the "tragic natures" or "Immortals" who have transcended the narrow bourgeois concept of egoism and have burst forth into the cosmos by embracing a belief in the fundamental unity of life. They are aware of the fact that supreme existence consists in the recognition and acceptance of all aspects of life, and this attitude demands transcendence of the ego in the bourgeois sense. In order to preserve his "Ich," his ego, the *Bürger* must resist every impulse to lose himself in extremes: he must sway toward neither pole; he wishes to be neither profligate nor saint. Moreover, in maintaining this position of moderation, the *Bürger* assumes a definite standpoint with regard to the world, relative to which certain of its polar opposites must be condemned as evil.

Thus, for the *Bürger,* whose very way of life requires the utmost order in the world, the opposite extreme of disorder or chaos must be anathema. The Immortals, on the contrary, accept chaos as the natural state of existence, for they inhabit a realm where all polarity has ceased and where every manifestation of life is approved as necessary and good. In their eyes the polarity of nature and spirit does not exist, for their cosmos is expansive enough to encompass all of the apparent polar extremes in the *Bürger*'s limited sphere.[3]

If the Immortals and the *Bürger* represent the two extremes in Hesse's scale of individuation, the Steppenwolf occupies a tenuous and anomalous perch between them:

Prüfen wir daraufhin die Seele des Steppenwolfes, so stellt er sich dar alas ein Mensch, den schon sein hoher Grad von Individuation zum Nichtbürger

> bestimmt—denn alle hochgetriebene Individuation kehrt sich gegen das Ich
> und neigt wieder zu dessen Zerstörung. (p. 238)

Yet not every person of this nature is strong enough to transcend the *principium individuationis* completely; many are destined to remain in the world of the *Bürger* despite their longing for the reaches of the cosmos. If we adapt this fact to the sphere-image, we must place the Steppenwolf in an orbit within the sphere, cruising close to the surface, but never penetrating into the cosmos for more than a brief, tantalizing moment. The fact that he belongs to neither realm completely accounts for the Steppenwolf's dissatisfaction with existence and demonstrates why Harry Haller, the case in point, can find no satisfactory solution to his dilemma and often contemplates suicide.

The "Tractat" goes on to point out that only humor[4] can make it possible for the Steppenwolf to exist peacefully in a world whose values he despises:

> In der Welt zu leben, als sei es nicht die Welt, das Gesetz zu achten und doch
> über ihm zu stehen, zu besitzen, "als besässe man nicht", zu verzichten, als sei
> es kein Verzicht—alle diese beliebten und oft formulierten Forderungen einer
> hohen Weisheit ist einzig der Humor zu verwirklichen fähig. [p. 240]

But humor in this sense is possible only if the individual has resolved the conflicts in his own soul, and this resolution is the result of self-recognition. To this end the "Tractat" mentions three contingencies for Haller:

> Möglich, dass er eines Tages sich erkennen lernt, sei es, dass er einen unsrer
> kleinen Spiegel in die Hand bekomme, sei es, dass er den Unsterblichen be-
> gegne oder vielleicht in einem unsrer magischen Theater dasjenige finde, wes-
> sen er zur Befreiung seiner verwahrlosten Seele bedarf. [p. 241]

Thus the "Tractat" proposes a reconciliation of the conflicting themes which have been discussed. If Harry Haller can peer deep into the chaos of his own soul by any of the suggested means, then he will be able to live happily in the world or even dare to make "den Sprung ins Weltall" (p. 240)—to join the Immortals. The final section of the "Tractat" explains, however, that this is a more difficult task than Harry had previously imagined, for his personality comprises not only the two conflicting poles which he had named, but literally thousands of divergent aspects which cry for recognition.

It becomes clear that the "Tractat" is ostensibly the work of the Immortals, for no one else could have this lofty and all-encompassing view of the world. Thus it represents a study of Haller from still a third standpoint. If we pause now to survey the preliminary material of the novel, a pattern seems to emerge. These three sections (introduction, the opening pages of the manuscript, and "Tractat") present three treatments of the conflicting themes in Haller's soul, as perceived respectively from the three points of view outlined in the theoretical tract: *Bürger*—Steppenwolf—Immortals. The introduction states the two themes theoretically; the second section brings the development in which the significance of these themes for Haller's life is interpreted; and the "Tractat" recapitulates the themes, theoretically again, and proposes a resolution of the conflict. But this scheme, exposition—development—recapitulation, can be found in any book of music theory under the heading "sonata form" or "first-movement form," for it is the classical structure for the opening section of the sonata.

The terms *sonata* and *sonata form* are two of the most confusing designations in music theory, for the latter does not refer to the form of the former. The sonata is a generic name for any major composition of one to four movements, of which one (usually the first) must be in sonata form. If the composition is written for piano, it is a piano sonata; if written for orchestra, it is called a symphony; and so forth. The term which interests us here, sonata form, refers to the structure of the first movement alone. The exposition states two themes with one in the tonic, the other in the dominant; the development follows in which the potentialities of these themes are worked out; and the recapitulation restates the themes as they occurred in the exposition, but this time both are in the tonic; the conflict has been resolved.

In the novel the difference in keys is approximated by the contrasting attitudes of Harry Haller as Steppenwolf, on the one hand, and as *Bürger* on the other: The first represents, as it were, the tonic, and the second the dominant. The *a-b-a* structure of the sonata, which is achieved through the general repetition of the exposition in the recapitulation, is imitated by Hesse insofar as the exposition and recapitulation are views of Haller from the outside and are largely theoretical; this gives them the effect of unity. The development, however, differs from these in tone and style since it is written by Haller himself, and it stresses the practical significance of the two themes for his own life. The resolution of the tonic and dominant in the recapitulation is an obvious parallel to the proposed reconciliation of Steppenwolf and *Bürger* in Harry Haller. In view of this rather close correspondence between the musical form and the first part of *Steppenwolf,* it seems safe to assert that the preliminary material of the novel reveals "first-movement form." And in view of Hesse's chosen analogy, it would not be unreasonable to assume that this structure is a conscious one.

In case this assertion seems to force one art-form willfully into the Procrustean bed of another, it might be mentioned in passing that "first-movement form" has been applied to various literary genres before now. Otto Ludwig, in his essay on "Allgemeine Form der Shakespearischen Komposition,"[5] evolves a general structural tendency in Shakespeare's plays which he compares to sonata form. Oskar Walzel, ever the advocate of "wechselseitige Erhellung der Künste," suggests that the same application can be made to certain poems.[6] H. A. Basilius has shown that Thomas Mann's *Tonio Kröger* is consciously constructed according to the pattern of sonata form;[7] and Calvin S. Brown, in *Music and Literature: A Comparison of the Arts,* devotes an entire chapter to the analysis of literary works—mainly poems—which employ this structure more or less successfully.[8]

On the other hand, there have been objections to the application of musical form to literary works, and one of the most lucid and convincing of these is stated in *Theory of Literature* by René Wellek and Austin Warren. With regard to romantic notions concerning musical form, the authors contend that "blurred outlines, vagueness of meaning, and illogicality are not, in a literal sense, 'musical' at all."[9] But we have seen that Hesse presents his material clearly, is specific in meaning, and proceeds according to a highly logical system. Wellek and Warren go on to say:

Literary imitations of musical structures like leitmotiv, the sonata, or symphonic form seem to be more concrete; but it is hard to see why repetitive motifs or a certain contrasting and balancing of moods, though by avowed intention imitative of musical composition, are not essentially the familiar literary devices of recurrence, contrast, and the like which are common to all the arts.[10]

Yet Hesse, though he makes ample use of the leitmotiv, depends neither upon this nor upon contrast in order to produce his musical effect; he is not concerned with vague synesthesia. Rather, he has devised a novel which consciously adheres to the rigid structure of sonata form, and the other musical devices which he employs are merely embellishments within the entire framework. Thus the criticism, which is justifiable with regard to many so-called "musical" works of literature, is not applicable in the case of *Steppenwolf.*

II

Before going on to the second part, we must pause to consider a matter which contains the key to the entire work: the question of double perception.

In the "Tractat" we read: "Und dies alles ist dem Steppenwolf, auch wenn er niemals diesen Abriss seiner innern Biographie zu Gesicht bekommt, sehr wohl bekannt. Er ahnt seine Stellung im Weltgebäude, er ahnt und kennt die Unsterblichen ..." (p. 241). This seems to suggest a satisfactory solution to the mystery of the "Tractat." The device of causing a figure in a novel to read his own biography, written by some unknown hand, is an approved romantic practice,[11] and Hesse is certainly an heir of romanticism. Yet it must not be forgotten that up to this point the entire work has taken place on the level of everyday reality. Why should there be this sudden intrusion of the supernatural? Is it not more reasonable to assume that Haller himself reads this strange message into the text of the pamphlet since it is all familiar to him? This is an intriguing speculation, but it requires substantiation.

In his essay "Vom Bücherlesen" (1920) Hesse considers three types of readers. The first type is the naïve person who accepts the book and its story objectively; the second type comprises those who read with the imagination of a child and comprehend the hundreds of symbolic connotations latent in every word and image. But the third reader is one who uses the book simply as a *terminus a quo:* on this level

lesen wir ja überhaupt nicht mehr, was vor uns auf dem Papier steht, sondern schwimmen im Strom der Anregungen und Einfälle, die uns aus dem Gelesenen zukommen. Sie können aus dem Text kommen, sie können sogar nur aus den Schriftbildern entstehen. Das Inserat einer Zeitung kann zur Offenbarung wreden.[12]

This delightful conceit is not the whim of an instant; it is a recurrent theme in Hesse's works. An example can be found, for instance, as much as ten years later in *Narziss und Goldmund* (1930). After his rude awakening by Narziss, Goldmund lives in a new world:

Ein lateinisches Initial wurde zum duftenden Gesicht der Mutter, ein langgezogener Ton im Ave zum Paradiestor, ein griechischer Buchstabe zum rennen-

den Pferd, zur bäumenden Schlange, still wälzte sie sich unter Blumen davon,
und schon stand an ihrer Stelle wieder die starre Seite der Grammatik.[13]

In the light of this idea, why should the action in *Steppenwolf* not be con-
strued similarly? Let us briefly reconstruct the scene. In a fit of depression Haller
goes out for his evening stroll; he is willing to grasp eagerly after any ray of
hope which would alleviate his desperate condition. Thus, when he notices a
smudge or crack in the wall of the alley, set off by the sparkle of the damp plas-
ter, his overwrought mind reads an imaginary message in fleeting letters. In the
course of the evening he consumes a considerable portion of wine: "Ich brauchte
keinen Wein mehr. Die goldne Spur war aufgeblitzt, ich war ans Ewige erinnert,
an Mozart, an die Sterne" (p. 219). In this inebriated and rhapsodic state he
meets a weary placard-bearer, fortuitously, in the same fateful alley. But the tired
worker, anxious to get rid of the troublesome drunk, brusquely shoves a pamphlet into his hands—*any* pamphlet—which Haller's acrobatic and stimulated mind
converts, at home, into the "Tractat." These are essential thoughts from a remote
and more perceptive area of Haller's intelligence—an area which is usually
blocked by the problematics of his dual personality and the exigencies of his existence. Here, for an instant, his higher acumen seeps through.

This concept of double perception plays an increasingly important role in the
novel, for it is necessary throughout the remainder of the book to make a clear
distinction between two levels of reality: the everyday plane of the *Bürger* or the
placard-bearer, and the exalted, supernal plane of the Immortals and the magic
theater. Haller might be called an eidetic, i.e., "an individual capable of producing subjective (visual or other) images or 'Anschauungsbilder' of virtually hallu-
cinatory vividness."[14] Accordingly, his experiences on the upper level of reality
assume fully as much intensity for him as the action on the level of mundane
reality.

Here again we are concerned with a highly musical device corresponding
closely to counterpoint, which the *Harvard Dictionary of Music* defines as "the
combination into a single musical fabric of lines or parts which have distinctive
melodic significance."[15] By means of double perception almost any given action
of the book may be interpreted on two distinct levels, and this produces the effect of simultaneity or concomitance of the two planes or melodic lines. This
particular device comes much closer to the musical concept of point-
counterpoint than the technique employed, for instance, by Aldous Huxley in
his novel of that title or by André Gide or by many of their imitators. The latter
achieve their effect by the sudden juxtaposition of various moods and points of
view, but Hesse consciously attempts to produce authentic counterpoint by
bringing the two lines of action into play at the same time.

In his chapter on "Timbre, Harmony, and Counterpoint," Calvin S. Brown
denies the possibility of true counterpoint in literature; but he cites the literary
pun as the closest approach. The limiting element in the case of the pun is the
fact that we have "not two things, but one word with different relationships."[16]
On the basis of this parallel, it might be stated that double perception achieves
the effect of a sustained pun, and the interplay of the two levels of reality produces a genuine contrapuntal effect. If this is not precisely what is understood by
the musical concept of counterpoint, it at least represents an advance beyond any
previous literary counterpart.

III

The second and longest part of *Steppenwolf* might be called Harry Haller's *Lehrjahre,* and it is interesting to note that the verbs "lernen" and "lehren" actually occur scores of times in this section of the book. Here Haller learns to accept many facets of life which certain inhibitions of his personality had previously caused him to reject; he discovers to his astonishment that the poles of his being are not so irreconcilable as he had imagined. This phase of Haller's education is rather elementary: it is kept on the level of everyday life in preparation for and in conscious anticipation of the more metaphysical scope of the magic theater.

The motif of "chance" and "destiny," as in *Wilhelm Meisters Lehrjahre,* lends an aura of inevitability to the initial events of the denouement, and it is an obvious corollary to the technique of double perception. One day Haller happens to see a man who resembles the placard-bearer of his recent adventure. With a conspiratorial wink Haller asks him if there is no entertainment that evening: " 'Abendunterhaltung' brummte der Mann und sah mir fremd ins Gesicht. 'Gehen Sie in den Schwarzen Adler, Mensch, wenn Sie Bedürfnisse haben!' " (p. 260). The repeated use of the word "schien" in connection with these incidents indicates clearly that Haller is not dealing with the same man as before. Moreover, it is just chance that the stolid citizen happens to respond indignantly to the misunderstood question and advises Haller to go to an obviously notorious prostitute den if he wishes to satisfy his needs. It is likewise chance (or destiny?) which leads Haller that very evening to this particular night club, where he meets Hermine, who becomes his teacher during these *Lehrjahre.*

The entire first day of the action represents an accumulation of impossible situations which bring Haller to the point of suicide. One incident after another convinces him that his life has become intolerable. The conflict of themes which was introduced in the preliminary material is elevated in the course of this first day to an unbearable pitch. Late in the night Haller weaves wearily from bar to bar, determined to put an end to his miserable existence yet hesitant to go home and do so. Then he finds himself outside the bar "Zum schwarzen Adler," and since he recalls the name from that morning, he goes in.

It is made sufficiently clear in the course of the book that Hermine is a high-class prostitute or call-girl, and she greets the errant Haller with an intimate, hearty tone which has no deep metaphysical implications whatsoever (as some scholars assume[17]), but which is simply customary in her profession. She immediately perceives that he is weary, dejected, and drunk; like any sensible woman she advises him to sleep it off. Haller, drunk as he is and happy to be able to stave off his suicide as long as possible, is delighted to obey her. He feels that her immediate comprehension of his situation is almost preternatural. Actually, any reader will recognize that most of Hermine's remarks, like the utterances of the Delphic oracle, are open to two interpretations. In this case Hermine's words are precisely what one would expect from a prostitute with long experience in handling drunks and mothering would-be suicides. Only Haller's lonely and despondent state allows him to ascribe any higher significance to her casual remarks.

Hermine, who becomes genuinely interested in Haller, makes a tremendous impression on the naïve intellectual. In his eyes she stands for a wholly new

aspect of life—one which he had previously regarded with distrust. His experiences with her must be viewed continually in double perspective. On the one
hand, the whole episode is anticipated in the "Tractat," which, as an example of
Haller's dual nature and bourgeois limitations, cites his attitude toward
prostitutes:

> Ausserdem war er in kleinbürgerlicher Erziehung aufgewachsen und hatte von
> dorther eine Menge von Begriffen und Schablonen beibehalten. Er hatte theo-
> retisch nicht das mindeste gegen das Dirnentum, wäre aber unfähig gewesen,
> persönlich eine Dirne ernst zu nehmen und wirklich als seinesgleichen zu bet-
> rachten. [pp. 235-36]

Yet in order to overcome these bourgeois inhibitions he must expand his soul to
the point of embracing every aspect of life (p. 250). Hermine, then, is a test case:
On a higher level Haller's acceptance of her and her world—dancing and jazz, the
love orgies of Pablo and Maria, narcotics, and the elemental pleasures of life—is
only symbolic for his repudiation of the entire narrow world of the *Bürger* and
his new dimensions as an aspirant to the kingdom of the Immortals.

Haller learns much from and through Hermine. She teaches him to enjoy
and appreciate many new aspects of life, and her friends, Pablo and Maria, aid
her in Haller's education. For Haller she becomes almost a symbol; he calls her
"eine Tür . . . durch die das Leben zu mir herinkam!" (p. 290). On the brink of
a suicide of despair he has found someone who can bring him back to life:

> Sie war die Erlösung, der Weg ins Freie. Sie musste mich leben lehren oder
> sterben lehren, sie mit ihrer festen und hübschen Hand musste mein erstarrtes
> Herz antasten, damit es unter der Berührung des Lebens entweder aufblühe
> oder in Asche zerfalle. [p. 294]

Hermine, too, realizes why he needs her: "Du brauchst mich, um tanzen zu
lernen, lachen zu lernen, leben zu lernen" (p. 300). And at first she feels that the
task is almost insurmountable: "Ich glaube, du musst alles erst lernen, was sich
bei andern Menschen von selber versteht, sogar die Freude am Essen" (p. 301). It
is the art of life in which Hermine is Haller's preceptress:

> Wofür ich aber zu sorgen habe, das ist, dass du die kleinen leichten Künste
> und Spiele im Leben etwas besser erlernst, auf diesem Gebiet bin ich deine Leh-
> rerin und werde dir eine bessere Lehrerin sein, als deine ideale Geliebte es war,
> darauf verlasse dich! . . . Ideal und tragisch lieben, o Freund, das kannst du ge-
> wiss vortrefflich, ich zweifle nicht daran, alle Achtung davor! Du wirst nun ler-
> nen, auch ein wenig gewöhnlich und menschlich zu lieben. [p. 318]

But all that Haller learns from Hermine on this level of mundane reality is only
symbolic for an entire new world of experiences: "Wie das Grammaphon die
Luft von asketischer Geistigkeit in meinem Studierzimmer verdarb . . . so drang
von allen Seiten Neues, Gefürchtetes, Auflösendes in mein bisher so scharf um-
rissenes und so streng abgeschlossenes Leben" (p. 319).

Yet on a higher level of reality Hermine and Pablo, the jazz musician to
whom she introduces Haller, are equally important—as reflections of his own
thoughts! For occasionally these two representatives of the sensual world utter
deep and significant statements which ill conform to the very realistic picture
drawn of them. Hermine, for example, expresses quite lucidly the central tenet of

the novel, which Haller is unable to formulate articulately for himself; she confirms his inchoate belief in the eternal spiritual kingdom of the Immortals. She tells him what people of their sort, the Steppenwolf-natures, live for:

> Der Ruhm ist es nicht, o nein! Aber das, was ich Ewigkeit nenne. Die Frommen nennen es Reich Gottes. Ich denke mir: wir Menschen alle, wir Anspruchsvolleren, wir mit der Sehnsucht, mit der Dimension zuviel, könnten gar nicht leben, wenn es nicht ausser der Luft dieser Welt auch noch eine andre Luft zu atmen gäbe, wenn nicht aussr der Zeit auch noch die Ewigkeit bestünde, und die ist das Reich des Echten. [p. 345]

Just as Haller read his own speculations on the Steppenwolf into an indifferent pamphlet, so has he transplanted his own thoughts into the words of a clever courtesan. This fact is stressed: "Dies alles waren, so schien mir, vielleicht nicht ihre eigenen Gedanken, sondern die meinigen, die die Hellsichtige gelesen und eingeatmet hatte und die sie mir wiedergab, so dass sie nun Gestalt hatten und neu vor mir standen" (p. 346). It is again made explicit at the end (p. 411).

In the case of Pablo, who is presented consistently as a monosyllabic sensualist, it is even more striking. At the beginning of the magic theater, when Pablo is speaking so astutely on the nature of the personality, Haller muses:

> War nicht vielleicht ich es, der ihn sprechen machte, der aus ihm sprach?
> Blickte nicht auch aus seinen schwarzen Augen nur meine eigene Seele mich
> an . . . wie aus den grauen Augen Herminens? . . . Er, den ich nie zusammenhängend hatte reden hören, den kein Disput, keine Formulierung interessierte, dem ich kaum ein Denken zugetraut hatte, er sprach nun, er redete
> mit seiner guten, warmen Stimme fliessend und fehlerlos. [pp. 367-68]

Thus, Hermine, Pablo, Maria, and the entire demimonde of *Steppenwolf* exist on a realistic plane consistently throughout the book. Only Haller's sense of double perception bestows upon them the added dimension by which they assume symbolic proportions. In the "Tractat" he tells himself that he must expand his soul to encompass the world; accident with an element of destiny places him in a position to carry out this self-admonishment, and he sparks his contact with this other world with reflections which he imputes to the minds of his new acquaintances. This entire sequence of development, on both levels of reality, culminates in the experience of the magic theater, which takes place a little less than four weeks after the initial encounter with Hermine.

The occasion which Haller designates as the *magisches Theater* on the upper level of reality is no more than the aftermath of a great ball—according to the season probably a *Faschingsball*. Haller is prepared for it on both levels: He has learned to dance and to love; by implication he has embraced and affirmed all aspects of life. Symbolic for this acceptance of the cosmos, including its most abysmal depths, is the fact that Haller must descend to a basement bar, called quite pointedly "Die Hölle," in order to meet Hermine (p. 357). From that point they gradually ascend to a small room in the upper stories (p. 367) where Haller later experiences the magic theater. This upward progression is interrupted by a symbolic wedding dance which Haller performs with Hermine (p. 365) and which represents the imminent marriage of the two poles of existence in his soul: the intellectual or spiritual with the sensual or natural. In this passage Hermine is no longer "*a* woman"; she is "womankind": "Alle Frauen dieser fiebernden Nacht

... waren zusammengeschmolzen und eine einzige geworden, die in meinen Armen blühte" (p. 365).

In the course of the symbolic ascent, on both planes, Haller loses the last vestiges of his bourgeois notion of individuality. Here the concept of fluidity, so important in other works by Hesse (for example *Siddhartha*), is touched upon: "Ich war nicht mehr ich, meine Persönlichkeit war aufgelöst im Festrausch wie Salz im Wasser" (p. 362). These rites are the final stage in Haller's initiation for the supreme experience. Only now can he agree to Pablo's invitation to the magic theater, which involves the stipulation: "Eintritt nur für Verrückte, kostet den Verstand" (p. 367).

The words "nur für Verrückte," which occur in leitmotiv fashion at several significant points in the book, sum up still another major motif of the novel: namely, the concept of magical thinking. This idea is most succinctly stated in the essay "Gedanken zu Dostojewaskis 'Idiot' " (1919),[18] in which Hesse declares that the "Verrückte" are those rare individuals, like Myschkin in Dostoevski's novel, who have perceived the total relativity of good and evil; they are the inhabitants of this world who have learned to regard life with the eyes of the Immortals. They live for a higher reality where polar opposites have ceased to be reciprocally hostile, where every aspect of life is affirmed, where there is no dichotomy between *fas* and *nefas*. They think "magically," for they look beyond the apparent "reality" of the bourgeois phenomenal world to the essential reality of cosmic harmony.

After his symbolic descent into hell and the wedding dance with his opposite and complement, Hermine, Haller is able to think magically and to accept Pablo's invitation, even on the condition that he become "verrückt." This acceptance concludes Haller's *Lehrjahre:* the second part of the novel has portrayed the full course of his development from a schizophrenic intellectual contemplating suicide because of an imaginary conflict between two poles of his being to a man with a healthy awareness and appreciation of the world around him. To extend the analogy, he is now ready to embark on his *Wanderjahre,* to plumb the very depths of the potentialities of his life. The magic theater is the vehicle through which he is to be introduced symbolically to the full extent of his personality in all its manifestations, and the consummation of his symbolic marriage to Hermine is to represent the complete welding of all aspects of his nature.

It would be gratifying if we could demonstrate that this second part conforms strictly to the form of the second movement of the sonata, but that would be an extension of the truth. The second movement offers various possiblities to the composer; but since no precise correspondence exists between the novel and the musical forms, it will be best not to go into the matter. It might be mentioned in passing that the structure of many modern sonatas is far less rigid than that of the classical sonata, and we have seen that Haller's *Lehrjahre* are highly musical in nature owing to the device of double perception or counterpoint. In this restricted sense, then, the second part is equivalent to a second movement.

IV

The "magisches Theater," like every other incident in the novel, is open to interpretation on two levels. On the realistic level it is nothing more than an

opium fantasy in which Haller indulges after the ball in the company of Hermine and Pablo. From the very beginning of Haller's acquaintance with Pablo it
is emphasized that the jazz musician is familiar with all the exotic refinements of
narcotics. At their first meeting Pablo offers Haller a powder to improve his
spirits:

> In der Tat wurde ich in kurzem frischer und munterer, wahrscheinlich war
> etwas Kokain in dem Pulver gewesen. Hermine erzählte mir, dass Pablo viele
> solche Mittel habe, die er auf geheimen Wegen erhalte, die er zuweilen Freun-
> den vorsetze und in deren Mischung und Dosierung er ein Meister sei: Mittel
> . . . zur Erzeugung schöner Träume. . . . [p. 322]

Later Haller admits: "Nicht selten nahm ich etwas von seinen Mitteln an" (p.
336). On the last evening Pablo again offers Haller one of his stimulants:

> Jeder von uns rauchte nun . . . langsam seine Zigarette, deren Rauch dick wie
> Weihrauch war, und trank in langsamen Schlucken die herbsüsse . . .
> Flüssigkeit, die in der Tat unendlich belebend und beglückend wirkte, als
> werde man mit Gas gefüllt und verliere seine Schwere. [p. 368]

Everything Haller is to see in the magic theater, then, is a reflection of his
own soul and a product of his eidetic vision under the influence of narcotics.
Pablo makes this clear:

> Sie wissen ja, wo diese andre Welt verborgen liegt, dass es die Welt Ihrer eige-
> nen Seele ist, die Sie suchen. Nur in Ihrem eigenen Innern lebt jene andre Wir-
> klichkeit, nach der Sie sich sehnen. Ich kann Ihnen nichts geben, was nicht in
> Ihnen selbst schon existiert. . . . Ich helfe Ihnen Ihre eigene Welt sichtbar
> machen, das ist alles. [pp. 368–69]

The "Tractat vom Steppenwolf," as we recall, stated that the Immortals are
those who have transcended the *principium individuationis*. Pablo now restates
this theme:

> Ohne Zweifel haben Sie ja längst erraten, dass die Überwindung der Zeit, die
> Erlösung von der Wirklichkeit, und was immer für Namen Sie Ihrer Sehnsucht
> geben mögen, nichts andres bedeuten, als den Wunsch, Ihrer sogenannten
> Persönlichkeit ledig zu werden. [p. 370]

The magic theater gives Haller a chance to do precisely this. Peering into Pablo's
magic mirror, Haller perceives simultaneously thousands of faces of his personality: he sees himself as a child, a youth, an adult, an old man; as a serious scholar
and a comical buffoon; bald and with long hair; every potentiality of development and expression is there in the mirrored image.[19] When he accepts the
fact that all of these Harrys are part of his own personality, he is prepared to enter the magic theater and to enjoy the multifarious activities offered there for his
amusement.

Structurally the theater which he visualizes in this dream is on the order of a
penny arcade. There are thousands of booths which he has only to enter in order
to undergo a new experience. Hesse mentions fifteen of these sideshows by
name, and Haller enters only four of them. But it is obvious that these few sen-
sations are symbolic for the world of experience which lies open to him.

Individually each sideshow recapitulates a motif which has been developed in the course of the entire novel, and each one can be analyzed separately in order to demonstrate how carefully Hesse has constructed his work. Let us examine the first one as a typical example. While Haller is peering into Pablo's magic mirror, two aspects of the personality which he sees reflected there leap out of the mirror: one, an elegant young man, embraces Pablo and goes off with him; the other, a charming youth of sixteen or seventeen, dashes down the corridor to a booth marked "Alle Mädchen sind dein!" (p. 373). In the second part of the novel it is indicated that Pablo, apart from his proficiency in heterosexual love, is also homosexually inclined; on two specific occasions he makes overtures to Haller, who rejects them indignantly. Now Haller sees that part of his personality is not only willing but eager to explore this particular side of life. Yet at the same time another part of his nature goes into a booth where (as we learn later when Haller finally comes back to the same booth himself) he experiences the love of every woman Haller has ever known or even seen and desired during his life. The complete resolution of any polarity in matters of physical love is clearly implied.

The following sideshows pick up various other motifs from the novel: In the second one Haller learns that he, the confirmed pacifist, is able to enjoy war and killing. The motifs of metamorphosis, suicide, the decline of western civilization, the nature of music, humor, the structure of the personality—all these are mentioned; and each one, whether Haller actually enters the booth or not, conjures up a very concrete image because it represents the culmination of a motif which has been subtly suggested again and again throughout the book.[20]

The final tableau, however, requires a more detailed consideration, for there the two levels of reality become so entangled as to be almost inextricable. As the effect of the opium begins to wear off, Harry has his most sublime experience: direct contact with the Immortals in the person of Mozart (like an earlier encounter with Goethe in a dream). But this exposure is too much for his overtaxed nerves: he feels despondent of ever attaining the stature of the Immortals, whom, for an instant, he felt that he had approximated. In this feeling of despair he suddenly becomes aware that Pablo and Hermine, far from spending their time in idle dreams, are lying on the carpet, locked in a passionate embrace. On the dream level Haller seems to take a knife and kill Hermine (p. 406). Yet the actual event probably amounts to no more than an exclamation of jealousy and disgust when he realizes that the woman whom he had elevated to symbolic stature, rather than being the ethereal personification of an ideal, is indeed very much of the flesh. It is, to be sure, a murder on this level of reality also, for in his mind he eradicates the idealized image of Hermine which had obsessed him. As he contemplates her (imagined) corpse, he meditates: "Nun war ihr Wunsch erfüllt. Noch eh sie ganz mein geworden war, hatte ich meine Geliebte getötet" (p. 406).

This realization marks the climax of the novel, for the whole structure is calculated to bring Haller to the consummation of his wedding with Hermine, to the total acceptance of all that she represents to him—namely, the opposite of every pole of his personality. He fails because he allows a touch of bourgeois reality to creep into the images of the magic theater; he allows bourgeois jealousy to destroy the image of Hermine as the complement of his being. Pablo's words indicate that Hermine, in the last analysis, is simply an aspect of Haller's being with which he is not yet reconciled: "Mit dieser Figur hast du leider nicht umzugehen verstanden – ich glaubte, du habest das Spiel besser gelernt. Nun, es lässt sich korrigieren" (p. 414).

After the deed Haller slumps back in his chair, and when Pablo fetches a blanket to cover Hermine from the cool morning air (on the level of ordinary reality), he interprets it to be a cover to conceal the knife wound (on the dream level). When Pablo brings in a radio (first level), Haller thinks that it is Mozart again (second level), and the ensuing conversation is once more on the plane of dream or higher reality. Mozart-Pablo's message is a reiteration of the thought which Haller had once before inferred from Hermine's words. Mozart experiments with the radio and, at length, locates a Munich broadcast, where the strains of a Handel concerto are scarcely recognizable through the maddening static and interference of the instrument. When Haller objects to this, Mozart replies:

> Sie hören und sehen, Wertester, zugleich ein vortreffliches Gleichnis alles Lebens. Wenn Sie dem Radio zuhören, so hören und sehen Sie den Urkampf zwischen Idee und Erscheinung, zwischen Ewigkeit und Zeit, zwischen Göttlichem und Menschlichem. [p. 409]

Haller must learn to perceive the eternal spirit behind the spurious phenomena of external reality; he must learn to take seriously only those things which deserve it: the essence, not the appearance. Mozart goes on to chastize Haller for the murder of the image of Hermine, and it is revealed that the stabbing took place only on the dream level. Before the jury of Immortals he accuses Haller: "Haller hat ... die hohe Kunst beleidigt, indem er unsern schönen Bildersaal mit der sogenannten Wirklichkeit verwechselte und ein gespiegeltes Mädchen mit einem gespiegelten Messer totgestochen hat" (p. 412). For this crime against the higher reality of the Immortals Haller is punished by "Ausgelachtwerden" (p. 412).[21] The only penance imposed is the following:

> Sie sollen leben, und Sie sollen das Lachen lernen. Sie sollen die verfluchte Radiomusik des Lebens anhören lernen, sollen den Geist hinter ihr verehren, sollen über den Klimbim in ihr lachen lernen. Fertig, mehr wird von Ihnen nicht verlangt. [pp. 413–14]

At this point Haller begins to realize that the figure which he had taken for Mozart is actually none other than Pablo, who is reproaching him for his previous outburst against Hermine. He comprehends that he was too weak to sustain the rarified stratosphere of the Immortals; he had confused the two levels of reality and had taken seriously the prostitute Hermine of the first level, whereas he should merely have laughed at her. By taking her seriously and allowing himself a tirade against her, he had destroyed the image of Hermine as the symbolic woman, which he had meticulously constructed during his four-week acquaintance with her.

However, the novel ends on an optimistic note, for Haller understands his situation and his shortcomings: "Einmal würde ich das Figurenspiel besser spie-

len. Einmal würde ich das Lachen lernen. Pablo wartete auf mich. Mozart wartete auf mich" (p. 415). Haller knows now that Mozart and Pablo are only two
aspects of the same person (just like Narziss and Goldmund in Hesse's next novel): Between the two of them they represent the complete union of the poles of
spirit and nature. Haller's last words, with their tacit understanding and affirmation of this metaphysical union, indicate that he, too, may hope to learn magical
thinking and to enter the ranks of the Immortals. He has experienced it briefly,
but must transcend himself in order to be able to maintain constantly this new
view of life.

   Thus the novel ends. In retrospect the structure of the magic theater might
be called a theme with variations. The theme, which is borrowed from the
"Tractat," is the notion that Haller's personality comprises a multiplicity of opposite elements; but when he views these opposites from the new perspective
gained through the magic mirror, from the standpoint of the Immortals, he realizes that they are not mutually exclusive. For the duration of the magic theater—
until the murder of Hermine's image—he observes life from a point outside the
polar sphere of the *Bürger*, and he is able to accept all its aspects. Each booth in
the magic theater represents a variation on this theme; in each one he sees a specific instance of the opposite tendencies in his nature, and yet he affirms all of
them completely.

   The *Harvard Dictionary of Music* defines the theme with variations as "a musical form based upon the principle of presenting a musical idea (theme) in an
arbitrary number of modifications (from 4 to 30 or more), each of these being a
'variation.' "[22] It also has a statement that the variation is sometimes employed as
the form of the finale in the sonata or symphony.[23] Calvin S. Brown mentions
that the obvious danger of formal repetition and variation in the literary genres
is tedium,[24] and in conventional works of literature that criticism holds true. By
making use of a dream sequence Hesse is able to maintain a constant theme
while providing in each case a different setting and new details. The setting and
details, in turn, are drawn from motifs which occur in the preceding parts of the
novel. Thus, the finale knits the book into a tightly constructed whole.

   Der Steppenwolf might be compared to a sonata in three movements. The first
movement shows unmistakable first-movement form, or the so-called sonata
form; the second movement, though it does not reveal any form typical of the
adagio of the sonata, employs the highly musical device of double perception or
counterpoint throughout; the third movement, finally, is constructed according
to a pattern remarkably similar to a finale in variations. As in the modern symphony, the themes are not limited to one movement alone, but appear in all the
parts, thus creating an effect of structural unity in the whole: The second and
third movements are based, respectively, upon the first and second points of the
"Tractat." Although the work abounds in so-called musical devices, like leitmotiv and contrast, it does not depend upon such hazy concepts in order to attain
its musical effect. Instead, it reveals a structure which, consciously or unconsciously on Hesse's part, corresponds in general to a specific musical form and, in
certain places, seems to adhere rigidly to the accepted pattern of musical composition. To this extent it might be permissible to designate Hesse's *Steppenwolf* as a
sonata in prose.

Notes

1.   Hermann Hesse, *Briefe* (Berlin: Suhrkamp Verlag, 1951), p. 34; or Hermann Hesse, *Gesammelte Schriften* (Berlin: Suhrkamp Verlag, 1957) 7:495 (hereafter cited as *GS*).

2.   All page references to *Steppenwolf* are taken from Hesse's *Gesammelte Dichtungen* ([Frankfurt am Main]: Suhrkamp Verlag, 1952), vol. 4 (hereafter cited as *GD*).

3.   This concept of chaos is explained more programmatically in Hesse's essay volume *Blick ins Chaos* (1920); cf. *GS*, 7:161–86.

4.   It is immediately apparent that the attitude which Hesse defines here as "humor" is identical with "romantic irony." Interestingly enough, Novalis also refers to it as "Humor"; cf. Novalis [pseud.], *Blütenstaub* 29, any edition.

5.   Otto Ludwig, *Gesammelte Schriften,* ed. Adolf Stern (Leipzig: Franz Wilhelm Grunow, 1891), 5:89–91.

6.   Oskar Franz Walzel, *Gehalt und Gestalt im Kunstwerk des Dichters* (Berlin-Neubabelsberg: Akademische verlagsgesellschaft Athenaion, 1923), pp. 351–54. All of ch. 14, "Dichtkunst und Musik," is of interest in this connection.

7.   H. A. Basilius, "Thomas Mann's Use of Musical Structure and Techniques in *Tonio Kröger," Germanic Review* 19 (1944):284–308.

8.   Calvin S. Brown, *Music and Literature: A Comparison of the Arts* (Athens: University of Georgia Press, 1948), pp. 161–77. This is unquestionably the most comprehensive and most perceptive book on the subject; it is regrettable that it does not include a historical survey of critical theory regarding the relationship of the two arts.

9.   René Wellek and Austin Warren, *Theory of Literature* (New York: Harcourt, Brace, 1949), p. 126.

10.   Ibid.

11.   Cf. the Provençal manuscript examined by the hero in ch. 5, "Heinrich von Ofterdingen." Hesse knows Novalis extremely well.

12.   Hermann Hesse, *Betrachtungen* (Berlin: S. Fischer, 1928), p. 164; or *GS*, 7:245.

13.   *GD* 5:67.

14.   Walter Silz, "Otto Ludwig and the Process of Creation," *Publications of the Modern Language Association of America* 60 (1945):873–74. With reference to Ludwig and to Heine, Silz points out that narcotics can stimulate and accelerate these visions; see footnote 90, p. 874. This might be borne in mind for the discussion of the "magic theater" in *Steppenwolf.*

15.   Willi Apel, *Harvard Dictionary of Music* (Cambridge, Mass.: Harvard University Press, 1955), p. 189.

16.   Brown, p. 42.

17.   Richard B. Matzig, *Hermann Hesse in Montagnola: Studien zu Werk und Innenwelt des Dichters* (Basel: Auerbach-Verlag, 1947), p. 65. Matzig's chapter on *Der Steppenwolf,* incidentally, is a perfect example of the confusion which reigns with regard to the structure of the novel: The elaborate plot summary which the author attempts is a hodgepodge of inexactnesses, shifts in sequence, and outright errors.

18.   Hermann Hesse, *Blick ins Chaos* (Bern: Seldwyla, 1922), especially pp. 24–29; or *GS*, 7:181–84, especially.

19.   This effect, which has much in common with the painting "Ich und das Dorf" by Chagall, is a favorite motif in Hesse's works and may be found also in *Klingsors letzter Sommer* (1919), *GD,* 3:611–12, as well as in *Siddhartha* (1922), *GD,* 3:731–32.

20.   It is almost superfluous to mention that all of these motifs play a major role in most of Hesse's other works and do not belong exclusively to *Steppenwolf.*

21.   Harry Haller, in Hesse's *Morgenlandfahrt* (1932), is punished more mildly for a similar transgression against the eternal spirit by being smiled at by the assembled Immortals; cf. *GD,* 6:65. In the same book, moreover, Mozart appears disguised as Pablo; cf. *GD,* 6:63.

22.   Apel, p. 782.

23.   Ibid., p. 265.

24.   Brown, pp. 111, 134.

Musical Form and Principles in the Scheme of *Ulysses*

Don Noel Smith

One need not apologize for any approach to Joyce's *Ulysses* that attempts to render more comprehensible the overwhelming complexity of its design, for still debatable are the basic questions of what structural considerations determine its form and what underlying view of life gives coherence to its bewildering profusion of meaning. My own approach draws frankly upon analogies supplied by music, an art with a formal system perhaps complex enough to illustrate that of *Ulysses*.

I would not insist that Joyce intended such an analogy, that musical form and principles actually determined the scheme, but I believe that the evidence strongly suggests a deliberate and comprehensive relationship. The importance of music in the life and work of Joyce is of course well known. His works are full of allusions to it, an essential point sometimes depending on a fragment of song; we know that the Sirens episode of *Ulysses* is based upon the fugue; and Joyce insisted in later life that *Finnegans Wake* is music. Pater's contention that music is the perfect art toward the condition of which all other arts aspire might well have been taken literally by later artists, such as Joyce, who felt Pater's influence and took perfection seriously. One notes, for instance, Ezra Pound's saying that when his *Cantos* reached a hundred their structure will resemble that of a Bach fugue. Moreover, among Joyce's critics, there has been a persistent recourse to musical terminology to describe his techniques and effects, and a number of studies have examined the function of music in his work. Convincing evidence of an intended analogy of course remains for exegesis and not circumstances to demonstrate.

Analogies are troublesome, for writer or critics, in that they allow ingenuity a great deal of latitude and, however ingenious, yet remain no more than what they are. Although music and literature may share certain principles of construction, a reliance upon identical principles would yet result in different forms and effects. *Ulysses* compounds the problem by being so rich in technical and thematic possibilities. As Harry Levin pointed out years ago: "... The very form of Joyce's work is an elusive and eclectic *Summa* of its age: The montage of the

Reprinted from *Twentieth Century Literature* 18 (1972):168–80 by permission.

cinema, impressionism in painting, leitmotiv in music, the free association of psychoanalysis, and vitalism in philosophy."[1] Examining the novel in relation to any one of these possibilities would no doubt be profitable but could hardly proceed greatly beyond analogy.

But if analogy has inherent limitations, always stumbling over the distinction between *similar* and *same,* it can be effective for analytic, or synthetic, purposes. I should expect my analogy, used as an exegetical device, to account for the nature of the larger divisions of *Ulysses* and the order in which they appear, as well as to indicate their relation to each other. It should take into consideration the correspondences to Homer's *Odyssey* and account for the development of major themes and significant technical departures. And it should clarify the view of life that emerges from, or dictates to, the textural detail and indicate the relation of this to the structural scheme. I suspect that my analogy and my interpretation may stray apart occasionally, but I hope that they may do so without fatal damage to either.

The analogy that immediately suggests itself for the structure of *Ulysses* is the sonata form. The *Oxford Companion to Music* (under "Development") provides a succinct definition of this musical term:

> In examining the forms of music we shall find often three processes: (a) the statement of musical themes or subject, (b) the treatment of them by breaking them up into their constituent members, and making new passages out of these (often very modulatory), and (c) the repetition of them. Compound binary form (otherwise called "Sonata Form" and "First Movement Form") is, indeed, nothing but a realization of this scheme exactly as above outlined.

In addition to statement, development, and recapitulation, the sonata form usually includes a coda, in which the themes are resolved.

The similarity of the novel's structure to the sonata form has not gone without comment. Ezra Pound remarked the resemblance as early as 1922, the year of the first edition: "Ce roman appartient à la grande classe de romans en forme de sonate, c'est-à-dire, dans la forme: thème, contre-thème, rencontre, développement, finale."[2] Enlarging somewhat upon Pound's impression, Harry Levin has noted: "Its introductory theme would be Stephen, its main theme Bloom; each, after a preliminary exposition, undergoes his own development, then a treatment in combination, and at last a recapitulation."[3] Having thus commented, Levin goes on to other matters without indicating any more specific correspondences or what bearing the correspondences he has suggested might have on an interpretation of the novel. More recently, Robert Boyle, also acting on Pound's impression, has attempted to analyze *Ulysses* in terms of a more technical and quite specific relation to the sonata form. Although Boyle endorses the usefulness of his approach, he finds it ultimately frustrated by his interpretation of the work: "Those who choose to see Molly as a jolly Irish Earth goddess and her 'yes' as a vital, positive assent to life, and to find Stephen enlivened by the paternity so symbolically bestowed on him by Bloom, could perhaps get my scheme to work out as successful sonata form, with Stephen, Bloom, and Molly all brought into the unity of triumphant assertion like the conclusion of Beethoven's Ninth Symphony. But I have been unable to see the characters, and especially Molly, in any such optimistic light."[4] In effect, Boyle is saying that he will not allow his analysis to generate any change in his interpretation of the novel—which is, I believe, at odds with that of most other critics. I hope to show that the unity he suggests does indeed take place.

Since I first saw the resemblance of *Ulysses* to the sonata form independently of Pound, Levin, or Boyle, I must conclude that it is rather obvious. In fact, as a general pattern the sonata form is rather inescapable. The setting forth of a concept, the development of it, and the repetition of it is a formula as common to freshman themes as to Beethoven's Ninth. But such reduction is mere facetiousness in view of possible correspondences on a sophisticated level—and one might note that the formula is certainly not characteristic of narrative works. The question is whether one can demonstrate similarities between *Ulysses* and the sonata form that are specific enough to be useful and yet not so specific as to end in a technical impasse. The usefulness of the analogy is to be measured by its descriptive accuracy and by the economy and inclusiveness of the interpretation it can generate. Let me, then, present a general outline of *Ulysses* as sonata form—after my own fashion, which need not be taken absolutely *de rigeur*. I will stress its descriptive value and then go on to more intrinsic musical correspondences.

One may find of course a variety of themes in *Ulysses*, but I will emphasize only the three commonly mentioned, generally agreed upon ones, derived from the Homeric parallel: (1) the search for the father, or for protection, guidance, authority, and most of all identity; (2) wandering and return; (3) usurpation, perceived as disorder or an unrightful order by those who feel displaced. These themes could be designated in other ways, but if properly qualified they are meaningful and I think central. One could speak of Stephen as the first theme and Bloom as the second, as does Levin, but it seems better to regard them as subjects, in relation to whom various themes accrue, notably the three above. For convenience' sake, I have numbered the chapters and have titled them according to the familiar chart of the episodes, first published in Stuart Gilbert's study of *Ulysses* and since reprinted variously.

I. Chapters 1-6 ("Telemachus" through "Hades"); 8:00 a.m.–noon. Exposition, or statement, of themes.

A. 1-3: First subject. The three themes are here initiated in relation to Stephen. Proud, tormented, and helpless, he struggles with meaning and value in a world become fluid and uncertain, where fathers have abdicated and mothers are "beastly" dead, trying to define his world and his relation to it. His life in the tower with Mulligan has been disrupted by the intrusion of the Englishman Haines. He begins his wanderings of the day, in effect, burning bridges behind him. His mother's death and the fiasco of his attempted flight have left him without a center: His wandering is dominated by search, for he has yet no established point of return. In Stephen's case, the themes will not be resolved except in a projected sense.

B. 4-6: Second subject. The same themes are reiterated in relation to Bloom, except that the search for the father is inverted, appearing in its obverse form, the search for the son—someone to care for, rely upon, share with, in an exclusively masculine sense. Bloom too begins his wanderings but, unlike Stephen, he has a home, a point from which he starts and to which he returns. Usurpation is of course present in the person of Blazes Boylan. The themes are resolved in Bloom's case, the latter paradoxically.

II. Chapters 7–15 ("Aeolus" through "Circe"); noon–midnight. Development of themes.

Tracing the modulation of subject and theme throughout these nine middle chapters lies beyond the scope of this study, but to insist that it does take place is no more than to insist on the obvious. With chapter 7 the focus shifts as abruptly from Bloom as it has from Stephen with chapter 4, and although Bloom is without doubt the major figure throughout them, he is by no means the sole center of attention. His day is interwoven with that of Stephen: paralleling, counterpointing, intersecting, and finally merging with it. One might note that Stephen's reflections on Shakespeare and *Hamlet* (chapter 9, Scylla and Charybdis) provide a particular instance of modulation of the three themes. Worth noting also is that chapter 7 (Aeolus) represents the first radical change in style and point of view. The shift is from an impressionistic combination of narrative and internal monologue, from a relatively limited point of view, to expressionistic technique and an omniscient point of view. Edmund Wilson has remarked this change in his early commentary on the novel, pointing out that in the first six chapters "the characters' perceptions of the external world are usually distinct from their thoughts and feelings about them. But in the newspaper office, for the first time, a general atmosphere begins to be created, beyond the specific minds of the characters."[5] To be sure, we return again and again to the consciousness of the characters, but their consciousness no longer measures our distance from the action. Throughout the middle chapters we cannot anticipate just how Joyce will handle his materials, though we come to expect virtuosity. In other words, he reserves the right to modulate as he sees fit.

III. Chapters 16–17 ("Eumaeus" and "Ithaca"); midnight–2:00 a.m. Recapitulation.

A. 16: This chapter can be seen as a bridge between the development and recapitulation rather than as a part of the recapitulation proper. Although Stephen and Bloom have been joined together in a group two chapters previously, they are here brought into intimate conversation for the first time; and by the end of the episode they have actually begun to communicate, to interpenetrate in thought, though they retain their distinct, characteristic concerns: While Stephen lifts his heart in song, Bloom calculates the amount of money such a "phenomenally beautiful tenor voice" could command (p. 663).[6] One should resist the temptation to write this troublesome chapter off to the Homeric parallel, even though a definite similarity exists: The Eumaeus episode in *The Odyssey* seems also long, tedious, and nearly irrelevant. Perhaps a test of either episode's function would be to imagine the work without it. The father needs a chance to feel out the son, determine his suitability and dependability; the shift from the last wayward adventure to the home scene seems to demand a transition: For better or worse the Eumaeus episode fulfills these functions.

B. 17: Ithaca may be seen as a recapitulation in the abstract of that which has been previously experienced or explored. Joyce has called it a "mathematico-astronomico-physico-mechanico-geometrico-chemico sublimation of Bloom and Stephen . . . to prepare for the final amplitudinously curvilinear episode of Penelope." He has also said of it: "I am writing Ithaca in the form of a mathematical catechism. All events are resolved into their cosmic, physical, psychical, &c equivalents . . . so that not only will the reader know everything but know it in the baldest and coldest way. . . ."[7] Joyce seems to have overestimated the ability of his readers to understand even the baldest, coldest presentation, but he does imply that he intends the episode to be, at least in part, recapitulatory.

Joyce's enigmatic commentary aside, the recapitulatory element in this chapter is present in various ways: in Stephen and Bloom's deliberating upon the considerations and incidents of the past day (p. 666), in their noting the circumstances of their previous acquaintance (p. 680), in their exchanging their respective vital statistics (p. 682). We see it also in Bloom's going over his expenditures of the day (p. 711) and in his relating the events of his day to Molly (p. 733). Moreover, this chapter finds Bloom reminiscing to a greater extent than in any other. The similarity of the Ithaca episode to recapitulation in music remains, nonetheless, admittedly tenuous. It differs in proportion and effect, though it is similar in position and general intent.

IV. Chapter 18 ("Penelope"); after 2:00 a.m. Coda.

Little explanation seems necessary here. The purpose of the coda is to resolve the themes and give a greater sense of finality to the piece. The term has often been used impressionistically to describe Molly's monologue. The sense in which her section does represent a resolution of the themes should become clear later.

Analyzing *Ulysses* in relation to the sonata form yields, then, a meaningful outline of its development, relating the parts to each other and to the whole. The analogy surely provides a more accurate description of the arrangement and relation of parts than that which *The Odyssey* can supply. In fact, viewing the structure of *Ulysses* in relation to the Homeric parallel has perhaps led to more exegetical problems than solutions. Certainly there is no overlooking the three larger, designated divisions in the novel nor the evidence that Joyce intended them to correspond to the three greater divisions of *The Odyssey:* the so-called Telemachia, the wanderings, and the homecoming or Nostos.[8] But there is also no overlooking the fact that other divisions in the novel are just as pronounced, if not more so. Actually, there are only three basic points of view in *Ulysses:* the limited narrator of 1-6, the unlimited narrator of 7-17, and the absolutely banished narrator of 18.

Attempting to explicate the novel in terms of the threefold division puts the first three chapters in problematic relation to the rest of the work. Regarding their function as similar to that of the first four chapters of *The Odyssey* quickly results in an impasse. Homer begins with Telemachus in Ithaca to set the central conflict in motion and so give unity and a certain suspense to the action—to make a plot of the story, in Forster's sense of the words. But the beginning of Stephen's day and exposition of his problems has nothing ostensibly to do with the situation in the Bloom household; it is merely a parallel situation, which initiates the common themes. There has been a tendency to regard these first three chapters as a somewhat puzzling appendage to a novel about Leopold Bloom. Stuart Gilbert describes them as a "prelude to Bloom's day" and says that they "may be regarded as a 'bridgework'" between *Ulysses* and *A Portrait of the Artist*.[9] Although Gilbert probably does not mean that this is their only function, the impression suggested is one that simply belies the evidence of the novel. The middle chapters chart the course of Stephen's day as well as Bloom's. As noted earlier, the focus shifts from Bloom with chapter 7, and although it does return to him for brief and for considerably extended periods he does not always remain uppermost in view. Bloom's role is the major one throughout them, but whereas it does not assume the proportions of its Homeric counterpart, Stephen's role acquires even greater importance than that of Telemachus. The development includes both the subjects presented in the exposition. The first three chapters serve the same function as the second three.[10]

One need not think of *Ulysses* as subscribing at all literally to the structure of *The Odyssey*—in the way, for instance, that *The Aeneid* imitates the structure of both Homer's epics. Rather, the sequence of events has been broken up and abstracted; the incidents have been redistributed, superimposed, given different emphases. This is not to deny the meaningfulness of the threefold division nor, certainly, the myriad of correspondences that exist between the two works. It is simply more in keeping with the evidence of the novel to look upon it as an orchestration of the themes, incidents, characters of *The Odyssey* in a modern context.

In designating the structural divisions as I have outlined them, one could of course use the terminology of literary analysis: Chapters 1-6 would be the exposition; 7-14, the complication; 15, the climax; 16, the resolution; 17, an abstract or summary; and 18, an epilogue. But this terminology is finally misleading. Not only are epilogues rarely seen in fiction and summaries never, but the terms have a reasonably well circumscribed meaning that prevents their being readily applied to Joyce's last two chapters. Similarly, the other terms indicate a linearity and expeditiousness of action that is not present in *Ulysses*. As Samuel Johnson said of *Pamela*, if you read it for the story, you would hang yourself. Joyce is more concerned with repetition, variation, and elaboration than with what happens next. Here again Edmund Wilson provides a pointed observation: "There is a tremendous vitality in Joyce, but very little movement ... he is symphonic rather than narrative. His fiction has its progressions, its developments, but they are musical rather than dramatic."[11]

The musical analogy goes beyond a resemblance in form, though this in itself is instructive. The interpretation of reality, or creation as a whole, on which *Ulysses* is based and which gives coherence to its textural detail, is one in which events bear essentially the same relation to time, space, and motion that sounds bear to them in music. If I may resort to a rather simplistic and somewhat ludicrous definition, *music* is an ordering of sounds based on their consecutive, concurrent, and recurrent occurrence—in other words, melody, harmony, and rhythm. I speak only of Western music, the principles of which presumably had their origin in ancient Greece. And it is perhaps worth the digression to point out that Bloom, whose problem has its origin, or at least epitome, in the literature of ancient Greece, often escapes to the East in reverie (as do so many of Joyce's characters); to him it represents a different order of reality, just as, in truth, its music rests upon different principles of composition from those derived from the Greeks. That the principles passed on to us have undergone considerable modification over the centuries presents no difficulty: So has the concept of the hero, as seen in the difference between the mythic Odysseus and the modern Leopold Bloom.

Turning to the beginning of the Proteus episode and a difficult passage of this very important chapter, we find Stephen quite literally stumbling upon what is essentially a musical conception of creation, that is, the order or composition of reality. The formulae may be expressed thus: melody = succession, or consecutiveness, of events (in relation to space of consciousness, in which past and present may coexist); rhythm=cyclic recurrence of events. The formulae can be related to the major themes, with wandering representing succession; usurpation, simultaneousness; and the father-son relation, recurrence. The following explication of the passage is tedious, but seems necessary to substantiate my point.

Walking on the beach, Stephen reflects: "Signatures of all things I am here to read, seaspawn and seawreck, the nearing tide, that rusty boot" (p. 37). Perhaps considering that signatures appeal as well to one's aural perception, he decides that it might be possible to "Shut your eyes and see." The "ineluctable modality of the visible" may bear some relation to the fixed modes of the audible. Stephen's feet follow each other consecutively—*nacheinander,* or one after the other: "A very short space of time through very short times of space." Beginning to grasp the concept, he starts to open his eyes, but then immediately reflects: "No. Jesus! If I fell over a cliff that beetles o'er his base, fell through the *nebeneinander* ineluctably. I am getting on nicely in the dark." Like Hamlet, whom the reference suggests, Stephen is repelled by chaos, not as a fatal, meaningless void but as an incomprehensible existence in which incompatibles lie side by side. *Nacheinander,* with its German conciseness, has suggested *nebeneinander* as a compliment, and the literal meaning of the world again connects with his walking feet to give him his second insight. He remembers he has on Mulligan's boots; hence, two identities are proceeding concurrently, harmonizing in step: "My two feet in his boots are at the end of his legs, *nebeneinander.* Sounds solid: made by the mallet of *Los Demiurgos.*" Los Demiurgos is of course the divine smith, the personified principle of creation. A bewildering succession of associations then follows, bringing Stephen to his final realization. He muses:

> Am I walking into eternity along Sandymount strand? Crush, crack, crick, crick. Wild sea money. Dominie Deasy kens them a'.
> *Won't you come to Sandymount,*
> *Madeline the mare?*
> Rhythm begins, you see. I hear.

Sea shells crackling under Stephen's feet remind him of the sea shells he has fingered earlier in the school office, which reminds him of the money paid him there, which reminds him of Mr. Deasy, who reminds him of horses. Horses, the fact that he is on the beach, the Latinate *Los Demiurgos* associate in a pun on *mare,* producing the snatch of verse. *Mare,* as tide (and female) suggests recurrent motion, and so "rhythm begins." With a typically Joycean twist, the "I hear" converts the preceding "You see" from empty idiom to grammatical sense. At the same time, Stephen disassociates himself from the rest of mankind and implies the superiority of his mode of perception to the common one. Like the speaker of Marvell's "Coy Mistress," he can "hear" that which should shock our complacent vision, though the perception compels enervation and not urgency. The melody, harmony, and rhythm of creation sound upon his senses not as music but as a horrible din of birth and death. God is mere noise, "a shout in the street" (p. 34).

Stephen perceives only blind forces engaged in an endless transmutation of matter. Creation, or reality, is mere Protean process, the identity of which can never be fixed and without any meaning to yield. Yet it is, like music conceived as pure mechanism, a very constraining and uncompromising process, with its ineluctably circumscribed possibilities. Stephen of *A Portrait* thought that he could be free of it; Stephen of *Ulysses* has begun to realize that he cannot, yet he still rebels, not only against its constraint but against its unholy harmony, its lack of distinction between the vulgar and the sublime. To the artistic temperament, striving toward freedom and purity, confinement and crudity are the perennial anathemas.

Stephen's problem, which Joyce implies is peculiar to masculine kind, is a too-exclusive conception of beauty, or what he conceives to be pleasing and appropriate order. He projects dichotomies upon his world, then chafes when they victimize him. As the young artist he has engaged in a histrionic insistence on schisms. To mix a metaphor, he would create in the smithy of his soul a music exclusive of vulgar, constraining reality. He finds himself not in key, out of tune, for he would place himself and his art outside God's octave.

That Stephen's harkening to a phantom drummer has got him out of step with the rhythms of reality is reflected in several ways. Consider, for instance, what one might call the eat-excrete and birth-death rhythms, which seem the most prominent ones. In a novel in which eating and drinking go on continually, Stephen has bad teeth, a poor stomach for drink, and irregular eating habits. His disregard for physical well-being, which betokens his scorn for the material, contrasts with the well-regulated habits of the better adjusted, more mature Bloom, who gives pleasurable attention to routine physical need. And one notes the conventional respect and duty Bloom pays at the birth of Mina Purefoy's child and at the funeral of Paddy Dignam. His behavior does not, however, imply empty conventionality; these are serious matters in relation to which he assumes involvement and obligation. One contrasts Stephen's drunken irreverence at the hospital while the child is being born and his high-minded refusal to perform a duty his mother desires at her death. The ghost conjured by this latter default rattles its chains around his conscience throughout the novel so that, considered in retrospect, his bravado at the end of *A Portrait* sounds hollow indeed: "Free. Soulfree and fancyfree. Let the dead bury the dead" (p. 248).[12] Stephen is beginning to discover that it is the living who must bury the dead and that agenbite of inwit can be sharper than a toothache.

Stephen is of course at that stage in a young man's development when the dreams of youth have undergone bitter chastisement and reality has offered no consolation. He has yet to discover a relationship which will, if not forever bind up and make whole the scattered fragments of his world, at least provide him with an emotional center from which to relate to it. The experience that Stephen lacks seems to be quite simply love: Love as a divine principle infusing creation, of which the relation between man and woman is a particular manifestation. As the author interjects in the first chapter: "Pain, that was not yet the pain of love, fretted his heart" (p. 5). Insofar as the analogy is concerned, Joyce might well have seen love as corresponding to the miracle of the octave: The sense of wholeness and completion achieved by two distinct tones yearning across an interval to assert a shared identity, a departure from center anticipatory of ultimate return.

But Stephen, who has spent his life seeking an identity, has no conception of sharing one. He looks upon the forces of generation and degeneration as simply locked indistinguishably in a terrible and meaningless embrace. In the poem he writes, these forces, immediately suggested by his mother and death, assume the guise of awful lovers: "He comes, pale vampire, through storm his eyes, his bat sails bloodying the sea, mouth to her mouth's kiss." It then becomes "mouth to her womb. Oomb, allwombing tomb" (p. 48). Stephen's poem, itself in the process of creation, is a dismal reflection on the Greek myth of how order began. Supposedly, from the union of darkness and night, children of chaos, love was born. Love then put chaos in order, creating light and day, making beauty possible. And it was love that united earth (Gaea) and her offspring heaven (Uranus), who went on to produce both gods and monsters. But Stephen cannot get beyond the awful, mechanical fact of intercourse to recognize any positive investment in the activity. The whole history of human relationships he views in purely mechanistic terms. He envisions them as stretching back to the womb of Eve, like a vast telephone exchange, with umbilical cords forming the network: "The cords of all link back, strandentwining cable of all flesh. . . . Will you be as gods? Gaze in your omphalos. Hello. Kinch here. Put me on to Edenville." (p. 38). The centuries of love, of man for woman, parent for child, are left out of his metaphor. Stephen feels himself simply trapped in a vulgar, meaningless concatenation of material forces. To such an existence he would prefer nothingless, yet his conscience, which clearly has not been created in the smithy of his soul, insists upon assigning value to a relation that should now mean nothing, death having ended it. Small wonder he should believe that "History . . . is a nightmare from which I am trying to awake" (p. 34).

In the Circe episode, chided to frenzy by conscience in the form of his mother's ghost, Stephen attempts to break the spell of the nightmare. In confronting the ghost, he continues to insist upon a purely naturalistic scheme of things: "Cancer did it, not I." "Bloody bones!" "Shite!" And he still maintains his defiance of that in which he no longer believes: *"Non serviam!"* At last, lifting his ashplant and screaming *"Nothung!"* he strikes out at the source and divine symbol of order, the light. *"Time's livid final flame leaps and, in the following darkness, ruin of all space, shattered glass and toppling masonry"* (pp. 580-83). Stephen's cry is one of romantic nihilism, naming the mythic sword of Siegfried and the preferred alternative to the existing scheme: nothing. *Not hung* also asserts his resistance to the fate of Christ, for he cannot appreciate the value of love that made that sacrifice meaningful.[13] In the rhetoric that follows his cry, time and space, the very principles of order, are destroyed. But only in the rhetoric. Anyone who attaches serious significance to Stephen's deed might note that he has merely smashed a lampshade, and a rather cheap one at that (p. 569). Creation survives his blow, and so does Stephen.

Leopold Bloom, the second subject, is really no more pleased than Stephen with what he feels to be the unholy harmony of things, nor is he less the lonely wanderer, seeking an alter ego who might assist him to put his house in order, according to his exclusive view of that. But like his Homeric counterpart, he is resourceful in adjusting himself to the exigencies of the situation. No man of violence, as Odysseus could be, he is yet a strategist, though one who practices the somewhat self-deceptive arts of substitution, subterfuge, and spite to try to keep the score, as it were, even. As if to avenge the death of his son on nature, he produces no further offspring. He counters his wife's lover by taking himself a mistress, in whom he seems scarcely interested; and he makes up for her most recent act of adultery by masturbating on the beach. When his race is insulted, he responds with an insult, albeit veiled in truth, to his antagonist's religion. The imprint of his wife's lover and flakes of Plumtree's potted meat apprise him that his bed has served double duty during his absence, and his reaction is to demand breakfast in bed. "Toothless Kinch" has his counterpart in a toothless Leo. Bloom's petulant strategems have a kind of hopeless but humorous pathos about them; they reflect the lonely little boy who feels himself unloved and forsaken. To Molly he is, like all men, "some kind of big infant" (which is not to imply that she feeling toward him can be so simply described). Except for his relation to Molly, the difference between him and Stephen is one of age, experience, and intellectual inclinations—of degree, not kind. As the chart of the episodes would indicate, they are men of the same kidney, at heart the same: Stephen is not assigned organs, because his are identical to Bloom's.

We may see Stephen and Bloom as both literally and figuratively keyless because they do not like the tune called by the scheme of things. The condition of their keylessness differs, however, in that Stephen's relation to his tower home is unstable to begin with: No woman's love asserts a constant attraction on him to return. But there is love, however unidealistic, between Bloom and Molly. She is the center from which he begins and to which, throughout his wanderings, love compels his return. Bloom of course forgets his key—perhaps a Freudian slip—but, being resourceful, he manages to enter his home anyway. Once there, after Stephen has gone, he finds on the piano "music in the key of G natural for voice and piano of *Love's Old Sweet Song*" (p. 706). One might well think of *Ulysses* as being specifically in the key of G, as in *geo-* or *Gaea,* Greek for *earth*.

The theme of wandering and return is, then, resolved for Bloom, and in Stephen he seems satisfied that he has found an appropriate son substitute. But Stephen is left to wander, without a center, still seeking the identity he lacks. The projection, however, seems clear: The musical scheme of things admits no possibility of keylessness; the principle of the octave allows for a kind of protean metempsychosis but no escape. Stephen's fate is evident in Bloom's and no doubt in Joyce's own. Joyce's choosing to set *Ulysses* on the day of his first date with Nora provides one of those important clues he was fond of supplying from his own life. On June 16 in Joyce's life, Stephen Dedalus became Leopold Bloom.

The usurpation theme, or that of an undesirable harmony, is, as I stated earlier, paradoxically resolved. Both Stephen and Bloom establish an order of life that subsequently comes to grief because of what they see as intrusion and betrayal. The case of Bloom is obvious, but that of Stephen's seems to need clarification. In the first place, we must see Buck Mulligan as parallel to Molly. His jolly earthiness and acceptance of life are much like hers. His judgment of Stephen is as shrewd as hers is of Bloom. He is Antinous not because he is a suitor but because Stephen sees him as a false friend (in *The Odyssey* Antinous of course pretends to be a friend of Telemachus). Buck's indiscreet reference to Stephen's mother as being "beastly dead" marks him, in Stephen's eyes, as a betrayer; the callousness it indicates spoils his image of a true and beautiful friendship. Moreover, when the Englishman Hains, who is the parallel to Boylan, moves in, Stephen feels that his position has been both betrayed and usurped; and so he moves out. He will maintain no adulterous friendships.

Bloom is too old and experienced, and too much in love, to behave like Stephen. To be sure, he idly contemplates leaving toward the end of the Ithaca episode, but he also thinks of all the practical objections (p. 276 ff.). So he endures his betrayal and plots to overcome the usurper and restore what he considers more perfect harmony in his household. Stephen becomes a fortuitous element in this, Bloom's master strategem of the day. By enlisting Stephen's aid, if not his conspiracy, he will drive out the usurper Boylan. This is the resolution Bloom projects, but Molly has a less exclusive view of what constitutes proper harmony. The resolution she projects is quite different: Stephen is to become, if she has her way, yet another usurper—though Molly, as ultimate female, as earth and the embodiment of life, makes no distinction between usurpers and rightful lords or between the vulgar and the sublime (and one notes her lack of distinction between art and life in her reflections on the naked male statue, pp. 775-76). Molly finds no metaphysical impasse and therefore no Yeatsian profundity in Love's having pitched his mansion in the place of excrement, for she perceives no necessary disharmony. Such dichotomies provide play for big infants. Secure within her identity, she feels no need to wander in search of one that will in some way confirm her own. She does not remove from home all day, remaining at center, in key; and in the menstrual cycle, which has just completed a rotation within her (p. 769), one may see a microcosmic representation of the macrocosm's octave.

At the conclusion of the Penelope episode the two subjects, with their common themes, unite and resolve in relation to Molly. The father figure Bloom lies curled up beside her in a fetal position,[14] while his spiritual son Stephen has attained the status of lover in her imagination. Stretched out in bed, Molly is reminiscing of a day on Howth head with Bloom—but Bloom as he was sixteen years ago, when he was twenty-two, the exact current age of Stephen. The present image of the one thus merges with the past image of the other. And the fusion is further reinforced by the fact that Molly, presently reclining, imagines herself as she was then, lying supine, stretching her arms upward to embrace her lover—in the semblance of Gaea proffering herself to Uranus, who is both her son and lover and who constantly revolves around her.[15] Father and son, returning wanderer, usurped usurper—the themes thus unite and resolve, figuratively at least, in this final chord.

Not every intricacy of the novel's form and substance need be, or ever could be, related to music (though there are certainly more possibilities than I have been able to note here), and one should be ready to admit the tenuous and too pat. But the analogy does provide a fascinating and, I think, valuable way of looking at *Ulysses*. Moreover, the use of music as a system could be seen as quite compatible with the use of certain other systems: in history, certainly Vico's cyclic theory; in philosophy, perhaps Hegel's dialectic. In all these systems, one might contend, the penultimate stage of any development anticipates as ultimate not perfect realization but its opposite, a return to the beginning of the process. Applied to the development of Joyce, or Stephen-Bloom, this would mean that the furthermost degree of estrangement, which begins with birth, from the female and all she represents does not anticipate an ideal state of estrangement but rather a reunion with the female, given a difference of vibrations.

The analogies music provides are teasing, remaining no doubt more interesting than convincing; but the evidence of them might well lead one to suppose that the conception of the octave as the basic principle of order, with love
as the attractive force infusing it, could have as much validity for the scheme of
Ulysses as the conception of unity in Trinity has for the scheme of Dante's *Divine
Comedy.*

Notes

1.   Harry Levin, *James Joyce: A Critical Introduction,* rev. ed. (Norfolk, Conn.: New Directions, 1960), p. 89.

2.   Ezra Pound, *"James Joyce et Pecuchet,"* *Mercure de France* 156 (1922):313.

3.   Levin, p. 79.

4.   Robert Boyle, *"Ulysses* as Frustrated Sonata Form," *James Joyce Quarterly* 2 (1965):249.

5.   Edmund Wilson, *Axel's Castle* (New York: Scribner, 1931), p. 207.

6.   Page references are to The Modern Library edition, 1961.

7.   Letter to Claud W. Sykes, Spring 1921, and letter to Frank Budgen, February 1921,
Stuart Gilbert, ed., *Letters of James Joyce* (New York: Viking, 1957), pp. 164, 159–60.

8.   See letter to John Quinn, Sept. 1920, Gilbert, p. 145.

9.   Stuart Gilbert, *James Joyce's Ulysses* (New York: Alfred A. Knopf, 1930), p. 3.

10.   Stanley Sultan has reached essentially the same conclusion in approaching the structure from an entirely different point of view. *The Argument of Ulysses* (Columbus: University of Ohio Press, 1964), p. 21.

11.   Wilson, p. 209.

12.   Viking Compass edition, 1968.

13.   Robert Ryf notes these three meanings of the word but attaches a different interpretation to them. *A New Approach to Joyce* (Los Angeles: University of California Press,
1962), p. 85.

14.   See p. 737. Bloom is described as resembling "the manchild in the womb" and
Molly as "in the attitude of Gea-Tellus." The cryptic statement following "when?" at
the bottom of the page seems obviously another reference to the Greek myth of
creation.

15.   Speaking of the Ithaca episode, Joyce says that Stephen and Bloom "become heav-
enly bodies, wanderers like the stars at which they gaze" (Gilbert, *Letters,* p. 160).

Six

Beyond Classical Form

Strindberg's *The Ghost Sonata* and Sonata Form

Raymond Jarvi

One of the recurring projects that occupied August Strindberg to greater and lesser degrees during all phases of his career as a playwright was the founding of an independent theater where his own dramas would be staged. During his pre-Inferno years (1869-92), the closest he ever came to achieving this goal was two performances of the triple bill *Pariah, Creditors,* and *The Stronger* which the Scandinavian Experimental Theater gave in Copenhagen and Malmö respectively on March 9 and 16, 1889. Before withdrawing into the isolation of the Inferno period itself (1894-97), Strindberg formulated with varying degrees of imagination plans for this kind of theater in Berlin, as his correspondence with Adolf Paul of 1893 indicates, and in Paris, where in 1894 he thought about opening with Leopold Littmansson: "A *chat noir*–or *Procope*-Strindberg. I am going to make decorative wall paintings and to produce *Keys to the Kingdom of Heaven* as a shadow play. My guitar will also be of help. Littmansson is going to conduct a small orchestra in a new manner."[1] In 1900 he discussed with Gustaf Uddgren the possibility of converting a shed in Djurgarden (Stockholm) into a small theater plant; and in September of 1905 he proposed to Harriet Bosse that the two of them create a miniature ambulatory stage: "But I must have three people. If I have you and two more, I shall borrow money and engage for screens to be painted for my miniature stage. We shall even include monodramas and adaptations of older great beautiful plays from antiquity, Shakespeare, Schiller."[2]

What chiefly compelled Strindberg to speculate about a functional theater was that for unaccountably long stretches–years at a time occasionally–he was relegated by circumstances and a tragicomic series of misunderstandings to the frustrating status of an unperformed dramatist. His letter to his German translator, Emil Schering, dated January 18, 1902, is especially helpful in filling in the gap that exists in his dramatic production[3] between the completion of *A Dream Play* somewhere around the change of year from 1901 to 1902 (as the evidence

This article originally appeared in *Mosaic: A Journal for the Comparative Study of Literature and Ideas,* published by the University of Manitoba Press, 5 (1972):69-84, to whom acknowledgement is herewith made.

below suggests) and the onset in January of 1907 of the terminal phase within his career as a playwright:

> What shall I write, what [shall I] say about *Engelbrekt* and *Easter* and every-
> thing else? I become silent in adversity because I cannot throw the blame on
> anyone and I cannot change my fate. Sometimes you have the wind with you;
> now I have the wind against me and can only wait. The worst of it is that I am
> beginning to lose interest in my work when encouragement is systematically
> withheld. Moreover, it seems to me that I should have said everything [that] I
> have to say for this period; especially in a newly finished dream-play which is
> not [yet] copied.[4]

Strindberg's negligible dramatic output between 1902 and 1906 had really little to do with his own inner resources. These years embraced, in fact, a period of intense productivity during which he wrote the bulk of his post-Inferno non-dramatic prose works[5] in addition to his most important collection of poems.[6] The sporadic and generally fragmentary results of his concurrent dramatic output were the immediate effects of neglect on the part of the Swedish theater of his entire production for three consecutive seasons. The waiting to which Strindberg referred in the letter quoted above lasted for all intents and purposes until January of 1906 when *Creditors* was staged with moderate success at the Vasa Theater in Stockholm. Two months later the Royal Dramatic Theater revived *Crimes and Crimes,* and in the fall of that year the administration of the Swedish Theater announced both a revival of *Gustav Vasa* and the première of *A Dream Play* for the subsequent winter and spring seasons respectively. The Ostermalm Theater put in its bid for a revival of that perennial favorite, *The Travels of Lucky Peter.* By the winter season of 1907, Strindbergian drama was, thus, once again a viable commodity in the current theatrical bill of fare.

During the fall of 1906, Strindberg made the acquaintance of August Falck, who at the age of twenty-four was on the threshold of his career in the theater. Falck was not at the time associated with any of the established performing companies in Stockholm; he did have, nevertheless, a considerable amount of theatrical apprenticeship behind him as well as an unshakable faith in the practical and esthetic potentials of Strindberg's plays. His début as a producer of Strindbergian drama was noteworthy in and for itself. In September of 1906 Falck assembled in Lund a company of actors and actresses and successfully presented the first public performances in Sweden of *Lady Julie.* He toured the provinces with this production and finally unveiled it in Stockholm on December 13, 1906, at the Folk Theater, receiving both critical acclaim and public support for his directorial achievement. This production of *Lady Julie* brought Falck initially into contact with Strindberg. The latter immediately recognized in the younger man the colleague for whom he had been waiting for many years. On the occasion of their first meeting, they discussed the possibility of establishing a new theater in Stockholm, a theater devoted to the production of intimate dramas in general and Strindberg's plays in particular.

Fortunately for Strindberg, Falck possessed training, talent, energy, will, and vision which, combined with the artist's corresponding qualities, enabled the two of them to pursue this idea beyond the scope of mere discussion. What Falck did not have was the capital to underwrite the project in general, but this

Strindberg was largely able to amass on his own and then put at Falck's disposal. Strindberg was not, of course, a rich man; and the range of repertory which they envisioned in the early stages of their planning necessarily had to be abandoned. At any rate, approximately one year after their initial acquaintance, August Falck, under the patronage of August Strindberg, presented on November 26, 1907, in Stockholm the première of *The Pelican* at the Intimate Theater, inaugurating the first of three and one-third seasons consisting, except for the production of Maeterlinck's *L'Intruse,* of a repertory of twenty-three Strindbergian plays.[7]

The *Kammerspiele* that Max Reinhardt established during the fall of 1906 in Berlin provided Strindberg with the immediate point of reference concerning the fundamental purpose that he envisioned for his own experimental theater. He conveyed this purpose in the first of his open letters to the members of the Intimate Theater accordingly: "The idea of chamber music transferred to the drama. The intimate procedure, the significant motif, the careful treatment."[8] The idea of chamber music presupposes, of course, the principle of an ensemble of three or more individual voices blending and adjusting their dissimilar personalities and capabilities in order to deal effectively with the essential thematic content of the work itself. While an application of the ensemble principle has been increasingly achieved in the general theatrical development of the last six decades—most substantially in that of the Scandinavian- and German-speaking countries—the concept of performance that Strindberg wanted to impose on the Stockholm stage of 1907 contrasted sharply with the dominant kind of thinking that governed the majority of activities in the professional theater of the turn of the century,[9] a kind of thinking that is by no means obsolete, as the figurations of charismatic stars whirling about in the firmament above our own theatrical horizons indicate.

In matters of artistic significance Strindberg largely ignored the stars that flourished at the turn of the century. For example, when Sarah Bernhardt descended on Stockholm for a guest performance on September 12, 1902, Harriet Bosse procured for herself a seat in the loges of the Royal Opera in order to behold the celebrated actress; her husband spent the evening at home, achieving his own entertainment by sitting at his piano and playing as best he could manage the Largo e mesto from Beethoven's Piano Sonata in D Major, op. 10 no. 3.[10] Strindberg was not alone, however, in disliking what many people considered to be the epitome of theatrical artistry. Max Reinhardt in Berlin, Constantin Stanislavsky in Moscow, and Gustav Mahler, who in 1907 completed the cycle of his work as artistic director of the Vienna Court Opera—these men not only shared with August Strindberg an essential commitment to the principle of ensemble art as opposed to the enthronement of the performing artist but also expended a great amount of energy in order to establish this principle in the realm of the theater during the first decade of this century.

In the winter and spring of 1907 Strindberg once more programmed his morning hours for the writing of works for the stage. One after the other, he produced *Storm Weather, The Burned House, The Ghost Sonata,* the fragment *Toten-Insel,* and *The Pelican* (his diary for the month of April that year notes an additional drama which he burned because it was too ruthlessly honest), in order to provide a set of plays for the initial series of productions at the Intimate

Theater—a repertory that corresponded with his theoretical understanding just then of what the performance of serious drama *should* be. Working independently with the same programmatic concept that Mahler and Reinhardt also maintained, he coined his own term, *chamber play,* using it as the root idea for the writing of each of these plays and listing them already in his diary by means of opus numbers. Beyond the limits of the texts themselves, Strindberg's definition of this term consists of a single paragraph in the first of his open letters to the members of the Intimate Theater:

> If one asks what an Intimate Theater is all about and what is indicated by a Chamber-play, then I can answer like this: In the drama we look for the strong, significant motif, but within limitations. In our treatment we avoid all pride, all calculated effects, places for applause, star roles, solo numbers. No determined form is to bind the author because the motif determines the form. Accordingly, freedom in our treatment, bound only by the unity of the conception and the feeling for style.[11]

Strindberg obviously used this term in order to communicate more effectively with his theatrical, rather than his strictly literary, colleagues. The designation "chamber play" pertains, in other words, more to the specific conditions upon which the performance of these theater pieces depends than it does to an arbitrary literary classification or genre. These conditions are, in effect, the consequences of a systematic application of the idea of chamber music to the correspondingly time-oriented art of drama. Maintaining the idea of chamber music at every point in the re-creative process of staging these plays negates, as Strindberg has pointed out, the catalog of clichés which even in the 1970s habitually provides the general notion of what theatricality is all about.

Strindberg isolated the crux of the matter by means of the following key phrase: *The motif determines the form.* As in writing *A Dream Play,* Strindberg's purpose in each of the chamber plays centered exclusively on thematic exposition, development, and resolution. The inherent substance which these texts afford emanates, accordingly, not from a deftly constructed plot in the manner of Scribe and Ibsen, nor from the cumulative process of characterization that Chekhov employed with such incomparable skill (not that these plays are plotless or without their kind of characterizations), but rather from a comprehensive statement of theme. In contrast, however, to the symphonic qualities of *A Dream Play,* as well as the dream consciousness that conveys its imagined reality, are the restricted performing mechanism and the plane of waking consciousness which indicate, in turn, the principal functional aspects of the chamber plays. I cannot find any primary source material, either in the manuscripts or in the documents surrounding them, which gives definitive coherence to the assortment of modified "dream-play" theories (not to mention such non-Strindbergian terms as "expressionism" and "theater of the absurd") that scholars and theater people have attached especially to *The Ghost Sonata.*[12] By trying to explain away the fact that Strindberg was wide awake when he wrote his chamber plays, we really deprive ourselves of ever being able to come to terms with what is essentially significant about these dramas. Now Strindberg's wakefulness pertains very much to all of us. The waking consciousness that the artist demands from an individual audience member will inform him beyond any shadow of doubt that when he is

watching the performance of one of the chamber plays, except for the Gentleman in *Storm Weather,* the Stranger in *The Burned House,* the Student and above
all the Mummy in *The Ghost Sonata,* he is in the presence–figuratively speaking–of sleepwalkers.

Unlike the one who created them, the overwhelming majority of the people
who inhabit the chamber plays possess no consciousness, no awareness, no real
knowledge–especially of themselves. Not that any of them inherently lack the
basic equipment–that is to say, mind, heart, and body–the coordinate function-
ing of which potentially will open, so to speak, those headdoors that lead to the
perspectives which self-consciousness involves. When they are compared, however, with Strindberg's own consciousness, with his own awareness of what is
possible here on the plane of material existence, and with the real knowledge for
which he daily worked and worked in order to acquire, most of the characters in
the chamber plays are simply figments of each other's imaginations in the worst
sense of the word, sleeping daydreamers at the mercy of an infinitude of acciden-
tal happenings to which not infrequently our thoughts magnetically are drawn,
victims first and foremost of the tragedy of having been born.

A world of appearances (life-lies, illusions, subjectivity, Maya) obscures the
reality of the world (objective truth): Each of the chamber plays traces its own
particular form from its relative proximity to this general thematic statement. In
Storm Weather appearances retain most effectively their tenuous, veillike qualities;
objective truth here is a matter of nuance and indirect statement. Degrees of exposure to the reality of the world become increasingly acute in the subsequent
three plays.

The Ghost Sonata not only enjoys the reputation of being the most viable of
the chamber plays, from both a theatrical and an intellectual point of view, but
also is commonly regarded as the most formidable achievement of the final phase
in Strindberg's literary career. It has frequently been cited as the artist's most significant contribution to the range of development that has occurred in European
drama during the last six decades. Its curious and bizarre theatricality has sorely
perplexed a sizable number of scholars–Martin Lamm maintained that this play
was "the most difficult of Strindberg's works to interpret";[13] the text itself has
been rendered disturbingly memorable, nevertheless, by a number of eminent di-
rectors from Max Reinhardt to Ingmar Bergman. The notion of difficulty will
not obsess the interpreter who seriously considers and applies what Strindberg
said to Emil Schering in a letter dated March 27, 1907, wherein he initially acquainted the latter with this work:

> With today's mail will be posted another chamber play (Opus 3), called *A
> Ghost Sonata* (with the subtitle Kama Loka, which need not be included). It is
> *schauderhaft* as life, when the scales fall from one's eyes and one sees *Das Ding
> an Sich.* There is form to it, and content, the wisdom that comes with the years
> when the material of life is increased and the capacity to survey the entirety has
> been attained. That's how "the World-weaver" threads human beings' des-
> tinies, that's how many secrets are found in *every* home. People are too proud
> to confess it, most of them brag about their imagined happiness, and in general
> they hide their misery. The Colonel plays his auto-comedy to the end; illusion
> (Maya) has turned into reality for him–the Mummy finally wakens but cannot
> wake up others. . . .[14]

Like the other three chamber plays, *The Ghost Sonata* essentially has to do with the layers of appearances that obscure the reality of our world. Unlike the rest of the chamber plays with their respective treatments of one significant theme, the substance of *The Ghost Sonata* gravitates alternately toward two contrasting subjects, namely, the Arkenholz and the Hummel themes. The former sets into motion within the framework of the drama the same degree of waking consciousness that *through* suffering and penitence the Mummy alone among the other characters also has attained; and the latter corresponds, in turn, to the condition of the sleepwalker for whom, as Strindberg pointed out in the letter above concerning the Colonel, illusion has turned into reality. The stripping away of those illusions upon which the Hummels—specifically in the environment of the play, father and daughter—depend in order to take the breath of life, and without which these unfortunate people literally manifest the dying that their eighty- and twenty-year journeys from the cradle has been, as well as the ironic irrelevance of the exceedingly few Arkenholzes with respect to a race of human beings that mechanically crucifies its liberators: This is the comprehensive statement that the artist has drawn from these two contrasting subjects, the coordinate presentation of which shortly will be examined by means of a detailed analysis of the form of *The Ghost Sonata.*

Before making such an analysis, one needs to consider the specific denotative value of the title itself. The earliest chronological indication of the play is found in Strindberg's diary on March 8, 1907, at which time the artist used his title in order to point directly to the chief narrative occurrence in the second section, that is, *The Ghost Supper.*[15] The letter quoted above to Schering later that month cites the play, however, as *A Ghost Sonata;* and in the acknowledgement of his German translator's affirmative response to the manuscript, which is dated April 1, 1907, Strindberg first indicated his final thinking as far as the title of the play was concerned: "*The Ghost Sonata* (we are able to call it this after Beethoven's Ghost Sonata in D minor and his Ghost Trio. Hence not Spook [Sonata].)"[16] Strindberg has referred here to two of Beethoven's compositions, the Piano Sonata in D Minor, op. 31 no. 2, and the Piano Trio in D Major, op. 70 no. 1. Early in the nineteenth century, the latter of these compositions received the identifying label, *Geister* (Ghost) Trio, because of a prominent motif in the second movement which John N. Burk has described as "a soulless cry,"[17] and which also is found among the composer's sketches for an unfinished setting of the text from the opening scene of *Macbeth.* On the basis of his own subjective response, Strindberg evidently applied this identification to the D Minor Piano Sonata, the third movement of which he previously had used in the second act of *Crimes and Crimes.*[18]

Nowhere in the text of *The Ghost Sonata* has Strindberg actually specified music from either of these compositions. This being the case, Göran Lindström[19] has suggested that the reason for the artist's having chosen this title exists primarily beyond the limits of the text itself, that its significance is a matter of connotation strictly within the realm of Strindberg's own subjectivity. The denotative value of this title remains nevertheless. I agree with the point of view that Evert Sprinchorn,[20] among others, has advanced in the introductory essay to his English translation of the play, namely, that *The Ghost Sonata* cannot really be understood other than by means of a musical analysis of its form. I question,

however, the musical terminology upon which Sprinchorn's analysis depends–
that is to say, his curious mixture of concepts which pertain to the idea of the
sonata as a whole with those that have to do with the ideas of sonata form. It
will be argued in this article that the title *The Ghost Sonata* suggests the basic
structural concept, what in music is generally referred to as sonata form, upon
which the technical scheme of this drama depends.

The term *sonata form* is misleading because it does not denote the form of a
sonata (i.e., a composition consisting of several contrasting movements), but the
complex musical structure frequently used for single movements of the sonata.
Such alternate designations as sonata-allegro and first-movement form do reflect
how and where composers generally have used sonata form within their compositions; but they are not entirely definitive because the form appears many times
in slow (andante, adagio, and so on) second movements as well as fast (allegro,
presto, and so on) fourth ones. Generally speaking, the term refers not to a form
of music, but to a form that western composers have used within their
compositions.

> [It is common knowledge that] a movement written in sonata form consists of
> three sections: exposition, development, and recapitulation, the last usually fol-
> lowed by a coda. In the exposition the composer introduces the musical ideas,
> consisting essentially of a first and second theme connected by a bridge passage.
> The second theme is in a different key from the first, normally the key of the
> dominant if the tonic is major, or the key of the relative major if the tonic is
> minor. In practically all early sonatas the exposition is repeated. The devel-
> opment is the central section of the movement, in position as well as emotion-
> al impact. Such devices as melodic fragmentation, rapid harmonic modulation,
> and contrapuntal combination of different motifs are used to produce the spe-
> cial character of "development," "dynamic tension," "increased temperature,"
> "fighting forces," etc., one or both of the themes from the exposition being
> used as the point of departure. The recapitulation normally contains all the ma-
> terial of the exposition, though usually with certain modifications in the bridge
> passage. One modification is obligatory, namely, that the second theme appear
> in the tonic (not, as before, in the dominant or relative major). Thus the
> whole movement closes in the tonic. The coda, usually a closing statement of
> moderate length, sometimes assumes considerable proportions and even be-
> comes another development section.[21]

Exactly as they are explained here, the terms of this definition can and
should be applied to the technical scheme of *The Ghost Sonata* in order to clarify
the artistic coherence of this exceptional theater piece. Working exclusively with
the precedents of dramatic tradition, many commentators have assessed this play
as a highly interesting but potentially anticlimactic work;[22] however, what to
the dramatic imagination seems perilously close to the danger of an anticlimax
makes explicit musical sense.

Neither in his manuscript nor in the published editions of the text that appeared during his lifetime, nor in what has been preserved of his own commentary on *The Ghost Sonata* in letters, memorandums, and the like, addressed to
a wide range of his colleagues and friends, did the artist actually indicate that the
structure of this play was to be considered in relationship to the standard concepts of dramaturgy. Where most of his English translators in their renderings of

this work have provided their readers with scene divisions, Strindberg simply put asterisks. It should go without saying that the artist did not think of the three sections into which the play can be divided as maintaining the kind of linear segment that the dramatic *scene* implies. There are, on the other hand, definite indications that Strindberg was entirely aware of the musical nature of this drama. The following postcard to Emil Schering dated July 31, 1907, however telegraphic the wording of its contents, reemphasizes the pertinence in Strindberg's own understanding of the matter, specifically of Beethoven's D Minor Piano Sonata:

> My oldest brother, Axel, is travelling on Thursday from here to Berlin, to my old Linden hotel. He is a Beethoven performer, [and] if you will acquaint him with the musical news in Berlin, he will play the Ghost Sonata for you. . . .[23]

If the title *The Ghost Sonata* had been finally decided on simply for an additional connotative reference, Strindberg would not likely have called Schering's attention again to this composition. That the artist actually made the arrangements whereby his German translator was able to listen to Beethoven's D Minor Piano Sonata, while he was preparing his own edition of the text, indicates the proximity of this musical composition to the creative process that the writing of *The Ghost Sonata* was for Strindberg himself. Either the student in general or the re-creative artist in particular, whoever wants to penetrate the meaning of *The Ghost Sonata,* is well advised to listen carefully to Beethoven's D Minor Piano Sonata, the first movement of which—with its deliberate and studied blending of an introductory largo tempo with a dominating allegro, its darkly agitated passages, and its exploration of the silence within sound—serves as a specific example of sonata form with which August Strindberg was intimately conversant and to which the technical scheme of this play corresponds. There is a muted bridge passage, an atypical fragment consisting of a single melodic voice expressed by means of the largo from the introduction, between the recapitulation and the coda of this movement about which A. Forbes Milne has observed: "It is as if the music were trying to become articulate."[24] *The Ghost Sonata* shows that this music is more than capable of being articulated.

The technical scheme of *The Ghost Sonata* should be considered as an unbroken progression of three basic sections: (1) the introductory exterior environment, (2) the series of unmaskings in the "round room," and (3) the concluding exterior-interior restatement of the "hyacinth room." These primary units of the technical scheme are sections of an all-inclusive structural whole; there is no justification in the text for separating them either into a set of "dream-like" scenes or into a group of contrasting "musical" movements (as, on the other hand, there obviously is in the case of *A Dream Play* because of Strindberg's having divided his manuscript copy of this work with Roman numerals into three distinct structural entities). There is, moreover, every reason for calling attention to the overall structural design of *The Ghost Sonata*—to the oneness of the movement that it is—because of the thematic interdependence of its three basic sections, each of which will now be closely examined with regard to how it functions within the totality of the work itself.

Taking into account the ordering of *The Ghost Sonata*'s thematic content by means of the idea of sonata form, the following is an analysis of the structure of the introductory exterior environment as it corresponds with the theory of the section in this form that is called:

I. The Exposition:

A: Introduction: The intitial pantomime involving the Dark Lady, the Portress, the Old Man (Hummel), and the Milkmaid (pp. 49–50).[25]

B: Statement of first theme: The entrance of the Student (Arkenholz). Definition of Arkenholz by means of two confrontations: (1) Arkenholz and the Milkmaid (pp. 150–51), (2) Arkenholz and Hummel (pp. 151–56).

C: Bridge passage: Arkenholz's speculation about the house and its inhabitants countered by Hummel's exposure of the tangled web of reality that binds the inhabitants of the house to each other. The simultaneous shifting of focus from Arkenholz to Hummel (pp. 157–62).

D: Statement of second theme: Definition of Hummel by means of Arkenholz's consciousness: "But let go of my hand, you're taking my strength, you're freezing me, what do you want?" (pp. 162–63). Note well that Strindberg has punctuated the Arkenholz-Hummel dialogue with an asterisk at this point (p. 163).

E: Repetition of first theme: The entrance of the Young Lady (Hummel's daughter); the shifting of focus again to Arkenholz (pp. 164–65).

F: Bridge passage: Hummel's further exposure of the tangled web of reality; the apparition of the dead Consul, visible only to Arkenholz, the "Sunday child"[26] (pp. 165–68).

G: Repetition of second theme: Definition of Hummel by means of what Johansson says to Arkenholz (opposed to what Hummel previously has said about himself but corresponding with the impression from Arkenholz's consciousness); the reentrance of Hummel accompanied by a crowd of beggars; the acknowledgment of "the noble youth, Arkenholz," by Hummel, the beggars, and the "ghost-supper" set (the Colonel, the Fiancée, etc.) (pp. 168–72).

H: Coda: The second apparition of the Milkmaid; Hummel's collapse into his wheelchair; Arkenholz's question which ends this portion of the play (p. 173).

The introductory exterior environment is not, accordingly, dominated exclusively by the character of Hummel, nor is the subject of vampirism, manifested by the essential reality of Hummel's condition, the only significant idea to which the substance of *The Ghost Sonata* can be abstracted; nor is Arkenholz a mere listener and answerer of questions here in the expository portion of the play. This section is, rather, a balanced presentation and a deliberately repeated initial statement of the two opposing subjects that Arkenholz and Hummel are. The meaning of *The Ghost Sonata* pertains, then, as much to Arkenholz (the savior of human lives in a world where accident and chance are the fundamental laws, and the impoverished student of languages who, nevertheless, is endowed with the expanded consciousness of the "Sunday child") as it does to Hummel (the well-to-do elderly businessman who claims to look mildly on the shortcomings of, and flaws in, his fellow human beings, but whose grasp literally sucks the life force from Arkenholz, and who is finally characterized as anything but tolerant and kind by his manservant Johansson).

A secondary aspect of the exposition is the initial statement in the bridge passages of the crucial "exposure" motif—that is, the stripping away of the layers of appearances that the specific world of the play affords. Hummel chiefly commands the "exposure" motif in this portion of the drama. Whether or not he actually possesses the moral credentials to command this motif is a question that is decisively answered in the substance of the middle portion.

The following is an analysis of the second section, the series of unmaskings in the "round room," as it corresponds with what in sonata form is called:

II. The Development:

A: Bengtsson and Johansson; Bengtsson's *exposure* of the general conditions within the house; his opening the wallpapered door where the Mummy, who, as Bengtsson puts it, "thinks she is a parrot," keeps herself (pp. 174–78).

B: Hummel's intrusion into the "round room"; his confrontation with the Mummy; her admonition: "Jakob, think about what you are doing! Spare him . . ." (i.e., her husband, the Colonel) (pp. 178–83).

C: Introducing himself as the creditor demanding payment and compensation for what he owns, Hummel confronts the Colonel; Hummel's systematic *exposure* of the life-lies and the delusions behind every aspect of the Colonel's appearance: The aristocratic family he claims to represent has been extinct for one hundred years; his military title has been revoked; his hair, teeth, and waistline are false; he is not the father of the Young Lady! (pp. 184–89).

D: The gathering of the "ghost-supper" set (in addition to Hummel and the Colonel, the Fiancée Miss Holsteinkrona, the Aristocrat Baron Skansborg, and the Mummy); Hummel's vindictive *exposure* of the pervasive and criminal fraudulence that their tangled existences are; Hummel's exaction of revenge on the "ghost-diners": His revelation to them that he is the father of the Young Lady and that his mission in their house is "to pull up the weeds, expose the crimes, settle the accounts, so that the young people can begin anew in this home that I have given them!" (pp. 189–92).

E:(i) The Mummy's *exposure* of what her acquired waking consciousness affords: "But I can stop time in its course—I can make the past into nothing, what was done undone; but not with bribes, not with threats—rather through suffering and penitence. . . ."

(ii) The Mummy's turning of the process of *exposure* onto Hummel: ". . . But that you, Jakob Hummel, with your false name are going to sit [as our] judge, this shows that you are worse than we poor ones! You are not either the one you appear to be!"

(iii) The third apparition of the Milkmaid, visible only to a terrified Jakob Hummel; Bengtsson's definitive *exposure* of the network of criminality that is the essential nature of Jakob Hummel; Hummel's collapse, his transformation into a parrot; his death in the same closet where the Mummy has done penance for the crime of adultery she once committed with him (pp. 192–95).

F: Connecting passage: Arkenholz's "Sun Song":[27]

Solen såg jag, så mig syntes
som jag skådat Den Fördolde;
sina verk var mänska njuter, säll är den det goda övar.

För din vredes gärning som du övat
gör ej bot med ondska;
hugna den du har bedrövat med din godhet, har du batnad.
Ingen fruktar som ej illa gjorde;
gott är menlös vara.

(I saw the sun, it seemed to me
that I beheld the Concealed (Hidden) One;
his own work each human being receives,
blessed is the one who does what is good.
For deeds of your anger that you have done
do no penance with evil;
comfort the one that you have grieved
with your goodness and you will gain.
No one fears who did no evil;
good is being innocent.)

The exposure motif from the bridge passages of the exposition becomes, accordingly, both the point of departure from which the development initially proceeds and the recurring thematic idea that gives coherence as well as progression to the five episodic units within this portion of the play. As far as appearances go, the Hummel subject is aggressively dominant; but the virtual absence of the Arkenholz figure from this middle portion does not preclude a development of what expositorily was presented as *his* subject, as the intervention of the Mummy—waking up the way she does there in the fifth episode—indicates. That consciousness which she has attained through suffering and penitence savagely and inexorably destroys Jakob Hummel, a creature whose formerly disastrous lifestyle has made him so totally void of inner essence that it is absurd to attribute his ultimate disintegration to the sudden impact of a "bad" conscience. Hummel has, putting it in an expression that is currently fashionable, played too many games far too long to have given himself any conscience at all!

Arkenholz's "Sun Song" between the second and third sections of the play not only extends the intrinsic knowledge that was initially unveiled when the Mummy unmasked herself, and then Hummel's non-self, but also stands as a pithy distillation of the moral vision in the light of which Strindberg conceived *The Ghost Sonata* (not to mention the other thirty-three completed dramas that were written between the chronological extremities of *To Damascus, Part I* and *The Great Highway*): "His own work each human being receives!"

The development section attains, indeed, a tempestuous spiraling of dramatic intensity as well as a final penetration of the forces in conflict that obviously results in the first of *The Ghost Sonata*'s two climactic moments—namely, the death of Hummel. Retiring Hummel to the dugout, so to speak, with approximately one-third of the action remaining to be played is not necessarily the strategic blunder that a routine reading of the text or a stage presentation, the authority of which emanates from individual characterizations rather than a collective understanding of the overall thematic design, can make it appear to be. Transposed from the dominant to the tonic, the Hummel theme survives with ghastly effectiveness in the concluding section of the play, the exterior-interior restatement of the "hyacinth room," the first three units of which correspond with what in sonata form is called:

III. The Recapitulation:

A: Restatement of first theme: Arkenholz and the Young Lady (Adèle); their contemplation of the beams of love that the hyacinth, the snowflakes, the star Sirius, the narcissus, and the shallot all manifest, the culmination of which becomes: "Our [thought]!−We have given birth to something together, we are wedded . . ." (pp. 196–99).

B: Bridge passage: Adèle's denial of Arkenholz; her initial exposure of the nongenerative reality that exists beneath the apparent well-being of her home environment; her concentration of their attention on the person of the Cook (pp. 199–201).

C:(i) Restatement of second theme: The first appearance of the Cook, who belongs to "the vampire-family Hummel."

(ii) Adèle's exposure, in so many words, of the unwholesome injustices and absurdities that undermine the apparent harmony of her own condition (note well the following remark from Strindberg's preliminary sketches for *The Ghost Sonata,* useful in maintaining perspective on Adèle's behavior here: "She is so evil that she feels sorry for herself sometimes . . ."[28]); her assessment of what the essential activity of her existence amounts to: "Keeping life's unclean [things] at a distance."

(iii) The second appearance of the vampire Cook (pp. 201–5).

That which is expressed within the third portion of *The Ghost Sonata* is only incidentally a matter of narrative extension from the preceding two sections. Strindberg's thought in this drama has not really organized itself horizontally with regard to time−that is to say, in the implicit chronological fashion to which the general notion of dramatic structure subscribes. The third portion of *The Ghost Sonata* becomes uninteresting or difficult to understand, in consequence, when the interpreter (reader, stage director, actor) arbitrarily puts primary emphasis on the relatively unimportant factor that narrative continuity here is. What we do have in the terminal section of the musical structure of this play is, rather, a reconsideration of the opposing Arkenholz and Hummel themes from the exposition achieved here by means of a confrontation between Arkenholz and Hummel's daughter, Adèle. The motion of the imagined experience that this drama postulates, in effect, doubles back on itself after the death of Hummel, and the movement of the entirety of the drama begins, accordingly, all over again.

The literal radiance of the introductory exterior environment is repeated here in the figurative sunshine that spills over from the central image of the connecting passage between the second and third sections and that Arkenholz's rays of thought clearly maintain. When we resist the temptation to bury the Cook in the grave of the artist's isolated subjective bias (in other words, when we try to determine her meaning within the context of the work), we perceive with her appearance on stage extreme anxiety. We are here reminded, in turn, of the angry cloud masses that heralded the apparition of the dead Consul and the subsequent rainstorm that prevailed during Johansson's responses to Arkenholz's questions about the identity of Jakob Hummel back in the penultimate units of the first section. If our senses and imaginations are alert, we now share Arkenholz's penetrating vision of the horrifying sickness that, so to speak, permeates Adèle's environment and life.

What remains of the third section (pp. 205-11) is an extensive coda—a second development, if you will—in which the cyclical processes of the recapitulation proper are further and further expanded because of a blend of the "exposure" motif with the waking consciousness that Arkenholz by nature possesses. As the Mummy's articulation of this motif in the terminal phase of the development proved fatal to the personality which masqueraded as essence in the "life" of Jakob Hummel, so also is Arkenholz's definitive statement of the "exposure" motif, here in the concluding moments, that force which thrusts the action of the drama itself into its second and final climactic moment, namely, the death of Adèle.

This is not, however, the end. As the Mummy petitioned God for mercy for the soul of Jakob Hummel, so also does Arkenholz extend his compassion to the soul of Adèle after her embarkation with the "Liberator" that, in the context of this play, death is. Strindberg finally directs our eyes to Arnold Böcklin's magnificent painting *Die Toteninsel*[29] and asks that "soft music, quietly, pleasantly, sorrowful [music]" reach our ears from the island of Böcklin's vision. The Adagio from Beethoven's D Minor Piano Sonata corresponds perfectly with the music that the artist has indicated here. This being the case, would not the staging of *The Ghost Sonata* be unmistakably realized, in terms of the artistically unified experience that it inherently affords, if a director were to place the whole of the drama between the first and the second movements of Beethoven's D Minor Piano Sonata: In other words, if he were to use the Largo; Allegro from this composition as a prelude to the peformance of this play and the Adagio as its necessary meditational epilogue?

Notes

1. This letter has been reprinted in August Falck's *Fem år med Strindberg* (Stockholm: Wahlström & Widstrand, 1935), p. 24. This passage in the original runs: "En 'chatnoir'—eller 'Procope-Strindberg.' Jag gör dekorativa väggmålningar och uppför 'Himmelrikets nycklar' som skuggspel. Gitarren kommer också att få hjelpa till. Littmansson dirigerar en liten orkester på nytt vis."
   All translations of the Swedish quotations in this article are my own.

2. Harriet Bosse, *Strindbergs brev till Harriet Bosse* (Stockholm: Bokförlaget Natur och kultur, 1932), p. 173.
   Men tre personer måste jag ha. Har jag Dig och två till skall jag låna pengar, engagera och låta måla min miniatyrscen med skärmar. Afven monodramer skola med; och apteringar af äldre stora vackra saker, antik, Shakespeare, Schiller.

3. With the exceptions of *Gustav III* (1902) and the four installments that were completed for the projected cycle of plays about world history, namely, *The Nightingale of Wittenberg* (1903) and the *Moses-Socrates-Christ* trilogy (1903), none of the ideas for dramatic works that Strindberg more or less formulated between the completion of *A Dream Play* and the writing of *Storm Weather* ever materialized into a viable and definitive text.

4. Strindberg's letters to Schering have been deposited at the archives of the Bonnier Publishing House in Stockholm.
   Hvad skall jag skrifva, hvad säga om Engelbrekt och Påsk och allt annat? Jag blir stum i motgången, ty jag kan icke skylla på någon, och mitt öde kan jag icke ändra. Man har medvind ib land, nu har jag motvind och kan bara vänta. Det värsta är att jag börjar förlora intresset vid arbetet när uppmuntran systematiskt uteblir. För öfvrigt synes mig att jag skulle ha sagt allt jag har att säga för denna period; särskildt i ett nytt slutadt Drömspel som ej är kopieradt.

5. *Fairhaven and Foulstrand,* 1902; *Alone, Tales, Gothic Rooms,* 1903; *Black Banners,* 1904; *Historical Miniatures,* 1905; *The Rearing Feast, The Scapegoat,* 1906.

6. *Word Play and Minor Art,* 1905.

7. Regarding the source material here, Strindberg's five open letters to the personnel of the Intimate Theater are obviously the point of departure for any serious inquiry and have been published in the fiftieth volume of the Landquist edition of the *Samlade skrifter* (see note 8). Walter Johnson's translations of these letters, augmented with introductions and extensive annotation, are available in the "Washington Strindberg" as *Open Letters to the Intimate Theater* (Seattle: University of Washington Press, 1966). August Falck's *Fem år med Strindberg* (Stockholm: Wahlström & Widstrand, 1935) contains a wealth of firsthand information about the genesis, method, procedure, achievement, and disbandment of the Intimate Theater as well as a comprehensive assessment of the role which this performing group played in the introduction of Strindbergian drama to Swedish theatrical life. Gösta M. Bergman in his definitive study *Den moderna teaterns genombrott: 1890-1925* (Stockholm: Albert Bonniers, 1966) devotes an entire chapter to the Intimate Theater as one of the most important harbingers of present-day usage on the Stockholm stage.

8. John Landquist, ed., *Samlade skrifter ar August Strindberg* (Stockholm: A. Bonnier, 1919), vol. 50, *Öppna brev till Intima teatern,* p. 11.
   Kammarmusikens idé överförd på dramat. Det intima förfarandet, det betydelsefulla motivet, den soignerade behandlingen.

9. For an excellent discussion of this matter, see Bruno Walter, *Theme and Variations: An Autobiography,* trans. James A. Galston (New York: Alfred A. Knopf, 1946), pp. 59-60.

10. Strindberg Archive of *Nordiska Museet,* deposited at the Swedish Royal Library (*Kungliga Biblioteket*), Stockholm, Carton 72, *Ockulta Dagboken* (ms.), p. 162.

11. Landquist, 50:12.
   Om man nu frågar, vad en Intim Teater vill, och vad som åsyftas med Kammarspel, så kan jag svara så här: I dramat söka vi det starka betydelsefulla motivet, men med begränsning. I behandling undvika vi all flärd, alla beräknade effekter, applådställen, glansroller, solonummer. Ingen bestämd form skall binda författaren, ty motivet betingar formen. Alltså frihet i behandlingen, endast bunden av konceptionens enhet och stilkänslan.

12. C. E. W. L. Dahlström, *Strindberg's Dramatic Expressionism,* 2d ed. (New York: B. Blom, 1965), pp. 195-201.

13. Martin Lamm, *August Strindberg,* 2d ed. rev. (Stockholm: A. Bonnier, 1948), p. 360.

14. This letter has been reprinted among other places in Torsten Eklund's biographical selection of Strindberg's letters, *Från Fjärdingen till Blå tornet* (Stockholm: A. Bonnier, 1946), pp. 377-78.
   Med dagens post avgår ett andra kammarspel (Opus 3), kallat *En Spöksonat* (med undertitel Kama Loka, som ej bör medtagas). Det är schauderhaft, såsom livet, när fjällen falla från ögonen och man ser Das Ding an Sich. Det är form på det, och innehåll, visdomen som kommer med åren, då livsmaterialet ökats och förmågan att överskåda infunnit sig. Så där väver 'Världsväverskan' mänskors öden, så där mycket hemligheter finnes i *varje* hem. Människorna äro för högfärdiga att erkänna det; de flesta skryta med sin inbillade lycka, och i allmänhet döljer man sitt elände. Överstens spelar sin autocomedie till slut; illusionen (Maya) är bliven verklighet för honom – Mummien vaknar dock först, men kan icke väcka andra. . . .

15. *Ockulta Dagboken,* p. 251.

16. See n. 4.

Gespenster Sonaten (vi få kalla den så efter Beethovens både Spöksonat D-moll och Spöktrio. alltså icke Spuk.)

17. John N. Burk, *The Life and Works of Beethoven* (New York: Modern Library, 1946), p. 399.

18. Elizabeth Sprigge, trans., *Five Plays of Strindberg* (Garden City, N.Y.: Doubleday, 1960), pp. 74–80.

19. Göran Linström, ed., *Spöksonaten* (Lund: Gleerup, 1963), p. 93.

20. August Strindberg, *The Chamber Plays,* trans. Evert Sprinchorn et al. (New York: Dutton, 1962), p. xx.

21. Willi Apel, ed., *Harvard Dictionary of Music,* 2nd ed. rev. (Cambridge, Mass.: Harvard University Press, 1970), pp. 791–94.

22. Lamm, p. 362; Gunnar Ollén, *Strindbergs dramatik,* 2d ed. rev. (Stockholm: Sveriges Radio, 1961), p. 471; and Maurice Valency, *The Flower and the Castle* (New York: Macmillan, 1963), p. 354.

23. See n. 4.

Min äldsta bror, Axel, afreser om torsdag härifrån till Berlin, till mitt gamla Lindenhotel. Han är Beethovenspelare, vii Ni visa honom på leüsta musik i Berlin, så spelar han Gespenstersonate för Er. . . .

24. A. Forbes Milne, *Beethoven:* I. *The Pianoforte Sonatas* (London: Oxford University Press, 1925), p. 35.

25. The page references in the analytical sections of this article are to *Samlade skrifter ar August Strindberg,* vol. 45, *Kammarspel.*

26. Strindberg is using the idea from folklore and Scandinavian tradition, namely, that a child born on a Sunday can see supernatural phenomena and possesses the gifts of prophecy and of healing; cf. J. P. Jacobsen's *Marie Grubbe* (1876): "You are as diligent as a Sunday child, their eyes are more open, all of their senses are more subtle in what they can perceive."

27. The "Sun Song" (*Solsangen*) is an Icelandic poem written probably about 1200 and often included with the body of Eddic poetry because of its form, although its content is Christian. Strindberg previously borrowed from this poem in his folk drama *The Crown Bride* (1901). For an interesting present-day consideration of the "Sun Song," see Bo Bergman's *Predikare* (Stockholm: A. Bonnier, 1967).

28. Strindberg Archive of *Nordiska Musset,* deposited at the Swedish Royal Library (*Kungliga Biblioteket*), Stockholm, Carton 4, No. 4, *Fragment ar Spöksonaten.* "Hon är så ond att hon får medlidande med sig sjelf ibland. . . ."

29. The Swiss artist Arnold Böcklin (1827–1901) produced between 1880 and 1900 five versions of *Die Toteninsel* ("The Island of the Dead"), surely the crowning glory of his life's work. Many consider this expression of death's dream kingdom among the highest manifestations of the German romantic spirit. During his post-Inferno period, Strindberg repeatedly cited this as his favorite painting.

Parallel Attitudes to Form in Late Beethoven and Late Goethe: Throwing Aside the Appearance of Art

R. T. Llewellyn

In a celebrated passage in Thomas Mann's *Doktor Faustus* Wendell Kretzschmar, the music-teacher of Adrian Leverkühn, plays and at the same time comments on Beethoven's last piano sonata (op. 111 in C minor). Toward the end of the arietta, at that point where the music dissolves into seemingly endless trills, becoming almost something other than merely music,[1] Kretzschmar shouts to his small audience that there the appearance of art is thrown aside, that in the end art always throws aside the appearance of art. And, later, he speaks of the B-flat String Quartet (op. 130), which in its first version had the frighteningly taut and difficult Grosse Fuge as the last movement of this monster of all string quartets, and goes on to talk of a new attitude to form in late Beethoven—a more indulgent, complaisant, and easygoing one than had previously been the case with this composer.[2] One thinks immediately of the last three piano sonatas, the two cello sonatas (op. 102) and of the late string quartets, especially of the A Minor, B-flat, and C-sharp Minor quartets, where for the most part Beethoven has rejected conventional form for arrangements of highly contrasting movements, running as in the C-sharp Minor Quartet to seven movements, arrangements in which the listener is presented with the blunt juxtaposition of seemingly alien elements—the sublime and the commonplace, the ethereal and the grotesque, the refined and the rustic. One recognizes in the late sonatas and quartets Beethoven's rejection of the conventional three- or four-movement work with its expected and familiar contrasts for aggregates of surprisingly disparate movements, both as regards their character and their length. One exception is, however, the first of the late quartets (op. 127 in E-flat) which is formally closer to the middle period Rasoumovsky quartets than to its immediate successors. Beethoven's last quartet (op. 135 in F Major) also has four movements, but this resemblance to the earlier quartets is only the superficial numerical one. In their essentials the four movements of the F Major Quartet are far removed even from the quartets of the middle period.

Reprinted from *Modern Language Review* 63 (1968):407–16.

Very frequently in the late quartets and sonatas the appearance of art is indeed thrown aside. These works seemed opaque and uncouth to Beethoven's contemporaries and they continued to dismay later generations (Tchaikovsky regarded them as chaos itself). Only well into the present century did they come to be acclaimed and now it is generally recognized that, despite their apparent lack of artistic organization, they do possess a certain degree of integration, due mainly to the use of leitmotiv technique and cyclical thematic development. Indeed, in this respect there is perhaps a stricter artistic control at work than was the case with the more conventionally constructed earlier works. But now the polished artifice is deliberately eschewed.

This approach, a superficially offhand one with, however, a certain degree of artistic control present and the attempt to hold together the most disparate elements by means of the leitmotiv is one that has influenced not only later musicians but also writers, particularly in the twentieth century. In the novel Thomas Mann, Aldous Huxley, James Joyce, and Hermann Broch come to mind and in poetry, above all, T. S. Eliot. The novelists were of course looking for something more subtle than the sustained narrative of the traditional novel and they adopted from time to time a montage technique, assembling diverse sections alongside one another and employing recurrent symbols in order to secure an underlying unity. It is well known that Thomas Mann "musicalized" his novels, taking over the leitmotiv from Wagner who in turn had found it in late Beethoven in particular. Mann claimed, for example, that *Der Zauberberg* should be read a second time for its musical qualities. These developments are familiar and anyway it would be misleading to talk comprehensively about late Beethoven and the novelists mentioned in this respect, for there are fundamental differences present between the style of the late Beethoven and similar developments in twentieth-century music and prose. What seems to have escaped notice is that, at the very time when Beethoven was composing his late quartets, a literary work appeared which exhibits virtually the same approach to form. The work is Goethe's *Wilhelm Meisters Wanderjahre,* a novel which is as quirky, strangely beautiful, remote, sometimes theoretically dry but again often as startlingly direct in physical impact as the late quartets. Like the latter it went long unrecognized and is still perhaps Goethe's most neglected major work. Only since about 1930 have critics begun to do justice to the work, whereas previously it had been regarded as an interesting compendium of the wisdom of Goethe's old age, as a document with only a very limited aesthetic appeal. It was even suggested that formally it was the work of a man who declined into senility.[3] Recently, however, claims as regards the unity and integration of the novel's material have been put forward which appear to be exorbitant.[4] This work cannot really be viewed in the light of traditional aesthetic judgments as regards its form.

It would of course be unwise to bring the late quartets and *Wilhelm Meisters Wanderjahre* too close together as regards content. It is the peculiar excellence of most music that it does not admit of such intellectual precision and the most one can say is that both the work of Beethoven and Goethe is characterized at this stage by a profound sense of resignation. The very subtitle of Goethe's novel indicates the tone of the work and in the late quartets a sense of resignation is found above all in the last movement of the A Minor Quartet, a dark, bittersweet, intensely poignant movement; in the coda of the last movement of the

C-sharp Minor Quartet; and in the last movement of the F Major Quartet with its heading, "Der schwer gefasste Entschluss: Es muss sein!" But whereas Goethe's resignation has mainly social relevance, his novel being concerned with the future of European society, Beethoven's, one feels, is more absolute.

Closer parallels can be elicited, however, if the attitudes of Goethe and Beethoven within their respective media to form at this period in their lives are compared. *Wilhelm Meisters Wanderjahre,* like the late quartets, is an aggregate (the word is Goethe's own)[5] of the most diverse elements. It consists of the mere outline or framework of a novel proper into which are interpolated a number of Novellen of widely varying tone, thematic character, and narrative technique, a Märchen, poems and songs, a passage of art-criticism, sections on the technicalities of spinning and weaving (this being almost purely factual information in the manner of the pages of scientific knowledge inserted by Mann into *Der Zauberberg*), letters by various hands, diary entries, and two collections of aphorisms. It is at once evident that Goethe's attitude toward form at the end of his life was more radical than that of Beethoven in his late period, even if allowance is made for the scope which their respective media allowed them (the string quartet is one of the most restrained and economical combinations in music).

The general circumstances in which the late quartets and Goethe's novel came into being clearly reveal their more indulgent and easygoing attitude to form; both men allowed external, fortuitous factors to determine the proportions and order of their materials—and this in works which contain their profoundest ideas. Beethoven, at the request of his publisher, Schott, who considered his Grosse Fuge too long and too difficult for both performers and audience, dropped this movement, his greatest shaping of the problem of grace and energy with which he had grappled so often in his life, and supplied a shorter, less complex movement. Beethoven also swapped around movements from one quartet to another and told Schott that the C-sharp Minor Quartet was put together from things he had stolen from here, there, and everywhere.[6] And he told Ries who proposed to play the *Hammerklavier* Sonata to omit movements or play them in any sequence as he wished. Much the same is true of the genesis and publication of *Wilhelm Meisters Wanderjahre.* Most of the Novellen were published separately before they were finally taken into the novel. One intended for the novel was put aside and became an independent novel in its own right, namely, *Die Wahlverwandtschaften.* Another of the Novellen, *Die pilgernde Törin,* is not even Goethe's own work but a translation from the French. Again, there are two editions of the novel and they differ considerably. In the second there are substantial additions to the novel proper and the Novellen are introduced in a different order. Like Beethoven, Goethe altered the proportions of his work to comply with the demands of his publisher. When Goethe submitted his manuscript to his publisher in 1829, the latter found that the material was not enough for the proposed three volumes and he asked Goethe for more material to this end. Goethe was, however, unable to extend what he had written and he found himself, as Eckermann puts it, in some embarrassment. But Goethe was soon equal to the situation. He placed before Eckermann two bundles of papers, aphorisms and short prose passages on science, the arts, and life in general and asked him to sort out sufficient matter from these papers in order to fill the required space. This explains the presence of the two collections of aphorisms and short prose passages which stand at the end of the second and third books of the novel respectively. For good measure Goethe also included two new poems, "Bei Betrachtung von Schillers Schädel" and "Vermächtnis." Understandably, as Eckermann reports, there was widespread bafflement amongst Goethe's readers. Eckermann was authorized by Goethe to omit the aphorisms and the two poems in subsequent editions of the novel and this wish was respected throughout the nineteenth century. But recently some editors have felt that these accretions are after all an integral part of the novel and have reintroduced them.[7]

Then there is the use of the conventional in the late quartets and *Wilhelm Meisters Wanderjahre* in such a way that it becomes unnerving and sometimes startling. In the rarified world of late Beethoven and late Goethe the conventional, the cliché almost, becomes something peculiarly striking and worthy of notice. Two outstanding examples are the pedantic little recitative which leads into the variations of the C-sharp Minor Quartet, into the very heart of the work; and the pathetic, trite march episode which follows on the withdrawn mysticism of the slow movement of the A Minor Quartet which has as its title "Heiliger Dankgesang eines Genesenen an die Gottheit, in der lydischen Tonart." In such a context their ordinary aspect becomes something extraordinary or, as Wendell Kretzschmar is reported to have said of the last five piano sonatas:

> Das Verhältnis des späten Beethoven, etwa in den fünf letzten Klaviersonaten, zum Konventionellen sei bei aller Einmaligkeit und selbst Ungeheuerlichkeit der Formensprache ein ganz anderes, viel lässlicheres und geneigteres. Unberührt, unverwandt vom Subjektiven trete die Konvention im Spätwerk öfters hervor, in einer Kahlheit oder, man möge sagen, Ausgeblasenheit, Ich-Verlassenheit, welche nun wieder schaurig-majestätischer wirke, als jedes persönliche Wagnis.[8]

And it is much the same in Goethe's novel where there is from time to time a stiffly conventional presentation of character, scene, and opinion—in particular a stereotyped use of adjective—amidst the richness of Goethe's mature prose which fluctuates between unnerving the reader and strangely impressing him.[9] He feels the precarious achievement of these conventional sentences with their slightly too recurrently insistent adjectives, denoting admirable human qualities, noble manners, and restrained passions.

Another feature of the late quartets is, of course, their laconic and enigmatic style. Not only is there a certain general spareness of outline typical of most composers' late periods (one thinks in particular of Mozart's Piano Concerto in B-flat K. 595, of Mahler's *Das Lied von der Erde,* and of Bartok's Sixth String Quartet), but there is also a deliberate abruptness in utterance and a pervading enigmatic quality even in the more extrovert movements.[10] Whereas in the earlier quartets two very different themes were linked by means of a resolving transitional passage, in his late period Beethoven merely juxtaposes them without attempting to fill in between them in the usual manner. Akin to this there is also a strong tendency to eschew obvious beginnings and endings to the movements in most of the late quartets. This is clearly seen in the C-sharp Minor Quartet, in which all the movements are linked and beginnings and endings are virtually sublimated. The casually enigmatic first movement of the F Major Quartet is a

further example of Beethoven's rejection of self-conscious onsets and closing per-
orations in music. Here the music seems to have been going on for some time
before we actually hear it and it comes to rest much in the same indefinite manner. Generally in this period Beethoven adopts swift, abrupt endings, two or
three sforzando chords or a violent pizzicato bring the proceedings to a sudden
end with very little in the way of prior preparation.

Now very much the same procedure may be observed in *Wilhelm Meisters
Wanderjahre.* The Novellen are introduced, for example, in the most casual and
arbitrary manner. Some do not end conclusively within their allotted space and
run over into the novel proper. Throughout the work Goethe's attitude is a deliberately enigmatic one. He withholds information, puzzles the reader for no
obvious reason and constantly balks him by leading him to the brink of an important scene or discussion only to break off, saying that this cannot be displayed
to the reader at this point. Sometimes the omission is made good later, but more
often it is not. Goethe is constantly thrusting himself in editorial guise between
the novel and the reader to shatter the illusion of the work of art. And this is
only due in part to Goethe's didactic aims. Instead of dominating his material,
Goethe allows himself to be dominated by his material and makes the material
seem more recalcitrant than it actually is. He is constantly working against the
grain as it were.[11] On other occasions it is apparent that Goethe just cannot be
bothered to shape his material. His editorial role in the novel, for example, is
very different in tone and function from the pseudoeditorial fussiness of Wie-
land and Sterne. It is not playfully omniscient as is the case with these novelists
but rather it conceals Goethe's impatience with his material and his general re-
luctance to sustain the artifice. His interventions nearly always serve to avoid a
well-constructed transitional passage or the rounded presentation of a conversation between his characters.[12] Perhaps the most striking example of Goethe's re-
luctance to portray events in a sustained manner and his tendency to leave things
unresolved is contained in the Novelle, *Nicht zu weit,* a brief and highly com-
pressed tale of marital infidelity in which the ironically contrasted experiences of
a married couple are presented. The husband, Odoard, exasperated by the failure
of his wife, a coquettish socialite, to return for a birthday party, is driven out of
the house by anger and meets by pure chance his former mistress at an inn. In
the meantime his wife has been involved in a coach-accident in the course of
which her lover shows more solicitude for the injuries of her friend, thereby be-
traying the affair between them. But Goethe breaks off abruptly at this point
and does not resolve the tale. Does Odoard sleep with his former mistress? Does
he return to his wife? Does their marriage founder? The reader is not told.
Odoard appears before the story and soon afterwards in the novel proper but no
mention is made of his earlier life apart from a vague passing reference to laby-
rinthine passions during a nocturnal conversation in which he takes part.[13]
Goethe has deliberately withheld the consequences of such a story and has con-
tented himself with an account of the interaction of foolish behaviour and
chance which brings about such extreme situations in people's lives. In the context of a novel like this which is permeated with the idea of *Entsagung* the rest
does not matter. This apparently unresolved Novelle is really most subtly resolved in the general ambience of the novel proper.

Then there is the use of the leitmotiv in Beethoven's late quartets and *Wilhelm Meisters Wanderjahre*. Not only are the individual quartets held together by this means but the entire corpus of the late quartets is pervaded by thematic association. With Goethe the disparate elements of the novel are also related by means of thematic association and an incipient leitmotiv technique. Thus the Novellen are not the mere points of relaxation within the didactic whole which they appear to be at first, but are variations on the idea of *Entsagung*. for example, *Die pilgernde Törin* and *Der Mann von fünfzig Jahren* both deal with the love of a father and his son for the same young girl, situations which are reflected in the novel proper by the fascination which Wilhelm and Felix feel for the young Hersilie. Other important motifs are the small chest which Wilhelm and Felix find in the depths of a maze of mountain-caves and the case of surgical instruments which Wilhelm possesses. Of these the small chest is the more important binding-agent. It is introduced frequently into the various aspects of the novel proper and occurs in a slightly transposed form in the Märchen, *Die neue Melusine,* where it is spoken of as a *Schatulle* rather than as a *Kästchen*. The use of the small chest as a recurrent leitmotiv is a rather arbitrary one for it has to do duty in a number of contexts and it is introduced into various aspects of the plot in an often artificial and contrived manner. It represents the essential mystery of life, the secrets of nature which should be respected and not violated (the link with Goethe's attitude as a scientist is obvious here), and it also represents the mystery of the personality, the last secrets of the self, a mystery which lovers in particular should respect in one another (in this sense it plays an important part in the relationship between Felix and Hersilie and in that between the Barber and his sprite-wife in the Märchen *Die neue Melusine*). It is of no striking poetic invention and does not convey in any profound sense the mysteries involved; it merely indicates or denotes them and does not embody them as the true symbol should. Wilhelm Emrich describes it as being "gleichsam Symbol des Symbolischen selbst" and then goes on to give the work a distinctly twentieth-century interpretation in this respect, seeing the chest as a symptom of Goethe's sceptical attitude toward language:

> Das Äusserlichste, ein Kästchen, ist zugleich das Innerlichste dieser Dichtung. Dort, wo das Symbol *nur* noch leblos dinghafte Erscheinung ist, offenbart es zugleich das Wesenhafteste alles Seins. . . . Der Schein einer unmittelbaren Einsichtigkeit oder Totalität erlischt. Nur mittelbar wird Verständnis erzielt, Totalität erreicht. Das Wort von der bruchlosen Einheit zwischen Erscheinung und Wesen im Kunstwerk—seit je ein fragwürdiges Wort, das ja letztlich nur für das religiöse Symbol (Eucharistie) in vollem Ernst und Wahrheitssinne zutrifft—wird endgültig in Frage gestellt.[14]

Can the chest be interpreted in such a far-reaching manner? It seems to be an allegorical device rather than a symbol and what we have here is perhaps the somewhat impatient artistic shorthand of the writer at the end of his life which is in keeping with the late Goethe's tendency towards allegory. It is not so much that Goethe is sceptical about the possibilities of art, but that he is impatient and high-handed with it from time to time. One does not have to look very far elsewhere in the novel for examples of Goethe's subtle use of symbol and masterly prose-writing.[15]

There is something similar in Beethoven's last quartet (op. 135 in F major).
Above the music at the beginning of the final movement Beethoven wrote:
"Der schwer gefasste Entschluss. Muss es sein? Es muss sein!" It is said that this
arose from the question of one of Beethoven's unpaid bills and was used by him
among his friends as a jocular catch-phrase. Here in his last quartet this unadorned phrase underpins the movement which is his final word in his lifelong
struggle with the mystery of life. The ground covered in all those C-minor bat-
tles, in the onslaught of the *Hammerklavier* Sonata and the Grosse Fuge is light-
heartedly illuminated once more in this deceptively simple movement built up
on a motif which had its origin in a joke arising from the petty exigencies of
life. Only the artist in his late period can allow himself such devices; in the
hands of a younger man they inevitably become shallow and flippant.

That critical response to Beethoven's late quartets and *Wilhelm Meisters Wanderjahre* has evolved along much the same lines provides further proof of their
kinship as regards their creators' attitude toward form. Now that these works are
no longer generally viewed as eccentric conglomerations, exaggerated claims for
their unity and integration have been advanced. Thus Deryck Cooke in a "Third
Programme" talk some years ago spoke of the entire complex of the late quartets
as being bound together thematically. This may be so; but it is only an abstract,
theoretical unity, not one which the listener recognizes in practice. Each of the
late quartets has its own enclosed, musical logic which does not refer in any
clinching manner to that of the other quartets. Deryck Cooke may be right as far
as abstract musical analysis is concerned but wrong concerning the actual business of assimilating the music of any one of these quartets.

Possibly the most exorbitant claim in this respect with regard to *Wilhelm
Meisters Wanderjahre* arises from the question of the two collections of aphorisms
and the two poems to which I referred earlier and which have now been reintroduced into the work by editors who believe that they are an integral part of the
work. But even here some measure of disagreement exists as Erich Trunz in the
Hamburger Ausgabe includes the aphorisms but not the poems, whereas Wilhelm Flitner in the Gedenkausgabe (Artemis Verlag) has both the aphorisms and
the poems. Of course many of the aphorisms deal with ideas discussed by the
characters in the novel; these discussions crystallize from time to time in aphoris-
tic utterances similar to those in *Betrachtungen im Sinne der Wanderer* and *Aus
Makariens Archiv*.[16] Now these two collections of aphorisms are to a large extent
the shavings and offcuts from Goethe's workshop—elements he could have included in the novel, had he wished to shape sustained conversations between his
characters. But Goethe, mainly because he was impatient with art and pressed for
time (the unfinished second part of *Faust* lay at hand), was unwilling to do this
and left much of the novel in a fragmentary state, contenting himself with mere
bare outlines for long stretches of the work. The aphorisms are clearly relevant
and this is why Goethe felt able to interpolate them when it later emerged that
the novel was not long enough for the planned three volumes and more material
was needed for the edition in hand. But the all-is-relevant approach of the editors who have insisted on reintroducing them together with the poems whilst
claiming a unified formal organization for the novel seems excessive. If the two
poems are to be retained, then why not introduce other related poems from the
Weltanschauliche Gedichte? Or why not include additional aphorisms from else-

where in Goethe's output?[17] Indeed, this approach, whilst claiming a thorough-going unity for the work, tacitly admits that the novel is basically an expandable portfolio containing a variety of papers, sketches, and notes.[18] Yet it is apparent that Goethe attempted to secure a certain binding element in the work, princi-pally, as Beethoven did, by means of the recurrent motif and thematic associ-ation. They both strove to achieve what one could perhaps call the unified aggre-gate. How successful were they in their respective media? Few today will deny the cogent impact which every one of the late quartets, despite all their dis-parities, makes on the listener.[19] Almost invariably such devices as the leitmotiv and thematic association function more profoundly and convincingly in music than in prose. But what of *Wilhelm Meisters Wanderjahre?* With a work like this it is difficult, perhaps inadvisable, to talk about success or failure as regards its form, since it is obvious now that Goethe both cared and did not care about the shape and presentation of his novel. If one insists on looking for a unified organ-ization in the work of the order of that in *Der Zauberberg,* which has much in common with Goethe's novel, then the latter must be counted unsuccessful or, to phrase the matter in different terms, not fully worked out, despite the claims of Trunz and Emrich, since what we have here is an only partially unified aggre-gate in which perfunctoriness has prevailed from time to time. *Der Zauberberg* enjoys a high degree of unity of character and place–the all-assimilating Hans Castorp and the sanatorium with its recurrent, secular ritual–whereas *Wilhelm Meisters Wanderjahre,* despite its eponymous hero, does not really have a central character because Wilhelm is merely just one representative of Goethe's new so-ciety. Lenardo and Odoard are just as important and they accordingly dominate large sections of the novel. This arrangement is in agreement with the concept of *Entsagung* upon which the novel rests and it signifies the suppression of individ-uality in the service of the community; the introspective hero of the earlier Bil-dungsroman can no longer hold the center of the stage in a work like this. But the work fails (from the point of view of traditional aesthetic judgments, that is) because of this very multiplicity. Too much is attempted in too short a span. The work could well have been expanded into a trilogy which presents the fun-damentals of the new society from the standpoints of Wilhelm, Lenardo, and Odoard, the same problems seen from a variety of perspectives, a much favored technique in the twentieth-century novel. But such a procedure exists only in rudimentary outline in Goethe's novel.[20] As it stands, it is a mixture of highly successful passages which often evince a brilliant narrative technique with pas-sages which are either deliberately flat and unadorned (Goethe's dislike of "das Gefällige" merely in art manifests itself here) or which reveal very summary treatment indeed from their author.[21] Toward the end of his life Goethe was evi-dently often impatient with art and the appearance of art is discarded to a greater extent in this novel than elsewhere–more so, I believe, than in late Beethoven, for whom, isolated in his deafness, art was the only consolation. But even he, it is obvious, became impatient with it from time to time.

The question which presents itself at this point is of course whether Goethe and Beethoven had fully exhausted the possibilities of their respective genres. This brings us to another of Wendell Kretzschmar's famous remarks about

Beethoven's last piano sonata. When asked why there was no third movement after the arietta, Kretzschmar replied that it was the end of the sonata, not only of this particular one but of the sonata in general. This is largely the case, or perhaps one should say, rather, that for *Beethoven's* purposes sonata form and the classical three- or four-movement pattern was no longer adequate and was, indeed, somewhat false in its familiarly well-proportioned representation of reality.[22] But a similar claim cannot be made with regard to Goethe, most of whose prose is experimental in nature and who was always far removed from the mainstream of the European novel (only in *Wilhelm Meisters theatralische Sendung* and its revised version in the *Lehrjahre* did Goethe employ sustained narrative and realism), whereas Beethoven stands at the end of the classical tradition of the sonata as evolved by C. P. E. Bach, Haydn, and Mozart. In the last works of Beethoven it can be clearly observed that the sonata has been fully exploited and then totally reforged into something new. Mostly this is done ingeniously, sometimes willfully and high-handedly.[23] With Goethe arbitrariness is far more in evidence.

Here then, side by side, the two greatest artists of this period in Germany developed, unknown to each other, much the same approach to the question of organization in their respective arts. It is a development which, it is true, has greatly influenced twentieth-century music and literature. But one must beware of the danger of falsifications, should one insist too much on this relationship between the last works of Goethe and Beethoven and many of those in the twentieth century.[24] The originalities and enigmatic peculiarities of the late quartets and *Wilhelm Meisters Wanderjahre* are the result of a lifetime's preoccupation with the form of art and recourse to twentieth-century parallels (or even to the temporally nearer concept of romantic irony) can never yield more than slight illumination. The pressures which shape the work of twentieth-century musicians and novelists who adopt these devices are very different indeed. It must be recognized that the attitudes of Goethe and Beethoven toward their later work were highly complex ones and it is doubtful whether their true intentions regarding this or that aspect of their work can ever be totally divined.[25]

Notes

1.   There is a similar moment toward the end of the variation movement in the C-sharp Minor Quartet (Eulenburg Miniature Score, Edition Eulenburg No. 2, bars 241–54).

2.   Thomas Mann, *Doktor Faustus* (Stockholm: Bermann-Fischer, 1947), p. 84. Most of Mann's ideas concerning Beethoven were derived from Theodor W. Adorno; see Gunilla Bergsten, *Thomas Manns Doktor Faustus* (Stockholm: Svenska Bokförlaget, 1963), and Adorno's short essay "Spätstil Beethovens" which was first published in *Der Auftakt* in 1937 and has now been reprinted in the collection, Theodore W. Adorno, *Moments Musicaux* (Frankfurt am Main: Suhrkamp, 1964), pp. 13–17. The 1959 essay on the *Missa Solemnis,* "Verfremdetes Kunstwerk," on pp. 167–85 of the same volume, is also highly relevant.

3.   Hermann Hettner, *Geschichte der deutschen Literatur im achtzehnten Jahrhundert,* 4 vols. (Berlin: Aufbau-Verlag, 1961), 2:735.

4.   See the otherwise excellent commentary by Erich Trunz in vol. 8 of Johann Wolf-gang von Goethe, *Werke,* ed. Erich Trunz, 14 vols. (Hamburg: C. Wegner, 1958–   ) (hereafter referred to as *Hamburger Ausgabe;*) and Wilhelm Emrich, "Das Problem der Symbolinterpretation im Hinblick auf Goethes *Wanderjahr,*" *Deutsche Vierteljahrsschrift* 26 (1952):331–52.

5.   See A. Henkel, *Entsagung: Eine Studie zu Goethes Altersroman* (Tübingen: Max Nie-meyer Verlag, 1964), p. 17.

6.   Edition Eulenburg No. 2, p. iv.

7.   Erich Trunz in the *Hamburger Ausgabe* and Wilhelm Flitner in Johann Wolfgang von Goethe, *Gedenkausgabe der Werke, Briefe und Gespröche, 28 August 1949,* ed. Ernst Beutler, 25 vols. (Zurich: Artemis-Verlag, 1948–   ).

8.   Mann, p. 82. See also Adorno, p. 16.

9.   The most striking example of this procedure may be found at the beginning of Wil-helm's arrival at the castle of Makarie (the tenth chapter of the first book), a passage which teems with the favorite adjectives of the late Goethe and yet at the same time is pervaded by a strange note of ceremony.

10.   Adorno, p. 14.

11.   Compare Adorno, p. 171, where the late quartets are described as being "gegen den Strich komponiert."

12.   For example, *Hamburger Ausgabe,* 8:118, 125.

13.   Ibid., 8:393.

14.   Emrich, pp. 350–51. Emrich refers to Montan's "Sprachskepsis" which he rightly says was shared by Goethe. But this scepticism is directed mainly at everyday language as a means of communication and not at the language of literary invention.

15.   For example, the ice-skating scene in *Der Mann von fünfzig Jahren,* the episode on Lake Maggiore, or the final chapter of the work.

16.   See the discussion between Wilhelm and the Astronomer at the castle of Makarie or the utterances of Montan.

17.   Beethoven kept his smaller pieces, the six Bagatelles (op. 126) separate from the so-natas with which they, nevertheless, have a great deal in common.

18.   Those who claim a thoroughgoing unity for the work invariably quote Goethe's re-mark, "Ist es nicht aus Einem Stück, so ist es doch aus Einem Sinn" (*Hamburger Aus-gabe,* 8:575), without seeming to realize that this very sentence conveys clearly the nature of the limited form of the novel. Meaning alone does not guarantee formal unity. And they significantly fail to quote another statement by Goethe to Kanzler von Müller in 1830 which warns of "die alberne Idee, das Ganze systematisch konstruiren und analysie-ren zu wollen." The truth regarding the form of the novel lies somewhere between these two statements.

19.   But their success is of a different order from that of the earlier works. See Adorno, p. 184:

> Der Wahrheitsanspruch des letzten Beethoven verwirft den Schein jener Identität des Subjectiven und Objektiven, der fast eins ist mit der klassizistischen Idee. Es erfolgt eine Polarisierung. Einheit transzendiert sich zum Fragmentarischen. In den letzten Quartetten geschieht das durch das schroffe, unvermittelte Nebeneinanderrücken kahler, spruchähnlicher Motive und polyphoner Kom-plexe. Der Riss zwischen beiden, der sich einbekennt, macht die Unmöglichkeit ästhetischer Har-monie zum ästhetischen Gehalt, das Misslingen in einem obersten Sinn zum Mass des Gelingens.

Goethe seems to have attempted much the same approach but with less success.

20.   Goethe employs what one might call the polyphony of the collective.

21.   A particular example is Goethe's final grouping of almost all the characters of the novel at the castle of Makarie, each of them showing some facility in a trade or a profession. Goethe's irony emerges when Philine, the "angenehme Sünderin" of the *Lehrjahre,* appears as a competent, if garrulous, seamstress.

22.   See Adorno, pp. 182–83.

23.   The latter is more in evidence in the *Diabelli* Variations than in the sonatas.

24.   Emrich claims (p. 352) that the fragmentation of form in Goethe's novel reflects the breakup of society into specialized separate entities, which Goethe foresaw.

25.   "It seems that art, almost perversely, creates tasks that cannot be mastered by our normal faculties. Chaos is precariously near." Anton Ehrenzweig, *The Hidden Order of Art* (Berkeley: University of California Press, 1967), p. 31. This highly stimulating book which appeared when the present essay had been completed focuses at one point on the "fractures" and "lack of surface coherence" in late Beethoven and Goethe, recommending "unconscious scanning" or "syncretistic vision" as the approach needed to assimilate the hidden order of their work, an order which a self-conscious, intellectual approach will not espy or, as Ehrenzweig puts it: "Art is a dream dreamt by the artist which we, the wide-awake spectators, can never see in its true structure; our waking faculties are bound to give us too precise an image produced by secondary revision" (p. 79). Now surely this recommendation is not universally applicable. It is feasible with regard to a great deal of painting, "pure poetry," music, and some forms of drama, but Ehrenzweig does not consider whether several hundred pages of narrative prose can be unconsciously scanned (he does not mention *Wilhelm Meisters Wanderjahre* but concentrates on *Faust II,* which is more fruitful for his psychoanalytical approach but less interesting in my view than the novel as regards formal innovations). Admittedly, *Wilhelm Meisters Wanderjahre,* consisting as it does of an aggregate of short sections, would seem to lend itself more readily to unconscious scanning than a novel with a sustained narrative, but it is also to a large extent a novel of ideas and the lengthy discursive passages certainly obstruct such an approach.

Acknowledgments

Clark, Marden J. "Blending Cadences: Rhythm and Structure in *Moby-Dick*." *Studies in the Novel* 8 (1976):158–71.

Freedman, William. "*Tristram Shandy:* The Art of Literary Counterpoint." *Modern Language Quarterly* 32 (1971):268–80.

Adams, Stephen J. "Are the *Cantos* a Fugue?" *University of Toronto Quarterly* 45 (1975):67–74.

Stanley, Patricia Haas. "Verbal Music in Theory and Practice." *Germanic Review* 52 (1977):217–25.

Frye, Northrop. "Wallace Stevens and the Variation Form." In *Literary Theory and Structure: Essays in Honor of William K. Wimsatt,* edited by Frank Brady, John Palmer, and Martin Price. New Haven, Conn.: Yale University Press, 1973, pp. 395–414.

Brown, Calvin S. "Theme and Variations as a Literary Form." *Yearbook of Comparative and General Literature* 27 (1978):35–42.

Chancellor, Paul. "The Music of *The Waste Land.*" *Comparative Literature Studies* 6 (1969):21–32.

Gardner, Helen. "The Music of *Four Quartets.*" In *The Art of T. S. Eliot,* by Helen Gardner. London: The Cresset Press, 1949, pp. 36–56.

Brotman, D. Bosley. "T. S. Eliot: 'The Music of Ideas.'" *University of Toronto Quarterly* 18 (1948):20–29.

Howarth, Herbert. "Eliot, Beethoven, and J. W. N. Sullivan." *Comparative Literature* 9 (1957):322–32.

Gross, Harvey. "Music and the Analogue of Feeling: Notes on Eliot and Beethoven." *The Centennial Review of Arts and Science* 3 (1959): 269–88.

Rees, Thomas R. "The Orchestration of Meaning in T. S. Eliot's *Four Quartets.*" *Journal of Aesthetics and Art Criticism* 28 (1969–70):63–69.

Basilius, H. A. "Thomas Mann's Use of Musical Structure and Techniques in *Tonio Kröger.*" *Germanic Review* 19 (1944):284–308.

Wallace, Robert K. "'The Murders in the Rue Morgue' and Sonata-Allegro Form." *Journal of Aesthetics and Art Criticism* 35 (1977):457–63.

Carlile, Robert Emerson. "*Great Circle:* Conrad Aiken's Musico-Literary Technique." *Georgia Review* 22 (1968):27–36.

Ziolkowski, Theodore. "Herman Hesse's *Steppenwolf:* A Sonata in Prose." *Modern Language Quarterly* 19 (1958):115–33.

Smith, Don Noel. "Musical Form and Principles in the Scheme of *Ulysses.*" *Twentieth Century Literature* 18 (1972):168–80.

Jarvi, Raymond. "Strindberg's *The Ghost Sonata* and Sonata Form." *Mosaic: A Journal for the Comparative Study of Literature and Ideas* 5 (1972):69–84.

Llewellyn, R. T. "Parallel Attitudes to Form in Late Beethoven and Late Goethe: Throwing Aside the Appearance of Art." *Modern Language Review* 63 (1968):407–16.

Index

Adams, Stephen, 5, **36–43**

Aiken, Conrad, "simultaneity in dissimilarity," 28; verbal music, 26; WORKS: *Blue Voyage*, 187; *Great Circle*, 8, sonata form in, 187–193 *passim; Ushant*, 187

Bach, J. S., counterpoint in, 29, 33; fugues, 37; toccatas, 44–45; WORKS: *Die Kunst der Fuge*, 38; Goldberg Variations, 55; Passacaglia and Fugue in C Minor, 77; Toccata in G, BWV 915, 45

Barth, Karl, 62–63

Bartók, Béla, Quartets 2–6, 142

Basilius, H. A., 7, 9, **153–174**, 175, 200

Baudelaire, Charles Pierre, 87–88

Beethoven, Ludwig van, WORKS: Archduke Trio, 71; Coriolan Overture, 123; Diabelli Variations, 55, 71; *Grosse Fuge*, 38, 123; late quartets, 9, 107, 117, 133, 242, compared with Goethe's *Wilhelm Meister's Wanderjahre*, 243–250; Quartet in B-flat Major, 242; Quartet in C-sharp Minor, 7, 8, 133–39, 242–44; Quartet in A Minor, 7, 113–114, 117, 243; Quartet in F Major, 242; Quartet in E-flat Major, 242; Piano Sonata in D Major, 229; Piano Sonata in C Minor (*Pathétique*), 8, 176–83; Piano Sonata in D Minor, 9, 232–234; Third Symphony (*Eroica*), 133; Fifth Symphony, 3, 13; Sixth Symphony (Pastoral), 133; Ninth Symphony, 127, 132, 214; Violin Concerto, 97

Berlioz, Hector, *Symphonie Fantastique*, 144

Bernstein, Leonard, 175

Bhagavad-Gita, 98

Böcklin, Arnold, *Die Toteninsel*, 239

Bosse, Harriet, 227, 229

Boyle, Robert, 214, 215

Broch, Hermann, 243

Bronowski, Jacob, 4

The Brothers Karamazov, 13

Brotman, D. Bosley, 6, **107–116**

Brown, Calvin S., 1, 6, **70–82**, 175, 192, 200, 202

Browning, Robert, *The Ring and the Book* as variation form, 79–82

Bull, John, 71

Byrd, William, 71

Cabezón, Antonio de, 71

Cadilhac, Paul-Emile, 26